Paralegal's Litigation Handbook

Second Edition

Paralegal's Litigation Handbook

Second Edition

——— • ———

Carole A. Bruno

WEST PUBLISHING COMPANY
Minneapolis/St. Paul   New York   Los Angeles   San Francisco

Copyediting: Margaret Jarpey
Design: Tara Bazata
Cover design: David J. Farr, ImageSmythe, Inc.
Art: Rolin Graphics
Composition: Carlisle Communications

Production, Prepress, Printing and Binding by West Publishing Company.

WEST'S COMMITMENT TO THE ENVIRONMENT

In 1906, West Publishing Company began recycling materials left over from the production of books. This began a tradition of efficient and responsible use of resources. Today, up to 95 percent of our legal books and 70 percent of our college and school texts are printed on recycled, acid-free stock. West also recycles nearly 22 million pounds of scrap paper annually— the equivalent of 181,717 trees. Since the 1960s, West has devised ways to capture and recycle waste inks, solvents, oils, and vapors created in the printing process. We also recycle plastics of all kinds, wood, glass, corrugated cardboard, and batteries, and have eliminated the use of styrofoam book packaging. We at West are proud of the longevity and the scope of our commitment to the environment.

Library of Congress Cataloging-in-Publication Data

Bruno, Carole A.
    Paralegal's litigation handbook / Carole A. Bruno. — 2nd ed.
       p.   cm.
    Includes bibliographical references and index.
    ISBN 0-314-01177-3 (hard)
    1. Civil procedure—United States—Outlines, syllabi, etc.
    I. Title.
    KF8841.B78 1993
    347.73'5—dc20
    [347.3075]   92-40067
                        ∞ CIP

To MARY,

a perfect sister.

About the Author

———•———

Carole Bruno has been involved in the paralegal profession for over 20 years. A pioneer paralegal of the '70s, she wrote her first book in 1980. Since then she has written *The Standard Legal Secretary's Handbook,* and numerous articles for various legal publications, including *Legal Assistant Today, The National Law Journal, The American Lawyer Management Services, Law Office Economics and Management, Practicing Attorneys Newsletter, The Pennsylvania Lawyer, The Oklahoma Bar Association Journal, The State Bar of Georgia Bread 'N Butter, Boston Association of Legal Administrators' Newsletter, The Law Marketing Exchange, The Georgia Association of Legal Assistants' Newsletter,* and *The National Federation of Paralegal Associations Newsletter.*

Ms. Bruno is the former editor of *Attorneys Computer Report, Attorneys Marketing Report* and *CPA Marketing Report.* She continues to give seminars nationally to various colleges, universities and paralegal schools through the National Institute for Continuing Paralegal Education. Carole started the first paralegal placement agency in Georgia in 1979. Ms. Bruno consults with firms on paralegal utilization and law office management. In 1986, Carole became the first in-house law firm marketing director in Georgia. She has been a marketing consultant for over six years and in 1990, she founded Professional Services Marketing in Atlanta.

Contents

—————•—————

Preface

————•————

I originally wrote *Paralegal's Litigation Handbook* with one primary goal in mind—to provide paralegals and paralegal students with a book that was written from the perspective of a practicing paralegal. This second edition is intentionally written to offer hands-on techniques and skills. An added benefit to this approach is that this book will not become outdated quickly.

Written in the logical sequence of the litigation process, this second edition begins with an introduction to the courts and procedures, then follows through the initial filing of the lawsuit, and the response by the defendant. Continuing through the litigation process, chapters on motions, negotiations and pretrial, discovery, trial preparation, judgment and post-judgment follow. Finally, the last chapter is on appeals. Scattered throughout the book are additional chapters covering specific skills needed by the litigation paralegal, including legal writing, legal research, and legal interviewing.

One of the highlights of this second edition are two new chapters on computers and automated litigation support. Today paralegals need a good working knowledge of computers and how they are used in law. While not all paralegals will use automated litigation support, most paralegals will come in contact with computers in some fashion. Chapters 13 and 14 are packed with valuable information that the industrious paralegal can use to improve his or her computer savvy.

In writing this second edition, I have the following goals:

1. To provide paralegals and paralegal students with a practical hands-on approach to performing their tasks;
2. To be as comprehensive and up-to-date as possible;
3. To offer step-by-step procedures to perform most functions;
4. To serve as a handy guide for reference for most litigation tasks;
5. To be a resource for usable forms and checklists; and
6. To give practical examples for reference.

• Learning Tools

The text contains the following pedagogical features designed to help paralegals and paralegal students learn and comprehend the material.

• Outline, Introduction, Summary

Each chapter begins with an outline, an introduction and ends with a summary of the key points of the chapter. Each term in the text that is printed in **bold** is defined in the glossary at the end of the book.

• Forms, Exhibits, Pleadings, Checklists

This second edition contains over 105 valuable forms and checklists that the paralegal can use in his or her daily functions. The forms included in this second edition are meant to serve as a guideline only and not to be used verbatim. Likewise, the checklists are guides and are not all-inclusive. The facts of the particular case must always be taken into consideration when using these forms. It is anticipated that the reader will add items to them so they will be more valuable. Merely photocopying the forms and filling in the blanks is not only flirting with error but indicates a lazy attitude towards one's job. Use the forms creatively as a guide and mold them to fit the specific facts of the case on which you are working.

• Step-by-Step Procedures

Wherever possible, step-by-step procedures are given, but in all instances, the reader should check the local and state codes before beginning a task. Procedural rules also go out-of-date, and an astute paralegal will double-check to make sure the particular procedure applied is still valid.

• Appendix

The Appendix contains much useful information including valuable sources of information about paralegal associations and schools. The Paralegal Skills Inventory Test in the Appendix is a composite test covering not only litigation tasks, but also legal duties in most general areas of law. This test may be used by employers when interviewing paralegals to determine their experience and skills. An experienced paralegal may use this inventory to assess his or her growth in skills.

• Ethical Discussion

Every attempt has been made to include ethical considerations throughout the body of the text. The Appendix also contains the codes of ethics for the two major national paralegal associations—a must-read for all paralegals.

• What's New to the Second Edition

The first edition of *Paralegal's Litigation Handbook* was revised in its entirety and includes the following major changes:

Five new chapters have been added:

Chapter 4 Writing Skills;

Chapter 5 Legal Interviewing Techniques;

Chapter 9 Handling Medical Discovery;

Chapter 13 How Computers Are Used in Litigation; and

Chapter 14 Automated Litigation Support.

These chapters are a valuable addition to this second edition because of their technical approach to the specific duties of the litigation paralegal today.

- An instructor's manual has been added to this second edition.
- A Paralegal Skills Inventory Test has been added to the Appendix.
- Information regarding databases and relational databases, as well as a litigation support software evaluation form has been added to the Appendix.
- The paralegal evaluation form has been updated.
- An updated list of affiliated associations and member associations for the National Federation of Paralegal Associations (NFPA), and the National Association of Legal Assistants (NALA) is included in the Appendix.
- Since the directory of paralegal schools is too voluminous to include in this second edition, the address and telephone number where you may request a list of paralegal schools is noted at the beginning of the Appendix.
- A glossary has been added to this second edition. Again, the words which appear in the glossary are indicated in **bold** through the text.

• Acknowledgments

Writing a book is an arduous task but there is no question that without the support of my friends and colleagues, this book could not have been written. I am most appreciative of the tremendous assistance of my friend and colleague, Paula Turner for her valuable expertise on computers in the law office. My special thanks go to Dr. Todd W. Rudner whose specialized knowledge on medical discovery makes Chapter 9 very valuable. I also am indebted to Professor Corneill Stephens, Georgia State University College of Law and judge of the magistrate court of DeKalb County, Georgia, for his gracious assistance with the chapter on courts. I sincerely thank Frank Bird, Jr., attorney at law, for assisting in the expansion of the chapter on judgments. Numerous other friends and colleagues made helpful suggestions and provided material. They include:

Robert Hochdorf	Steve Reiff	Tammy Griner
Connie Coe	Robin Lepore	Vanessa Stogsdill
Don Keenan	Isadora Vardaros	Sallye Thornton
David Bills	Jeff Finkel	Kathy Allen
Joe Hansen	Leuveda Phillips	

Other friends were very gracious in offering me assistance in many ways. My friend, Gary Wall kept my computer running—often saving the day. Another friend and colleague, Janice Hoover, director of the Atlanta regional office of the

American Institute for Paralegal Studies, Inc., carefully went through the first edition pinpointing necessary updates, as well as editing several chapters. Other friends and colleagues were very gracious in offering me assistance in many ways:

Celena Bullard	Marlene Barton
Dianne Duffin	Sandra Korey

Hidden behind the publication of every book are some very important people. Behind the scenes at West Publishing Company were my colleagues who helped to make this book come to fruition. Elizabeth Hannan, my editor, who guided me through every step of the long process of publishing; Patty Bryant, developmental editor, whose professional skills gave a certain polish to the book; Peggy Brewington, assistant production editor and confidante who cheered me on; Carrie Kish, promotion manager, whose creativity was an inspiration; and finally, Bill Statsky, author and consultant for West. His kind recommendation to West Publishing Company to publish this second edition started the project.

• Reviewers of the Second Edition

1. Eileen Mitchell
   University of New Orleans
2. Pamela Matarrese
   Sussex Community College
3. Kathleen Reed
   University of Toledo
4. Allan Gordon
   Oakland University
5. Virginia Noonan
   Northern Essex Community College
6. Edie Koonce
   Tulane University
7. Theresa (Perky) Lewis, Legal Assistant

If you have any additions, suggestions or comments, please write me in care of West Publishing Company. I promise to answer every single letter that I receive.

Carole Bruno

Atlanta, Georgia
October 1992

Concise Guide to Courts

• Introduction

This chapter[1] gives you an overview of the state and federal court systems and the laws of jurisdiction and venue. Your paralegal work will be easier when you can distinguish between these two types of laws. You are also introduced to forum shopping and long-arm statutes.

In whatever court system you work with, be sure to get a copy of the local court rules. Check them frequently.

• Laws of Jurisdiction

Since the laws of jurisdiction are extremely complex, this section is merely an overview of the subject.[2] *Jurisdiction* is the authority or power of a court to hear a particular cause of action and to render a lawful and binding judgment against one or more defendants.

A court must have jurisdiction over both the *subject matter* of the litigation and the *person* of the parties to hear a case and render a lawful judgment. *Subject-matter jurisdiction* refers to the type of action, such as divorce, personal injury, or property damage. *Personal jurisdiction* refers to the individual parties, corporations, fiduciaries, or other litigants.

Limitations of subject-matter jurisdiction include the following:

1. *The matter of the case.* A probate court would not have jurisdiction over a traffic violation.
2. *The amount involved.* Small claims court could not hear a suit for $1 million.
3. *The remedies that the court can provide.* A traffic court would not have jurisdiction to impose the death penalty.
4. *The location (situs) of the property.* A California court could not hear a suit for foreclosure of property in Nevada.

---

[1]Contributions to this chapter were made by Professor Corneill A. Stephens, Georgia State University College of Law, judge of the magistrate court of DeKalb County, Georgia.

[2]Consult your state code or Title 28 of the United States Code to determine the applicable subsection.

5. *The identity of the litigants.* A small claims court could not hear a suit against an ambassador.

The court automatically gets personal jurisdiction over the *plaintiff* when he or she commences the civil action. The court gains jurisdiction over the *defendant* through proper *service of process* upon the defendant, meaning that applicable rules of law and constitutional limitations are followed. If the service of process upon the defendant is defective, the court will not have jurisdiction over the defendant. The defendant, however, can usually waive defects in personal jurisdiction.[3]

Concurrent versus Exclusive Jurisdiction

When two or more courts have jurisdiction over the same case, they have *concurrent jurisdiction*. For example, a domestic case may be heard in family court, but it may also be heard in a state superior court. Just because the federal court may hear a case does not exclude it from being heard by a state court. In many instances, the state courts may hear cases involving federal issues. For example, both the state court and the federal court may hear a civil rights action involving sexual harassment.

A court has **exclusive jurisdiction** over cases that only that court can hear. For instance, the federal courts must hear cases involving a federal question or diversity of citizenship (discussed later in this chapter). Antitrust actions and maritime suits are examples of cases that only the federal courts can hear.

Forum Shopping

Forum shopping is the term given to the process whereby attorneys choose among courts of concurrent jurisdiction, trying to provide the best "forum" for their clients. (Obviously, forum shopping does not apply to cases that involve exclusive jurisdiction.) Attorneys may look for certain judges who have ruled favorably in cases involving similar issues. Or they may seek a particular environment or culture favorable to the issues involved in the action.

Types of Jurisdiction

There are three types of jurisdiction: original, appellate, and federal-question.

Original Jurisdiction
The term *trial court jurisdiction* is synonymous with *original jurisdiction*. It refers to the court that has the authority to hear a case originally, that is, the court where the suit is commenced. The case may possibly be appealed to a higher court, removed to another court, or transferred to a different location of the same judicial system.

Appellate Jurisdiction
Statutory or constitutional provisions determine a court's *appellate jurisdiction*, that is, its authority to hear an appeal from the lower courts. Principally, in the state and federal court systems, both the intermediate courts of appeal and the

---

[3]U.S.C.A. §404.

highest courts of appeal have appellate jurisdiction. The Supreme Court of the United States has original jurisdiction in some matters and appellate jurisdiction in others. Like the highest state court of appeals, it normally hears appeals from the lower courts.

Federal-Question Jurisdiction

Federal-question jurisdiction is based on the U.S. Constitution, a federal law, or a treaty of the United States. District courts (discussed later in this chapter) have jurisdiction over all civil actions arising under the Constitution, federal statutes, or treaties of the United States. Special federal statutes or diversity of citizenship (discussed shortly) is the basis for federal-question jurisdiction.[4]

Federal Jurisdiction Based on Federal Statutes. Federal courts such as the United States District Court hear cases that arise from certain statutes voted by Congress to allow tort actions, including the following:

1. *Federal Tort Claims Act.* When a federal employee commits a tort designed in this act, the United States can be sued for money damages.
2. *Civil Rights Act.* A plaintiff deprived of federal rights under color of law can obtain money damages against the defendant.
3. *Federal Employers' Liability Act.* Railroad employees engaged in interstate commerce may recover from injuries, similar to the way workers' compensation laws operate.
4. *Consumer Product Safety Act.* A violation under this act may result in money damages.

Federal Jurisdiction Based on Diversity of Citizenship. One important basis of federal jurisdiction is *diversity of citizenship,* which applies only when the matter in dispute is greater than $50,000. In this case, the controversy is between:

1. Citizens of different states.[5]
2. Citizens of a state and foreign states or citizens or subjects thereof.
3. Citizens of different states, in which foreign states or subjects thereof are additional parties.[6]

A corporation is considered a citizen of the state wherein it is incorporated and where it has its principal place of business.[7] The tests for determining the principal place of a corporation are:

1. The location of the nerve center—that is, where principal administrative and financial transactions are conducted.

---

[4]U.S.C.A. §1331.

[5]The word "state," as used herein, includes the territories, the District of Columbia, and the Commonwealth of Puerto Rico.

[6]28 U.S.C.A. §1332.

[7]In questions of diversity jurisdiction involving corporations, the most frequent litigation arises out of the question of where the principal place of business is.

2. The state that the corporation declares as its principal place of business or where it has a representative.
3. The state where the corporation makes its most frequent contacts.

• Long-Arm Statutes

Most states have *long-arm statutes,* which give a court personal jurisdiction over nonresident defendants who commit civil wrongs in a state other than the state in which they reside.

Example 1: A resident of Mississippi is involved in an automobile accident while traveling through North Carolina. By statute, the plaintiff can obtain personal jurisdiction over the Mississippi resident in North Carolina where the accident occurred.[8] The theory is that the nonresident motorist, by operating his vehicle in a foreign state, consented by implication to be sued in any litigation resulting from an automobile accident occurring in that state. In addition, the statute is designed for the convenience of the resident plaintiff.

Example 2: A renowned physician is visiting his relatives in Kentucky. He is asked by the local hospital to assist with emergency surgery, because the local doctor is unavailable. He is negligent in conducting the operation, and afterward returns to his home in Illinois. By statute, the plaintiff patient could obtain personal jurisdiction over the doctor by his consent to the operation. The statute is designed to protect the resident plaintiff.

Similar long-arm statutes create personal jurisdiction over nonresident property owners, aircraft operators, or vessel owners.

Foreign Corporations

In addition, every state has a long-arm statute that applies to *foreign corporations,* meaning those incorporated in and located in another state, but which are "doing business" in that state, at least with respect to any disputes arising out of business transacted within the jurisdiction. Many state statutes require that foreign corporations become "qualified," that is, formally registered with the secretary of state in the state where they wish to do business.

Service of Process on Nonresident Defendants

Service of process can be accomplished on a nonresident defendant where jurisdiction is properly based on a long-arm statute. Generally, the plaintiff is required to serve a copy of the complaint on an official designated in the state, usually the secretary of state, who then forwards a copy to the nonresident defendant. Since this procedure varies from state to state, be sure to check your state statutes for the proper procedure. In the federal courts, the law of the state where the suit is filed governs the procedure for service of process on a nonresident defendant.[9]

---

[8]N.C. *Gen. Stat.* §1–75.4.
[9]*Federal Rules of Civil Procedure* Rule 4(d)(7).

• Laws of Venue

Venue is the place or location (i.e., city, county, district, or other geographical division) in which an action is to be heard and tried. It is usually the most convenient forum. Various states have venue statutes that limit the choices of where an action may be heard.

Although some requirements of venue and jurisdiction are similar, venue is the *actual location* of the forum and the territorial limits from which a jury is drawn whereas jurisdiction is the power, or authority, the court has to hear a particular action.

Criteria for Proper Venue

Proper venue is ultimately determined by the state based on these criteria:

- Residence of defendant.
- Place where cause of action arose.
- Place of business of defendant.
- Place where defendant has an office or representative.
- Residence of plaintiff.
- Location of seat of government.
- Location of defendant.

In actions involving property, or *res*, the location of land determines the proper venue.

Since the local statute that determines venue varies considerably from state to state, it is best to check with your local statutes and court rules. Venue usually lies where the cause of action occurs, but it may lie in the county of the plaintiff's residence instead. Venue is usually determined according to what is most convenient for the parties and, unlike subject-matter jurisdiction, it may be waived.

Actions Involving Real Property

For example, in a civil action involving *real property*, the cause of action occurs in the county where the real property is located. However, several factors determine jurisdiction, or the proper forum, such as the amount in controversy, the citizenship of the defendants, or the nature of the case (as previously discussed).

Actions Involving Torts

Generally speaking, in a *tort action*, proper venue is in the county where the loss or injury occurred. However, the action may also be tried in the county of the residence of the defendant.

Actions Involving Breach of Contract

Proper venue in a *breach of contract* action is usually the county where the contract was to be performed or the county of the defendant's residence. Some state statutes further provide that in an action involving a contract, the county where the contract was executed may also be the proper venue. Again, check your state code for specific requirements of venue in various civil actions since they vary from state to state. For specific venue requirements in the federal court system, see Title 28 of the United States Code, §1391, et seq.

Change of Venue

If venue is improper, the defendant may request a *change of venue* before or with the responsive pleading. If the request is not made then, the defendant waives his or her right to change the venue. In some state courts, a motion to dismiss may be made where venue is improper. Generally speaking, in the state courts, grounds for a change of venue include:

1. A violation of one of the criteria for proper venue (listed on page 5).
2. Reasons why an impartial trial cannot be had.
3. Reasons why bias or prejudice of the judge or jury is likely, if provided by statute.
3. The convenience of the parties and/or witnesses.
4. Reasons why a change would be in the interest of justice.

Some state court rules (e.g., California) require that you file an affidavit or a declaration of merits with the motion for change of venue. In most states, however, parties may stipulate to a change of venue. You should consult your state code.

In some jurisdictions, when both parties stipulate to a change in venue, the attorneys do a procedure called *striking of counties* in which each attorney eliminates a county, by turn, until there is only one county left for venue.

Change of venue may be an important tool for avoiding judges with a reputation of being plaintiff- or defendant-oriented. Often attorneys rely heavily upon their ability to obtain a change of venue for this reason.

In the federal courts, the grounds for change of venue are as follows:

1. Subject matter jurisdiction.
2. Personal jurisdiction and service.
3. For the convenience of the parties and/or witnesses. (Such a change can be made only to another court where the original action could have been brought.)

To change venue or to correct the defect of improper venue in the federal court system, a motion, consent, or stipulation of all parties must be filed, except in proceedings brought by or on behalf of the United States. Venue may be transferred without the consent of the United States when all other parties request a transfer.[10] A motion to dismiss may be filed in the federal court for improper venue.[11]

• Federal Court System

The federal court system, much like the state court system (discussed next), consists of the trial courts, appellate courts, and various specialized courts. The primary federal court at the trial level is the *U.S. District Court*. The intermediate appellate court is the *U.S. Courts of Appeals*. The highest level appellate court is the *U.S. Supreme Court* (Exhibit 1.1).

---

[10]28 U.S.C.A. §1404. (See also §1406.)
[11]28 U.S.C.A. §1406(a).

Exhibit 1.1
•
U.S. (Federal) Court System

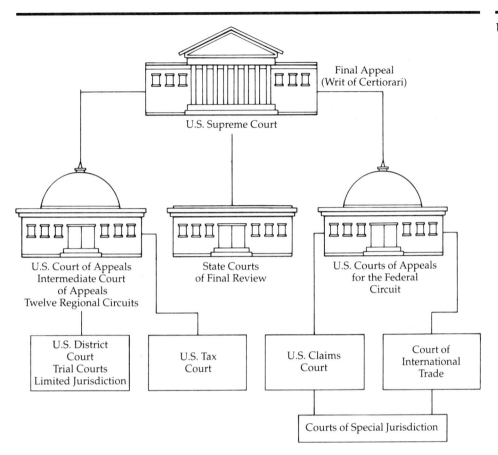

Generally speaking, federal courts have original jurisdiction in writs of mandamus, habeas corpus, prohibition, certiorari, and certain other civil actions as specified in the U.S. Constitution. The trial courts have limited jurisdiction that require them to take only cases falling under federal law. Generally, these two courts have appellate jurisdiction.

U.S. District Courts

The trial courts in the state systems (discussed later), such as the superior, circuit, district, and common pleas courts are similar to the U.S. District Court in the federal system. The United States is divided into almost 100 judicial districts, each of which has a U.S. district court. Some larger states (24 of them) have two or more districts, and every state and territory of the United States contains at least one district court. In the 24 states with two or more districts, courts are named Northern, Southern, Eastern, or Western and many are divided into divisions—for example, U.S. District Court for the Northern District of Iowa, Cedar Rapids Division (Exhibit 1.2).

Because the U.S. District Court is essentially a trial court in the federal system, its powers are limited to entering a monetary or equitable decision subject to appeal. It might be compared to a superior court in the state system that renders a judgment then open to appeal in the state system.

Exhibit 1.2

U.S. District Courts and Courts of Appeals

Name of State, Commonwealth, or Territory	Only One District	Northern District	Southern District	Middle District	Eastern District	Western District	Central District	Judicial Circuit
State of Alabama		X	X	X				5th
State of Alaska	X							9th
State of Arizona	X							9th
State of Arkansas					X	X		8th
State of California		X	X		X		X	9th
Canal Zone	X							5th
State of Colorado	X							10th
State of Connecticut	X							2nd
State of Delaware	X							3rd
District of Columbia	X							D.C.
State of Florida		X	X	X				5th
State of Georgia		X	X	X				5th
Guam	X							9th
State of Hawaii	X							9th
State of Idaho	X							9th
State of Illinois		X	X		X			7th
State of Indiana		X	X					7th
State of Iowa		X	X					8th
State of Kansas	X							10th
Commonwealth of Kentucky					X	X		6th
State of Louisiana					X	X		5th
State of Maine	X							1st
State of Maryland	X							4th
Commonwealth of Massachusetts	X							1st
State of Michigan					X	X		6th
State of Minnesota	X							8th
State of Mississippi		X	X					5th
State of Missouri					X	X		8th
State of Montana	X							9th
State of Nebraska	X							8th
State of Nevada	X							9th
State of New Hampshire	X							1st
State of New Jersey	X							3rd
State of New Mexico	X							10th
State of New York		X	X		X	X		2nd
State of North Carolina				X	X	X		4th
State of North Dakota	X							8th
State of Ohio		X	X					6th
State of Oklahoma		X			X	X		10th
State of Oregon	X							9th

Exhibit 1.2

Continued

Name of State, Commonwealth, or Territory	Only One District	Northern District	Southern District	Middle District	Eastern District	Western District	Central District	Judicial Circuit
Commonwealth of Pennsylvania				X	X	X		3rd
Puerto Rico	X							1st
State of Rhode Island and Providence Plantations	X							1st
State of South Carolina	X							4th
State of South Dakota	X							8th
State of Tennessee				X	X	X		6th
State of Texas		X	X		X	X		5th
State of Utah	X							10th
State of Vermont	X							2nd
Virgin Islands	X							3rd
Commonwealth of Virginia					X	X		4th
State of Washington					X	X		9th
State of West Virginia		X	X					4th
State of Wisconsin					X	X		7th
State of Wyoming	X							10th

The federal district courts have limited jurisdiction that allows them to hear only cases denoted by federal law. They are **courts of record,** meaning they keep a permanent written record of proceedings and have the power to fine or imprison for contempt.

Original Jurisdiction in Federal Courts

Federal district courts have original jurisdiction, exclusive of the courts of the states, of all criminal offenses against the United States.[12] They have broad jurisdiction over civil actions arising under the U.S. Constitution and federal laws. That is, when a controversy involves a *federal question,* one involving the U.S. Constitution, laws, or treaties of the United States, the federal courts have original jurisdiction. (In any action brought against the United States, any agency thereof, or any officer of employee thereof acting in his or her official capacity, no sum or value is required.)[13]

They also have original jurisdiction in all civil actions wherein the matter involves *diversity of citizenship*—where the parties to the lawsuit are from two different states and the amount in controversy exceeds the sum or value of $50,000, exclusive of interest and costs.

---

[12]28 U.S.C.A. §3231.

[13]28 U.S.C.A. §1331.

Concurrent Jurisdiction in Federal Courts

When two courts have concurrent jurisdiction over a particular case, either court may accept the case. Frequently, concurrent jurisdiction occurs in cases of diversity of citizenship. In this case, citizens of two different (or diverse) states can choose to sue in either state's court. This cause of action need not arise out of a special federal statute. Likewise, a cause of action based on a federal statute need not show diversity.

Exclusive Jurisdiction in Federal Courts

The federal district courts have exclusive jurisdiction, that is, it is the only court that can handle certain kinds of cases. Generally, the federal district courts have exclusive jurisdiction in the following matters:

- Admiralty and maritime cases.
- Bankruptcy matters and proceedings.
- Matters arising out of patent or copyright laws.
- Actions against consuls or vice consuls.
- Actions wherein the amount in controversy, exclusive of interest and costs, exceeds $50,000 between:
  - Citizens of different states.
  - Citizens of a state and foreign states or citizens or subjects.
  - Citizens of different states, with foreign states or citizens or subjects as additional parties ("state" here includes the District of Columbia and the Commonwealth of Puerto Rico).
  - Civil actions arising under the Constitution, laws, or treaties of the United States.
  - Stockholders' derivative suits.
  - Actions against the United States, eminent domain proceedings.
  - Actions for partition of lands wherein the United States is one of the tenants in common or joint tenants.
  - Any civil action of a local nature against defendants residing in different districts in the same state or involving property located in different districts.

U.S. Court of Appeals (Right to Appeal)

The U.S. Court of Appeals is the intermediate appellate court in the federal system. It is divided into 12 regional circuits plus the specialized Court of Appeals for the Federal District located in Washington, D.C. (refer again to Exhibit 1.2). The volume of litigation in the federal courts in a given circuit usually determines the number of judges for that circuit.

The U.S. Court of Appeals is a court of record, which, as you will recall, means that the proceedings of this court require a complete transcript. Courts of appeals have no original jurisdiction but have appellate jurisdiction over the decisions of the federal district courts. Also, they have the right to hear appeals from the U.S. district courts and review orders of certain administrative agencies located within their circuits. They can affirm, deny, or remand a case to a lower court. Further, they determine whether the trial court committed prejudicial error.

The U.S. Court of Appeals also has the power to review orders issued by certain federal administrative agencies. For example, these courts may review orders issued by the Federal Trade Commission, the Labor Department, the Federal Aviation Administration, and other federal administrative agencies. The U.S. Supreme Court may hear an appeal from the court of appeals. Cases get to the U.S. Supreme Court by appeal, by right, and by writ of certiorari (explained later).

U.S. Supreme Court (Final Appeal)

There is only one U.S. Supreme Court. It is located in Washington, D.C. The Supreme Court consists of one chief justice and eight associate justices, any six of whom shall constitute a *quorum*, meaning the number of members who must be present before any action may be taken. It has original jurisdiction in all cases affecting ambassadors, other public ministers and consuls, and those cases in which the states may be a party.

The Supreme Court has the highest level appellate jurisdiction in the federal court system, including all cases in law and equity arising under the Constitution and the laws of the United States and its treaties. Appeals in this court, however, are discretionary and a privilege. They may come from the U.S. Court of Appeals and from the supreme or highest court for any states.[14]

The typical way an appeal reaches the Supreme Court is on a *writ of certiorari*, where the court is asked to hear a specific case. The Court takes only those cases that, in its opinion, are of national importance. A very small percentage of appeals are actually accepted for review. The Court may accept or reject the *writ*, but does not have to explain its denial of *certiorari*.

The U.S. Supreme Court will also hear cases involving a major conflict in the decisions of the various circuits of the U.S. Court of Appeals. The Supreme Court must hear appeals regarding specific types of constitutional issues. Its decisions often include *majority, concurring,* and *minority* opinions. A *majority* opinion is the opinion of the Court in which the majority of its members join. A *concurring* opinion is a separate opinion delivered by one or more judges which agrees with the decision of the majority of the court but offers its own reasons for reaching that decision. A *minority* opinion disagrees with the result reached by the majority and thus disagrees with the reasoning and/or the principles of law used by the majority in deciding the case. Supreme Court decisions have significant effects on the entire U.S. legal system and constitute its most important legal precedents.

The power of the Supreme Court is limited to review of decisions of the state courts that involve a federal question. However, it has the power to declare unconstitutional any federal or state statute that is contrary to the U.S. Constitution. The Supreme Court has original jurisdiction in some instances. In cases involving ambassadors or other public ministers or consuls, and those where a state is a party, the Supreme Court has original jurisdiction; that is, it acts as the trier of fact as well as deciding issues of law. The cases over which the Supreme Court has original jurisdiction, however, are few. Usually a case reaches the Supreme Court only when a party petitions the Court for a writ of certiorari.

---

[14]U.S. Const. Art III, §2.

Special Federal Courts and Panels

The special federal courts include the U.S. Court of Claims, Customs Court, and Court of Customs and Patent Appeals, all of which are courts of record. The U.S. Tax Court and the U.S. Court of Military Appeals are not true courts but are quasi-judicial agencies.

There is also a Judicial Panel on Multidistrict Litigation, which handles coordinated or consolidated pretrial proceedings of actions that (1) involve similar questions of law and fact, and (2) are filed simultaneously by different parties against the same defendant(s).[15] This panel does not necessarily hear "class action" suits, wherein one or a few individuals sue an entire class (whose members are too numerous for a joinder). For example, an automobile owner whose automobile was defective might sue the company on behalf of all other similarly situated automobile owners.

U.S. Court of Claims

The U.S. Court of Claims has jurisdiction to render judgment upon any claim against the United States founded upon (1) the Constitution of the United States, (2) any act of Congress, (3) any regulation of an executive department, (4) any express or implied contract with the United States, or (5) for liquidated or unliquidated damages in cases not sounding in tort.[16]

The district courts have concurrent jurisdiction with the court of claims on general claims in which the United States is a party in controversies where the dispute involves more than $50,000.

U.S. Customs Court

The U.S. Customs Court, which consists of a senior judge and several judges, has exclusive jurisdiction of civil actions involving violations of customs laws. This includes review or protest of decisions of customs officials involving imported merchandise. More particularly, the U.S. Customs Court has exclusive jurisdiction when any of the following issues are involved: appraisement, classification, and rates of duties; exclusion from entry or delivery, liquidation or reliquidation; and refusal to pay claims or reliquidate an entry.[17]

U.S. Court of Customs and Patent Appeals

The U.S. Court of Customs and Patent Appeals is an appellate court having jurisdiction over appeals from (1) all final decisions of the U.S. Customs Court, (2) the Board of Appeals and the Board of Interference Examiners of the Patent and Trademark Office as related to patent applications and interferences, (3) the Commission of Patents and Trademarks as related to trademark applications and proceedings, and (4) the U.S. Court of Appeals for the Federal Circuit.

• State Court Systems

As paralegals, most of you will be working primarily with your local county and state court system. Familiarize yourself with the court system of your particular

[15]28 U.S.C.A §1407.
[16]28 U.S.C.A. §1491.
[17]U.S.C.A. §1582.

state, especially the court rules, jurisdictional subjects and amounts, filing fees and procedures. Your local court should have a book of local court rules and schedules of filing fees. The court rules may differ from county to county.

The organization of the various state court systems in the United States is not uniform, but most consist of the following courts:

1. A supreme court, or court of last resort.
2. An intermediate appellate court, usually called the court of appeals.
3. Numerous courts of regional jurisdiction, that is, trial courts where suits are commenced.
4. Lower courts, such as small claims, probate, juvenile, and other specialized courts.

Some states have more than one intermediate appellate court to handle the congestion of cases in the state's highest court. In California, for example, there are five appellate districts, each with a district court of appeals composed of one or more divisions and three justices. Usually a case is originally brought and tried in a trial court. Under proper circumstances, it may be appealed to higher courts having appellate jurisdiction until it reaches the state's highest appellate court—or, in some cases, the U.S. Supreme Court.

Several states are divided into circuits or districts with a court for each. Other states have only one original trial court that is composed of geographical divisions. The captions of any documents filed in such courts should reflect the geographical division. The courts in one state do not have control over, or relation to, the courts of another state. (See Exhibit 1.3 for a typical state court system.)

State Supreme Court

Most state *supreme courts,* or *courts of last resort* (they are not always called the supreme court), have appellate jurisdiction over all controversies arising in the state trial courts unless the state has an intermediate court of appeals. Generally speaking, they have original jurisdiction in writs of mandamus, habeas corpus, prohibition, certiorari, and certain other civil actions as specified in the state's constitution.

There is only one supreme appellate court in each state. In Oklahoma and Texas, the criminal courts of appeals are the courts of last resort in criminal cases.

In 45 states the highest court is designated as the supreme court. In the remaining five states, the highest court is designated as follows:

Maine	Supreme Judicial Court
Maryland	Court of Appeals
Massachusetts	Supreme Judicial Court
New York	Court of Appeals
West Virginia	Supreme Court of Appeals

State Intermediate Court of Appeals

State courts of intermediate review, or *intermediate courts of appeals,* exercise appellate jurisdiction over decisions of the lower courts (i.e., superior, circuit, etc.). In some states, such as California, they have original jurisdiction to issue writs of mandamus, habeas corpus, certiorari, and prohibition proceedings.

Exhibit 1.3

Typical State Court System

SUPREME COURT
Court of Final Review. Also referred to as Court of
Appeals, Supreme Judicial Court, or Supreme Court
of Appeals

COURT OF APPEALS
Intermediate Appellate Courts. Acts as an
intermediate appellate tribunal between the trial
court and the court of final review. Almost half the
States in other states appeals go directly to the
Supreme Court.

SUPERIOR COURT
Highest trial court with general jurisdiction. Also
called Circuit Court, District Court, Court of
Common Pleas, and in New York, Supreme Court

PROBATE COURT	COUNTY COURT	MUNCIPAL COURT
Called the Surrogate Court or Orphan's Court in some states. A special court which handles wills, administration of estates, guardianship of minors and incompetents.	Often called Common Pleas or District Courts. Limited jurisdiction in both civil and criminal cases.	Also called magistrates courts. Tries less important cases.

JUSTICE OF THE PEACE AND POLICE MAGISTRATE	DOMESTIC RELATIONS COURT
Lowest courts handling relatively minor cases. Limited in jurisdiction in both civil and criminal cases.	Also called Family Court or Juvenile Court

In many states, the decisions of lower courts are first appealed to an appellate court, such as a superior court (discussed next). In California, for instance, appeals from a municipal court are presented to the appellate department of the superior court. However, an appeal from the superior court would be presented to the state's district courts of appeals. In all states an appeal may be taken to the state's court of last resort.

In a few states, the appellate jurisdiction of the intermediate courts of appeals is restricted. In Illinois, for example, the appellate courts do not have jurisdiction over criminal cases involving felonies. In Georgia, the appellate courts have jurisdiction only over appeals involving the constitution of Georgia, the Constitution of the United States, divorce cases, and other types of equity proceedings.

State Superior Courts

The *superior courts* are the highest state courts of original jurisdiction. In some states these courts are called *circuit courts, district courts,* or *courts of common pleas.* They are frequently referred to as *trial courts.* (In New York the highest state court of original jurisdiction is designated as the *supreme court.*) They have general jurisdiction over civil, criminal, and equity matters. Their jurisdiction frequently extends to two or three counties.

In addition to original jurisdiction in the first instance, the state superior courts often have appellate jurisdiction over cases originated in the lower courts, such as municipal, justice, and small claims courts. In some states their appellate jurisdiction extends to the probate court.

The superior courts in some states have separate "departments" that have jurisdiction over special matters, such as matters of law or equity. These courts have a civil division (with no equity jurisdiction) and a criminal division. The monetary jurisdiction of the superior court in most states is $5,000 or more.

State Lower Courts

Lower courts include those whose proceedings are directly subject to review by a higher court, such as municipal courts, justice-of-the-peace courts, small claims courts, city courts, traffic courts, police courts, justice courts, magistrates' courts, recorder's courts, village courts, mayor's courts, and town courts.

All of these types of lower courts have limited jurisdiction. In criminal cases, they are generally restricted to misdemeanors, preliminary hearings, or inquiries in felony cases. In civil actions, they typically have jurisdiction over cases involving small amounts of money. For example, the jurisdiction of the municipal court in California is limited to civil actions of $10,000 or less. In Alabama, however, courts with similar monetary jurisdiction are designated as district courts.

Generally speaking, lower courts are not courts of record. In many instances, the judges are frequently not lawyers and are appointed (rather than elected) to office. However, some states require qualifying examinations for these judges. The decisions of these courts are subject to review by the higher courts.

Small Claims Courts

Small claims courts are frequently designated as conciliation courts, general sessions, magistrates' courts, city court, or civil courts. Generally, small claims courts handle small monetary claims such as those involving property damage, wages, collection of rent, breach of contract, delinquent accounts, and even small personal injury claims.

A client may come to your attorney with a case that belongs in small claims court. Since small claims courts normally do not allow an attorney to be present except upon appeal, you might want to provide some information for the client strictly as a courtesy. However, there is no uniform system for small claims courts, and in some states attorneys are allowed to participate. Most parties find that the amount of money involved, which can be anywhere from $100 or less to $5,000, does not warrant the expense of legal representation.

Most small claims courts will provide you with a pamphlet explaining their procedure. The procedures are kept informal so the most laypersons can understand them. The parties simply tell their stories to the judge, who then asks questions as necessary. These courts have subpoena power, but it is seldom used. The exclusionary rules of evidence are rarely employed. The parties may bring witnesses, and if a business entity is involved, an attorney or other agent may appear on its behalf.

The procedures involved in bringing an action in a small claims court are often simple. The plaintiff prepares a sworn complaint that contains the plaintiff's narrative statement of facts, and pays a nominal filing fee. The clerk of the court mails a copy of the complaint to the defendant's last known address. The defendant is directed to appear on a specified date to defend the plaintiff's allegations. No written answer is usually required from the defendant. The judge subsequently hears the matter.

Special State Courts

Courts of special jurisdiction have original jurisdiction over certain restricted matters. The most common *special courts* are probate courts, criminal courts, justice-of-the-peace courts, chancery courts, juvenile courts, and various other county courts. *Probate courts* have jurisdiction over the probate of wills, administration of a decedent's estate, and the guardianship of minors and incompetents. *Criminal courts* have original jurisdiction over criminal cases. *Justice-of-the-peace courts,* which are quickly disappearing, are usually found in rural areas.

• Summary

The attorney will make any determination as to jurisdiction of a particular case, but to be effective in performing your paralegal tasks, you should be able to differentiate among the various types of jurisdiction. Your attorney will also make any decision regarding the choosing of forums, but if you have a good working knowledge of how to forum shop, you will better understand the reason for many of your assignments. Also, a good familiarity with the court system will aid you in working with the courts. Knowing the purpose of long-arm statutes likewise will give you a better understanding of why your attorney is taking certain actions in a case. Thus, this chapter provides a foundation to which you can refer again and again as questions arise.

How to Initiate a Civil Action

• Introduction

The purpose of this chapter is to familiarize you with the various procedures involved in commencing a civil action. Causes of actions and counts are explained, and the importance of parties, capacity, and status is examined. One cannot work in a law office without knowing the significance of statutes of limitations.

Techniques for preparing the basic parts of a civil action—the complaint, any counterclaims, crossclaims, and third-party claims—are presented, along with two detailed checklists. Understanding service of process and the issuance, form, and service of summons is absolutely necessary. Because you frequently will have to locate a potential defendant in order to have him or her served, 20 useful techniques are given on how to find defendants.

• Paralegal's Role in Commencing Civil Actions

As a litigation paralegal, you may be given varying degrees of responsibility in the initiation of a lawsuit. One attorney may give you the entire file and ask you to draft a complaint without further direction. Another may give you specific allegations to be inserted in the complaint.

This chapter gives you essential information and techniques to help you assist your attorney in preparing a civil action on behalf of the plaintiff. The sample pleadings are based on the *Federal Rules of Civil Procedure* rather than the rules of any particular state. Although many states pattern their civil codes of procedure after the *Federal Rules of Civil Procedure*, be sure to check the statutes in the forum state where the civil action is to be commenced in a state court. The local court rules should also be checked.

To be proficient as a paralegal and to save time on future work, refine your procedures and techniques. Build a solid forms file by copying forms that may be adapted to other cases.

If the suit is to be filed in a federal district court, you must check that particular district court's rules. The federal courts have increasingly used local rules in efforts to manage discovery time limits. Accordingly, federal judges themselves have promulgated rules for actions filed in these districts. When an action is filed in federal court, call the clerk's office and obtain a copy of the court's and the specific judge's rules.

• Causes of Actions and Counts

For purposes of this discussion a *cause of action* is defined as "the claim upon which relief may be granted" in an action. In other words, a cause of action is a *right to sue*. People are not legally responsible, or liable, for every injury that they cause, only those injuries specified by the law. Therefore, a cause of action is simply a legally acceptable reason for bringing a lawsuit against another party.

A cause of action may arise out of various civil wrongs committed by one party upon another. Examples are tort, breach of contract, libel, slander, defamation, trespass, fraud, breach of statutory duty, abuse of process, alienation of affections, assault, battery, deceit, criminal conversation, public nuisance, interference with contractual relations, trespass to chattels, and malicious prosecution, among many others.

A cause of action is described in a complaint by *statements*, that is, allegations that set forth the facts supporting the charge that a wrong was committed or is being committed by one party against another, or that there is a failure to perform or an anticipatory breach of duty.

Essentially, there are six elements in a cause of action:

1. The plaintiff's right.
2. The defendant's duty.
3. Proximate cause.
4. A breach of that duty occurred.
5. Injury or damage to the plaintiff resulted.
6. The breach of that duty was the substantial cause of injury; therefore, the plaintiff is entitled to compensation for damages from the injury.

The cause of action is the heart of the complaint. If the cause of action is written incorrectly, it may result in a dismissal of the complaint, or possibly require an amendment to the complaint.

It is imperative that before drafting the complaint, you study the particular jurisdiction in which the complaint is to be filed. Become familiar with the rules of procedure and the case law applicable to that particular court. Study the case law on adequate pleadings or examine the pleadings in the form file in your office or the law library.

The plaintiff must also allege that the breach of the defendant's duty proximately caused the plaintiff's injuries. To have a valid claim, the plaintiff must suffer damages of some kind, for example, medical bills, or something like psychological trauma, damages that may have been unknown at the time of the filing of the complaint.

Counts may be set forth as either alternate theories of recovery or wholly separate causes of action, for example, negligence, fraud, or intentional tort. Several counts may appear in one complaint. If so, you should number each count and set forth each one separately from the other. Certain paragraphs may be re-alleged and included in the beginning paragraph of each count.

• Parties, Capacity, and Status

Real Party in Interest

Rule 17 of the *Federal Rules of Civil Procedure* provides that every action shall be prosecuted in the name of the *real party in interest*, that is, the person who is entitled to recovery under the cause of action. An executor, administrator, personal representative, guardian, bailee, trustee of an express trust, a party with whom or in whose name a contract has been made for the benefit of another, or a party authorized by statute may sue in his or her own name without joining with the party for whose benefit the action is brought. When a statute of the United States so provides, an action for the use or benefit of another can be brought in the name of the United States.

No action can be dismissed on the grounds that it is not prosecuted in the name of the real party in interest until a reasonable time has been allowed after objection for ratification or commencement of the action by, or joinder or substitution of, the real party in interest. Such ratification, joinder, or substitution shall have the same effect as if the action had been commenced in the name of the real party in interest.

Capacity To Sue or Be Sued

In federal courts, the capacity of an individual, other than one acting in a representative capacity, to sue or be sued is determined by the law of the individual's *domicile,* that is, the place where the fixed and permanent home and principal establishment exists, and to which the individual returns or has the intention of returning when absent. In other words, states look to their individual statutes to determine domicile.

The capacity of a corporation to sue or be sued is determined by the laws of the state under which the corporation was organized. In all other cases, capacity to sue or be sued is determined by the laws of the state in which the district court is held. However, a partnership or other unincorporated association that has no such capacity by the laws of the state may sue or be sued in its common name. The capacity of a receiver appointed by a court of the United States to sue or be sued in a court of the United States is governed by Title 28, U.S.C. §§ 754 and 959(a).

Status of Infants or Incompetent Persons

Whenever a party has the status of an infant or incompetent person, that is, a person incapable of acting on his or her own behalf, a representative, (e.g., general guardian, committee, conservator, or similar fiduciary) can sue or defend on behalf of that party. If an infant or incompetent person does not have a duly appointed representative, a *next friend* or a *guardian ad litem* can assume that role. The next friend is usually a relative, and is responsible for the property of the proceedings and the court costs. A guardian *ad litem* is a person appointed by a court to have the control or management of the person or property, or both, of the infant or the person deemed incompetent.

The court may appoint a guardian *ad litem* for an infant or incompetent person who is not otherwise represented in an action. The court may make any order necessary for the protection of the infant or incompetent person.

Many state statutes provide that trusts be set up with a bond posted by the trustee whenever money is awarded to an incompetent person or minor. Always check local statutes to ascertain the correct procedure.

• Importance of Statutes of Limitations

A statute of limitations is a period of time fixed by statute within which a lawsuit must be commenced, or the claimant will be forever barred from the right to bring the action. A statute of limitations may be as short as one year or as long as 20 years, or even more. It begins to run against the claim once the cause of action has occurred. For example, in a contract action, the cause of action becomes actionable from the day the defendant breaches the contract. In a personal injury action, the right to a cause of action begins the day the accident occurs.

Minors are exempt from the statutes of limitations and normally have one year from reaching the age of majority in which to bring their cause of action.

In an action based on account stated—that is, a suit based on an account between the parties that has been assented to as correct, either expressly or by implication of law from the failure to object—the right to a cause of action starts from the date of the last entry.

The failure of a plaintiff to bring suit within the specified statutory period is an affirmative defense to the action that must be raised by the defendant or it is considered waived by the defendant.

One of the purposes of statutes of limitations is to prevent "stale" claims that make it more difficult to locate evidence and available witnesses, and that have become stale due to plaintiff's negligence or inattentiveness. Some states base their statutes upon the nature of the plaintiff's claim, whether it is a breach of contract or injury to person or property. Often a cause of action may have a combination of injuries; therefore, one statute of limitations may have run out, partially barring the plaintiff's claim, while another has not. Carefully check all potential statutes of limitations that may apply, and be sure your firm has some sort of docket or tickler system to track statute of limitation dates (see Chapter 13).

• What Is a Complaint?

There are three parts to a complaint:

1. a caption.
2. a body, with jurisdictional averments or allegations, facts, plaintiff's rights, defendant's duties, breach of those duties, resulting injuries and damages.
3. the relief area known as the *wherefore clause,* where the remedy sought is specified.

Exhibits 2.1, 2.2, and 2.3 are three samples of typical complaints: personal injury, medical malpractice and breach of contract. Some of these complaints may be a bit more detailed than is necessary in your state. Check the form files for your state and the applicable codes to ensure conformity.

• Solid Techniques for Preparing Complaints, Counterclaims, Crossclaims, and Third-Party Claims

A *pleading* is any of the formal papers filed with the courts that states the facts each party will try to prove as to the other party's claim or defense. Court pleadings include complaints, answers, replies, counterclaims, crossclaims, and third-party claims. Other court papers may include notices, interrogatories, requests for admissions, motions, and briefs.

Exhibit 2.1

**Complaint for
Personal Injury**

IN THE UNITED STATES DISTRICT COURT
FOR THE NORTHERN DISTRICT OF GEORGIA
ATLANTA DIVISION

EVINS KEISLER and)
CATHIE KEISLER,)
)
    Plaintiffs,)
)   Civil Action
)
v.)
)   File No. _____
JOSEPH L. HANSEN, and)
STEPHENS, INC., a Delaware)
Corporation, Jointly)   COMPLAINT
and Severally,)
)
    Defendants.)
)

COME NOW EVINS KEISLER and CATHIE KEISLER, Plaintiffs in the above action which is over and above the jurisdictional amount of $50,000. Plaintiffs are residents of 70 Delk Road, Cobb County, Georgia, and now state their Complaint as follows:

1.

The Defendant STEPHENS, INC., is a Delaware Corporation qualified to do business in the State of Georgia and is subject to the jurisdiction of this Court. Its agent for service is Laddin Corporations Systems, Inc., 2200 Carnegie Building, Atlanta, Fulton County, Georgia 30301.

2.

The Defendant JOSEPH L. HANSEN is a resident of 1401 Emory Drive, Apartment "G," Decatur, DeKalb County, Georgia 30329, and is subject to the jurisdiction of this Court.

3.

On November 17, 1990, at approximately 2:50 p.m., Plaintiff EVINS KEISLER, was driving a 1990 Toyota MR-2, License No. DNK 968, which automobile is owned by him, in a northerly direction on Peachtree Street in Atlanta, Fulton County, Georgia 30301.

4.

On November 17, 1990, at approximately 2:50 p.m., Defendant, JOSEPH L. HANSEN, was driving a 1990 Mazda Miata, License No. BZB 626, owned by the Defendant, STEPHENS, INC., in a northerly direction on Peachtree Street in Atlanta, Fulton County, Georgia 30301.

5.

Defendant JOSEPH L. HANSEN owed Plaintiff a duty of reasonable care in operating his vehicle in a safe and prudent manner. Defendant JOSEPH L. HANSEN breached that duty by driving in a negligent and careless fashion so as to collide into the backside of the automobile driven by Plaintiff EVINS KEISLER. Defendant is the proximate cause of the injuries suffered by Plaintiffs because they were the foreseeable consequence of the original injury created by the Defendant's negligence.

Exhibit 2.1

Continued

6.

On November 17, 1990, at approximately 2:50 p.m., the Defendant, JOSEPH L. HANSEN, was the agent of Defendant STEPHENS, INC. At the time the automobile driven by Defendant JOSEPH L. HANSEN ran into and hit the automobile driven by Plaintiff EVINS KEISLER, Defendant JOSEPH L. HANSEN was acting within the scope of and in the employment of Defendant STEPHENS, INC.

7.

Plaintiff EVINS KEISLER's leg had been previously injured and operated on approximately nine times and was almost completely healed prior to the date of the accident on November 17, 1990. Plaintiff EVINS KEISLER had gained almost total use of his leg. As a result of this injury, the metal shank in Plaintiff EVINS KEISLER's leg that gives support and alignment to the fibula between the knee and the ankle shifted position. This shift caused the screws used to hold his shank to break, causing further injury to Plaintiff EVINS KEISLER's leg. Plaintiff EVINS KEISLER has suffered and continues to suffer from the infection and drainage of his knee. Because of this injury described, the bones have further separated to the extent that Plaintiff EVINS KEISLER has lost extensive use of his leg and may have to undergo amputation in the near future.

8.[1]

The negligence of Defendants JOSEPH L HANSEN, and STEPHENS, INC., and each of them, was a direct and proximate cause of the resulting collision, and of the injuries to Plaintiff EVINS KEISLER. Plaintiff EVINS KEISLER was injured and has suffered great pain and suffering to his damage in the sum of ONE HUNDRED THOUSAND DOLLARS ($100,000).[2]

9.[3]

Defendants' negligence, and each of them, was the direct and proximate result of the substantial damage to Plaintiff EVINS KEISLER's automobile in the amount of EIGHTEEN HUNDRED AND NO/100 DOLLARS ($1800), plus towing charges of ONE HUNDRED AND EIGHTY-FIVE AND NO/100 DOLLARS ($185) totaling NINETEEN HUNDRED EIGHTY-FIVE AND NO/100 DOLLARS ($1985). Plaintiff EVINS KEISLER has been without the use of his vehicle since the date of the accident.

10.

Further as a result of Defendants JOSEPH L. HANSEN and STEPHENS, INC.s' negligent conduct, and each of them, Plaintiff EVINS KEISLER has lost his job and has suffered lost wages in the approximate amount of EIGHTY-EIGHT THOUSAND NO/100 DOLLARS ($88,000). In addition, Plaintiff EVINS KEISLER has incurred medical and pharmaceutical expenses for his care in the approximate amount of ONE HUNDRED FIFTEEN THOUSAND AND NO/100 DOLLARS ($115,000). As a result of the negligence of the Defendants, and each of them, Plaintiff EVINS KEISLER will incur extensive additional medical and hospital expenses in the future.

11.

As a result of Defendants' negligent conduct, and each of them, Plaintiff CATHIE KEISLER has suffered loss of consortium of her husband, Plaintiff EVINS KEISLER, in the amount of THIRTY THOUSAND DOLLARS ($30,000).

WHEREFORE, Plaintiffs EVINS KEISLER and CATHIE KEISLER demand:

1. That service be perfected upon Defendant JOSEPH L. HANSEN, and Defendant STEPHENS, INC.;
2. That Plaintiff EVINS KEISLER be awarded damages against Defendant JOSEPH L. HANSEN, and Defendant STEPHENS, INC., jointly and severally, in the sum of FIVE HUNDRED THOUSAND DOLLARS ($500,000) for past and future physical and mental pain and suffering;
3. That Plaintiff EVINS KEISLER have and recover the sum of TWO HUNDRED FIVE THOUSAND NINE HUNDRED EIGHTY-FIVE DOLLARS ($205,985) against

Exhibit 2.1

Continued

Defendants JOSEPH L. HANSEN and STEPHENS, INC., and each of them, jointly and severally, for special damages plus all costs of this action; and

4. That Plaintiff CATHIE KEISLER be awarded damages against Defendants JOSEPH L. HANSEN, and STEPHENS, INC., and each of them, jointly and severally, in the sum of THIRTY THOUSAND DOLLARS ($30,000) for loss of consortium of her husband, Plaintiff EVINS KEISLER; and

5. That Plaintiffs EVINS KEISLER and CATHIE KEISLER have such other and further relief as this Court may deem just and proper.

JONATHAN, BRUINS & SNEAD
Attorneys at Law

_____

Samuel A. Jonathan

SANDRA KOREY
Attorney for Plaintiffs
2165 Northview Drive
Atlanta, Georgia 30318
(404) 223-4567

EVINS KEISLER, under oath hereby states that he has read the foregoing complaint, and that the matters stated therein are true to the best of his knowledge, information and belief.[4]

_____

EVINS KEISLER

Subscribed and sworn to before
this 3rd day of March 1991.

_____
Notary Public

My commission expires _____

CATHIE KEISLER, under oath hereby states that she has read the foregoing complaint, and that the matters stated therein are true to the best of her knowledge, information and belief.[5]

_____

CATHIE KEISLER

Subscribed and sworn to before
this 3rd day of March 1991.

_____
Notary Public

My commission expires _____

[1] Paragraph 8 is not used in no-fault states.

[2] Check your local or federal rules to determine the minimum jurisdictional amount of damages required to file an action in that particular court. As of the date of this publication, the minimal jurisdictional amount in the federal courts is $50,000.

[3] Paragraph 9 is not used in no-fault states.

[4] This clause is not required in some states.

[5] This clause is not required in some states.

Exhibit 2.2
•
**Complaint for
Medical Malpractice**

IN THE UNITED STATES DISTRICT COURT
NORTHERN DISTRICT OF GEORGIA
GAINESVILLE DIVISION

Gary Wall,	)	
	)	
Plaintiff,	)	
	)	
vs.	)	CIVIL ACTION FILE NO.:
	)	
REBECCA PETERS, M.D.,	)	
and REBECCA PETERS, M.D., P.C.	)	
	)	
Defendants.	)	

<u>COMPLAINT</u>

COMES NOW, the Plaintiff Gary Wall by and through his counsel Don C. Keenan and The Keenan Ashman Firm, and George Peacock, and Peacock & Peacock, co-counsel, and files this Complaint with this court against the above-named Defendants and states as follows:

1.

Plaintiff, Gary Wall, is a natural person, more than eighteen years of age and is a citizen of the United States and a resident of the State of North Carolina.

2.

Defendant Rebecca Peters, M.D., is a resident of Hall County, City of Gainesville, Georgia, and is subject to the jurisdiction and venue of this court. Service of process may be perfected at Defendant's office, located at 230 Live Oak Trail, N.E., Suite 168, Gainesville, Georgia 30501.

3.

Defendant Rebecca Peters, M.D., P.C., is a professional association with its principal place of business at 230 Live Oak Trail, N.E., Suite 168, Gainesville, Georgia 30501. Service may be made on the Defendant through its registered agent for service, Rebecca Peters, M.D., P.C., at 230 Live Oak Trail, N.E., Suite 168, Gainesville, Georgia 30501.

4.

Jurisdiction of this Honorable Court is based upon diversity of citizenship pursuant to 28 U.S.C., §1332, and venue is proper by virtue of 28 U.S.C., §1391.

5.

This is a personal injury action, alleging medical negligence on the part of the Defendants and injury in excess of $50,000. Accordingly, the amount in controversy in this action exceeds $50,000.

6.

At all relevant times, the Defendant Rebecca Peters, M.D., was acting as agent of the corporate Defendant, Rebecca Peters, M.D., P.C., and was acting within the scope of that agency, rendering the corporate Defendant Rebecca Peters, M.D., P.C., legally responsible for any and all damage to Plaintiff Gary Wall proximately caused by negligence of Defendant Rebecca Peters, M.D.

Exhibit 2.2

Continued

7.

On or about 2 March 1988, the Defendant Rebecca Peters, M.D., undertook the care and treatment of Plaintiff Gary Wall.

8.

Defendant Rebecca Peters, M.D., diagnosed the Plaintiff, Gary Wall, by physical examination as having pseudotumor cerebri, and began treating the patient for this condition.

9.

Plaintiff Gary Wall saw the Defendant Rebecca Peters, M.D., on at least six additional office visits between 12 November 1988 and 14 February 1990, during which time his vision got progressively worse and he continued to experience excruciating headaches.

10.

Despite the Plaintiff's persistence of headaches with increasing visual field defects and progressive visual loss leading to blindness, the Defendant Rebecca Peters, M.D., failed to appropriately treat Gary Wall's symptoms or diagnose that he was suffering from the effects of a tumor.

11.

Due to the negligence of the Defendants Rebecca Peters, M.D., and Rebecca Peters, M.D., P.C., Gary Wall is blind.

COUNT I - NEGLIGENCE

12.

The allegations contained in Paragraphs 1 through 11 set out herein are hereby and herewith reasserted and re-alleged by reference as if more fully and completely set out in this second count.

13.

Defendant Rebecca Peters, M.D., was negligent in failing to exercise reasonable degree of care, and but not limited to, the following:

A. Failure to obtain a lumbar puncture to confirm a diagnosis of pseudotumor cerebri;

B. Failure to perform visual field studies and visual acuity studies to follow the course of Plaintiff's condition; and

C. Failure to timely intervene with appropriate surgical treatment to alleviate persistent intracranial hypertension and obviate blindness.

See attached Affidavit of expert.

14.

As a direct and proximate result of the negligence of the Defendants, Gary Wall is blind.

COUNT II - BREACH OF CONTRACT

The allegations contained in Paragraphs 1 through 14 set out herein are hereby and herewith reasserted and re-alleged by reference as if more fully and completely set out in this second count.

Exhibit 2.2
●
Continued

16.

Defendants Rebecca Peters, M.D., and Rebecca Peters, M.D., P.C., have breached their implied contract with the Plaintiff by failing to exercise the requisite standard of care and skill for the diagnosis and treatment of brain tumor. In one or more, but not limited to, the following:

A. Failure to obtain a lumbar puncture to confirm a diagnosis of pseudotumor cerebri;

B. Failure to perform visual field studies and visual acuity studies to follow the course of Plaintiff's condition; and

C. Failure to timely intervene with appropriate surgical treatment to alleviate persistent intracranial hypertension and obviate blindness.

See attached Affidavit of expert.

17.

As a direct and proximate result of the breach of said contract by Defendants Rebecca Peters, M.D., and Rebecca Peters, M.D., P.C., Gary Wall is now blind.

18.

ACCORDINGLY, the Plaintiff requests the following damages:

A. past loss of income;

B. future loss of income;

C. past pain and suffering;

D. future pain and suffering;

E. permanent disability; and

F. such other relief as the evidence and justice demands.

Further, Plaintiff demands that a jury be empaneled to resolve all factual issues in this case.

This 12th day of November, 1990.

Respectfully submitted,
THE KEENAN ASHMAN FIRM

DON C. KEENAN
Georgia State Bar No.: 410650
Lead-counsel for Plaintiff

THE KEENAN BUILDING
148 Nassau Street, N.W.
Atlanta, Georgia 30303
(404) 523-2200

PEACOCK & PEACOCK

George C. Peacock
North Carolina State Bar No.: 3434

218 Lake Forest Road
Raleigh, North Carolina 27604
(919) 599-4821

Exhibit 2.2
•
Continued

AFFIDAVIT OF W. J. JOHNSON, M.D.

Before the undersigned, an officer duly authorized to administer oaths, personally appeared Dr. W. J. Johnson and after being duly sworn, deposes and states under oath as follows:

1.

I, Dr. W. J. Johnson, am over 18 years of age and am giving this Affidavit as required by O.C.G.A. 9-11-9.1. I understand that it will be used by Mr. Gary Wall in a civil action against Dr. Rebecca Peters, a Gainesville, Georgia, neurologist.

2.

I reside in Garden City, Kansas. I am a 1966 graduate of University of Tennessee Medical School, Memphis, Tennessee, with an M.D. degree. I am board certified by the American Board of Neurology and Psychiatry as a neurologist, and have been so certified since 1975. I have been a Professor of Neurology and Ophthalmology at the College of Medicine, University of Kansas, since 1986. I have practiced medicine since 1966, and have been a practitioner and teacher in the field of Neurology since 1971.

3.

A copy of a professional resume current as of 1990 is attached which summarizes my qualifications, practice experience, academic appointments, publications, research projects and research interests.

4.

I served as a consulting medical expert for the purpose of evaluating medical care provided to Gary Wall. I have reviewed the following medical records:

1. Chattahooche Family Practice 8/2/87 - 8/20/90
2. Dr. James Bowen 2/16/88 - 4/10/88
3. Dr. Rebecca Peters 2/19/88 - 2/22/90
4. Dr. Ida Laccabue 2/23/90 - 8/3/90
5. Dr. Sam Sears 8/6/90 - 10/3/90
6. Dr. Paul Nehring 4/25/90 - 7/23/90
7. Dr. Ross Grumet 3/2/90 - 5/7/90
8. Dr. James W. Bruno 12/6/90 - 1/9/90

5.

Based upon my personal knowledge and experience in the field of medicine, and specifically neurology and ophthalmology, and based upon my review of the records enumerated above, it is my opinion that the minimum standard of care for treatment by a neurologist of Mr. Wall, who presented as a patient with symptoms over a two-year period which included papilledema, transient vision loss, diminished visual fields, diminished visual acuity, and headache, required the following:

1. A lumbar puncture to confirm the diagnosis of pseudotumor cerebri. This is necessary because the diagnosis can only be confirmed when there is documented increased opening pressure of the puncture with normal cerebrospinal fluid (except for an anticipated subnormal protein content).
2. Verification of vision by performing tests to measure visual fields and visual acuity. This is necessary because visual loss, particularly peripheral vision loss, can result from persistent intracranial hypertension.
3. Use of appropriate surgical treatment to alleviate persistent intracranial hypertension. This is necessary when visual loss persists to prevent permanent vision loss.

Exhibit 2.2
●
Continued

6.

Based on my review of the records enumerated in paragraph 4, it is my opinion that Dr. Rebecca Peters, a neurologist of Gainesville, Georgia, was negligent in that she failed to treat Gary Wall with the reasonable degree of care and skill generally practiced by physicians, and failed to provide care within the standard of care enumerated in paragraph 5.

In particular, the medical records reflect that Dr. Rebecca Peters provided professional services to Gary Wall over a two-year period and treated him for pseudotumor cerebri without doing a lumbar puncture to confirm the diagnosis, without testing for visual acuity and visual fields, without conducting tests to determine the extent of vision loss being experienced by Gary Wall during the course of his treatment, and without considering surgical treatment to reduce intracranial pressure.

7.

It is my opinion that the failure of Dr. Rebecca Peters to meet the standard of care was a proximate cause of the irreversible loss of vision which Gary Wall has experienced and, had Gary Wall received care within the enumerated standard of care, Gary Wall would not be blind.

DATED: _____

_____

W. J. Johnson, M.D.

STATE OF KANSAS
COUNTY OF _____

Personally appeared before me W. J. Johnson, M.D., who, being by me first duly sworn, stated and affirmed that he has read this document, that the statements contained therein are true, and that he signed this affidavit on the date above written.

_____

Notary Public

My Commission Expires: (SEAL)

A pleading is included in the term *legal document,* although there is a technical difference. A pleading consists of formal written allegations or statements of the parties who file it with the court to maintain the suit, or to defeat it, for the judgment of the court. The original pleading is filed with the court and stamped by the clerk. A service copy is filed simultaneously, and stamped.

If the attorney wishes for the sheriff or marshall to serve the service copy, it is either left with the clerk of the court or delivered to the sheriff's or marshall's office. Many attorneys have private process servers serve the complaint. In this case, the process server must take the original stamp-filed complaint with him or her at the time of service. After service the process server completes the "return-of-service" section that may appear on the back of the complaint or on a separate document.

Finally, the original is filed with the court with the return-of-service information completed by either the sheriff, marshall, or process server. Marshals no

Exhibit 2.3

**Complaint for Breach
of Contract**

IN THE UNITED STATES DISTRICT COURT
FOR THE NORTHERN DISTRICT OF GEORGIA
ATLANTA DIVISION

SONO GROUP, INC.,   )
a Georgia corporation,   )
)
)
)
        Plaintiff,   )
)   Civil Action
)
v.   )
)   File No. _____
GEORGE C. PEACOCK, and   )
JACQUELINE C. M. PEACOCK,   )
)
        Defendants.   )
)   COMPLAINT FOR BREACH
)   OF CONTRACT
)
_____)

COMES NOW Plaintiff the SONO GROUP, INC., and alleges and complains as follows:

1.

Plaintiff is and at all times mentioned herein was a corporation in good standing with the State of Georgia with its principal place of business in the County of Fayette.

2.

Plaintiff is informed and believes and thereon alleges that at all times herein mentioned each of the Defendants sued herein was acting within the scope of employment at all times mentioned herein.

3.

The contract upon which this action is based was made and was to be performed in the County of Fayette, State of Georgia.

4.

On or about March 14, 1990, Defendants, and each of them, entered into a written agreement to purchase a 1988 IBM PS/2 computer and a Deskjet Plus Printer for $1000 from Plaintiff.

5.

Plaintiff delivered the 1988 IBM PS/2 computer and Deskjet Printer to Defendants, and performed all of the conditions, covenants and promises required by it to be performed in accordance with the terms and conditions of the contract, by delivering the computer and printer to Defendants.

6.

Defendants, and each of them, breached their written agreement with Plaintiff by failing and refusing to perform in good faith their promise to pay Plaintiff $1000 for the computer and printer, and refusing to communicate with Plaintiff.

Exhibit 2.3

●

Continued

7.

As a result of the breach of the Defendants, and each of them, in the obligations pursuant to the written contract, the entire sum of $1000 due Plaintiff from Defendants, is now due, owing, and unpaid. Demand has been made on Defendants, and each of them, for said sum, but Defendants, and each of them, have failed and refused, and continue to fail and refuse, to pay said sum. Defendants, and each of them, have therefore breached their written contract with Plaintiff, who has been damaged thereby in the sum of $1000 plus interest at the legal rate from and after the date due according to proof.

WHEREFORE Plaintiff prays for judgment against Defendants, and each of them, as follows:

1. For the sum of $1000 for breach of contract and the value of its performance;
2. For interest thereon at the legal rate from and after March 14, 1990;
3. For costs incurred herein; and
4. For such other and further relief as the court may deem just and proper.

Robin M. Lepore
Attorney for Plaintiff

longer serve complaints in many states. Check your local rules. A copy of the pleading or court paper must be mailed to the attorney(s) for the other party(s) under most court rules.

The following step-by-step procedure will help you prepare complaints, counterclaims, crossclaims, and third-party claims more efficiently, based on the *Federal Rules of Civil Procedure:*

- **Step 1:** Set forth a short statement of the grounds for jurisdiction unless the court already has jurisdiction, and the claim needs no new grounds of jurisdiction to support it [Rule 8(a)(1)]. If you are filing in a state court, include a statement setting forth venue.

- **Step 2:** Make the pleading simple, concise, and direct. No technical forms of pleadings for motion are required [Rule 8(e)(1)].

- **Step 3:** Set forth two or more statements of a claim alternately or hypothetically, either in one count or in separate counts. State as many separate claims as the party has, regardless of consistency and whether based on legal, equitable, or maritime grounds [Rule 8(e)(2)].

  Again, if filing in a state court, determine if that particular court has jurisdiction over an equitable matter. Some state courts can hear only legal matters; others can hear both legal and equitable matters.

- **Step 4:** State the capacity of the parties only to show jurisdiction of the court [Rule 9(a)].

- **Step 5:** Set forth statements of fraud and mistake [Rule 9(b)].

- **Step 6:**   Set forth allegations of malice, intent, knowledge, and/or other conditions [Rule 9(b)].

- **Step 7:**   Set forth performance or the occurrence of conditions precedent with generality, i.e., show that all conditions precedent have been performed or have occurred [Rule 9(c)].

- **Step 8:**   If alleging that a document was filed or an official act was done, it is sufficient to just state compliance. The allegation need not be specific [Rule 9(d)].

- **Step 9:**   Set forth judgments or decisions of domestic or foreign courts, judicial or quasi-judicial tribunals without specifying the jurisdiction for the judgment, decision, etc. [Rule 9(e)].

- **Step 10:**   Set forth statements of time and place [Rule 9(f)].

- **Step 11:**   Set forth items of special damages (medical and hospital bills, etc.) giving a description of item, amount of damages, date of expense (damage), etc. [Rule 9(g)].[6]

- **Step 12:**   Set forth a short and plain statement of the claim, showing that the pleader is entitled to relief [Rule 8(a)(2)].

- **Step 13:**   Set forth a demand for judgment for the relief to which the pleader claims to be entitled. Relief of an alternative type or of several different types may be demanded [Rule 8(a)(3)].

- **Step 14:**   Include a verification, with a notary public's signature and seal.

Exhibit 2.4 is a checklist for drafting complaints, counterclaims, crossclaims, and third-party claims. Exhibit 2.5 is a checklist for the final preparation of these documents. The verification referred to in item 14 on the checklist is shown in Exhibit 2.6.

• Perfecting Service of Process

Service of process is governed by Rule 4 of the *Federal Rules of Civil Procedure.*[7] After a complaint is filed, the clerk of the court issues the summons and delivers it to the marshal or to a person specifically appointed to serve it. The plaintiff may request separate or additional summons to be issued against any defendants. In many states, an attorney can issue a summons rather than having it issued solely by the court.

---

[6]Some state courts, e.g., California, set forth allegations in the pleading that, "The specific or actual amount of damages is unknown, and the party requests leave to amend the pleading when the amounts are known."

[7]Check your state statutes and procedural rules for specific rules in your state court regarding service of process.

General

Document captioned correctly with

- Name of court-county-city.
- Case name and number.
- Statement of the name of the document, e.g., complaint, petition, amended complaint or petition, answer, or reply.
- Parties and capacity.
- If the pleading is not a complaint, include the judge's name in the caption, as well as all attorneys of record.
- Paragraph numbering if required in this state.
- Separate statement of causes or defenses joined in the same pleading. All possible theories for recovery set forth.
- Prayer for relief based on theory of case. (Is a prayer for general relief sufficient, or should a prayer for specific relief be included?)
- Document signed by the party or the representative attorney, and the telephone number and address given.
- Pleading verified as required. (See Exhibit 2.6)

Style

- Pleading confined to the issuable facts, as distinguished from evidentiary facts and conclusions of law, under the codes. Under rules of court based upon the *Federal Rules of Civil Procedure,* pleading must be a short, plain statement free from vagueness and ambiguity.
- Pleading brief and stated simply and directly, with repetitions eliminated.
- Statements direct and positive, leaving nothing to inference
- Pleading adheres to the rule of definiteness, certainty, and clarity, so that the opposing party is reasonably informed as to what is proposed to be proved.
- Written instrument(s) upon which the case is founded are attached to the pleading.

Content

- Every material fact essential to the statement of a cause or a good defense is alleged.
- Allegations, if proved, would show as a matter of law the essential elements of the cause or defense to be in the pleader's favor.
- Pleading sufficient with respect to statements and affirmative defenses, such as
    Notice.
    Demand.
    Performance of statutory conditions precedent.
    Ownership.
    Possession.
    Contributory negligence.
    Assumption of risk.
    Lack of consideration.
    Limitation.
- Items of damages specially pleaded where necessary.

Exhibit 2.4

Continued

Parties, Jurisdiction, Venue

○ All appropriate parties included as plaintiff(s) and defendant(s). (Is there a local statute allowing a "Jane or John Doe" party until additional discovery has been made?)

Husbands or wives.

Heirs.

Personal representatives, e.g., guardians.

Partners.

Proper parties; necessary parties.

○ Parties have legal capacity to sue or to be sued.

A partnership or a corporation is involved in the litigation.

Infants or incompetent persons are represented by guardians, next friends, or guardians *ad litem.*

○ Plaintiff has a real interest in the cause, either as an individual or a representative, as distinguished from the holder of a mere naked legal title when the beneficial interest is vested in another.

There been some injury to the plaintiff's personal or property rights.

The plaintiff's interest is a present, substantial interest as distinguished from a future or contingent interest.

The plaintiff will derive benefit from a judgment.

○ The real party in interest is the one bringing the action (if statutes require it to be so brought).

○ The cause is within the jurisdiction of the court.

Requirements as to amount in controversy are satisfied.

Jurisdiction is correct according to residence of the parties, situs of the property involved, and the transitory or local nature of the action.

○ Venue is proper.

Venue is proper according to the local or transitory nature of the action, residence or domicile of the parties, and place of the transaction.

A change of venue should be requested on the grounds of bringing the action in the wrong county, belief that a fair and impartial trial cannot be had in the present forum, or convenience of the parties.

The summons must be signed by the clerk with the clerk's seal. It must indicate the name of the court, the names of the parties, the names of the defendant(s), and the name and address of the plaintiff(s)' attorney. If the plaintiff(s) does not have an attorney, the summons must indicate the address of the plaintiff(s).

The summons must indicate the time by which the defendant(s) must appear and defend the action according to the *Federal Rules of Civil Procedure.* Most states have a printed summons form. If you draft a summons, make sure it states that if the defendant(s) does not appear, a default will be entered against the defendant(s) for the relief demanded in the complaint.

Service of process must be made by a U.S. marshal, deputy, or by some person specially appointed by the court. The server must not be a party to the action and must be over 18 years old.

Service of the summons and complaint must be made in one of the ways listed in Exhibit 2.7.

- Proper court designation.
- Correct spelling of parties' names.
- Properly completed summons. (In many states, an attorney can issue a summons rather than having it issued solely by the court.)
- Sufficient instructions to party serving the documents.
- In states that require them, proper court covers, or *bluebacks* (heavy paper used to cover complaints, some with a return-of-service form printed on one side).
- Correct amount of filing fees.
- Use of mandatory standard (printed) forms.
- Proper use of Arabic numbers (1, 2, 3) or Roman numerals (I, II, III).
- Sufficient number of copies.
- Exhibits attached and properly marked.
- Verification made where necessary (see Form 2.6).
- According to local federal and state courts' rules, proper size of paper upon which pleading is prepared. The most commonly used is 8 and one-half by 11 inches, with 1-inch margins around the entire sheet. [5]
- Proper signatures, i.e., attorney and client, where necessary.
- Proper spacing. (All pleadings should be double-spaced, except for legal descriptions and excerpts from cases, which may be single-spaced.)
- Copies of complaint conformed. (To conform a signature in a complaint insert "/s/" together with the person's name either typed or handwritten. For example: /s/ Kim A. Turner.)
- Errors, omissions, and deletions conformed on copies of pleadings.
- New subjects beginning on a new page.

• What You Should Know About Service and Filing of Complaints, Counterclaims, Crossclaims, and Third-Party Claims

The process of initiating a civil action involves much more than drafting the complaint. You must be familiar with the procedures and local court rules involving the service and filing of the complaint, counterclaim, crossclaim, or third-party claim. The local rules and fees change frequently, and it is important for you to keep your notes up to date to prevent the embarrassment of having a pleading returned and perhaps missing a statute of limitations.

When Service Is Required

According to Rule 5(a) of the *Federal Rules of Civil Procedure,* all orders, pleadings, discovery documents, written motions, notices, appearances, demands, offers of judgment, and designations of record on appeal must be served upon all parties of record in the lawsuit. Service does not need to be made on parties in default for failure to appear. Pleadings asserting new or additional claims for relief against those parties in default shall be served upon them in the same manner that a summons is served.

Exhibit 2.6
•
Verification

VERIFICATION

STATE OF GEORGIA,

COUNTY OF _____

Personally before the undersigned Notary Public of the State of _____ ,
an officer authorized by law to administer oaths therein, came and appeared _____ ,
who after being duly sworn, deposes and says that affiant is (plaintiff/defendant), and
that the facts set forth in the foregoing pleading are true to the best of affiant's knowledge
and belief.

_____

Sworn to and subscribed before me
this _____ day of _____, 19

_____
          Notary Public

(Affix Seal)

Service is usually accomplished by mail and a certificate of service (or *proof
of service* or *acknowledgment of service*, as it is referred to in some states) may be
prepared, showing that the particular pleading or other paper was mailed to all
parties of record or their attorneys.[8]
In an action for seizure of property in that no person is named as a defendant, any service required to be made prior to the filing of a response, claim, or
appearance must be made upon the person having custody or possession of the
property at the time of its seizure.[9]

How Service Is Made

According to the *Federal Rules of Civil Procedure*, service upon a party represented
by an attorney shall be made upon the attorney by delivering a copy of the
document to the attorney, by mailing the document to the attorney at the last
known address or, if no address is known, by leaving it with the clerk of the
court. Delivery of a copy means

1. Handing it to the attorney; or
2. Leaving it at the attorney's office with the clerk or other person in
   charge; or
3. If there is no one in charge, leaving it in a conspicuous place;[10] or

---

[8]See Exhibit 8.1.

[9]Rule 5(a).

[10]In some states, e.g., California, this is not considered proper service. Check the state code of
the forum state.

Exhibit 2.7

Federal Rules for Service of Process

Party To Be Served	Manner of Service
Individual	By delivering a copy of the summons and complaint to him personally, or by leaving copies at his residence with a person of suitable age and discretion residing therein, or by delivering a copy of the summons and complaint to an agent authorized by appointment or by law to receive service of process [Rule 4(d)(1)].
Infant or incompetent	By serving the summons and complaint in the manner prescribed by law of the state in which the service is made for the service of summons or other like process upon any such defendant in an action brought in the courts of general jurisdiction of that state [Rule 4(d)(2)].
Domestic or foreign corporation, partnership, or other unincorporated association that is subject to suit under a common name	By delivering a copy of the summons and complaint to an officer, managing or general agent, or to any other agent authorized by appointment or by law to receive service of process and, if the agent is one authorized by statute to receive service and the statute so requires, by also mailing a copy to the defendant [Rule 4(d)(3)].
United States	By delivering a copy of the summons and complaint to the U.S. attorney for the district in which the action is brought or to an assistant U.S. attorney or clerical employee designated by the U.S. attorney in a writing filed with the clerk of the court and by sending a copy of the summons and complaint by registered or by certified mail to the attorney general of the United States at Washington, D.C., and in any action attacking the validity of an order of an officer or agency of the United States not made a party, by also sending a copy of the summons and complaint by registered or certified mail to such officer or agency [Rule 4(d)(4)].
Officer or agency of the United States	By serving the U.S. officer or agency and by sending a copy of the summons and complaint by registered or certified mail to such officer or agency. If the agency is a corporation, the copy shall be delivered in the same manner as a domestic or foreign corporation [Rule 4(d)(5)].
State or municipal corporation or other government organization subject to suit	By delivering a copy of the summons and complaint to the chief executive officer thereof or by serving the summons and complaint in the manner prescribed by the law of that state for the service of summons or other like process upon any such defendant [Rule 4(d)(6)].
Nonresident defendant	For service of summons and complaint upon an individual or corporation or party not an inhabitant of or found within the state in which the district court is held, service may be made in the manner prescribed by the law of the state in which the district court is held, e.g., by publication [Rule 4(e)].
Party in foreign country	Where federal or state law authorizes service upon a party not an inhabitant of or found within the state in which the district court is held, service may be effected upon the party in a foreign country in the manner provided in Rule 4(i).

4. If the office is closed or the person to be served has no office, leaving it at the attorney's home or usual place of residence with some person, preferably over the age of 18, who resides in the home.[11]

---

[11]See *Encyclopedia of Federal Procedure*, 3d ed., §1201.

Service by mail is deemed complete upon mailing.[12] If there is an unusually large number of defendants, the court may order limited services upon the parties.[13]

Filing Pleadings

Under the *Federal Rules of Civil Procedure,* all papers after the complaint that are served upon a party must be filed with the clerk of the court either before service or within a reasonable time thereafter.[14] In some instances, the judge may allow documents to be filed with him or her. If so, the clerk will note the filing date on the document and will send it to the clerk's office for filing in the court's file.[15]

Due to the voluminous nature of the legal business, some courts (federal and state) do not require filing of copies of pleadings such as interrogatories and requests for production. Always check local court rules to ascertain whether the court accepts filing of these pleadings or if the court merely requires a notice of service.

Also check the discovery cutoff date for filing certain pleadings and documents prior to trial, such as answers to interrogatories, responses to requests for production, responses to requests for admissions and depositions.

• Twenty Dependable Ways to Locate Defendants

In addition to the numerous investigative methods used to locate missing persons and defendants outlined in Chapter 7, the following techniques will be helpful. Because the least expensive and most practical methods are listed first, it is better to use these methods in the order given. The *Federal Collections Act* and various state statutes affect the limitations of creditors in contacting and investigating debtors and using other collection procedures. Therefore, be sure to review your state's statutes to determine the legality of the following methods in your state. For example, some states consider contacting a previous employer or neighbors to be harassment. Exercise caution in this sensitive area of the law.

1. Write the defendant at his or her last known address and request a corrected address from the postmaster by writing "Address Correction Requested" under the return address. If the post office has a new address, it will submit it to you for a nominal charge.

2. Send a certified or registered letter, marked "Return Receipt Requested." Check the box on the card provided by the post office entitled, "Show to whom, date, and address of delivery." Use a plain envelope, addressed in longhand, but do not indicate a return name or address. The postal carrier will deliver the letter to the (defendant) addressee and request his or her signature on the card. Include a brief note in the letter inviting the defendant to work out a suitable arrangement to the dispute, for example, payment of money owed. Send the letter to the defendant's last known address.

---

[12]Rule 5(b).

[13]Rule 5(c).

[14]Rule 5(d).

[15]Rule 5(e). See also *Encyclopedia of Federal Procedure.*

3. Conduct a *postal search* by obtaining a form from your local post office, filling out the subjects's last known address, and sending it to the post office in that location. The post office will send you any information available for a nominal charge.

In a small town or rural area, check with the local postmaster for information regarding the defendant's whereabouts.

4. Send a telegram via Western Union's "Report, Delivery and Address" service.

5. Check with the local credit bureaus in the area where the defendant previously resided to determine (a) if they have had recent inquiries from creditors, employers or out-of-town credit bureaus; and (b) if they have a record of lenders, bankers, employers, previous addresses, aliases, previous spouses, charge accounts, real estate owned, automobile registrations, or any other pertinent information.

6. Contact the defendant's landlord and previous landlord to determine

  a. If the new or forwarding address is known.

  b. Names of references given by the defendant prior to taking occupancy.

  c. Name of the moving company for date moved, and location of where furniture was delivered or stored.

  d. Number and age of defendant's children and schools attended. Contact the schools for record of transfer.

  e. Physical description, i.e., race, age, sex, color of hair and eyes, and other characteristics.

If landlord is a neighbor, ask the questions pertaining to neighbors listed in item 8 of this list.

7. Contact mortgagee of property if still owned by defendant to determine current residence address. Also notify your attorney, who may want to consider reducing the defendant's debt to judgment to protect the client's interest. If you are able to determine the property is rented, ask the occupant to whom and where address payments are sent.

If property has been sold, ask who handled the closing, and ask that company or attorney the present address and the name of the bank where the defendant deposited the sales proceeds, the name of the store, or the party who cashed the check.

8. Contact neighbors, local stores, gas stations, and previous addresses, etc. In addition to the questions listed in item 6, determine

  a. If the present address is known;

  b. The defendant's wife's maiden name, if applicable, and the address of both the defendant's and his wife's parents or other relatives known;

  c. Names and addresses of friends, doctors, dentists, clubs, unions, churches, and veterans' organizations;

  d. If neighbors or the present occupant of last known address is holding mail for defendant, obtain the name and address of the sender;

  e. If gas stations or garages honor defendant's credit cards, from what companies?

9. Contact gas, electric, water, and telephone companies for record of changes of address and the names of references given when the accounts were opened. Contact companies that may have made home deliveries (e.g., milk, paper, etc.) to the defendant.

10. Check the civil and criminal divisions of local and county courts and the state police for relevant information on the defendant and his or her assets. If a criminal record is found, check with the parole officer if one was assigned (even though term of parole may have expired).

11. Check the county and/or local court records within the defendant's jurisdiction according to his or her last known and previous address for

    a. Current real estate ownership (if located, follow the same steps as in item 7 of this list); and

    b. Marriage licenses, births, divorces, voter registration, or other vital statistics' records that may reveal relevant leads.

12. Check all known lodges, clubs, unions, churches, veteran's organizations for

    a. Current address of record;

    b. Record of transfer to another branch, locale, etc.;

    c. Record of those who nominated, vouched, or stood for defendant;

    d. Record of other affiliation; and

    e. Record of insurance policy and name and address of beneficiary.

13. Contact all known relatives and friends of both defendant and his spouse to determine

    a. If present address is known;

    b. The names and addresses of other friends and relatives;

    c. Information that may lead to other areas of the country and information regarding conversations defendant may have had regarding a move to another area; and

    d. Ask the questions listed in item 8.

14. Contact the local army, navy, air force, and marine recruiting boards to determine record of defendant's enlistment.

15. Contact defendant's bank(s), both checking and savings. If unknown, ask previous employers to review old paychecks and to give the name of the bank where checks were deposited or the names of stores or individuals who cashed checks and to ascertain the bank account number indicated on the back of checks.

If defendant's bank account(s) is located, obtain defendant's current address. Consult your attorney regarding the advisability of attaching the defendant's account.

If defendant's bank account(s) is closed, determine

    a. The bank to which funds were transferred or the address where the closeout check was mailed by the previous bank;

    b. The name of payers and payees available from the bank's records that reflect deposits and disbursements; and

    c. The names of references given to the bank by the defendant when the account was opened.

If a loan was granted to the defendant, obtain relevant information from the bank's file if possible.

16. Contact defendant's present and past employers to determine if defendant is still employed, in which case ask for current address and hours and location of employment. If defendant travels, obtain defendant's itinerary.

If defendant is no longer with the employer, ask if present address is known. Keep in mind that the defendant must obtain a withholding tax form from his or her previous employers at the end of the year. If address is not known, obtain

    a. Name of defendant's former immediate supervisor (interview the supervisor, if possible);

    b. Length of employment and date defendant left and the circumstances;

    c. Exact nature of defendant's work;

    d. Names of friends and co-workers (obtain permission to interview them); and

    e. From personnel files, obtain if possible defendant's history and references, name of bonding company, beneficiary's name, and defendant's address indicated on insurance policy, name of employment agency, and the names of potential employers who may have contacted this employer regarding defendant.

From fellow workers determine names of clubs, unions, churches, veterans organizations, other occupation(s) or business(es), previous jobs, nicknames or aliases, and information from conversations defendant may have had about his future plans.

17. Contact trade references, finance companies, and banks to determine

    a. Date the defendant was last seen;

    b. Date credit was last extended and type of loan;

    c. How loan was paid and whose checks were cashed; and

    d. From company files, names and addresses of employers, relatives, friends, lodges, clubs, unions, and any other references.

18. Check your state and neighboring states for

    a. Current address of record on registration and driver's licenses for both defendant and spouse;

    b. Current license tag number and record of insurance carrier if such information has been recorded by the state;

    c. If state will permit, request to be notified if defendant or spouse makes new contact with the state agency.

19. Check with the principal seller of defendant's automobile, in addition to dealer's service manager and mechanics for

    a. Additional information the company may have in its files or that someone there may recall;

    b. Tag number issued at the time of automobile purchase by defendant;

    c. Color of automobile and unusual features; and

   d. Full details of the trade (check with the state for previous address, lien holders, etc.).

20. Offer a reward for information on the defendant.

• Summary

To draft a complaint, counterclaim, crossclaim or third-party claim effectively, you must understand all the various parts of the pleading, and their relation to each other. Careful attention must be given to statutes of limitations, and you must know the rules for service of process. Check your local and state codes for all details of procedure.

    In all instances, you should check and recheck your work. Any doubt about a particular portion of the pleading should be researched. Developing a form file is important to keep you from "reinventing the wheel," but always make sure your form is restyled to suit the particular facts of the case you are working on. In reality, there is no standard pleading, and every clause should be examined. In time you will develop shortcuts of your own.

3

Responding on Behalf of the Defendant

• Introduction

The purpose of Chapter 3 is to introduce you to the various types of responses, or answers, that a defendant may make to a complaint, counterclaim, and cross-complaint and to explain the various parts of the answer. Techniques to help you prepare the initial draft of the answer are given in a step-by-step procedure, along with a sample answer. A practical method for computing the time in which an answer to a complaint, or a response to a motion, must be filed is presented. The rules of amended pleadings are also discussed.

Defenses to negligence are explained to help you better understand the duties owed by one person to another in substantive law. No-fault statutes are briefly explained.

• Defendant's Response

Upon service of the complaint, the action is initiated and the legal process begins. The defendant may choose not to answer the complaint and thus default, or the defendant may choose to attack the complaint through appropriate motions, file a petition to have the case removed from state court to federal court, or respond to the complaint in the form of a pleading called an *answer*. The defendant may respond by amending, opposing, or replying as necessary within a specified period of time set by law.

Your contribution as a paralegal to the responsive pleading stage will depend upon the degree of responsibility your attorney gives you. Some attorneys will let you draft the initial draft of the answer and then they will make changes to your draft. Others will have you do the primary research so that they may draft the answer.

An Attack on the Complaint Is Not An Answer

An attack on the complaint is merely an assertion that the complaint is defective, but is not a proper answer. A detailed discussion of these attacks in the form of "demurrers," a "motion to strike," or a "motion for judgment on the pleadings," is in Chapter 6. Check with the forum state to see if these remedies are available to the defendant. If the attack is unsuccessful, the defendant then must answer the complaint.

Types of Answers

Possible responses by a defendant to a plaintiff's complaint include legal defenses, denials (untrue, no contest, or neither admitting nor denying), admissions, affirmative defenses, counterclaims and crossclaims. In the answer, the defendant can admit or deny the allegations in the complaint and present his or her defenses. In other words, if the complaint is sufficient in law, it must be overcome, if at all, on the facts. Thus, you may state, "Defendant Morrison is without sufficient knowledge and neither admits nor denies and leaves Plaintiffs to their proofs." Further, the defendant may admit a portion of the allegation and deny the balance. Be sure to check your state statutes and local court rules to determine the legality of these types of answers.

The primary function of the answer is to give the defendant an opportunity to respond to the complaint and raise defenses to the plaintiff's allegations of fact. It also serves to notify the plaintiff of the defenses and other allegations of the defendant in order to enable the plaintiff to prepare his or her proof and prevent the defendant from taking unfair advantage of the plaintiff by surprise or through a technicality.

The answer is the defendant's *defense* or *denial,* or both. It admits what is true and denies what is not. The defendant may use the answer to reject the allegations of the plaintiff set forth in the complaint because they are untrue or because the defendant's actions against the plaintiff were justifiable. In other words, the defendant may have committed the actions alleged, but have a defense to performing those actions. For example, Plaintiff Griner alleges that Defendant Kramer removed Plaintiff's CD player from his car after Defendant Kramer sold it to him. Kramer can deny he took the CD, or he can allege that he took the CD because Griner failed to pay for it. The first is a denial, the second a defense.

It is wise to use both denials and defenses in preparing an answer to a complaint, depending upon the facts of the case and the relevant legal theories, in order to maximize the protection available to the defendant.

When Are Verifications Necessary?

A verification is a sworn statement that accompanies a pleading, dated and signed by the party filing the pleading.[1] If your attorney wants a verified complaint, be sure not to plead inconsistent facts. In a verification to a pleading, the affiant declares that to the best of his knowledge and belief, all facts contained in the pleading are true and correct.[2] (See Form 2.4 in Chapter 2.)

Except for specific provisions (e.g., Rule 65(b)),[3] The *Federal Rules of Civil Procedure* does not require that pleadings be verified or accompanied by an affidavit executed by the party. However, answers to interrogatories must be verified. If the facts contained in the pleadings are not of record, some states require that pleadings be verified or accompanied by a sworn affidavit.

---

[1] Pleadings as discussed here include any documents filed with the court, e.g., complaint, answer, etc.

[2] Affidavits are executed under penalty of perjury in most states.

[3] Rule 65(b) pertains to complaints seeking temporary restraining orders.

In some states (e.g., California) the effect of filing a verified complaint compels the defendant to file a verified answer. This forces the defendant to answer specifically, paragraph by paragraph, each and every allegation of the complaint. If the defendant does not do this, any allegations unanswered are deemed admitted.

If the defendant files a general denial in his or her answer to a verified complaint, the plaintiff may file a motion to strike the answer on the ground that it is not a verified answer. On the other hand, if the complaint is unverified, the defendant, in turn, may file a general denial on that basis.

If someone other than the plaintiff verifies the complaint, the defendant can make a motion to strike the complaint on the grounds of improper verification. Any duly authorized officer of a corporate entity may execute the verification on the behalf of the corporation.

Verified pleadings can be used to support or oppose summary judgment motions, They are similar to affidavits. Again, check your state statutes and procedural rules to determine whether verifications are required in your state for the particular action for which you are preparing the pleading. (See Exhibit 2.6 in Chapter 2.)

• Techniques for Drafting the Answer

When you receive the complaint from your attorney with the request to make an initial draft of the answer on behalf of your defendant client, you will usually find that the attorney has written in the margin of the complaint, beside each allegation of the complaint, either "admit" or "deny," or a combination of both if there are separable allegations in the complaint. If your attorney has not written specific notes on the complaint, ask for specific instructions as to how to answer each allegation.

This section will lead you through the various steps in preparing the initial draft of the answer for your attorney. A sample answer to a complaint for medical malpractice is presented in Exhibit 3.1. The complaint was shown in Exhibit 2.2 in Chapter 2.

Waiver or Preservation of Certain Defenses

Rule 12(h)(1) of the *Federal Rules of Civil Procedure* provides that a defense of lack of jurisdiction over the person, improper venue, insufficiency of process, or insufficiency of service of process is waived if they are omitted from the first responsive pleading filed by the defendant.

Under Rule 12(h)(2) a defense of failure to state a claim upon which relief can be granted, a defense of failure to join a party indispensable, and an objection of failure to state a legal defense to a claim may be made in any pleading permitted or ordered under Rule 7(a)—that is, an answer, reply to a counterclaim, answer to a crossclaim, third-party answer, or a reply to a third-party answer. These defenses may also be made by motion or at the trial on the merits.

Rule 12(h)(3) further provides that whenever it appears by suggestion of the parties or otherwise that the court lacks jurisdiction of the subject matter, the court may dismiss the action.

Exhibit 3.1

**Answer To Complaint for
Medical Malpractice**

IN THE UNITED STATES DISTRICT COURT
NORTHERN DISTRICT OF GEORGIA
GAINESVILLE DIVISION

Gary Wall,   )
)
   Plaintiff,   )
)
vs.   )   CIVIL ACTION FILE NO.:
)
REBECCA PETERS, M.D.,   )
and REBECCA PETERS, M.D., P.C.   )
)
   Defendants.   )

A N S W E R

Come now Defendants, REBECCA PETERS, M.D., and REBECCA PETERS, M.D., P.C., and answer Plaintiff's Complaint as follows:

1.

Defendants admit the allegations contained in Paragraph 1 of Plaintiff's Complaint, except the allegation as to the residence of the Plaintiff, and Defendants are without knowledge sufficient to form a belief as to the truth of that allegation.

2.

Defendants admit the allegations contained in Paragraphs 2 and 3 of Plaintiff's Complaint.

3.

In answer to Paragraph 4, Defendants state that they are without knowledge sufficient to form a belief as to the correctness of the allegation concerning the jurisdictional basis of the case as they are without knowledge sufficient to form a belief as to the exact present residence of the Plaintiff. Subject to that, the allegations of Paragraph 4 are admitted.

4.

In answer to Paragraph 5, Defendants admit that the Plaintiff seeks recovery in an amount exceeding $50,000, but it is denied that the Plaintiff is entitled to recover in that amount or in any other amount.

5.

In answer to Paragraph 6, the allegation of agency is admitted, but it is denied that Rebecca Peters, M.D., P.C., is legally responsible for any damages, and it is denied that Defendant Rebecca Peters was negligent. Thus, it is denied that any act or omission on the part of either Defendant proximately caused any injury or damage to the Plaintiff.

6.

In answer to Paragraph 7, it is admitted that on or about 2 March 1988, Defendant Rebecca Peters, M.D., agreed to and did serve as a neurological consultant to Plaintiff's physician, Dr. Mark Schmidt. It is further admitted that insofar as the scope of the consultation was concerned, Defendant Peters undertook the care and treatment of the Plaintiff.

Exhibit 3.1

Continued

7.

The allegations contained in Paragraph 8 are denied, as stated. In further explanation, Defendant Peters made an initial diagnosis of anterior papillitis, and she began treating the Plaintiff for that. Furthermore, Defendant Peters did think that the Plaintiff had a very minimal picture of pseudotumor, but there was no actual diagnosis of such.

8.

The allegations of Paragraph 9 are admitted as to the number of visits, but it is denied that during those visits the Plaintiff reported progressively worsening vision or excruciating headaches. Furthermore, insofar as the use of the word "continued" implies that the Plaintiff was experiencing excruciating headaches at the time of the first visit, it is denied that he reported such to Defendant Peters.

9.

Defendants deny the allegations contained in Paragraphs 10 and 11 of Plaintiff's Complaint.

COUNT ONE

1.

In answer to Paragraph 12 of Count I, Defendants incorporate by reference their responses to Paragraphs 1 through 11 of the Complaint.

2.

Defendants deny the allegations contained in Paragraphs 13 and 14 of Count I including each and every subparagraph stated therein.

COUNT TWO

1.

In answer to Paragraph 15 of Count II, Defendants incorporate by reference their responses to Paragraphs 1 through 14 of the Complaint.

2.

Defendants deny the allegations contained in Paragraph 16 and 17 including each and every subparagraph stated therein.

3.

Though Paragraph 18 seems to be a demand for relief requiring no answer of Defendants, insofar as an answer may be required, it is admitted that the Plaintiff seeks the items of damages listed in Paragraph 18, but Defendants deny that the Plaintiff is entitled to recover for those items of alleged damage or any other.

WHEREFORE, Defendants REBECCA PETERS, M.D., and REBECCA PETERS, M.D., P.C., pray that they be discharged from liability with costs assessed against the Plaintiff.

Mark S. Schreiner
Attorney for Defendants
Georgia State Bar Number: 21466

• Step-by-Step Procedure for Drafting the Answer

Your attorney will probably heavily edit your draft of the answer and other defenses, but you can assist him or her by drafting as much of the answer as you can. Follow this step-by-step procedure to ensure that you prepare your draft as accurately as possible and point out areas of concern to your attorney:

• Step 1:   Check local procedures and forms for pleading guidelines.

Notice pleading and code pleading govern answers the same way they govern complaints. Notice pleading stems from the federal system in which the goal of the complaint is to give enough information to notify the defendant of the nature of the claims against him or her. There is no requirement that ultimate facts be alleged. Plaintiffs must simply provide a "short and plain statement of the claim showing the pleader is entitled to relief." The technicalities of pleading facts, conclusions of law, etc., are unimportant in notice pleading. The plaintiff does not have to state a cause of action in the sense of identifying all the essential facts that go to the elements of the cause of action.

In a notice-pleading court, the complaint will not be thrown out if it fails to plead an ultimate fact or if it includes conclusions of law—so long as the complaint gives adequate notice of the nature of the claim.

Notice pleading does not necessarily require a different kind of pleading from fact pleading; notice pleading is simply more liberal, or tolerant of what is acceptable.[4]

If code pleading governs in the applicable jurisdiction, the answer must contain more detail than in a notice pleading jurisdiction. As for other pleadings, there are specific requirements for the content of the answer, the time in which to answer, and manner in which a defendant must respond. Again, it is necessary to check the court rules governing the preparation of pleadings in the jurisdiction where the action has been commenced.

• Step 2:   Design the answer to fit the facts of the case.

If you have a form given to you by another paralegal or an attorney, or have obtained a standard form from a form book, always be sure to rewrite the form in line with applicable statutes and precedents. In other words, never use canned forms verbatim. Always question each sentence in a form to see whether it is applicable to the facts of the particular case on which you are working.

• Step 3:   Know the parameters of the answer.

The defendant cannot seek relief in the answer. The answer is the defendant's means of defending himself or denying the claims in the complaint, but the defendant cannot seek relief either in the form of monetary damages or other injunctive relief against the plaintiff in the complaint. Rather, he must file his own complaint, counterclaim, or cross-complaint to obtain relief. By denying or defending himself in the answer, the defendant is not automatically entitled to relief.

---

[4]William P. Statsky, *Torts: Personal Injury Litigation,* 2d ed., (Minneapolis/St. Paul, MN.: West Publishing Company, 1990), pp. 155–156.

In the example given earlier, Defendant Kramer may reject the allegations of the complaint, but cannot assert any right to relief against Plaintiff Griner. If Defendant Kramer wants payment for the interest on the debt while Griner had possession, he must file his own complaint or counterclaim to get relief.

Substantive law of negligence. Law is divided into two major areas: substantive law and procedural law. *Substantive law* defines the duties owed by one person to another and concerns the rights of the parties. *Procedural law* defines the steps that must be followed in a lawsuit. The *substantive law of negligence* states that all individuals have a duty to conduct themselves in their activities so as to not create an unreasonable risk of harm to others. The elements that must be proven to show that negligence exists include the following:[5]

    a. *Duty.* The existence of a duty of due care owed by one person to another.

    b. *A breach of that duty.* Failure to conform to the required standard of care, meaning that which is reasonable under the circumstances.

    c. *The cause of the injury.* The conduct in question was the natural and *proximate* (probable) *cause* of the resulting harm. Some states define this as the substantial cause of the injury.

    d. *Injury in fact.* An actual injury or loss must have resulted from the incident.

In an answer, each of these elements must be either admitted or denied. Also, any affirmative defenses should be raised (see Step 4). For example, the issue of duty must be addressed either by denying that the duty of due care was not met, or perhaps by addressing the degree of duty owed and whether it was met, and likewise for breach of that duty. Each element must be addressed separately to show that the defendant conducted herself in a reasonable manner so as not to create an unreasonable risk of harm to others.

• Step 4:   Include necessary parts of the answer.

Most state statutes do not require the answer to be in a specific form but they do require that it be in writing and signed by the defendant himself or his counsel of record. To be sufficient, the answer must (a) admit or deny the allegations upon which the adverse party relies, and (b) state in simple and brief terms the defendant's defenses to each claim asserted. Each of plaintiff's paragraphs in the complaint, counter-complaint, or crossclaim should evoke a paragraph response by defendant.

    Admissions and denials are part of the answer. The affirmative defenses and legal defenses are part of the affirmative defense claim following the answer. Counterclaims and crossclaims are separate from the answer, in that they are the defendant's claims against the other parties. These are not a part of an answer, but rather pleadings to go with the answer.

    As previously mentioned, your attorney may ask you to make an initial draft of the answer and may make notations in the margin of the answer to indicate how you are to draft the response to each particular allegation, such as "admit,"

---

[5]James W. H. McCord, *The Litigation Paralegal* (St. Paul, MN.: West Publishing Company, 1988) p. 46.

"deny," or "lack of knowledge to form a belief." Many answers are similar in nature and you will find yourself using similar phrases in your drafts of answers.

• Step 5:   Admit or deny each allegation in the pleading.

Every answer and subsequent pleading should contain a specific admission or denial of each allegation of the pleading to which it responds. *Admissions* are simply admitting facts, such as the defendant's name and address.

Example: "Defendant admits Paragraph No. 2 of Plaintiff's Complaint. Paragraph No. 2 correctly sets forth Defendant's name and address."

However, failure to deny any specific allegation in the complaint is also held to be an admission thereof. An example of a specific *denial* follows:

Example: The complaint alleges that Darryl was asleep at the wheel of his car at the time of the collision with Corneill. The allegation in the answer should read: "Defendant denies the allegations of Plaintiff's Complaint as set out in Paragraph No. 2 thereof and further denies that he was asleep at the wheel of his car at the time of the collision."

Denials can be general or specific. A *general denial* is a blanket denial of all the allegations in the complaint—the entire complaint. It may be used to respond to an unverified complaint. It is referred to as a general denial because it denies all of the allegations generally, without referring to them individually.

Example: "Defendant denies each and every allegation as set out in Plaintiff's Complaint." Preferably, Defendant should respond to each paragraph in the complaint and admit or deny each allegation separately, any allegation not denied is deemed admitted. Defendant must deny any allegation he wishes to dispute.

If a complaint is unverified, a general denial may be used to respond to it even if it contains true allegations that are included in the general denial. A verified complaint requires a specific denial that is also verified. The defendant may respond to an unverified complaint with specific denials without verification. Remember that a specific denial to both verified and unverified complaints must admit true allegations, whereas there is no such requirement with a general denial.

If individual allegations are partly true, admit the true portions of the paragraph and deny the balance so that some items are not inadvertently admitted. The best way to handle this is to repeat the true allegations verbatim and then deny the remainder.

Example: Suppose Plaintiff Griner alleged, "Defendant Kramer agreed to sell the CD player to Plaintiff Griner for $500, that sum being paid in full to Kramer." Kramer might respond, "Defendant admits that Defendant agreed to sell the CD player to Griner but specifically denies each and every other allegation as untrue except as specifically admitted."

It is not advisable to make affirmative allegations of facts in a specific denial. Even though it may refute the plaintiff's allegation, it may omit direct controversions of facts. For example, suppose Plaintiff Griner alleges that the CD player was given to him in used condition when he purchased it. Defendant Kramer may allege in his answer that plaintiff Griner knew the CD player was used. The allegation of fact by defendant Kramer obviously controverts that of plaintiff Griner. But is this fact helpful or harmful to Kramer? He may be admitting more than he intends to. It is better to use a specific denial of plaintiff Griner's allegation.

Denial based on insufficient information. Frequently, there are allegations in a verified complaint about which the defendant has no knowledge or insufficient personal knowledge to enable her to respond to the allegation under oath. The defendant must state this lack of knowledge, which has the effect of a denial.

Denial based on information and belief. When the defendant has some information with which to respond to the allegations in the complaint and believes the allegations are true (or untrue), she may state that she admits (or denies) "on information and belief." The defendant may choose to deny a part of the complaint and qualify her denial of an allegation. In this instance, she shall specify the portions she knows to be true and shall deny the remainder of the allegation. Denials of allegations must not be evasive, but must fairly answer the substance of the allegation denied.

Verification of answer. An answer need not be verified or accompanied by affidavits unless specifically provided by local rules or statutes. (See Form 2.4 in Chapter 2.)

Negative pregnant. A common error in pleading is to deny an allegation in such a manner as to imply an admission of part of the allegation. Such an evasive and ambiguous form of denial is called a *negative pregnant,* because it is an express denial "pregnant" with an implied admission. For example, if the allegation states, "On Friday, August 3, 1990, Defendant Kramer agreed to sell the CD player to Plaintiff Griner for $500, the sum being paid in full to Kramer," the defendant should be careful not to deny the whole allegation, because the denial is "pregnant" with an implied admission of all the facts in the allegation except for the date. Avoid negative pregnants by denying each allegation in the paragraph.

Example: "Defendant denies that he agreed to sell the CD player to Plaintiff Griner at any time," or "Defendant denies that he owes Plaintiff $500 or any other amount."

• Step 6:   Serve the answer within the statutory time.

Under Rule 12(a) of the *Federal Rules of Civil Procedure,* a defendant must serve his answer within 20 days after the service of the summons and complaint, except when service is made under Rule 4(e) and a different time is prescribed. An answer to a crossclaim and a reply to a counterclaim must also be served within 20 days. The United States, or an officer or agency of the United States, must serve its answer within 60 days after service of the Complaint.

Under most state statutes, you must serve an answer within 30 days after the service of the summons and complaint. Check your state statutes since they may require serving an answer within 5 days. Other kinds of actions have other time requirements. Refer to the summons, since it may designate a time period within which to respond.

Computing the time accurately. According to Rule 6(a) of the *Federal Rules of Civil Procedure,* when computing any period of time, including the time in which an answer to a complaint or a response to a motion must be filed, the day of the act, event, or default from which the designated period of time begins to run should not be counted. Include the last day of the period unless it is a Saturday, a Sunday, or a legal holiday, in which event the period runs until the end of the next day that is not a Saturday, a Sunday, or a legal holiday. If weather or other conditions make the office of the clerk inaccessible for the filing of a paper, exclude those days. Exclude intermediate Saturdays, Sundays, and legal holidays when the period is less than seven days.

"Legal holiday" includes any holidays and any other day appointed as a holiday by the president or Congress of the United States, or by the state in which a district court resides. For rules to use to compute time in your state, check your state statutes and procedural rules.

Add to the present date the number of days you have (e.g., 20 days for an answer). If the number of days is greater than the number of days in the current month, subtract the number of days in the current month to arrive at a due date.

Example: If the answer is due in 20 days, and the complaint is served on January 22, add 20 days to 22 days:

Date of service, January	22
Time allocated for response:	+ 20
Total:	42
Less number of days in Jan.	− 31
	11

February 11 is the due date, unless it is a weekend or holiday, in which case it would be the day succeeding the weekend or holiday, e.g., Monday).

Most lawyers' diaries contain tables for use as a guide in computing deadlines. While these guides are excellent, they are only guides, and you should check the result using the formula given above.

• Step 8:   Raise affirmative defenses.

The defendant must raise affirmative defenses and set them out clearly and affirmatively. You should make sure that the answer reserves the defendant's right to assert other defenses as they become known. The defendant should not rely on a general denial, such as a denial alleging an accord and satisfaction, but should use an affirmative defense that reveals facts that defeat the plaintiff's claim. Although these are not denials, they are new matters that can show that even if all the plaintiff's allegations are true, the defendant has a defense to the claim and should prevail. The answer is the proper vehicle for raising affirmative defense and not the motion.

Substantive law defines affirmative defenses. Each action or claim established by substantive law has one or more defenses that will defeat the claim. For example, you can prove self-defense to defeat a civil action for battery; prove the statement is true to defeat slander; and defeat negligence by proving *contributory negligence* in those jurisdictions still recognizing it as a defense. Assumption of risk, fraud in the inducement, duress, statute of limitations and statute of frauds are some of the other affirmative defenses available to defendant.

Defense based on written document. Where a written instrument is the basis for a defense, attach a copy to the answer as an exhibit or recite it in the answer, unless the affidavit shows the instrument inaccessible.

Default Judgment. The defendant must file the answer or other responsible pleadings within the period of time prescribed by statute. If a judgment by default will be entered against him.

New matter. An affirmative defense is *new matter* constituting a defense, that must be raised in the responsive pleading (e.g., the answer). In simple terms, it means that, assuming plaintiff's allegations are true, she cannot recover for a particular reason.

Example: If an affirmative defense is asserted as follows "Defendant Sam Sears shows that Plaintiff is barred from any relief sought by the applicable statute of limitations," you should state, "Defendant Sam Sears states that the applicable statute of limitations has expired, and therefore Plaintiff is barred from any relief sought in Plaintiff's claim."

In other words, the Defendant admits the truth of the allegation in the complaint; however, no cause of action existed at the time the complaint was filed due to whatever defense the defendant claims.

Rule 8(c) of the *Federal Rules of Civil Procedure* includes the following defenses:[6]

Accord and satisfaction.
Injury by fellow servant.
Arbitration and award.
Laches.
Assumption of risk.
License.
Contributory negligence.
Payment.
Discharge in bankruptcy.
Release.
Duress.
Res judicata.
Estoppel.
Statute of frauds.
Failure of consideration.
Statute of limitations.
Fraud.
Waiver.
Illegality.

Any other matter constituting an avoidance or affirmative defense is also accepted under this rule. In addition, the courts have held the following to be affirmative defenses:[7]

Circuity of actions.
Comparative negligence.
Active and passive negligence.
Election of remedies.

[6]See *Black's Law Dictionary* (Minneapolis/St. Paul, MN.: West Publishing Company, 1991) for a definition of these particular defenses.

[7]George Vetter, *Successful Civil Litigation: How to Win Your Case Before You Enter the Courtroom* (Englewood Cliffs, NJ.: Prentice-Hall, Inc., 1977), p. 47.

Exception or exemption created by statute.

Exclusion in an insurance policy.

Failure to mitigate damages.

Immunity.

Failure to raise a compulsory counterclaim in an earlier action.

Lack of authority.

Justification.

Novation and release.

Patent litigation defenses (e.g., late claiming, prior use, misuse).

Prescription.

Ratification.

Defamation litigation defenses (e.g., privilege, retraction, truth, fair comment, etc.).

Unclean hands.

Failure to comply with statutory provisions wrong party.

• Defenses to Negligence

In substantive law, there are certain duties owed by one person to another. Included in this are the following defenses to negligence: comparative negligence, assumption of the risk, last clear chance, and contributory negligence. Not all states have provisions for these defenses. For example, Louisiana no longer recognizes the defense of assumption of the risk.

Comparative Negligence

Most states have laws of comparative negligence, but be sure to check your particular state statutes. This doctrine permits a plaintiff who is contributorily negligent to recover based upon the percentage of the plaintiff's negligence.

Example: If Marlene Barton walked across a sidewalk where warnings of danger were posted, slipped on a banana peel, but tried to avoid it, a jury might find her 40 percent negligent. If Ms. Barton's total damages were $10,000, then the award would be reduced by 40 percent to $6,000. Some states bar recovery if the comparative negligence exceeds 50 percent.

Assumption of the Risk

Assumption of the risk is a principal of law whereby persons who knowingly place themselves in a dangerous situation may not recover.

Example: If Richard and Sam Sears were riding in their convertible and scooted around a detour sign, riding past it, and then were confronted with a tractor in the road which they subsequently hit, they would be barred from recovery from the driver of the tractor and his employer, because they assumed the risk of injury.

Last Clear Chance

The doctrine of last clear chance permits a plaintiff to recover in spite of the plaintiff's own contributory negligence. The doctrine applies when the plaintiff is in a position of danger, and the defendant knows that the plaintiff cannot save himself. If the defendant has such knowledge in sufficient time to enable him to prevent the injury by the exercise of reasonable care, but thereafter fails to exercise due care, the plaintiff may recover.

As an example, assume a young girl is riding a bicycle in the middle of the street in front of traffic, and the driver of a semi-truck realizes that the girl cannot get out of the way of the moving vehicle. The truck driver would be held liable if he had sufficient time to stop the truck but did not. The doctrine of last clear chance permits recovery even though the girl was contributorily negligent by being in the middle of the road.

Contributory Negligence

Although most states have abolished contributory negligence as a defense, its use should be understood. If the action of the plaintiff, the person suing for injuries, was a contributing factor in the accident, the plaintiff cannot recover her losses from the defendant, the person being sued.[8]

• No-Fault Statutes

Although no-fault statutes are being repealed in many states, some states still have such laws. Generally, no fault refers to a particular minimum level of insurance coverage for bodily injury regardless of fault. Also, the term *no-fault* is often used to refer to statutes that limit the filing of personal injury lawsuits to those reaching a particular dollar amount in medical specials or some other medical/injury criteria.

In no-fault auto insurance, each driver/owner accepts financial responsibility for some or all losses sustained by herself, pedestrians hit by her, and occupants of her own vehicle, in return for which she enjoys immunity from liability for losses to third-party persons. The need to establish fault before reparation is made is eliminated.

Some states have statutes requiring "a serious impairment of body function," or "permanent serious disfigurement," or similar language under the auspices of their no-fault automobile statutes. If the injuries claimed do not meet such a statutory requirement, then an affirmative defense could be raised. Check your state statutes.

• Filing Amended or Supplemental Pleadings

According to Rule 15 of the *Federal Rules of Civil Procedure,* a party may amend his pleading once at any time prior to the responsive pleading being served. If the pleading is one to which no responsive pleading is permitted, and the action has not been placed on the trial calendar, the party may amend it at any time within 20 days after it is served. Because the rules on amended and supplemental pleadings will vary by state, be sure to check your state statutes.

In all other instances, a party may amend her pleading only by leave of the court or by written consent of the adverse party. Such leave will be given freely by the court when the interests of justice so require.

---

[8]McCord, *The Litigation Paralegal,* pp. 46–47.

A party must answer an amended pleading within the time remaining for a response to the original pleading or within ten days after service of the amended pleading, whichever period is longer, unless the court orders otherwise.

When a claim or defense asserted in the amended pleading arose out of an allegation set forth in the original pleading, the amendment relates back to the date of the original pleading.

• Summary

To prepare the initial draft of the answer to a complaint, cross-complaint, counterclaim, or crossclaim, you must understand the various parts of the answer, and their part in the whole document. You must be careful in computing the time in which to respond. Understanding the local procedures and court rules is important to make sure the proper defenses and/or denials are raised. Affirmative defenses are a key part of the answer and must be drafted carefully. Work closely with your attorney and make no assumptions. In all instances, check your state statutes and local court rules before beginning your initial draft of the response.

4

Writing Skills for the Paralegal

• Introduction

You came to your paralegal job with a particular writing style, partly formed by rules of writing learned in school and perhaps influenced by a job in a law firm. Consequently, you may be going by some outdated school rules, and you may have acquired some bad habits of using "legalese," or legal jargon. The purpose of this chapter is to freshen up your writing skills, help you eliminate some unnecessary legal jargon, and refine your writing to a simple and direct style.

Writing well will improve your communication skills and help you advance your career. For instance, good writing skills are a must for a legal assistant manager or paralegal supervisor. In addition to advancing your career, good writing skills can save you time and money. Better communication reduces the chance of confusion, and even embarrassment, resulting from the mistakes that can arise from misunderstanding. Writing well improves self-esteem and confidence and will gain you the respect of the attorneys you work with. It is one of the primary parts of your job: it is communicating.

The good writer in any profession will advance faster than even more educated colleagues. In the law office, attorneys will delegate research assignments to the good writer and entrust him or her with greater responsibilities. In addition, the communication skills that make you a good writer also make you more effective in talking to clients. Attorneys sometimes intimidate clients with their use of legal jargon. If you develop a good rapport with clients, they will often call you before they call the attorney, one reason being that you are usually more accessible than the attorney. This skill of communicating with clients raises your value to the firm. Communication is clearly one of the primary ways to build a firm's practice.

• Learning to Write Simply and Directly

Writing simply and directly is like speaking very slowly and clearly. Words are useful only if they are necessary. Avoid rambling. Have you ever had someone say to you, "Would you get to the point?" You were obviously rambling—or indulging in preamble, that is, an unnecessary introduction to what you had to say. Furthermore, you do not have to tell your reader why you are saying what you are going to say. Just say it. Some people think an abundance of words will be more impressive. Quite the contrary—the reader will be more impressed if your writing is understandable, and an excess of words will make understanding difficult. If you don't write so that people can understand you, your career will suffer.

Remember, the purpose of writing a letter, memo, report or a brief, is to make something happen. The clearer the writing, the more likely you are to achieve the results you want.

First, to write simply and directly you should police your writing to eliminate unnecessary words and phrases. Brevity is important for clarity. You don't want to lose the attention of your reader. Most people receive so much paper; the first thing they want to do is to throw it away. Keep in mind when you write that people don't have much time. You have to get to your point quickly.

Have you ever received a letter like this? "Dear Susan, I just wanted to write this letter to remind you that I was going to send you the contract, but I wasn't quite finished with it." Obviously, most of the preamble in this letter is unnecessary. The only important point is that the contract will be sent soon. If you are not being clear and direct, you may be being emotional, or you may be giving the reader information he does not need or want. Rewrite until you have eliminated unnecessary information as well as unnecessary words.

Here are some practical tips to help you write better:

1. Write as if you were talking to someone in person, using practical English.

2. Tailor your language to fit your audience.

3. Give information people want in your writing. Do research to determine what information they need.

4. Have something to say. Do your homework and get your information together before you start. Develop your framework then take another look at it and rearrange it as necessary.

5. Use a three-pronged approach when writing about a general principle: 1) illustrate its application to a specific matter, 2) use a quote, 3) give a biographical, historical, or an entertaining account.

6. Think before you write. Visualize your ideas then create the best way to illustrate them. Use colorful verbal illustrations to make your writing more interesting.

7. Talk to a friend who is interested in the subject you plan to write about and test your ideas. Brainstorming will help you discover facts or interpretations, points of argument that you might have missed.

8. Use your stream of consciousness and just write without thought to how your words are structured. Later you can go back and revise them. Writing is rewriting.

9. Start with something related to your main theme. Put the reader in the proper frame of mind and get her interested in what is going to come.

10. Direct your writing to the reader. Writing is a romance between you and the reader. Court the reader by telling her about the reader's favorite character—herself. She will read about your problems and experiences only if she can learn from them and it is beneficial to her personally.

11. Write simply and directly. Say one thing at a time. KIS = Keep it simple.

12. When you give an example, first tell the wrong thing to do, then tell the right thing to do.

13. Make an outline before you write. If you use index cards to write down the separate topics as you think of them, then you can rearrange them easily in the way you want them.

14. Lead your reader by telling her what you are going to say, then say it.

15. End with a summary of your main points. Do not introduce any new ideas, but capsulize the most important points you have made.

16. Make your writing direct, personal, but lively.

17. Use the active voice. Go back through your writing to catch sentences written in the passive voice if you don't have grammar checker software on your computer that will highlight them.

18. Be careful in using facts and numbers. Always check them. Use only the facts necessary to express your point, and confront those against you. Eliminate unnecessary details. Don't stretch the facts to prove a point.

19. Don't exaggerate. Understate your point rather than overstate it. You are trying to build your reader's trust, and a single exaggeration will haunt you.

20. Make sure you separate fact from opinion. This is especially important in legal briefs and other pleadings.

Exhibit 4.1 presents some letter writing tips from an expert.

• Stamp out Legalese

For years attorneys have had their own language—legal jargon—often referred to as "legalese." The art of writing, in the hands of many attorneys, appears to be the art of confusing. Although there may be a lack of practical writing skills, lawyers more frequently use confusing legalese to impress the reader with their expertise. Sometimes, however, the goal is to write broadly enough to allow flexibility in interpretation during litigation or negotiation. Jokingly, many say that the idea is to increase the attorney's work by the need for further interpretation of legal documents. Certain words have been used by lawyers for so long that they don't know how not to use them anymore. Words like whereas, wherefore, heretofore—which come from old English common law—are usually meaningless, but attorneys are having a hard time letting go of these words after using them for so long.

Other words are routinely overused. The most notable example is "however." If you look through the correspondence file of most of the attorneys in your office, you will likely find the word "however" in almost every letter and memo. "Therefore" is almost as popular. Both words are good transition words, but they are often used when no transition is necessary. For example, a sentence might read, "I would like you to review these interrogatories first; therefore, please turn them in by Friday." The word "therefore" seems to help condition the second clause upon the first clause, but if you try removing it, you will find that it did not serve any necessary purpose. It almost serves as a pause for the writer. Because many attorneys dictate, they tend to use such words as a prop.

Exhibit 4.1

You probably have received a letter similar to the following:

Dear . . . ,

Pursuant to our telephone conversation, I have written a letter for my client to execute and directing the letter directly to said client.

Pursuant to the terms of the above-mentioned conversation, it is my understanding that upon receipt of these documents that the said client has agreed that. . . . , hereinafter referred to as the defendant, may be nonprossed of the above-referenced accusation.

What happened is that the writer was treating the message as an end in itself. As a result, he just wrote (or probably dictated) the words that came to mind, without considering whether the reader would understand.

In letterwriting, especially, the reader is of paramount importance. Even in long formal letters, the writer is addressing someone specific, and the purpose is to get a response, be it a reply or an understanding. To achieve this purpose the writer must think about who the reader is and what he or she will understand.

The main thing you should remember is to be brief. If you write a letter that is longer than one page, take it out and look at it. You need to get to the point, say what you have to say in the manner that you want to say it, in a manner that gets across what you want to get across. Just like when you write a cover letter for a resume, you probably write that letter twenty times, don't you? You want that job, so you gear that letter to get that job.

When you are writing a letter to the clerk to request the filing of certain papers with certain papers returned to you and certain papers stamped-filed, you must be clear. If not, you know what you are going to get—five days later you are going to get them back in the mail. What could happen? Your attorney may have a malpractice suit. Clarity is so important.

Keep your sentences short. You should count the number of words in a sentence. It makes you more conscious of how long your paragraphs are. Using big words doesn't impress people. It confuses them. It makes people think we are pretentious. The best way to impress somebody is to make them understand what you are trying to say.

Letter writers benefit from some general guidelines that have at their base three qualities, often called the three Cs of letter writing. These qualities—conciseness, courtesy, consistency—apply whether the reader is someone within the legal profession or without.

Whether writing to another attorney or to a client, you don't need to waste words. Being concise saves both you and your reader time. The letter cited at the beginning of this exhibit, for example, contains excess verbiage. Primarily, the needless repetitions tax the reader's attention. When the writer says, "direct the letter directly to the said client," he produces an annoying stutter. Similarly, the repetitions of "pursuant to," and "the said" and "the above" become sandspurs in the reader's comprehension. Thinking about the reader means focusing on your message, saying only what the reader needs to know, and finding the precise words to convey the meaning.

In an attempt to be objective and professional, some writers come across as being stilted, distant, and almost rude. If you identify your reader and keep that person in your mind throughout the letter, you will be able to choose the appropriate terminology and establish a courteous tone.

Source: The *Fulton County Daily Report* (Atlanta, Georgia: 1987). Reprinted with permission of Vee Nelson, V. Nelson and Associates.

Another overused phrase is "of course." When "of course" is used frequently, the flow of sentences is impeded, and the writing becomes cumbersome. If you stop and really think about how this phrase is used, you might find it insulting. The writer is implying that you must agree him, that what he has to say is "of course" true.

Another commonly used word, "notwithstanding," can be a confusing word if used improperly. The phrase, "needless to say," is useless; if something is "needless to say," why say it? The word, "nevertheless" might better be replaced by one-syllable words such as "still" or "yet." A common mistake is to use "irregardless" instead of the correct word, "regardless." Trite words and phrases should be avoided as well. Appendix N at the back of the book lists some of the trite phrases to avoid in legal correspondence.

Paralegals often pick up bad writing habits from the people they work with. Many attorneys and paralegals are very verbose, or develop a penchant for one particular word or phrase. For example, one attorney known to the author used the phrase, "among other things" in every few sentences, so that it might appear in the same letter four or five times. It was a "catch-all" phrase for him. A paralegal used "furthermore" in every other sentence. Such trite phrases as "hoping to hear from you in due course" are better substituted with "please call" or "please contact me." "Enclosed please find" is better said as, "Enclosed is."

Eliminate legalese wherever you can. Laypersons don't understand it, and in this media-oriented age, they insist on understanding the things that concern them. Attorneys cannot afford to lose good clients to competitors—and they will, if they don't clean up the cobwebs in their language. Clients prefer to deal with those they easily understand.

Courtesy is another reason to eliminate legal jargon. When directed toward a layperson, legal jargon can become offensive. It's like using a secret language to talk down to or to talk around someone. It excludes, rather than communicates with, the reader.

When writing to a lay person, you should replace the technical phrases with familiar ones. For instance, write "among other things" instead of *"inter alia"* or a "change of place of trial" instead of "a change of venue." If you must use a technical term, such as *"nolo contendere,"* define or illustrate it. Don't just leave it there for the lay reader to puzzle over.

Legal jargon is rife with terms that could confuse even lawyers and would surely baffle nonlawyers: alter ego, Blackacre, clean hands, exhaust the security, four corners of the instrument, John Doe, Whiteacre. You can probably think of many others that are part of an insider's vocabulary. Remember, your client is not an "insider," and in your letter your job is to communicate.

As one expert reminds us, "Of course, some legal language is necessary in your letters; after all, you are writing on a technical subject and you need a technical vocabulary. Yet, how much of this terminology you use should be determined by how much your reader will understand."[1]

Do your part to ensure that your attorney's writing as well as yours is readable and is written simply and directly. Often, your attorney will value your opinion since you are an objective listener. Times have changed, and more and more attorneys and paralegals are attempting to write more simply and directly. This has received a good response from clients.

Double Entendres[2]

Many terms that are unambiguously legal to you or your attorney may have another, common meaning for the lay reader. In this sense, certain phrases are *double entendres. Privileged communication, privy, alien, assigns, close,* and *suffer* are examples of terms that have common meanings as well as technical ones. If the

---

[1]Vee Nelson, *Fulton County Daily Report* (Atlanta, Georgia: 1987).
[2]Nelson, *Fulton County Daily Report.*

Good writing requires a sincere belief in the value of clear communication, a genuine desire to improve one's communication, and the ability to criticize one's own work and edit and re-edit it. It also requires perseverance. Though seldom instinctively easy, good business writing can become a habit.

Before You Write—Prepare

Experience shows that the more effort spent in preparation, the less time will be spent from the initial draft to the final memo—because the first draft will be better written than if preparation were skimpy. Here are some suggestions to help you write better the first time.

- **Step 1:   Determine who your reader is, and what action you want.**

What do you know about your reader? What background does your reader need? Do you want your memo read casually for information or studied in depth? Do you want a major decision made? Answer these questions before you begin writing.

- **Step 2:   Define what key information your reader will want to consider in making a decision.**

The information that your client will want in order to know whether to sign an agreement might be different from the information the opposing counsel will want in order to know whether to approve it. Give only the information necessary for the reader to make the decision. Too much information tends to confuse the reader and cloud the issues. Ask yourself what the principal risks or problems associated with your proposal are, and how you can present them objectively.

- **Step 3:   Gather all the necessary information relating to these key factors.**

Examine client files, reports, and records related to the issue. Review court pleadings if necessary. Draw upon the knowledge and experience of others who have worked on the file. Learn all you can, then sort the information you have gathered and discard that which you do not need.

- **Step 4:   Review available information and draw logical conclusions.**

Apply your knowledge, experience, and judgment to the data. Consider using these reasoning tools.

Inductive reasoning. Examine typical instances or examples to reach a general conclusion. Inductive reasoning moves from the specific to the general. However, to warrant the conclusions, there must be sufficient examples. For example, repeated evidence in the file that the plaintiff has been litigious may lead you to conclude that the firm's client has a good defense.

Deductive reasoning. Apply a general principle or rule to a specific example. Deductive reasoning moves from the general to the specific. For example, if you start with the general principle, "Cases that are filed in court settle more quickly," you might then recommend an early filing for the strategy of the case.

Cause-and-effect relationship. Search for the effect when you know the cause, or the cause when you know the effect. Check to determine whether the cause is sufficient in this case to produce the same effect as in previous cases. The link between cause and effect must be established directly and logically. For example, you know that every time you call a certain attorney's office and don't leave a detailed message, the attorney never returns your call. To get a return call, you must be sure to leave a message.

Analogies. Compare one instance with another to conclude that what happened in the first will happen in the second. For example, in a medical malpractice case involving a cesarean section, the doctor used a certain type of forceps known to cause damage to the infant's brain. There is a good likelihood that it caused the same damage in the present case.

• Step 5:   Outline the memo carefully.

List all the points you want to make, assess their relative importance, and arrange them in a logical sequence. Prepare a written outline before actually writing a single paragraph. Be sure this outline:

   a. Makes maximum use of historically successful documents on similar subjects. Do not "reinvent the wheel" on documents that your attorney is used to seeing in a familiar format.
   b. Includes a clear and complete statement of your purpose.
   c. Provides sufficient background data to enable the reader to properly evaluate the proposal—but no more.
   d. Presents conclusions, reasons, findings, and other information briefly and in order of importance.
   e. Includes necessary supporting data either in the body of the memo or as exhibits.
   f. Develops the memo in a logical order from start to finish.

Format of Memo

Your outline generates the basic *format* of your memo. Each format will vary depending on whether you are writing a research memo, a project status report, a personal request, or a major recommendation.

The All-Important First Paragraph of Memo

Your first paragraph is worth almost as much attention as the rest of your memo combined. This is your opportunity to tell management exactly what you are asking of them. The first paragraph should answer the following questions:

   • What is being recommended.
   • What key details, e.g., quantities, costs, timing, etc., influence this decision.
   • What other people are in agreement of what agreements are still needed.
   • What decisions are needed at this time.

Reread your first paragraph. Is enough information presented so clearly that your attorney or law office administrator can anticipate what your memo says? If not, you are not ready to proceed.

Background Information in Memo

The reader will only rarely be as familiar with the situations leading to your memo as you are. In most cases, some background information will be necessary. For example, a research analysis gives the reasons for conducting the research. A recommendation for a change in plans should state what the present plan is. In general, you should provide enough information to put the recommendation in perspective. This should include any pertinent statements of strategy principles or objectives. Exclude information not needed by your reader to understand the recommendation.

Detailed Recommendation in Memo and Discussion

Present a detailed recommendation, with a prioritized discussion of the key factors on which it is based. In other words, explain all the reasons, in order of importance, why you are making this recommendation. Also explain in detail how it can be carried out and what key qualifications must be kept in mind (e.g., the need for increased paralegal assistance for the associates, the number of computers necessary, the cost and location of printers needed). Note any basic assumptions that must be kept in mind (e.g., number of hours needed to input documents into litigation support.)

Also, outline alternatives open and reasons why you did not select them. Finally, give a candid, if brief, discussion of how you realistically regard the risks entailed in your proposal. Specify when the managing partner or law firm administrator can count on hearing from you next about the status of the project? Outline the next steps that are to be taken.

Goals to Strive for in a Memo

As you write, keep in mind that you are trying to write a memo that has the following qualities:

1. *Well-organized.* It will contain an early and complete statement of its purpose. The rest will fall in logical sequence with proper transitions from one thought to the next.

2. *Clear and precise.* It will not only be easily understood, it will be incapable of being misunderstood by all who read and act upon it. It will say exactly what you mean.

3. *Complete.* It will include all necessary information, including background information, supported by pertinent, reliable, and up-to-date facts. When stating a conclusion or a point based on figures, it will give significant figures. It will answer all of the reader's most important questions.

4. *Persuasive.* When the memo is a selling device (e.g., selling an idea, asking for a raise), lead from strength, citing the most compelling information first. The reader will seldom be antagonistic to your proposal, but will often be neutral. Let the facts speak for themselves when your case can be completely documented. Avoid superlatives; adjectives do not make up for facts.

5. *Concise*. Compactness is very important. Help your reader understand as quickly and easily as possible what you want to do. While you strive for brevity, do not sacrifice completeness (discussed earlier). You can make your point and be brief if you avoid repetition, wordiness, and unnecessary details. If your memo is over one page in length, the most important points should be on page one.

6. *Correct*. Your information should be completely accurate, and the memo perfect on a mechanical level (e.g., spelling, grammar, and punctuation). After all, your memo is the "packaging" for your ideas, your proposals, and your reports. A "perfect" memo signals to the reader how important the idea is to you. It signals how much you value his or her complete attention to the idea itself. Conversely, the imperfect memo may trigger this thought: "If this is wrong here, what else is the writer saying that may not be correct?"

7. *Inviting to read*. Your memo should have wide margins with plenty of spaced in between the different elements. White space makes a memo inviting to read. Eliminate something or run to more pages rather than present a memo that crowds the sheet and is loaded with type.

Words, Sentences, Paragraphs, Facts, and Figures

Here are some tips for writing a good memo.

Words

Simplicity, clarity, and precision are key in selecting words. Use words that express the exact meaning you wish to convey. This does not restrict you to one-syllable words. It does argue for avoiding stilted words or those with lofty and abstract meanings, especially legalese.

In choosing words, select the:

- Short over the long, e.g., "city" instead of "municipal."
- Familiar over the unfamiliar—that is, the commonly understood over the technical jargon, e.g., "eliminates confusion" for "imparts a state of chaos."
- Precise over the general, e.g., "17 out of 20 interrogatories" for "numerous interrogatories."

Sentences

The majority of your sentences should be short, simple, and direct. You will want to vary the sentence length and structure somewhat for variety and change of pace. However, your average sentence length should probably be no more than 15 to 20 words, preferably less.

Convey only one or two main thoughts in each sentence. Use proper emphasis to show the relative importance of ideas within a sentence.

Avoid complicating sentences with excess qualifications, conditions, or parenthetical expressions. Instead, use separate sentences.

Finally, make certain that relationships between subject and verb are clear in each sentence, and use enough conjunctions and transitional phrases to insure smooth reading.

Paragraphs

The paragraph is designed to assist the reader by grouping sentences around a central idea and developing that idea. You should distill each point to one simple topic sentence. The remainder of the paragraph will amplify that point with facts and logic. Avoid long paragraphs: do not depend on the weight of words to get your point across.

Headings

Proper use of headings makes your memo more readable. They outline the sequence of the memo and help break the text into smaller, easy-to-read units.

Facts and Figures

Use facts and figures instead of judgment or opinion where possible, and use them in their simplest form. Use only those that are essential to the subject.

Use actual numbers when possible. Indices or percentage figures when used alone can be quite misleading. Footnote important points. When discussing the progress of a case, you should footnote significant activity that could have an important effect of the outcome of the case.

Punctuation

Current punctuation practices give you much leeway.

For example, while commas are mandatory in a series, they are used at the writer's discretion to indicate a brief pause, or for clarity. The semicolon indicates a long pause; it is used, as in this sentence, to separate clauses not linked by a conjunction. The colon indicates a full stop to signify a forthcoming explanation. For example: "Two major agreements were reached: The firm will provide a preliminary decision by June 16." Use punctuation to speed up reading and to clarify the meaning of words and sentences.

After You Write, Wait Before Final Editing

Editing can be the most important step of the entire writing process. Review your memorandum thoroughly and objectively from the standpoints of organization, clarity, completeness, persuasiveness, conciseness, and correctness. Here is a checklist of some of the questions you should ask yourself:

- Is it well-organized with logical flow?
- Is it clear and precise? Could this possibly be misunderstood by someone less familiar than I with the subject? Is it completely clear what I want the reader to do?
- Are the words simple and concrete, and are the sentences and paragraphs short?
- Is it complete for:
  Early, complete statement of purpose.
  Necessary agreement spelled out.
  All necessary background.
  Key numbers and facts.
  Next steps spelled out.
- Is it persuasive? Does it lead from strength, with your attorney or firm administrator's questions anticipated and answered? Have you avoided superlatives and let the facts speak for themselves?

- Is it concise? Can it be cut? One of the most common faults in writing is wordiness, so the most important editorial job is cutting. Cutting unessentials makes essentials stand out and saves the reader time.
- Is it correct? Have I double-checked all facts and numbers? Are punctuation and spelling correct? Have I footnoted relevant citations, made reference to exhibits and made proper use of facts and figures?

Rewrite your memo if there is any question on any of these points. Now put the memo away for a few hours, or, better yet, overnight. Then, read your memo as if you were the recipient. Read it as if you had never seen it before. This isn't easy, but it's helpful. The memo that seemed so familiar, so perfect yesterday often looks different later. Ask yourself:

- Is it written for me (the recipient) so that I cannot misunderstand it?
- What questions does this memo trigger?
- If there are any weak points in this memo, what are they?

Consider asking a co-worker to glance at your memo for clarity. But, remember, you are the best qualified to edit your memo objectively from the reader's standpoint. After all, you know more about the subject matter than anyone else.

• How to Improve Your Brief Writing

Many of you may have the opportunity to write briefs or at least drafts of briefs in your duties as a litigation paralegal. But many attorneys may be reluctant to delegate brief writing to paralegals who do not have the proper training and education. If you like drafting briefs and want to do more of it, you are going to have to work a little harder to prove you can do it and do it well.

Because court rules vary from state to state, you should always check the rules of the forum state. Exhibit 4.2 gives some general guidelines for writing briefs presented by The Honorable Harold N. Hill, Jr., former justice of the Georgia Supreme Court.

• Eliminating Unnecessary Drafts

Many attorneys seem to write prolifically, resulting in a lot of rewriting. But there is no reason for ten revisions of the same brief. Excessive rewriting costs the client, is annoying to the secretary, and creates exorbitant word processing costs.

To prevent countless drafts, edit everything you write the first time you write it. Of course, the better the writer you are, the less satisfied you will be with your first draft, or even the second. Good writers consider editing to be an essential part of the writing process, not just a final polishing up. But your conscientious editing according to the following rules will help keep your drafts to a minimum of three.

1. If some information or comment isn't essential, cut it out. Go through your draft once with only this question in mind: What can I get rid of?
2. Eliminate unnecessary words. Mark Twain said that writers should strike out every third word on principle. Is each word in your draft necessary, and does it contribute to the whole?

3. Are you rambling? In putting together a first draft, it speeds things up to get something on paper, even if it only approximates what you want to say. But never settle for an approximation in your final draft.

4. Have you chosen the verbs and adjectives that express your meaning precisely?

5. Could you be less abstract and more down-to-earth? Scrutinize every important word.

6. Do you have things in the best order? Is there a chronology of events or time? For example, in writing this paralegal book on litigation, considerable thought was given to putting the book in the order and sequence that litigation matters follow.

7. Are there any holes in your argument? Put yourself in the reader's shoes. Does everything follow logically? Don't expect your reader to leap from point to point like a child skipping over rocks.

8. Are your facts right? Check all statistics, case citations, and statements of fact. A single error can undermine your reader's confidence in your paper. Make sure case citations are written in the proper form. Use the *Maroon book*[3] or *A Uniform System of Citation,* more commonly known as the *Harvard's Citator.*[4]

9. Is the tone right? Too stiff? Too chummy? Lacking in sympathy? Rude? Again, put yourself in your reader's place and change anything that you, as a reader, might find offensive.

Remember, writing is rewriting and editing. Here are five examples, taken from a single memorandum, of how editing shortened, sharpened, and clarified what the writer was trying to say.

First Draft	Second Draft
Consumer protection in regards to defective products has dwindled rapidly.	Consumer protection for defective products has dwindled rapidly.
Generate client referrals through high levels of client contact.	Generate client referrals through frequent contact.
Move from yellow page advertising to a referral campaign, one that would instruct clients on what we could do for their friends.	Move from yellow page advertising to an instructive referral campaign.
Using the resources of our firm in the suburban areas, in addition to our downtown office, we have been able to provide clients services they had previously been unaware of.	Using the resources of our downtown and suburban offices, we provided clients new services.
Based on their small budget, we have developed a litigation support database that is geared to meet their smaller caseload.	We have developed a litigation support database that fits their small caseload.

---

[3] *Maroon Book* is published by the Lawyers Co-operative Publishing Co. and Mead Data Central Inc. It was launched by students at the University of Chicago Law School.

[4] *A Uniform System of Citation* has been published since 1926 by a consortium of law reviews led by Harvard and Columbia law schools.

Cover Page	Every brief should have a cover page. Be sure to title it either "Reply Brief of Appellant" or, if there is a sequence of briefs, "Second Reply Brief of Appellant," etc. Never title it simply, "Reply Brief."
Index and Table of Authorities	Some courts require that briefs exceeding a certain number of pages contain an index and table of authorities. Even shorter briefs should contain indexes where more than one question is presented or where the argument portion of the brief contains more than one part. A table of authorities should be included when you cite more than five or six court decisions.
Organizing Your Brief	If the court has rules as to how you must organize your brief, follow those rules. If the rules do not specify the organization, here is a good sequence to follow: A. Orientation paragraph or page: (1) type of case and (2) type of judgment or order being appealed and its date. B. Brief statement of issues raised, with cross-reference to the corresponding enumeration of error (See D below). C. Statement of facts, generally. D. Enumerations of error. E. Argument, in sequence of the enumerations of error, including such additional factual details as may be needed and as relate to a particular topic of the argument. Note that item B appears to duplicate item D and to be out of logical sequence. The court has found that it can understand the significance of the facts better if it knows what the questions are going to be before reading the facts. You will also note that there is no suggested section in the brief entitled "Conclusion." Cases are won or lost before the "Conclusion." When you have something important to say, don't save it until the end.
First Page of Text	Your first brief in every case should have an orientation paragraph on the first page of text. It should show whether this is a divorce case, worker's compensation, criminal, etc. Also, it should show the procedural posture of the case: whether it is a direct appeal from the grant of a motion to dismiss, an appeal from the grant of a motion for summary judgment, an appeal from the overruling of a motion for new trial, etc. It is no longer necessary for you to show in your brief that you have complied with the procedural and time requirements in perfecting your appeal. If a motion to dismiss the appeal is made, you will have an opportunity to respond.
References to the Record and Transcript	In every case there will be references to the record or transcript. Traditionally, such references are made "R___" or "T___." The court sees "R"s and "T"s many times a day, so it is not necessary to explain what they mean unless there are several transcripts (e.g., transcripts of pretrial hearing as well as the trial) or more than one record (e.g., supplemental record).
References to the Parties	After once identifying the parties by name and capacity, strive for clarity. Use the most specific identification available. For example, "wife" is more specific and hence clearer than "plaintiff," and "plaintiff" is better than "appellant." Use proper names of family members but not of corporations. When referring to corporations, refer to their business identity, such as "insurance company," "manufacturer," "bank," "subcontractor," etc. When referring to government agencies, specify "Department" or "Commissioner" rather than saying "State" or "Federal Government."
Number of Questions and Enumerations	As appellant, you should list the questions (issues) and enumerations of error on scratch paper first. Then put them into final form only after the statement of facts and argument have been written. Although sub-questions may exist, the number of main questions should be equal to the number of enumerations of error. Also, the sequence of questions should be the same as the sequence of the enumerations, and both should be chronological.

Exhibit 4.2

•

Writing Briefs

Argue only your strongest points: *omit all weak arguments.*

After you have argued your strongest points, trim your list to not more than three enumerations of error. One sure winner is enough to get you a new trial, and there is no "law of the case" in the most trial courts. One winning argument may be overlooked among a half dozen losers. A brief that begins, "This appeal raises one issue and only one issue," is sure to get the court's interest because it shows that counsel has confidence in the cause.

If in writing your argument you find you can combine two or more arguments in one section, consider rewriting the corresponding enumerations of error into one.

Do not waste time trying to reshape the questions into persuasive arguments. Deal with the real questions in the case, resisting the temptation to recast them into the questions you wish they were. More cases have been lost or won over identification of the real issues than have ever been lost or won over the shading given those issues by the lawyers.

Statement of Questions Presented

The time consumed in formulating persuasive captions to head each section of argument is wasted for the reasons stated in item 8. Use captions to divide the argument according to the questions being considered, but use a simple caption, such as "ENUMERATION ONE."

Captions

State the facts accurately and completely (citing the transcript). Use facts, not adjectives and adverbs. State details rather than characterizations and conclusions. Use evidence rather than expletives.

Stating the Facts

As in arguing before a jury, you are better off dealing with unfavorable facts than trying to pretend they don't exist. Your opponent will highlight your omission. Avoid the unhappy situation of predicating your argument on the erroneous premise that such unfavorable facts do not exist.

If you have a desire to omit or abbreviate your statement of facts, it is probably because the facts are against your client. In such case, if you are an appellant, consider whether you really should appeal. If you are an appellee in such a case, *consider settlement.*

As an appellee, do not fear accepting the appellant's statement of facts. Specifically controvert those facts you consider to be misstated (giving transcript citations so the court can quickly verify your assertion). Add facts you consider needed (citing the transcript), but do not feel constrained to rewrite your opponent's statement of facts just to put your slant on the case.

Accepting Opponent's Statement of Fact

These errors won't win or lose cases for you, but they are embarrassing. Always proofread what you have written (and have your secretary run a spellcheck). Prepare your brief ahead of time so that you can let it sit one night, and then reread it in the morning. You are more apt to find typographical and spelling errors this way. If possible, have another lawyer review your work. Also double-check the citation to every case, since it is very easy for the numbers to be transposed.

Eliminate Typographical and Spelling Errors

Be careful not to mix plural and singular nouns and verbs. Particularly when referring to a jury, watch the use of the singular and plural. Avoid the following type of error: "The jury was free to make up their [sic] own mind [sic] based on all the facts shown by the evidence."

The Elements of Style by Strunk & White (paperback edition) contains less than 100 pages and is an excellent aid to perfecting your grammar and your style. Read it, at least once.

Be brief. Brevity is clarity. Use pronouns such as "he" and "she" when where the meaning is clear to avoid repetition of long phrases, such as "counsel for the respondent."

Use paragraphs. A page with no paragraphs gives the reader no place to rest on that page. There should be at least one paragraph indentation on every page, and preferably two.

Eliminate Grammatical Errors Also

Source: Harold N. Hill, Jr., Justice of the Supreme Court of Georgia, "Writing Briefs," presented to the Appellate Advocacy Seminar, Litigation Section, Atlanta Bar Association, September 21, 1978.

Again, your editing will be significantly improved if you let your drafts cool. Leave a draft at least overnight. Then come back to it in the morning. You will see it with new eyes. Imperfections that were invisible the day before will pop out at you. Through some magic of time, you will know what to do about them.

Solicit the advice of other people—colleagues, friends, anybody whose opinion you value. Others persons can spot your errors easily. Take their comments and decide whether the change will fit into the context of your work. Their point of view may give you new food for thought and often spark new ideas.

• Delete Excess Verbiage

Getting rid of excess verbiage is sometimes difficult, but it is the best way to enhance the clarity of your message. Vee Nelson, of the Atlanta-based V. Nelson and Associates, who conducts business and legal writing courses for colleges, industry, and government shares her thoughts on this subject:

> In earlier days of English law, it paid well to be verbose. Whether for warrant, pleas, or any other proceeding, the attorney received an additional fee for every page after the first. Thus, the longer the document, the larger the profit. Today attorneys don't get paid by the page for their legal documents, but some continue to write as if they did. Here is a paragraph taken from a letter that an attorney wrote to the Department of Education requesting information about a defaulted student loan: "I would like for you to review the materials enclosed herein, make a comparison with your records and provide me a list in writing of all obligations that the defendant owes at this time, the payments that have been made thereto, and the exact amounts still to be paid thereon. I am particularly interested in making a determination about whether either of the loans upon which payments are being made is the same as that upon which your Certificate of Indebtedness is based or whether that document concerns a wholly separate loan or series of loans."
>
> He uses 96 words to make his request. Are all of them needed? No, he could have cut out over a third of the words and lost none of the intent. As a bonus, he would have gained a lot of clarity. Compare the original with the rewrite of only 55 words: "Please review the enclosed materials, compare them with your records, and send me a list of the defendant's obligations, the payments made and the exact amounts due. Particularly, I want to know whether your Certificate of Indebtedness is based on the loan that the defendant is not paying off or whether it concerns other loans."
>
> The language could still be more precise, but just eliminating the verbiage makes the paragraph easier to read. It also saves both writer and reader time.
>
> Why does the writer waste time and effort on excess words? Primarily because verbosity is a bad habit, one that is instilled in lawyers at an early stage of their legal career and one that grows worse with years. Like any bad habit, verbosity is easy to acquire and difficult to overcome. Yet it can be one. One of the best ways to break the verbosity habit is to blue-pencil it away.
>
> The blue pencil has traditionally been the professional editor's tool of trade, and the term has become synonymous with carefully edited text. The professional editor knows almost instinctively what to cut from a text. With a few blue-penciling techniques, however, any lawyer can streamline his or her document. By practicing these techniques regularly, a writer can soon replace the old habit with the new.
>
> ### Strike through the Circumlocutions
> "Circumlocution" means taking several words to do the job of one. Usually a specific verb or adverb is turned into a noun and buried in a prepositional phrase.

Blue-penciling eliminates the circumlocution and inserts a direct word. Using this technique, the writer can replace phrases such as *bring to a conclusion* with *conclude: by the name of* with *named; from a legal standpoint* with *legally;* and *take action on the issue* with *act.*

These are only a start. Among other favorites to blue-pencil are *due to the fact that, at this point in time* and *in a great many instances.* The direct words *because, now,* and *often,* respectively, serve the purpose much better.

Strike through Archaic Modifiers

Legal language inherited many compounded words that are no longer used in modern English, but have stuck with the legal language. Every lawyer recognizes these immediately: aforesaid, foregoing, hereby; hereinunder, hereof, thenceforth, therefrom, therein, whereas, whereby. . . . The list goes on.

These words were once common—they were used even in casual speech. Today, however, the words are linguistic relics. They make writing appear stilted and out-dated; they also add clutter to the sentence. Certainly a writer sometimes needs a directional word, but a current one is better than an archaic one. (Why not "in" instead of "therein"?) Most of the time, though, these words can be deleted without any loss of specificity. Blue-penciling archaic modifiers streamlines the text and makes it much more readable.

Strike through False Starters

We can often eliminate unnecessary words by taking out the false starters. Phrases such as "it is" and "there is," for instance, are simply placeholders; they delay the message and often add clutter to the sentence. With the aid of the blue pencil, however, the writer can change, "There are three ways we can approach this case," into a more direct, "We can approach this case in three ways."

Occasionally these phrases can be used effectively, but only when the writer wants to build suspense, to delay the message until the last moment. In highly persuasive writing, the device works; in routine legal writing, it doesn't. These phrases are merely habits. They get the writer started, but then they should be removed.

Another frequent starter phrase in legal writing is "in that." With the blue pencil, "In that the defendant's lawyer had represented the complaining witness in prior unrelated cases, the district attorney moved to disqualify her as the defendant's attorney," becomes, "The district attorney moved to disqualify the defendant's lawyers because she had represented the complaining witness in prior unrelated cases." The rewrite is clearer and more direct.

Other padding occurs with starter phrases often found in correspondence. They can sometimes help the writer get thoughts on the page, but they should be struck before the final draft. Especially, strike these phrases from correspondence:

With reference to . . .

In answer to . . .

Pursuant to . . .

I am writing to . . .

This is to inform you . . .

Enclosed please find . . .

Writers often have difficulty taking the blue pencil to these phrases, but once they do, their letters will be stronger.

Blue Pencil Clauses and Phrases

Many times writers stretch out their sentences by using prepositional phrases and clauses. Most of these are modifiers, so the writer can cut down on words by substituting a single adjective or adverb.

The attorney who inquired about a loan default uses phrases and clauses where he could have single words.

At this time instead of **now**
list in writing instead of **written list**
payments that have been made instead of **payments made**
amounts still to be paid instead of **amounts due**

The blue-penciling makes his intent much clearer.

Of course, a writer doesn't want to reduce all clauses and phrases to single words; not all of them can be reduced. But if an idea can be expressed by a single word, it should be.

Another wordiness problem occurs if the writer lets clauses beginning with *which* or *that* run amuck in the sentence. When two or more clauses are embedded within another, the writer almost ensures that the reader will be lost. Notice what happens in the following passage: "The court held that, although UCC §9-204(3) provides that a security agreement may provide that collateral, when acquired, shall secure all obligations covered by the security agreement and UCC §9-110 provides that a description of property is sufficient if it reasonably identifies what is described, the failure of the security agreement to date, in so many words, that it applied to deliveries made after its date rendered it ineffective against third parties."

After a while the reader can't tell what clauses modify what words. A reader who must follow the discussion can take the sentence apart, in essence cut it up and find the meaning, but editing is not the reader's responsibility. The burden of the communication rests on the writer; the blue pencil needs to do the cutting first.

Strike through Repetitions

The attorney who wrote about a defaulted loan ended his letter with this statement: "I will withhold further action in this matter until April 25, but if the matters raised above have not been clarified by that date, I expect to voluntarily dismiss the within matter of entry of default without further action."

A nothing word—matter—is repeated three times here. Because the letter is about "this matter," the writer doesn't need to keep repeating the phrases. When the writer uses "further action" to refer to different events, he or she both clutters and confuses. By striking out repetitions, the writer can get right to the point: "I will withhold further action until April 25. If I do not receive your clarification by then, I will withdraw our request for entry of default."

Why do lawyers allow such underbrush to grow in their writing in the first place? A primary reason is that they have most likely been encouraged to verbosity in law school. How many law students have heard the criticism, "You can do better than that; what you have is just too simple." Later, as attorneys, they hear the same complaint: "Your argument is just too simple." To overcome this criticism, they pad, puff, and peregrinate through their documents, trying to make the argument more complex by making the writing more complex.

The attempt, of course, doesn't work. Brevity is not simplicity. By adding words, the writer complicates only the language, not the issue. Verbosity obscures the intent and gives room for error.

Realizing the need for conciseness, some lawyers have developed their own techniques for breaking the habit of verbosity. Justice Oliver Wendell Holmes, however, probably had the most unusual. After inheriting his father's manor, Holmes started writing his opinions while standing at his grandfather's high desk. When asked if writing that way tired him, he responded: "Yes, but it is salutary. Nothing conduces to brevity like a caving in of the knees."

If writers use the blue-pencil method consistently, they probably won't have to resort to Holmes' method for achieving brevity. Striking out the excesses again and again makes the writer aware of the problems, and soon he or she can avoid them in the first draft. The result is not simplicity, but brevity. The former may not work in practicing law, but the latter usually will.[5]

• The Artful Use of Ambiguity in Legal Writing

To be understood should be the writer's ultimate goal.

Will Rogers' quip that lawyers "make a living out of trying to figure out what other lawyers have written" has a ring of truth to it. From contracts and statutes to briefs and petitions, what one write's, another construes; and inherent in this process is the unavoidable risk that the meaning may be misconstrued. If the language is ambiguous, that risk increases significantly.

Ambiguity occurs when words have vague, broad and multiple meanings. Ambiguity in legal writing, when used artfully, can be a great boost to the writer's intent. When used artlessly, it can create a difficult situation in which the reader, and often the writer, gets lost.

In the artful use of ambiguity, the writer purposely selects a broad or vague term. A good illustration is *Bates v. State Bar of Arizona,* in which the U.S. Supreme Court addressed the problem of lawyers' advertising. Because the court did not, at that early state, want to draw an absolute and encompassing line on the issue, it allowed states to place "reasonable restrictions" on such advertising. Thus, the court could guide the states while allowing enough leeway for future review of specific cases.

Legal writers make good use of vague words like *reasonable, adequate, due,* and *undue.* In certain applications, they would do an injustice if they were more precise. Unfortunately, ambiguous language is not always carefully chosen. Instead, it creeps into the document while the writer's linguistic eye is half-closed. Artless ambiguity obscures the writer's intent and multiplies chances for misunderstanding.

Common catch-all phrases that are obvious examples of ambiguous language are *deal with* and *in terms of.* These phrases appear frequently in legal writing but rarely convey a precise meaning. A statement in a recent letter illustrates the vagueness of the first phrase. "The company must operate under federal regulations that are difficult to deal with. "Contrary to her intent, she says nothing about the problems that the federal regulations pose for her client, because *deal with* has too many varied definitions. It can mean administer, deliver, be concerned with, take action upon, understand, explain—the list goes on. It is about as precise as the phrase *do something with.* Neither has a place in precise legal writing.

In terms of is equally ambiguous. The phrase vaguely identifies a relationship or connects ideas; it is a weak substitute for the prepositions *at, as, by, for,* and *in.* Thus, the statement, "We have built a strong case in terms of our client's liability" has several meanings. It may say we have built a strong case for our client's liability, against our client's liability, or on our client's liability. The preposition makes a difference in meaning that should not be left to the reader's interpretation. *In terms of,* used correctly, shows the relationship of items when one is being converted into or expressed in the words of another. "Their agreement was expressed in terms of a contract" is an unambiguous statement.

Other words in everyday usage may seem at first to be more precise, but they are actually little more than place holders. One such word is *area.* In a memorandum, a lawyer wrote that his client's "first few investments were in areas that were considerably highly speculative." What does this mean? The client invested in Florida swampland? Alabama vineyards? Pet resorts? Baldness remedies? The multiple

---

[5]Nelson, *Fulton County Daily Report,* "Eliminating the Verbiage," 1987.

meanings of the word *areas* include surface of the ground, extent of space or surface serving a special function, scope of a concept, operation, activity, specialty or discipline. The word says nothing about the client's investments. The writer has wasted a line, if not an entire memorandum.

Another such word, *parameters,* varies so much in everyday usage that no one is quite sure what it means anymore. Precisely, a parameter is a variable or an arbitrary constant appearing in a mathematical expression. Generally, however, it has come to mean any set of physical properties whose values determine the characteristics of behavior of something; and it also means broadly a characteristic or element. So, if one writes of the "parameters of the case," does that mean the essential elements of the case, or the limits of the case? It means whatever the reader wants it to mean.

Even more descriptive words are sometimes too broad to be unambiguous. If a real estate contract, for instance, requires the seller to assure that "the heating and air conditioning units are in working order," what is actually being said? To the writer, "working order" may mean that the unit should heat the building to at least 68 degrees; to one reading the contract, it may mean only that the units have motors that run.

Ambiguity can crop up even with words that do have concrete or technical definitions. Some of these words, found frequently in legal writing, can be misinterpreted because they have many, sometimes conflicting, meanings. The noun *sanction,* for instance, means a law or decree, approval for a law or a penalty for noncompliance with a law. The verb *lease,* on the other hand, contains a polarity in its definitions: to grant use or occupation under terms of a contract; to occupy or use under terms of a contract. To write, then, that "the company leasing office space must pay all utilities" is ambiguous indeed.

When such ambiguous words are used, the reader automatically looks to the context to help determine the meaning. The legal maxim *noscitur a sociis,* literally "one is known by the company one keeps," justifies this impulse. In a legal document, words take on the nuance suggested by the context. The precise meaning of *sanction* or *lease* would, we hope, emerge if we read the entire passage.

The context aided the court's interpretation in *Shulton, Inc. v. Apex, Incorporated,* where the contract writer's lax usage opened the way for misunderstanding. The contract stated that the retailer was permitted to allow its customers a concession "in the form of a cash discount, trading stamps, cash register receipts or other device, provided that such concession shall be extended to all sales by the 'Retailer.' . . ." The ambiguous word is *device.* The retailer understood the contract to permit a tie-in sale of a fair-traded commodity with some other merchandise. Certainly, this reading is compatible with the main definition of *device*—a plan, procedure, object, or technique constructed for a particular purpose. By this definition, a retailer might well argue that he could include a free nutcracker with every 10-pound bag of unshelled pecans he sold.

The court, however, interpreted the contract differently. To determine the meaning of the passage, the court followed an additional maxim, *ejusdem generis,* or "of the same kind." According to this convention, general words following a listing of specific words should be construed as being of the same sort as the items listed. *Device,* therefore, could not be merchandise; it had to be of the same type as trading stamps and cash discounts.

Given legal maxims such as these, writers sometimes tend to relax a little too much when selecting their words. The word doesn't have to be too precise, they argue; the context will clear up any ambiguity.

Not always. Even in its context, an ambiguous word may be interpreted narrowly or broadly, as the reader sees fit. In a 1985 Georgia case, *Sevenningsen v. Knight,* the meaning of the word *property* was questioned. The ambiguous passage reads:

"Seller agrees to promptly have property inspected by a bonded pest control firm; to correct any structural damages found and to furnish at closing a certification from said firm stating that the property is free of termites and other wood-boring organisms."

From the context, it was clear that *property* did not mean jewels or furniture. The questions arose, however, about whether *property* meant all of the buildings situated on the lot or only the principal residence. The termite inspector, who treated only the principal residence, was accused of breach of contract; however, the ambiguity of *property* led the court to decide in the inspector's favor. In this case, as in many, the context worked against the writer's intent.

The writer who uses ambiguous terms carelessly, or who relies on the context for clarification, loses control over the meaning—and often over the case. Shadowing all instances of ambiguous language is the maxim *contra proferentem*, or "against the offerer." This means that uncertainties will be resolved against the one who created the uncertainties. With artless ambiguity, nothing is to be gained, and much is to be lost.

No one can eliminate all risks or interpretation in legal writing, but a careful writer can cut down on the opportunities for misunderstanding and misinterpretation. The primary way is by thinking about exactly what is intended and using as precise words as possible to convey that intention. If the writer of the inspection contract had clearly stated what structures were to be examined, there would have been little opportunity for misunderstanding on this point. The specific words, "all the buildings on the premises" or "the principal residence," do not exclude any crucial element, and they cannot be misunderstood.

In legal writing, there is no place for artless ambiguity. It serves no purpose. At best, it causes lawyers to spend their careers in the tedium of trying to figure out what their colleagues, and sometimes what they themselves, have written.[6]

• Improving Your Writing By Abolishing Sexism

Avoiding a sexist pronoun may also improve your writing. But how do you skirt around those "he"s and "she"s? While sometimes it is not easy, it can be done. Here are some more tips from Vee Nelson, writing consultant.

In *State v. Little*, a Georgia case, argument arose over the use of *he* in the instructions to the jury. The defendant, a woman, maintained that the trial court made a prejudicial error in the following: "Under our system of justice when a defendant pleads not guilty he is not required to prove his innocence, he is presumed innocent. The State must prove to you the defendant's guilt beyond a reasonable doubt."

In this instance, the judge overruled the assignment of error, asserting that the sentence puts forth a general principle applicable to all defendants. However, the complaint—and an increasing number like it—raise questions about the prudence of using *he, him,* or *his* as the universal singular pronoun. In business, politics and law, writers are becoming more aware of the problems surrounding the universal *he,* and they are making conscientious efforts to find solutions.

Although the search for solutions received renewed impetus from the feminist movement of the 1970s, people have been looking for alternatives since at least the 19th century. Charles Converse of Pennsylvania, for instance, suggested the word *thon* as a gender-neutral pronoun. The word remained in the dictionaries until the 1950s, though it was apparently little used.

More recently, there have been at least 16 other proposals for a new pronoun. Among them are *tey, co, E, mon, heesh, hesh, hir, per* and *na.* Books have been published using *na* and *per.* One university press and the American Management Association have published books using *hir.*

---

[6]Nelson, *Fulton County Daily Report,* "Ambiguity in Legal Writing," 1987.

But don't worry. You won't have to write, "A defendant has the right to the lawyer na wants." The language already has sufficient ways to address the pronoun problem without our inventing new words. Here are some of those ways that allow you to solve the pronoun problem with ease and with stylistic finesse.

• Change the singular to plural. Often the singular pronoun is not needed, especially when you are referring to a category of people, such as defendants or witnesses. Using the plural creates no ambiguity and eliminates the need for a singular pronoun. There is, for instance, no reason for the singular in this sentence: "Paragraph 5(e) requires an employer to ensure that his sales representatives comply with the order." The plural is much better: "Paragraph 5(e) requires employers to ensure that their sales representatives comply with the order."

• Strike the pronoun. Sometimes you don't need a pronoun, so eliminating *he* can solve both social and stylistic problems. The following compound sentence needs conciseness: "The contractor supplies copies of all employee time sheets, and he submits them with complete documentation of all expenses incurred." Striking the pronoun makes the sentence tighter: "The contractor supplies copies of all employee time sheets and submits them with complete documentation of all expenses incurred.

The next sentence needs better balance: "Information provided by a client to a consultant is privileged in the same way as are communications between a lawyer and his client or a physician and his patient." The balance is achieved by eliminating the pronouns: "Information provided by a client to a consultant is privileged in the same way as are communications between lawyer and client or physician and patient."

• Replace the pronoun with an article. A neutral word, such as *a, an* or *the* can easily substitute for *he.* The sentence, "Until the transaction is completed, the seller shall not take any actions that are outside his ordinary course of business," becomes "Until the transaction is completed, the seller shall not take any actions that are outside the ordinary course of business."

• Use the second person instead of the third person. Many times, particularly in giving instructions, writers use the third person (*he*) when the second person (*you*) is far more appropriate. Switching to the second person is not only clearer; it also circumvents any problems with the masculine pronoun. An instruction is implicit in this sentence: "If the shareholder allows his checks to remain uncashed for six months, his redistribution checks will be reinvested into his account at the then-current net asset value."

• *You* makes the sentence far more direct: "If you allow your checks to remain uncashed for six months, your redistribution checks will be reinvested into your account at the then-current net asset value."

Many writers hesitate to use the pronoun *you* because they think it makes the message either too informal or too didactic. Yet, in some contexts, especially instructions, *you* is clearly preferable.

• Use a noun. Often a noun can easily be substituted for the pronoun. When using this solution, writers usually choose a synonym. For example, the following sentence, "We want a geologist to be expert witness. We are sure he can supply the evidence we need," can just as well be written, "We want a geologist to be expert witness. We are sure this specialist can supply the evidence we need."

Sometimes, however, repeating the existing noun produces a desired rhetorical effect. The sentences, "A respondent must retain records for two years so compliance can be monitored. He must sanction employees who violate the order." can be rewritten as, "A respondent must retain records for two years so compliance can be monitored. A respondent must sanction employees who violate the order." Repeating the noun is a viable alternative here because it emphasizes the person who must act.

• Rewrite the sentence. Although it may take more time, rewriting the sentence is often the best way to solve the pronoun problem. Shifting words around can eliminate the need for a pronoun. For instance, "If a plaintiff loses faith in the system, he may never receive compensation for injury," can be written, "A plaintiff who has lost faith in the system may never receive compensation for injury."

• Use *they* for the singular. This suggestion is often frowned upon by those who are firmly fixed in the formal grammar. To them, it is totally unacceptable to use the plural *they* to refer to a singular. Although these people should be admired for holding to the principles of grammar, in this instance they soon may be grasping a grammatical fossil.

The word *they* is also found frequently in writing. Here is an example from *The Wall Street Journal:* "If another institution takes over the closed bank or thrift, all depositions are transferred to the new institution and no one loses any of their principal or interest." The phrasing sounds natural both in speech and writing. In addition, the expansion of the plural form to encompass the singular has a grammatical precedent. Originally in English there were two forms for the second person pronoun: *thou* as singular, and *ye* as plural. By the 16th century, however, the singular form had disappeared from the formal speech, and *ye*, which had become *you*, emerged as the only form for the second person.

We can see the same process occurring with *they.* The plural form probably will not replace the singular entirely; however, it will continue being a supplement. Considering the precedent and the obvious trend, we can safely use *they* in contexts where it sounds natural.

• Use a compound pronoun. One of the most common solutions, though not the best, is to use *he* or *she* every time the singular pronoun is needed. This approach works adequately when the pronoun is required only once or twice in a passage. If, however, the pronoun phrase appears frequently, it is very cumbersome, as it is in the following sentence: "The agreement requires that the salesperson specifically ask the individual placing the order whether he or she had authority to purchase the products in the dollar amount of the order and requires that he or she specifically state that he or she is authorized to do so."

Although at times *he or she* is appropriate, there are other, more effective ways to get around the problem. Any of these eight techniques can solve the problem posed by using the masculine pronoun in a universal meaning. One solution that is not advocated here, however, is *he/she* or *she/he.* These constructions are acceptable only in legal contracts and similar formats, in which the inapplicable pronoun will be crossed out. In other context, the use of this jury-rigged pronoun is both poor style and poor grammar. There are enough alternatives that produce polished, readable prose without relying on two pronouns tenuously held together with a slash.

• As the language evolves, the pronoun problem will undoubtedly work itself out. Until that time, however, you have many ways to eliminate sexist implications in your writing. These options are surprisingly easy to exercise, and as a bonus, they offer variety and strength to your legal writing style.[7]

• Punctuation of Legal Writing

Poorly placed punctuation can distort the intent of the writer. While content is important, without the proper punctuation, the context of the message may be unclear or misunderstood. Vee Nelson, gives the following suggestions to improve your punctuation and your writing.

Punctuation has its fashions like other aspects of writing style. While the basic definition of each mark has remained constant, the rules surrounding it vary from era to era.

---

[7]Nelson, *Fulton County Daily Report.*

In a widely used grammar text of 1878, *Practical English Grammar,* Thomas Harvey advocated the heavy use of punctuation to divide written discourse into parts of sentences. Recommending semicolons and colons for partitioning long, winding sentences, he gave the following example. "We do not say that his error lies in being a good member of society; this, though only a circumstance at present, is a very fortunate one: the error lies in his having discarded the authority of God, as his legislator; or, rather, in his not having admitted the influence of that authority over his mind, heart, or practice."

For most readers today this punctuation looks as outmoded as the frock coat and celluloid collar. And it is. Heavy punctuation—called "close punctuation"—is antiquated. Despite its mustiness, however, this punctuation style still characterizes legal writing. The following passage from a recently issued lease is fairly typical. "If Lessee defaults for three days after written notice in paying said rent; or if Lessee fails to abide by and perform any of the obligations resting upon him under this lease, including compliance with the regulations on the reverse side hereof: then Lessor, at his option, may at once terminate this lease by written notice to Lessee; except that Lessor may collect rent owing for the period prior to such termination."

Close punctuation is not confined to boilerplate documents; it pervades briefs, memorandums and even letters. This tendency is so characteristic of legal writing, in fact, that former congressman and New York Mayor Fiorella La Guardia dubbed attorneys "the semicolon boys."

The legal profession, and much of the academia, remains with the close style while other writers and editors have adopted "open punctuation," that requires marks only when necessary to prevent misreading. Open punctuation does not mean that a writer no longer needs semicolons and colons. Few would agree with writing consultant Robert Pinkert, who maintains that "semicolon is not much needed, if it's needed at all." What it does mean, however, is that the "rules" for both semicolons and colons have simplified considerably since Thomas Harvey's day. With a couple of ground rules firmly in place, any writer can use these marks successfully.

The semicolon connects *equals,* and it steps in when a comma is not strong enough to make the connection. Specifically this means the semicolon is used in two contexts: between sentences and between items in a list. The most frequent use of the semicolon is to connect sentences. Primarily it links sentences when there is no coordinating conjunction (and, but, or, nor, yet, so), as in the following example. "The neurologist set up an office appointment in order to complete his examination; the patient canceled this appointment and waited one month to see the original treatment doctor again."

But it can also be used when the sentences contain many commas already and need a stronger divider. "The investment of the vendor, a professional service corporation, in the property was not improper; and, we concluded, it was not a basis on which purchaser could seek to avoid specific performance."

A warning is perhaps in order here about using the semicolon with words like *however, hence,* and *therefore.* These words are not conjunctions; they are adverbs. Sentences, therefore, are not "connected" by these words. Notice that in the following example, *however* can move around. "The corporation's actions are indeed a contract; *however,* the costs to an individual of bringing a suit would be prohibitive." Or, "The corporation's actions are indeed a breach of contract; the costs to an individual of bringing a suit would be prohibitive, *however.*"

If a word can move around in the sentence, ignore it when deciding whether or not to use a semicolon.

The second use of the semicolon is to separate three or more items in a list. Of course if the items are short, commas are sufficient. If these items already contain commas, the semicolon provides a better break. In the following sentence, the semicolon is unnecessary: "The defendant said he had complained to the landlord; to the housing authority; and to the police."

When any of the items contains commas, use the semicolon to promote readability: "The defendant said he had complained to the landlord, who laughed at him; to the housing authority, which ignored him; and finally to the mayor's office."

With this use of a semicolon, a stronger warning is needed: If you start a pattern of semicolons, you must continue to put them between each of the equal items. Notice the confusion that occurs when the list is punctuated as follows: "In essence, the "Buyer's Guide" discusses any warranties that might apply or be offered, notes the major systems of the vehicle and problems that might occur; and addresses spoken promises, services, contracts and dealer information to include who to contact in the event of a complaint."

The reader automatically divides this list into two parts even though the writer intends three. Revised punctuation clarifies that the "Buyer's Guide" does three things: "In essence, the 'Buyer's Guide' discusses any warranties that might apply or be offered; notes the major systems of the vehicle and problems that might occur; and addresses spoken promises, services, contracts and dealer information to include who to contact in the event of a complaint."

Failing to use the semicolon between equal parts begs for misinterpretation. Such was the problem in a Kentucky case where confusion arose about how many parts an inheritance would be divided into. The passage reads: "I bequeath and devise my entire estate, both personal and real . . . in equal shares, absolutely and in fee to my cousin, the said Walter Cassidy; Robert Jamison and William Stivers, tenants on my farm; George E. Smith, who rents my property on Bland Avenue, Shelbyville, Kentucky; and the Kentucky Society for Crippled Children, of Louisville, Kentucky; Baptist Ministers Aid Society, of Owensboro, Kentucky; Baptists Orphan's Home of Louisville, Kentucky; King's Daughters' Hospital, of Shelbyville, Kentucky; and to the Clayville Baptist Church, of Clayville, Shelby County, Kentucky."

With the punctuation as it is placed, the estate should be divided into eight parts, with Robert Jamison and William Stivers dividing one eighth. This was the position that contester Walter Cassidy took. The Kentucky Court of Appeals disagreed, however. After reviewing the evidence, they decided that the intent of the deceased was that the estate be divided into nine portions. The lawyer who wrote the will distorted that intent with his punctuation.

Remembering that the semicolon stands only between equal parts you can use this mark to add rhetorical strength of the sentences. If the sentences are closely related and balanced, the semicolon works better than a conjunction by serving as a fulcrum that connects and balances the two sides. Here, the semicolon links alternatives: "For the purpose of this provision, in the case of items purchased on different dates, the first purchased is deemed the first item paid for; in the case of items purchased on the same date, the lowest priced is deemed the first item paid for."

When the balanced sentences contain opposites or contrasts, the semicolon is the best punctuation to use, as in the following examples: "First of all Plaintiff must prove that the product was the cause of the injury; the mere possibility that it might have caused the injury is not enough." And, "The Fourth Amendment protects people; it does not protect places."

The colon is used less frequently than the semicolon, but it does do more than preface a list. In today's punctuation style the colon follows a complete sentence and introduces an amplification. You can think of it as substituting for the words *that is* or *for example* and giving greater emphasis than a comma does. Most often the emphasis is directed toward lists, whether they are short or long. "Papers were strewn all over the room: on the floor, on the desk, behind the cabinets, under the furniture."[8]

[8]Nelson, *Fulton County Daily Report.*

• Summary

Writing is a skill that is developed with practice. Writing is rewriting and rewriting—editing your own material to eliminate unnecessary words, to make it short, direct, and simple. Avoiding long words and long sentences makes writing easy to read and simple. The proof of good writing is that the reader understands what he or she is reading. Challenge every word, sentence, or paragraph to make sure it is necessary, is short, and gets your idea across.

Legal Interviewing Techniques

• Introduction

This chapter[1] will cover legal interviewing techniques for interviewing clients. Interviewing methods for investigations are covered in Chapter 7. The purpose of this chapter is to help you clarify your role in conducting the client interview. Guidelines, forms, and checklists for conducting the interview and documenting it will be given, as well as procedures for following up the interview.

The client interview usually begins with the attorney, who then turns the client over to the paralegal for more comprehensive fact-gathering. This initial interview, called the *intake* interview is followed by a *follow-up* interview. The purpose of the intake interview is to identify the client's problem and gather sufficient information to enable the attorney to seek a solution on behalf of the client. The follow-up interview is intended to make sure certain things have been done or to decide another way or a further way to proceed in the matter.

Legal interviewing is a learned skill. You must make the client feel comfortable enough to reveal very personal information to a stranger—you. This requires an ability to build an atmosphere of trust and rapport. You must know what questions to ask as the interview proceeds and how to ask them properly.

• Preparing for the Client Interview

Preparing for the interview is as important as the interview itself. It is imperative that you have all the information and documents you need at hand and that you have carefully thought through the interview in advance. If you are unprepared, the client will pick up your uneasiness, and the tone of the interview will not be conducive to your purpose.

Setting the Appointment

The first step, of course, is to set up the date, time, and location for the interview. Most likely the interview will be in the firm's offices, either in your office or the conference room, depending upon the preference of the firm and your comfort zone. If the interview is to be conducted in the firm's conference room,

---

[1]Contributions to the checklists in this chapter were made by Steven N. Reiff, attorney at law, Atlanta, Georgia.

make sure that you schedule the conference for that time and that the receptionist is aware of it.

Confirming the Appointment and Requesting Information from Client

Once the date, time, and location of the interview is set, write the client a letter confirming these details. Make sure the appointment is entered on your personal calendar, the firm calendar, or tickler system. After you review the file, include in your letter any information or documents that you want the client to bring to the appointment. The best way to do this is to enclose a list with your interview confirmation letter. Exhibit 5.1 presents lists of items for certain types of litigation matters. These lists are not all-inclusive, nor are all the items necessary for all cases, but they give you a starting point for developing your own lists.

Reviewing the File and Other Documents

Gather all the files and other documents and information on the case prior to the date of the interview. Organize them and check to make sure all the information is there. Review the information to spot omissions, formulate questions in advance, check inconsistencies, and make lists to prepare for the interview. Make sure that your attorney takes the proper time to brief you on important items to cover during the interview.

Preparing the Interview Location

The interview area should be comfortable, clean, free of clutter, and non-distracting. No files pertaining to other clients should be in view. If one client sees another client's file, it is a breach of client confidentiality. Interruptions should be prevented by instructing that your calls be held. Picking up the phone will diminish the importance of the interview in the client's eyes. Close the door, and give the client your full attention.

Discuss with your attorney whether you should tape record an interview. Under no circumstances should you ever make a tape recording of the client without his or her knowledge. If it is the practice of your attorney to have the interview recorded, get the client's permission, and then put the tape recorder out of sight so the client is not so conscious of it that he or she is made nervous. Tell the client what the purpose of the recording is and that it will be used for that purpose only unless you obtain his or her consent to do otherwise.

Interview Forms and Other Forms

Most likely, you will develop your own set of interview forms for gathering information as you gain experience. Depending upon the type of practice in which your firm engages, you may have specialized forms such as personal injury or automobile negligence, or medical malpractice, workers' compensation, corporate information, and others. Included in this chapter are some forms that you may use as a skeletal form to gear to your firm's needs. Remember that forms should only be used as a *guide* for the interview, not a *control* of the interview. For example, when you ask one question, the response may prompt other questions that are not on the form.

Exhibit 5.1
•
**Checklists for Items Client
Should Bring to Interview**[1]

Automobile Accident Checklist

○ Insurance policy.

○ Name, policy number, automobile make and number, and other information about the other party.

○ Photos of the car(s), accident location, injuries, or other damage.

○ Rough diagram of the accident and location, and map, if available.

○ News clippings about the accident indicating the name and date of the newspaper.

○ Names, birthdates of family members.

○ Medical and dental bills.

○ Bills for damaged clothing and personal possessions.

○ Occupation, address, and phone number of the place of employment, annual income, time lost from work.

○ Social security number.

○ Information about prior accidents and prior illness.

○ Information about accidents and illness after this accident.

○ Correspondence concerning the accident.

○ Notes taken right after the accident, including utterances by the other party.

○ Property damage estimates.

○ Police report.

○ Insurance adjuster's card or I.D.

○ Car title.

○ Diary of out-of-pocket expenses, including travel to receive medical treatment.

Breach of Contract (Corporation) Checklist

○ The relevant contract.

○ Articles of Incorporation.

○ Minutes of meetings of directors and shareholders.

○ Stock records and transfers.

○ Tax filings (I.D. numbers, state and local tax registration numbers, Subchapter S elections, tax returns).

○ Bills of sales to transfer assets to corporation.

○ Promissory notes for loans to corporations.

○ Annual reports (secretary of state).

○ Profit-sharing and pension plans.

○ Annual meeting notices.

○ Amendments to Articles of Incorporation.

○ Amendments to Bylaws.

○ Certificate of Assumed Name.

○ Dissolution of corporation.

○ Merger documents.

○ Qualification and withdrawal of foreign corporations.

○ Reservation of name.

○ Registered agent or registered office.

○ Minute books.

○ Stock records.

Exhibit 5.1

Continued

○ Canceled checks, receipts.
○ A description of items or service in dispute.
○ Invoices.
○ Copies of related correspondence.

Real Estate Action for Quiet Title Checklist

○ Deed.
○ Easements.
○ Plat maps.
○ Title reports.
○ Title insurance.
○ Notices of sale or transfer.
○ Quitclaim deeds.
○ Foreclosure documents.
○ Zoning notices and documents.
○ Local ordinances and government resolutions.
○ Leases.

Medical Malpractice Checklist

○ Health care authorizations.
○ Patient history data.
○ Medical records, if in possession.
○ Family history data.
○ Photos of injuries, if any.
○ Medical and dental bills.
○ Documents from previous suits, if any.
○ Names and dosages of medicine taken.
○ Names, addresses, and telephone numbers of patient's doctor.
○ Names, addresses, and telephone numbers of hospitals and medical care facilities where patient was treated.

Also, keep in mind that you or the attorney may need to provide some of the information called for on the form, such as, for example, any statute of limitations information.

Hand in hand with conducting the interview is the art of listening. Try not to be so intent on filling out the form and going through the motions that you forget to listen to the client's answers. The answers the client gives you should serve as much as a guide to your next question as the form, if not more so.

Preparing an Instructional Folder for the Client

Consider various information, forms, checklists, and other documents that might be helpful to the client. Get your attorney's approval to include them in a folder that you will give to the client. For example, you might include a checklist on how to have your deposition taken, or a blank diagram for the client to diagram the accident.

To: (Doctor/Hospital)

I hereby authorize you to furnish to my attorney(s) of the law firm of _____ or any representative thereof any and all medical reports or findings and x-rays for inspection and copying and upon request, to discuss freely and render written opinions to my attorney(s) concerning diagnosis, treatment and prognosis of my physical condition. I hereby release you from all legal responsibility or liability that may arise from releasing the foregoing information.

Dated:_____.

_____
(Name of Patient)

_____
(Address)

_____
(Telephone Number)

_____
(Witness)

Getting Forms Ready for the Client's Signature

In preparing for the client interview, you should gather any forms that the client may need to sign so that the case can proceed. The Consent to Release Medical Information, Form 5.1, may not be honored by hospitals or doctors if it is more than 30 days old. It might be best not to have the client complete the date on the form in the event that there may be additional medical reports for future treatments. Other commonly needed forms are the Consent to Release Military and Personnel Information (Form 5.2), consent to Release Federal and State Income

To: (Name of Responsible Party or Department)

I hereby authorize and request you to furnish to my attorney(s) of the law firm of _____ or any representative thereof any and all information concerning my (my husband's) military and personnel records. I further authorize and request you to furnish my attorney(s) with copies of any of these records that they so request.

Dated:_____ .

_____
(Party or Widow)

_____
(Witness)

Form 5.3

Consent To Release Federal and State Income Tax and Estate Tax Information

To: (United States Internal Revenue Commission/State Department of Revenue)

I hereby authorize and request you to furnish to my attorney(s) of the law firm of _____ or any representative thereof certified true copies of the (United States Federal Tax Returns/ _____ State Tax Returns) filed by _____ for the

(Name of Taxpayer(s))

years _____. I also authorize and request you to furnish certified true copies of the (United States Estate Tax Returns/_____ State Estate Tax Returns) for the Estate of _____ filed by _____ ,

(Deceased)

as <u>Executrix/Executor</u> of the Estate of _____ .

(Deceased)

Social Security Number(s):_____.

Dated:_____

_____

(Executrix/Executor)

_____

(Witness)

Tax and Real Estate Tax Information (Form 5.3), School Record Authorization (Form 5.4), and Employee History Record Information (Form 5.5).

• Handling the Client Interview

One of the most difficult areas in which to define the paralegal's responsibilities is in the paralegal's relationship with a client. Most attorneys take the position that the paralegal may deal directly with the client as long as the attorney is the primary contact. Some give paralegals great latitude in dealing with and in advising clients, and it is the paralegal's responsibility not to overstep his or her abilities and training. Caution in this delicate area cannot be overemphasized. Always check with your attorney should you have any doubt about the parameters within which you may operate. There are ethical considerations in addition to the legal limitations on a non-lawyer giving legal advice to a client. Along with the attorney, the paralegal has a responsibility to protect the legal welfare of the client:

> A paralegal shall maintain the highest standards of ethical conduct.
>
> Discussion: It is the responsibility of a paralegal to avoid conduct which is unethical or appears to be unethical. Ethical principals are inspirational in character and embody the fundamental rules of conduct by which every paralegal should abide. Observance of these standards is essential to uphold respect for the legal system.[2]

---

[2]"NFPA Affirmation of Professional Responsibility," National Federation of Paralegal Associations, Inc. (NFPA), 5700 Old Orchard Road, Skokie, IL 60077-1057 (708)966-6066.

To: (School/College)

I hereby authorize you to furnish to my attorney(s) of the law firm of _____ or any representative thereof to examine, make or be furnished, copies of any records or information, including psychiatric and psychological reports, relating to my child, _____ , who is a student in the _____ .

DATED; _____ .

Signed,

_____

_____

Address:

_____

Phone (H)/(W)

(Name of Employer)
(Address)

Attention: ____ (Personnel Records Custodian) ____

Re: (Name of Client; Social Security Number)

Dear _____:

I hereby authorize you to furnish to my attorney(s) of the law firm of _____ or any representative thereof to examine, make or be furnished, copies of any records or information, relating to my employment by ____ (Employer) _____

DATED; _____ .

Signed,

_____

_____

Address:

_____

Phone (H)/(W)

Introducing Yourself to the Client

You and your attorney should realize the value of and the necessity for your proper introduction to the client. The following method of introducing the paralegal to the client has been used by numerous attorneys. However, you should discuss how to handle your introduction with your attorney and work out an arrangement comfortable to both of you.

Your attorney brings you into his office at one of the initial interviews with the client and introduces you to the client. He tells the client that you are a paralegal (or legal assistant), explains what you do, and states that you will be working closely with the client and with himself (the attorney). He tells the client to feel free to call you should the client have questions or problems, or in the event that the attorney is unavailable.

The attorney explains that you will be conducting an intake interview, and that the client will be billed at a lower rate for your services, specifying what your hourly billing rate will be. By telling the client how you will save the client legal fees, your attorney will make the client more receptive to your services and will help explain why you are involved in the legal handling of the case.

Establishing Rapport and Building Trust

In all communications that you have with the client and in all the work that you do on his behalf, you should always maintain the highest ethical standards of your profession. Exhibit a professional manner at all times, whether on the telephone or in person, and you will gain his confidence and respect. And it is important that the client have confidence in you and know that you are dependable, trustworthy, and loyal. Remember, he is entrusting you with his personal legal problems. The attorney is bound to exercise reasonable care to prevent her employees, associates, and others whose services she uses from disclosing or using confidences or secrets of a client. There should be the same bond of trust between you and the client as between the attorney and the client. Always preserve and respect all client confidences.

Rapport and trust are also important to client cooperation. To do an efficient and timely job, it is essential that you have this cooperation. For one thing, you will have less difficulty in obtaining necessary information and documents if you have the client's cooperation.

The following pointers should assist you in obtaining the cooperation of the client—or a witness in an interview situation:

1. *Be friendly, courteous, and polite at all times.* Keep a positive attitude toward the client or witness. Beware of any personal negative feelings affecting your manner. Always call the client or witness by his or her surname, e.g., Mr. Arnold or Ms. Arnold, unless otherwise requested.

2. *Practice the art of conversation.* In your communications with the client or witness, remember to spend a little time with the witness conversing about subjects other than business to establish a friendly rapport. In other words, begin your conversations with common pleasantries to break the ice.

Do not try to impress the client or witness with big words and stuffy conversation. The client or witness will be more impressed if you are at ease and conduct yourself in a businesslike manner. Many times the client or witness will look to you to interpret in layman's language what the lawyer has told him. He or she will be relieved when you explain seemingly complicated legal points in simplified terms.

3. *Exude confidence.* If you act confident, as if you know what you are doing, the client or witness will feel comfortable with you and will likewise be confident in your abilities. Consequently, she will be more apt to cooperate with you and relate confidences to you. This confidential relationship with the client or witness is essential for you to perform your job thoroughly, expeditiously, and efficiently. If the client or witness is inclined to reveal personal matters to you, then she will spend less time with your attorney, and you will succeed in saving her legal fees and in saving your attorney valuable time. In addition, you will be instrumental in your attorney having a satisfied client or witness.

4. *Maintain a good attitude.* If you maintain a positive and cooperative attitude toward the client or witness, you will most likely engender the same response from him. By offering assistance to the client or witness in every way you can, you will make him realize your value to him; as a result, he will be more cooperative with you. If you offer guidance—and consolation—when necessary, he will tend to rely upon you more. His satisfaction with you will become evident to your attorney. Your attorney wants to make the client or witness happy, and will be extremely pleased if you are helping in that endeavor.

Procedures for Conducting the Interview

Following are some guidelines for conducting the initial interview with the client or witness:

1. Explain that the purpose of your interview is to record information and facts.
2. Let the client or witness tell you the facts in her own words.
3. Extract the pertinent facts and information.
4. Ask specific questions regarding the information she gives you.
5. Answer basic questions without giving advice to the client or witness.
6. Take meticulous notes.
7. Have the client or witness sign the necessary authorizations that the attorney previously reviewed.
8. Obtain all necessary documents and other tangible evidence the client or witness has in her possession.
9. Make arrangements for follow-up information from the client or witness, if necessary.

The use of forms to be used as checklists will ensure that you obtain all the necessary information from the client or witness during the interview. You may develop your own forms or checklists or personalize any of the ones in this book or other books. Form 5.6 serves as a general checklist for any client or witness interview. It would be the beginning of any of the specific form or checklist that you develop.

The form for the initial interview in Form 5.7 is primarily for personal injury cases but may be adapted for medical malpractice cases. You may be able to send this questionnaire to the client ahead of time and have him bring it back into the office for review by you or your attorney. Form 5.8 serves as a checklist for automobile accident cases.

Form 5.6

General Client Interview

GENERAL CLIENT INTERVIEW CHECKLIST

PERSONAL DATA

FULL NAME: _____ ALIASES:

RESIDENCE: _____

DATE/PLACE OF BIRTH: _____ AMERICAN CITIZEN: YES ___   NO ___

MINOR: YES ___   NO ___   GUARDIAN: _____

SOCIAL SECURITY NO.: _____ MARRIED: ___ DATE/PLACE OF MARRIAGE: _____

MAIDEN NAME: _____ SPOUSE'S FULL NAME: _____

SPOUSE'S MAIDEN NAME: _____ CHILDREN/NAMES/AGES: _____

ADDRESSES (IF DIFFERENT): _____

REAL PROPERTY OWNED: _____

MILITARY RECORD: _____

NAME/ADDRESS-RELATIVE: _____

EMPLOYMENT HISTORY

NAME/ADDRESS-EMPLOYER: _____

WORK PHONE: _____ POSITION: _____ YRS EMPLOYED/CUR. POSITION: _____

PRESENT SALARY: _____ INCOME PAST 5 YRS: _____
(For injury claims—Copies of returns available?)

PRIOR CLAIMS: Made any previous claims?: _____

Details: (Who, What, When, Where, Why, How?)

_____

_____

_____

CRIMINAL RECORD: (ARRESTS, CONVICTIONS, PROBATIONS?)

_____

_____

Types of Interview Questions

One of your tasks in conducting the interview is to determine what types of questions to ask—and that will depend on the information you wish to elicit. A big part of the interview is to separate *facts* from *beliefs*. For example, if the witness says, "It happened around 12:15 P.M.," the interviewer should ask, "How do you know it happened around 12:15 P.M.?" to make sure that you are getting a solid fact, not a guess or belief.

In general, questions can be classified in terms of the breadth of information they seek to elicit.[3] Asking a question the right way can facilitate getting the

---

[3]David A. Binder and Susan C. Price, *Legal Interviewing and Counseling* (St. Paul, MN: West Publishing Company, 1977), p. 38.

**Initial Interview
(Personal Injury)**

Prepared by:_____ Date:_____

Date of Accident: _____

Statute of Limitations: _____

CAPTION:_____ vs._____

Was Accident Report Filed by State? _____

Deft.'s Ins. Carrier:_____

_____

Adjuster: _____

_____

Settlement Offer Before Employment: _____

By Whom: _____

_____

Pltf.'s Ins. Carrier: _____

_____

Plaintiff's Coverage: A.   Collision?_____

               B.   Med. Pay?_____

               C.   Uninsured Motorist _____

               D.   Liability _____

QUESTIONNAIRE

1. Client's Name _____ S.S. No.: _____ Spouse: _____

2. Occupation:_____

3. Address: Home _____ Telephone: Home: _____

        Business _____   Business _____

4. Age: _____Birthdate: _____ Mother's Name:_____

      Birthplace: _____ Father's Name:_____

5. Married _____ Divorced _____ Widow _____

    Single_____ Separated_____ Widower_____

6. Dependents' Names, Ages, Birthdates (Addresses If Married): _____

_____

_____

     a. Ever used any other name? _____

        When and why? _____

     b. All marriages and divorces (dates, names and places, names prior spouses): _____

_____

     c. Prior residences, go back 20 years (dates): _____

_____

_____

     d. Has any other birthdate or birthplace ever been used? _____ If so, details: _____

_____

7. Any Attorneys Consulted (Referred: Yes _____ No _____). Name and Address: _____

_____

_____

8. Who Recommended Case? _____ Ref.–Fee _____

8A. Atty. Credit:_____ 8B. Fee_____

Form 5.7

Continued

9. Any Statements Made (To Whom and When): _____

Remarks: _____

_____

PLAINTIFF'S FACTS

10. Personal Experience at Time of Accident: _____

_____

11. Length of Time Confined to Hospital and Bed (on Present Injury):_____ Charge:_____

11A. Home Confinement: _____ Charge:_____

12. Was Ambulance Called to Scene? Yes _____ No_____

Name and Address: _____

Charges: Conscious After Accident? Yes _____ No_____

13. Present Physical Condition, Scars, Marks, etc.: _____

13A. Any Appliances Used or Worn: _____Charges:_____

14. Names and Address, Dates of Confinement or Out-Patient Care of All Hospitals From This Injury:_____

15. Out-Patient X-Rays Taken: Yes _____ No_____

By Whom (Where?):_____

16. PHYSICIANS

From Present Injury: _____ Length of Time Treated: _____

Family or Defendant: _____ Charges:_____

1. _____

2. _____

3. _____

4. _____

5. _____

17. Total Medical Charges: _____

18. Remarks—Treating Physicians: _____

19. Time Missed From Work: _____

20. Injuries: _____

21. Age:_____ Birthdate: _____ Life Expectancy: _____ Job Expectancy:_____

22. Dependents—Names and Ages: _____

Relationship (Agency): _____

23. Present Employer, Wages, How Long, Types of Work, Work Record, Job Title:_____

_____

23A. How Many Hours Per Week Did You Average Prior to Accident?_____

_____

24. Previous Employment (Go Back 20 Years), Type of Work, Work Record (Names, Addresses and Dates): _____

_____

_____

25. Previous Year's Earnings: _____

25A. Qualified To Do What Kind of Work:_____

26. Previous Injuries (Be Specific), Dates—Recovered: Hospitals, Lawyers, Insurance Companies:

_____

Moving Traffic Violations: _____

27. Any Claims Made for Above and Amount Received: _____

28. Patient in Any Hospital Last 5 Years and Why: _____

29. Present Physical Condition and Prognosis: _____

30. Criminal Record: _____

31. Name of Desired Fiduciary and Address: _____

32. Other Assets in Estate:_____

33. If Death Action, Give Name and Addresses of Children, Spouse and Parents:_____
    _____

34. Doctors Seen in Last 10 Years, and Why (List Any Physical Exam, for Employment, etc.): _____
    _____

35. Politics:_____

36. Fraternal: _____

37. Religion:_____

38. Race: _____

39. Military Service (Dates, Branch, Type of Discharge, Serial No., Claims No., If Any, Service
    Connected Disabilities: _____
    _____

40. Nurses: Expenses _____

41. Medicines, Drugs, Bills:_____

42. Prop. Damage to Plaintiff's Vehicle: _____

43. Others (Bills or Expenses): _____

44. Make of Vehicle: _____ Year and Model:_____ Color:_____
    (Owner's Name and Address) _____
    _____

45. Cost:_____ Value Before: _____ Value After: _____
    _____

46. Name of Garage, Address Where Estimates Made, Where Car Is Now:_____
    _____

47. Years Driving Experience: _____

48. Was Car Equipped With Seat Belts? _____

48A. Were They in Use? _____

49. Any Driver's License Restrictions? _____

50. Do You Now or Have You Ever Used Any of the Following?
    a. Glasses ☐ Yes ☐ No If so, were they used at the time of the accident? ☐ Yes ☐ No
    b. Hearing Aid ☐ Yes ☐ No If so, was it used at the time of the accident? ☐ Yes ☐ No
    c. Back or Neck Brace ☐ Yes ☐ No If so, were they in use at time of accident? ☐ Yes ☐ No
    Details: _____
    _____

51. Present Condition of Mouth and Teeth: _____

52. Have You Received Any Payments From V.A., Social Security or Other Sources? ☐ Yes ☐ No
    If So, Give Details: _____
    _____

53. Names, Addresses and Passengers Pltf.'s Vehicle Positions

    a. _____ d._____

    b. _____ e._____

    c. _____ f._____

54. Immediately Following Injury, Did Any of the Following Occur? (Circle those applicable.)

    a. Bleeding   g. Shock   m. Sprains

    b. Broken Bones   h. Vomiting   n. Blindness

    c. Cuts   i. Paralysis   o. Noise in Ears

    d. Bruises   j. Limitation of Motion p. Soreness

    e. Dizziness   k. Numbness   q. Any Other

    f. Blackouts   l. Unconsciousness

55. Remarks: _____

56. Lost Time From Work Due to Prior Injuries, Dates, Length of Time Lost, Employer's Name and Address:_____

57. Was Workmen's Compensation Applied For? _____

57A. Result: _____

58. Any Accidents or Injuries Since This Accident? _____ Details:_____

59. Increases or Decreases in Pay Since Accident:_____

60. Any Increases or Decreases in Pay of Fellow Employees Not Received by Plaintiff: _____

61. List All Physical Exams in Last 10 Years for Employment, Promotions, Insurance, Social Security, or Armed Forces. Also List Dates, Names and Addresses of Doctors and Results. _____

62. Do You Now Have or Have You Ever Had Problems With Any of the Following? (Circle those applicable)

    Eyes   Heart   Neck
    Ears   Diabetes   Arms
    Nose   Alcoholism   Legs
    Blood Pressure   Headaches   Hands
    Circulation   Venereal Disease   Shoulders
    Wrists   Elbows   Wounds
    Feet   Abdomen   Scars
    Speech   Menstrual Periods Miscarriages
    Memory   Lungs   Knees
    Throat   Hernia   Ankles
    Chest   Fractures
    Hips   Back

62A. Give Details: _____

FACTS CONCERNING DEFENDANT

63. Name and Address of Operator: _____ Age:_____

    Op. Plate No.: _____

    Restrictions (on License): _____

    Agent of Owners: _____ Yes _____ No _____ in Doubt _____

64. Name and Address of Operator's Employer: _____

65. Name of Address of Owner of Vehicles: _____

    Owner of: Auto _____ Tractor _____ Trailer _____ Truck _____

66. License Number and Names on Vehicles: _____

67. Tractor: Trailer: Truck:

    P.U.C. No. _____ P.U.C. No. _____ P.U.C. No. _____

    I.C.C. No. _____ I.C.C. No. _____ I.C.C. No. _____

    I.C.C. Owner _____ I.C.C. Owner _____ I.C.C. Owner _____

68. Description of: Truck _____ Color: _____

                   Trailer _____

                   Tractor _____

                   Auto _____

69. Was Vehicle Empty or Loaded (Describe): _____

    Physical Defects Deft.: _____

70. Passengers and Positions in Vehicle: _____

71. Remarks or Notes: _____

ACCIDENT

72. Date of Accident (Give Day and Time): _____ Weather: _____

73. Location of Accident (Listing City, County, State): _____

74. Width of Street, Highway, Sidewalk, etc.: _____

    Condition of Street, Highway, Sidewalk, etc.: _____

	PLAINTIFF	**DEFENDANT**

75. Speed, Each Car: _____

76. Signal, If Given (Describe): _____

77. Lights: _____ Tires: _____   Lights: _____ Tires: _____

78. Condition of Brakes: Good Bad Unknown   Good Bad Unknown

78A. Remarks: _____

_____

_____

79. Parts of Autos Collided—Describe Damage: Location, Extent, etc.: _____

80. How Far Did Cars Travel After Impact: _____

81. Position of Vehicles After Impact: _____

82. Statement, If Any, After Accident: _____

83. What Objects in Cars: _____

84. How Did Parties Leave Scene? _____

85. Years Driving Experience: _____

86. Date of Last Inspection: _____ Where and By Whom: _____

87. Business Trip? _____

88. Glasses Needed? _____

89. If So, Were They in Use? _____

90. Any Medication Taken in Preceding 48 Hours? _____

91. If So, What, When, and Why? _____

_____

_____

Form 5.7

Continued

92. If Pltf. or Defendant Riding With Someone Else, Was Party Helping With Expenses or in Some Manner Reimbursing Driver? _____

93. If So, Give Details: _____

94. Personal Impression: (Note Any Antagonistic Mannerisms and Have Plaintiff Try To Avoid Them!) _____
_____

Presented by Judge Anthony A. Alaimo of Brunswick, Georgia, at the November 1969 seminar of the Institute of Continuing Legal Education in Georgia.

proper answer. Basically, there are four categories of questions: open-ended, leading, yes/no, and narrow.[4]

Open-ended Questions

Open-ended questions give the client or witness the latitude to control the subject matter. For example:

- What can we help you with?
- What have you been having problems with?

This type of question lets the client or witness tell his story in his own way. Usually, the interviewer loses control, and the client or witness tends to ramble. Some people will not talk at all when asked this question. In general, the use of the open-ended question is limited. There are times, however, when it can be very useful, as is illustrated later in this chapter under "Learning from Interview Models."

Leading Questions

Leading questions tend to call for a direct—possibly a yes or no—response, often suggesting the desired answer. For example:

- You didn't have your seat belt on, did you?
- You were going 65 mph, weren't you?

This type of question does not test the validity of the response and may distort the response. On the other hand, it tends to get an answer from the client or witness that she may not voluntarily give.

Yes/No Questions

Yes/no questions definitely call for a simple yes or no answer. For example:

- Were you driving the car?
- Was your driver's license valid at the time of the accident?

_____
[4]Ibid., pp. 38–40.

Parties—General Information

(   ) Plaintiff _____ Age _____ Sex _____ Phone _____

(   ) Address _____ City _____ County_____ State ____ Z.Code _____

(   ) Bus. Address _____ City _____ County_____ State ____ Phone _____

(   ) Ins. Carrier_____ Address _____ Phone _____

      Amount of Insurance: Liability _____ Property Damage_____

      Medical_____ Collision_____ Uninsured Motorist_____

      Any Coverage Deductible? Which? _____

      _____

(   ) Defendant 1. _____ Age _____ Sex ____ Phone _____

(   ) Address _____ City _____ County_____ State ____ Phone _____

(   ) Bus. Address _____ City _____ County_____ State ____ Phone _____

(   ) Ins. Carrier_____ Address _____ Phone _____

      Amount of Insurance: Liability _____ Property Damage_____

      Medical_____ Collision_____ Uninsured Motorist_____

      Any Coverage Deductible? Which? _____

      _____

(   ) Co-Defendants 2. _____ Age _____ Sex ____ Phone _____

               3. _____ _____ _____ _____

(   ) Address 2. _____ City _____ County_____ State ____ Z.Code _____

               3. _____ _____ _____ ____ _____

(   ) Bus. Address 2. _____ City _____ County_____ State ____ Phone _____

               3. _____ _____ _____ ____ _____

(   ) Ins. Carrier 2._____ Address _____ Phone _____

               3._____ _____ _____

      Amount of Insurance:

      Liability 2. _____ Property Damage _____ Medical _____ Collision_____

               3. _____ _____ _____ _____

      Uninsured Motorist 2. _____ Any Coverage Deductible? Which?_____

                    3._____

      2. _____

      3. _____

Facts of Accident

(   ) Date of Accident _____ Time_____ Material Facts_____

_____

_____

_____

(   ) Statements Made Immediately Prior to, During, or After the Incident _____

_____

(   ) Type of Case (Check Applicable Subject Matter)

      (   ) Animals (   ) Assault & Battery (   ) Drainage & Pollution

      (   ) Employer, Employee and Independent Contractor (   ) False Imprisonment

      (   ) Fraud and Deceit (   ) Invitees and Licensees (   ) Malicious Arrest or Prosecution

      (   ) Malpractice (   ) Municipal (   ) Products Liability (   ) Real Estate

Form 5.8

Continued

(   ) Slander or Libel (   ) Transportation—Airplane, Automobile, or Train

(   ) Trespass (   ) Wrongful Death (   ) Workers' Compensation (   ) Other _____

_____

(   ) Diagram Accident Scene if Physical Facts are Important

_____

_____

(   ) Indicate and Note on Diagram. Answer Yes or No Where Applicable

   (   ) Width of Streets or Roads Measured_____

   (   ) Number of Lanes _____ Any Peculiar Curves or Hills _____

   (   ) Yellow Lines _____ Stop Signs or Traffic Devices _____

   (   ) Skid Marks _____ Position of Vehicles after Accident _____

   (   ) Type of Road Surface, Asphalt or Concrete _____

   (   ) Dry or Wet _____ Weather—Fog, Rain, Drizzle, Sleet, or Snow _____

       _____

       _____

   (   ) Visibility—Good or Bad _____ Day, Night, Dusk or Dawn _____

       _____

       _____

   (   ) Clear or Cloudy _____ Other _____

   (   ) Were Pictures Taken of Accident Scene? _____

   (   ) When? _____ By Whom?_____

   (   ) Address _____ Phone _____

   (   ) If Not, Take Pictures of Accident Scene Immediately

   (   ) Place Pictures Obtained or Taken in Evidence File

   (   ) Miscellaneous Comments _____

       _____

(   ) Automobile Information

   (   ) Plaintiff Vehicle

      (   ) Year _____ Make_____ Model _____ Color _____

      (   ) Cylinders _____ Horsepower _____ Weight _____

      Manuf. I.D. _____

      (   ) Tag No. _____ Power Or Regular Steering?_____

      Brakes _____

      (   ) Defects of Vehicles—Brakes _____ Lights_____

      Motor _____ Steering _____ Tires _____

      Other_____

      Comments as to Condition _____

      (   ) Location of Vehicle—Garage _____

      Address _____ Phone_____

      Were Pictures Taken of Automobile? _____

      When? _____ By Whom?_____

      Address _____ Phone_____

      If Not, Take Pictures at Garage and Place in Evidence File Taken By _____

      When_____ Address_____

(   ) Note Alleged Speed Prior to Collision _____

_____

(   ) Indicate Impact Points on Vehicle Diagram and Note Interior Damage

Right Side   Front   Rear   Left Side
Length _____ ft.   Width _____ ft.

(   ) Owner of Plaintiff Vehicle _____ Age_____ Sex _____

(   ) Address _____ City _____ State ____ Phone_____

(   ) Business Address _____ City _____

State_____ Phone_____

(   ) Ins. Carrier _____ Address _____

Phone_____

Amount of Insurance: Liability_____

Property Damage _____

Medical _____ Collision_____

Uninsured Motorist_____Any Coverage?

Deductible? Which _____

_____

(   ) Driver Plaintiff Vehicle _____

(   ) Relationship to Owner_____

Driving with Permission? _____

(   ) Destination and Purpose _____

(   ) Impediments of Driver—Intoxication _____

Glasses _____

(   ) Hearing _____ Other Physical Defects_____

(   ) **Passengers**   **Seat Location in Vehicle**

_____

_____

_____

_____

(   ) Defendant Vehicle

(   ) Year _____ Make_____ Model _____ Color_____

(   ) Cylinders _____ Horsepower _____ Weight _____

Manuf. I.D. _____

(   ) Tag No. _____ Power Or Regular Steering_____

Brakes _____

(   ) Defects of Vehicles—Brakes _____ Lights_____

Motor _____ Steering _____ Tires _____

Other_____

Comments as to Condition _____

(   ) Location of Vehicle—Garage _____

Address _____ Phone_____

Form 5.8

Continued

Were Pictures Taken of Automobile? _____

When? _____ By Whom?_____

Address _____ Phone_____

( ) If Not, Take Pictures at Garage and Place in Evidence File Taken By _____

When?_____ Address_____

( ) Note Alleged Speed Prior to Collision _____

_____

( ) Indicate Impact Points on Vehicle Diagrams and Note Interior Damage

Right Side   Front   Rear   Left Side
Length _____ ft.   Width _____ ft.

( ) Owner of Defendant Vehicle_____ Age_____Sex _____

( ) Address _____ City _____ State ____ Phone_____

( ) Business Address _____ City _____

State_____ Phone_____

( ) Ins. Carrier _____ Address _____ Phone_____

Amount of Insurance: Liability _____Property Damage_____

Medical_____ Collision _____Uninsured Motorist _____

Any Coverage Deductible? Which? _____

( ) Driver Defendant Vehicle _____

( ) Relationship to Owner_____

( ) Driving with Permission? _____

( ) Destination and Purpose_____

( ) Impediments of Driver—Intoxication _____ Glasses _____

Hearing _____ Other Physical Defects_____

Passengers   **Seat Location in Vehicle**

_____

_____

_____

( ) Traffic Violations by Plaintiff and Defendant

Charges Against	Court	Hearing Date	Result

( ) Get Copy of Traffic Court Testimony if Recorded and Place in Evidence File

( ) Witness to Accident, Including Parties

Witnesses	Address	County	State	Age	Phone

(   ) Statements Taken from Witnesses, Including Parties

Name	Who Took Statement?	When?	Do we have a copy?

(   ) Place All Statements in Evidence File
(   ) Impeachment Of Parties and Witnesses (Note Unfavorable Military Record)

Name	Crime Conviction	Date	Good or Bad Character

(   ) Parties' Prior Accidents

Plaintiff _____

_____

Defendant _____

_____

Medical

(   ) Plaintiff—Summary Of Injuries (Indicate Degree Of Disability) (Restriction of Activities in work, sports, etc.) _____

_____
_____
_____
_____
_____
_____
_____
_____
_____
_____
_____
_____
_____
_____
_____
_____
_____
_____
_____
_____
_____
_____

Form 5.8

Continued

( ) Notes Injuries on Diagram

Parietal
Temporal
Zygomatic
Occipital
Cervical vertebrae (7)

Lumbar vertebrae (5)
Ilium
Sacrum
Pubis
Ischium
Femur
Patella
Tibia
Fibula
Tarsals (7)
Metatarsals (5)
Phalanges (14)

Frontal
Maxilla
Mandible
Clavicle
Scapula
Sternum
Ribs
Thoracic vertebrae (12)
Humerus
Ulna
Radius
Carpals (8)
Metacarpals (5)
Phalanges (14)

( ) Trunk
    ( ) Shoulders
    ( ) Spine
    ( ) Thoracic
    ( ) Scapula
    ( ) Lumbar
    ( ) Sacrum
    ( ) Coccyx
    ( ) Pelvis
    ( ) Hips

( ) Indicate Plaintiff's Area of Pain
( ) Symptoms
    ( ) Headaches
    ( ) Dizziness
    ( ) Nausea
    ( ) Nervousness
    ( ) Insomnia
    ( ) Appetite
( ) Head
    ( ) Brain
    ( ) Forehead
    ( ) Ears
    ( ) Eyes
    ( ) Nose
    ( ) Mouth
    ( ) Teeth
( ) Neck
    ( ) Muscles
    ( ) Spine
    ( ) Throat
( ) Chest
    ( ) Heart
    ( ) Lungs
    ( ) Ribs
( ) Abdomen
( ) Internal Injuries
    ( ) _____
    _____
( ) Arms (Right or Left)
    ( ) Upper
    ( ) Forearm
    ( ) Elbows
    ( ) Wrist
    ( ) Hands
    ( ) Fingers
( ) Legs (Right Or Left)
    ( ) Thighs
    ( ) Upper
    ( ) Lower
    ( ) Knees
    ( ) Ankles
    ( ) Feet
    ( ) Toes

( ) Indicate Radiations of Pain.
( ) *Note* Cuts, Bruises, Burns, Bumps, Sutures, Fractures, Missing Teeth, Swelling, Contusions, Points of Bleeding, Unconsciousness, etc.
( ) Same Information for Defendant's Injuries (if any)
( ) Ambulance, Hospital and Doctor Service, Findings, and Treatment

    ( ) Ambulance Service—By Whom? _____ Other_____

    Any First Aid Administered? If So What? _____

    Note Time Ambulance Arrived at Accident Scene _____

    ( ) **Hospitals**   **Address**   **Phone**   **Period of Treatment**   **Surgery**

    1. _____

    Treatment _____

    _____ X-Rays Taken? When? _____

2. _____

Treatment _____

_____ X-Rays Taken? When? _____

3. _____

Treatment _____

_____ X-Rays Taken? When? _____

(   ) **Doctors**   **Address**   **Phone**   **Period of Treatment**   **Surgery**

1. _____

Diagnosis, Treatment, and Prognosis _____

_____ X-Rays Taken? When? _____

2. _____

Diagnosis, Treatment, and Prognosis _____

_____ X-Rays Taken? When? _____

3. _____

Diagnosis, Treatment, and Prognosis _____

_____ X-Rays Taken? When? _____

4. _____

Diagnosis, Treatment, and Prognosis _____

_____ X-Rays Taken? When? _____

(   ) Summary Comments as to Percent Of Disability and Patient Prognosis

_____

_____

Prior Medical Treatment—Plaintiff and Defendant

(   ) Plaintiff—Prior Medical Treatment

    Doctors and Hospitals   **Address**   **Phone**   **Period of Treatment**

1. _____

2. _____

3. _____

Treatment _____

(   ) Note Relationships of Prior to Present Injuries _____

_____

_____

(   ) Prior Claims of any Nature? When? Where? _____

_____

_____

(   ) Defendant—Prior Medical Treatment

    Doctors and Hospitals   **Address**   **Phone**   **Period of Treatment**

1. _____

2. _____

3. _____

Treatment _____

(   ) Note Relationships of Prior to Present Injuries _____

_____

Form 5.8

Continued

(　) Prior Claims of any Nature? When? Where? _____
_____
_____

(　) Summary Degree of Prior Disability
　(　) Plaintiff _____
　(　) Defendant _____

Damages—Plaintiff

(　) Plaintiff Employment Subsequent and Prior To Accident

Subsequent to	Dates	Position	Annual Earnings	Per Diem

Prior To (Last 2 Yrs.)	Dates	Position	Annual Earnings	Per Diem

(　) Education and Job Training　(　) Elementary　(　) High School　(　) College
　(　) Graduate　(　) Other _____
　_____(　)

(　) Family

Spouse and Children	Relationship	Age

(　) Computation of General Damages—Note Age of Injured Party _____
　(　) Pain and Suffering (Past, Present, and Future) Estimate of Party—Value Assessed Per
　　　Day $_____ x _____ Days $_____ x Life Expectancy _____
　　　$_____
　(　) Diminution Capacity to Labor as Element of Pain and Suffering (Past, Present, and
　　　Future) Estimate of Party—Value Assessed Per Day $_____ x _____
　(　) Days $_____ x Life Expectancy _____　　　　　$_____
　　　Loss of Consortium—Estimate of Party—
　　　Value Assessed Per Day $_____ x _____
　　　Days $_____ x Life Expectancy _____　　　　　$_____
(　) Computation of Special Damages (Date Accident _____)
　(　) Loss of Earnings
　　(　) Past and Present to Date of Trial—(Days in Hospital _____)
　　(　) Past and Present Continued—(At Home _____
　　　　Returned To Work—Date _____)
　　　　Total Days _____ x Per Diem Wages
　　　　$_____　　　　　$_____
　　(　) Annual Average Earnings $_____
　　　　(Capacity Reduced _____ % Disability $_____)
　　　　x _____ (Use Annuity table _____ %
　　　　Column to Reduce to Present Cash Value)

or x _____ Life Expectancy (For Gross
when Reduction not Required) $_____
(   ) Hospitals, Nurses, Doctors, Drugs (Supports and Braces),
and Ambulance Expenses

Hospitals	Period	Amount	
			$_____
_____			
_____			
_____			
_____	$_____		$_____

Nurses	Period	Amount	
_____	$_____		
_____	$_____		$_____

Doctors	Period	Amount	
_____	$_____		
_____			
_____			
_____			
_____	$_____		$_____

Pharmacy	Period	Amount	
_____	$_____		
_____	$_____		$_____

Ambulance	Period	Amount	
_____			
	$_____		$_____

(   ) Funeral Expenses—Mortician's

Name and Address _____

_____ $_____

(   ) Property Damage
    (   ) Automobile—Fair Market
        Value before Accident $_____

    Less Fair Market Value after Accident $_____

    Diminution in Value $_____ $_____
    (   ) Reasonable Hire _____

    Days x Rental Value $_____ $_____
    (   ) Real Estate—Fair Market
        Value before Accident $_____

    Less Fair Market Value after Accident $_____

    Diminution in Value $_____ $_____
    (   ) Damages to Building—
        Reasonable Repair

    Repairs by _____

    Address _____

    Estimate $_____

    Repairs Completed $_____ $_____

Form 5.8

Continued

(   ) Exemplary
   (   ) Punitive
   (   ) Attorney Fees
   (   ) Other _____

                                                     $_____

   (   ) Other Miscellaneous Damages

                                                     $_____

   (   ) Total Damages Sued for _____ $_____

Summary Reminder

(   ) Client
   (   ) Obtain a Fee Contract from Client
   (   ) Obtain Signed Medical Authorizations from Client
   (   ) Obtain Financial Statements to Support Special Damages
   (   ) Obtain Income Tax Returns for Last Two Years
   (   ) Remind Client to Notify Own Insurance Carrier and File Accident Reports Required By Law
(   ) Investigation
   (   ) Obtain Medical Information from Doctors, Hospitals, and Other Sources
   (   ) Take Statements from All Witnesses
   (   ) Obtain or Take Pictures and Place Newspaper Clippings in Evidence
   File of:
      (   ) Accident Scene
      (   ) Vehicles
      (   ) Visible Injuries To Client
      (   ) Other _____
      (   ) Obtain Appraisals of Property, Warranty Deeds, Plats, and Surveys
      (   ) Obtain Engineer's Drawing of Accident Scene
      (   ) Obtain Copy of Accident Reports and Testimony Of Traffic Hearing
      (   ) Obtain Copy of Death Certificate where Applicable
   (   ) Notice Preparatory to Filling Suit
      (   ) Write Letter of Notice to Opposite Party or Party's Insurance Carrier if Known
   (   ) Office Information
      (   ) File Handled this Office _____
      (   ) Associate Attorney _____
      Address _____ Phone_____
      (   ) Referral By _____
      Address _____ Phone_____
   (   ) Obtain Letter in File as to Fee Arrangement in Associate and Referral Matters

Source: Thomas W. Elliott, and A. Elliott, 1ff., *Tort Resume for Use in Prosecution and Defense of All Damage Claims*, pp. 94–103.

Narrow Questions

Leading questions and yes/no questions are two types of narrow questions, which are the opposite of open-ended questions. They not only select the subject matter, but also can select certain aspects of the subject matter to be discussed. For example:

- Where was the stop sign located on Elm Street?
- Who was in the car at the time of the accident?

You should vary your questions to include all types. Determining the type of question that will elicit the desired information is a skill developed over time and through trial and error. Of course, the client or witness's personality will guide you as well.

Importance of Listening

Listening well is just as important as questioning well. First, by listening to the client or witness, you establish a good rapport. Everyone likes to talk, and client or witness will probably be eager to talk about the problem. He will appreciate your attentive listening. Also, by *controlled listening,* you will obtain a lot of information. Controlled listening is knowing when to interject a question and when to steer the client or witness in another direction. He will likely ramble at times, and you must redirect him to the point of the interview.

When you encourage the client or witness to keep talking by your silence, or by an expression indicating that she should continue, you are practicing *passive listening.* When you reflect upon what the client or witness is saying by a comment or a repetition of something she said, you are practicing *active listening,* meaning that you are participating openly in the listening process. You should probably practice active listening more often than passive. Also, you may summarize what the client or witness has said to let her know that you understand and to give her the opportunity to correct any misunderstandings on your part.

Learning from Interview Models

Here is a three-stage model for conducting a client or witness interview:[5]

> Before you enter any interview, it is imperative that you be properly briefed by your attorney. The paralegal-client dialogue typically begins with your having a preliminary understanding of the client's problem and having a grasp on what the salient points are in the attorney's eyes. Your goal is to assist your attorney in gathering the facts necessary so that your attorney can properly represent the client. When you understand what your attorney needs from the client, you can proceed to gather information.

A Three-Staged Interview

> There are undoubtedly several ways of approaching the task of ascertaining the facts relating to the client's problem and tentative or possible legal position. This general approach should be useful. Under this approach, the process of ascertaining the facts surrounding the client's problem and legal position is divided into three stages: (1) Preliminary Factual Identification, (2) Chronological Factual Overview and (3) Factual Development and Verification.
>
> A case may require one or more interviews for you to complete these three stages. It is important to gauge the time spent on the interview and to break into separate sessions. The client is usually emotionally charged during the first interview as he or she is thinking that he or she has been wronged and is seeking justice. Fatigue in you, as the intent listener, and on the part of the client, as he unravels emotionally, will make a long interview lose its effect. Consider having a second and perhaps a third interview before advancing to the Chronological and Factual Development and Verifications Stages.

---

[5]Portions of this model were taken from Binder and Price, *Legal Interviewing and Counseling,* Ch. 5.

Preliminary Factual Identification Stage. In [this] stage, the paralegal asks the client to provide a general description of at least the following: (1) the underlying transaction or incident which caused the problem, and (2) the facts surrounding the transaction or incident. During this stage, you should encourage the client to describe the foregoing matters in whatever way seems comfortable. You should refrain from imposing any particular order on the client's presentation and allow the client to proceed in a free-flowing narrative. You should ask only for a general description and refrain from asking for any details or interrupting with questions.

Chronological Factual Overview Stage. During [this] stage, encourage the client to provide a step-by-step chronological narrative of the past transaction or incident which underlies the client's problem. Ask the client to proceed from the point where the client believes the problem began, and follow through, step-by-step, up to the present. During the Overview, you should not attempt to obtain a detailed elaboration of the various points mentioned by the client during the chronological narration.

Factual Development and Verification Stage. At the conclusion of the Overview stage, you then should mentally review the entire story to determine what facts may be missing and what facts need further support. Using his or her knowledge of the information necessary to handle this case, consciously ask yourself, "What are all of the possible facts and information that my attorney will need to properly represent this client in this type of matter?"

When this tentative diagnosis has been made, commence the Factual Development and Verification Stage. Here you conduct a detailed examination to determine how many of the facts or information presented can be supported and which facts may need further support or evidence. Also assess which documents your attorney may need to proceed in this case. Based on the direction of your attorney, attempt to determine whether or not there are facts which will establish the existence of each of the substantive elements needed to invoke the causes of action and defenses which your attorney has seen as potentially applicable. Thus, if one cause of action seen as potentially applicable is that of breach of contract, your attorney may want you to determine in detail whether or not there are facts to establish: (1) the making of an agreement, (2) performance by the plaintiff, (3) breach by the defendant, and (4) damages. Of course, you may be gathering documents supporting the facts during the interview.

The Factual Development and Verification Stage is a phase devoted to exploring consciously, in a systematic manner, whether or not the specific facts and information have been obtained and which ones need further investigation and discussion. It is a stage when you must look at the facts and information that you have gathered and assess their applicability as a whole while determining if there are any missing elements.

The Purpose of the Three-Staged Interview. Why divide the process of ascertaining the client's problem and the information and facts surrounding the problem into three stages? The purpose of the division is to increase the thoroughness with which information and facts are gathered about so as to ensure that no time is wasted in the representation of the client and to ensure the thoroughness and efficiency of this representation by the attorney.

In legal interviewing, it is very common for an inexperienced paralegal to just gather the information that the client wants to give, which frequently is inadequate. One common omission involves the paralegal's failure to get enough of an idea of what the attorney needs prior to the interview with the client, thus causing additional follow-up.

Without proper briefing, you may tend to ask the client for information that may not include information and facts specific to this particular client's problem. It is always better to let the client talk and discard irrelevant facts later than to miss important lines to the story. Every client's problem is different in some way, usually in a factual way. You need to know what the attorney wants in order to bring about the desired result. If not, the questioning may turn out to be largely a waste of time since the information obtained is irrelevant in terms of the representation the client actually desires.

Techniques for Conducting the Three-Staged Interview

The Preliminary Factual Identification Stage. The process of Preliminary Problem Identification is usually begun with open-ended questions calling for a narrative description of the client's situation. Questions such as the following are typical: "Tell me in your own words what happened?" and, "What can you tell me about the incident?"

These open-ended questions leave the client free to set forth his or her dilemma in any manner which feels comfortable, and in as much detail as seems appropriate. The questions do not, however, explicitly suggest that the paralegal is interested in obtaining a general description of the past transaction which underlies the problem, and the relief which the client desires. To encourage the client to include each of these factors in the description, it is sometimes useful to provide a structural guide which outlines the information that your attorney desires. A structural guide can be worked somewhat as follows: "Give me a brief description of the facts surrounding your problem, how it arose, and what part you played in it." Or, "Tell me what your problem is, how it came about, and what you remember about it."

Such guides can be inserted into the dialogue either immediately after the initial open-ended questions, or after receiving the client's initial reply.

Chronological Factual Overview Stage (Using Questions). The principal form of questioning used during the Overview is an open-ended question which encourages the client to continue the narration and paves the way to the chronological stage. Thus, a typical question is one such as, "What happened next?" The use of the term "next" suggests the client proceed with the story in chronological sequence but in all other respects the question is open-ended. The client is left free to describe the incident in any way the client sees fit. Thus, the client can state what he or she observed, felt, thought, etc.

Given the purposes of the Overview and the restrictions against detailed probing, this form of question seems quite appropriate as the chief form of interrogatory. The question attempts to keep the client focused along a chronological track, and hopefully minimizes risks of interrupting normal paths of association. This form of questioning gives the client an opportunity to provide clues that might be lost if the paralegal were to try to discover all significant facts through a series of narrowly focused questions. As will be repeatedly noted in this chapter, the paralegal will not have the capacity to develop all the facts concerning a particular transaction by sitting back and thinking about how such an event might have occurred, and then asking did this, that, and the next thing happen.

Factual Development and Verification Stage (Determining What Facts Are Possibly Applicable). The objective of the Factual Development and Verification Stage is to conduct an investigation which will reveal what facts will be necessary to be supported or verified through investigation and evidence. To accomplish this objective, the paralegal should undertake at least two tasks. There should be an endeavor to determine (1) what facts need to be ascertained, and (2) which of the possibly applicable facts must be further explored or investigated.

Why the distinction between possibly ascertainable facts and the facts which need further study? One of the major defects that occur in legal interviewing by paralegals is distinguishing solid facts from weaker facts. The paralegal recognizes facts which suggest the possible applicability to the case, investigates these, and concludes the inquiry. The paralegal fails to look into other facts other than those that immediately "leap to mind." If the paralegal can learn to think of the Factual Development and Verification Stage as requiring, first of all, an effort to see how many facts might be applicable before trying to determine which are viable. Line up all points and let the attorney make the final judgment.

Determining what facts may possibly be applicable requires a very specific focus. At the conclusion of the Overview stage, you must consciously ask, "Given these facts and what I know about the attorney's desires and concerns, what other facts, regardless of how weak or strong they may now appear, might my attorney need to properly represent the client? Certain facts and information will perhaps be obvious, but your mental effort must be geared toward the development of the maximum number of possibilities. Critical to the success of this endeavor will be your knowledge of the substantive theories your attorney has determined may need support; the more substantive knowledge that you have in your head, the more successful you will be in executing this task.

What about the situation where you, for one reason or another, have little or no substantive knowledge of the legal theories that are potentially relevant and what facts are needed to support it? (By my definition, you have substantive knowledge of a legal theory when you have general familiarity with the basic substantive elements of the cause of action or defense involved as set forth by your attorney.) Where you lack adequate substantive knowledge the available choices seem to be: (1) adjourn the meeting and ask your attorney for guidance; or (2) go back through the Overview to learn more detail about the story in general since the additional detail might aid subsequent investigation. What must be noted, however, is that if the client appears to need immediate help, the latter choice will probably be called for. Keep the client's interests foremost in your mind and get guidance from your attorney when necessary.

This model is an example, but not a hard and fast way in which you must operate. Through time you will develop your own style of interviewing, and you should.

• Ending the Interview

You need to be aware of the time so that you end the interview within the time constraints you and the clients have in your schedule. If you begin the interview by telling the client or witness how much time you will spend with him, it will be easier to culminate the interview when necessary.

A good way to end the interview is to summarize what will be done next and what needs to be done. It is a good time to present documents that need to be completed or forms to be signed. Make sure that the client or witness understands completely what he is supposed to do next and also when you or your attorney will be back in touch with him. Letting the client know what steps you and your attorney will take next will ease the client's mind and prevent an unnecessary call from him.

Walk the client or witness to the door, shake her hand, give her your business card, and explain to her that you may have to call her again. (Even though you think that you have all the information, often you will find that you have to call her again and ask an additional question or clarify a point.) Exhibit 5.2 is a checklist of the basic instructions you might give a client in a personal injury case.

• Documenting the Interview

Documenting the interview is usually accomplished by preparing an *intake memo*, an end-product of the interview. The intake memo is comprised of the notes taken during the interview. It serves several purposes: (1) It documents the interview; (2) It prevents any future misunderstanding about the informa-

Exhibit 5.2
•
**Checklist of Basics to Tell
the Personal Injury Client**

○ Avoid speaking to anyone about the accident unless authorized by your attorney. (This includes the client's own insurance company unless otherwise directed by your attorney.)

○ Send to your attorney copies of all bills incurred as a result of the accident, including bills for property damage such as vehicle repair or vehicle rental expenses, personal property that was in the vehicle at the time of the accident and was damaged therein, medical and hospital expenses, pharmaceutical expenses, and medical supplies such as crutches, braces, etc.

○ Retain a record of mileage to and from doctors, hospitals, etc., including parking expenses.

○ Pay all bills by check, if possible. (The canceled check will be a receipt of payment for purposes of evidence.)

○ Do not give or sign any statements without prior authorization from your attorney. Telephone your attorney should anyone request a statement of information of any kind relating to the accident and, if possible, determine whom the inquirer represents.

○ Let your attorney review any official accident reports or forms prior to their filing.

○ Obtain written estimates from two or more repair dealers prior to making arrangements for your vehicle's repair. Photograph prior to repair all sides of the vehicle, even those not damaged.

○ Do not sell, trade, or dispose of the vehicle prior to its examination by the attorney or the representative, or prior to any photographs being taken of the vehicle.

○ Keep a record of dates on which anything important relating to the accident takes place regarding, for example, medical treatment, change of circumstances, degree of pain, falls, or other subsequent injuries of any nature, or any other unusual events regarding the effects of injuries.

○ Advise both your medical and automobile liability insurance carrier of the details regarding the accident, but check with the attorney before making any statements.

○ Keep a record of days lost from work and the amount of earnings lost, even if wages are paid as sick leave or vacation pay. Keep copies of check stubs showing lost days or sick pay.

○ To the best of your recollection, make a record of everything you remember about the accident, including:

1. Time of day.
2. Weather and visibility conditions.
3. The names and addresses of witnesses, if known, before and after events.
4. Any conversations or comments made by witnesses.
5. Road conditions and obstructions.
6. Damages to all vehicles involved.
7. Position of vehicles before and after the accident.
8. Diagram of the street and/or intersection.
9. Noises heard as a result of the accident.
10. Whether you gave statements or made comments regarding the accident to anyone and, if so, their names and addresses, if known.
11. Whether anybody took photographs of the vehicles and/or surrounding area after the accident.

Exhibit 5.2

Continued

12. Any particular defects you noticed in the other vehicles, i.e., broken windshield wipers, bald tires, etc.

13. Whether there were any pedestrians involved and, if so, their names and addresses, if known.

14. Notations regarding a description of the accident area and the immediately surrounding area.

15. Posted speed limits and position of traffic signs and/or signals.

16. Skid marks noticed after the accident, if any.

17. Passengers in involved vehicles.

tion the client gave the interviewer; and (3) It acts as a "tickler" to remind the attorney and paralegal what needs to be done. The intake memo is filed in the client's file, and a copy is given to the supervising attorney. The memo should note the following basic information:

1. The interviewer's name.

2. The supervising attorney's name.

3. The date the memo was written.

4. The date of the interview.

5. The title of the case, e.g., *Pittman v. Reiff.*

6. The client file number.

7. The type of case, e.g., negligence, contract.

8. The subject matter of the memo.

9. The client's name, home and business address and telephone, birthdate, marital status, and employer.

The memo should state the purpose of the interview as instructed by your attorney. The facts derived from the interview may be presented in chronological order, topical order, or in any other order requested by your attorney.

It is important to note your first impressions on the demeanor of the client, how truthful you think she was, and how knowledgeable she seemed to be. You might consider verbally communicating any doubts you have about the client in this regard—tactfully and diplomatically—rather than writing them into the memo, since the client may have access to this document.

The memo should serve as a "to do" list by indicating the next steps that you and your attorney should take. This may include research, telephone calls to make, discovery and investigation to be conducted, and other matters. The intake memo should also summarize what you told the client and what documents or information you have asked the client to give you. This will serve as a checklist of items to follow up on.

• Maintaining Contact with the Client

Some clients do not realize that their attorney handles numerous cases besides theirs. They tend to believe and act as if theirs is the only case that the attorney is handling. This can present a problem unless you step in and maintain the contact with clients that your attorney, for lack of time, cannot maintain. Keeping clients informed reassures them that their case is not being neglected, which will lead to client retention and fewer complaints. It also can prevent duplication of communications.

Follow Up on Every Reasonable Request of Client

Frequently the client will contact your office to ask seemingly obvious questions or to make apparently foolish requests. Always attempt to answer every question that the client may have regardless of how simple it may seem. What is obvious to you may not be obvious to everyone. However, remember to fulfill only those client requests that fall within the parameters of your job, and be mindful of the prohibitions against the unauthorized practice of law. If in doubt, ask your attorney.

If you are unable to answer a client's questions inform him or her that you will consult with your attorney or other proper authorities on the matter. Be sure to inform the client of the results as soon as possible.

Acknowledge Receipt of Correspondence Sent by Client

It is a good business practice to acknowledge by letter, if possible, or at least by telephone the receipt of any correspondence, important documents, pleadings, or other information that the client has sent to your office. As may be expected, most clients tend to worry about important things that they send through the mails. A simple telephone call or short letter will ease their minds tremendously.

Make Each Client Feel That She Is Your Most Important Client

Always bear in mind that each client feels that the legal matter she brought to your attorney's office is extremely important, or she would not have bothered to contact an attorney. You can easily offend a client by seeming to view her case as less important than she views it—or as less important than other cases your attorney may be handling. Therefore, you should make every effort to treat the client as if her case is your attorney's most important case.

• Summary

Interviewing is a very important task, one with a tremendous responsibility. Any time that you have personal contact with a client, your attorney is indicating significant confidence in you. Client relationships are delicate, so every contact you have with a client should be handled with care. Plan ahead when you are going to conduct a client interview. Rehearse, if necessary. Make sure you understand your ethical boundaries and adhere to them closely. Rather than say or do something you are unsure of, hold off and ask your attorney. Use checklists to standardize your information-gathering, and clarify anything that you do not understand while the client is still in conference with you. Once you have built the client's trust in you, work steadily to maintain rapport. Communicate openly and clearly with the client, and always follow up to let the client know what is happening on his case according to your attorney's guidelines.

6

The Paralegal's Role in Motion Practice

• Introduction

Motions are requests made by attorneys, either orally or in writing, for the court to take a particular action. They may seem hard to understand, mostly because they have separate parts with separate functions and seem to interrupt the normal litigation cycle. But a motion is merely a plea to the court for relief. They are a type of pleading that may be used before, during, and after trial, according to the stipulations of Rule 12 of the *Federal Rules of Civil Procedure.*

The paralegal can be extremely helpful to the attorney in motion practice. Many of the motions, stipulations, and notices can be initially drafted by the paralegal. However, before you can assist the attorney in preparing motions, you must have a thorough understanding of these pleadings. The goal of this chapter is to give you a brief overview of motion practice in the federal and state courts, but it is by no means a complete treatise on the subject.[1]

Motion practice comes into play once the complaint is received. The defendant may decide to attack the complaint through appropriate motions rather than (1) do nothing and default, (2) file an answer, or (3) file a petition to have the case removed from state court to federal court. The opponent may respond, amend, oppose, or reply as necessary.

During the motion stage, both sides may test the lawsuit with the goal of ending it through a motion for judgment on the pleadings, which is a motion filed by either party after the pleadings are closed but before the trial, similar to demurrer. Either party can also use a procedural device known as a motion for summary judgment when there is no dispute as to either material facts or inferences to be drawn from undisputed facts, or if only a question of law is involved. The difference between the two is that the party in a motion for summary judgment can introduce factual information that is outside the pleadings filed in the case. The court is not limited to the pleadings in making its decision.

Thus, motions are papers filed with the court by the moving party, opposition papers filed by the opposition, and a reply by the moving party. After the papers have been filed, the matter is heard by the court at a hearing, after which an *order* is rendered. The order, which either grants or denies the request of the moving party, is served on all parties to the action, resolving the dispute. An

---

[1]See Schweitzer, *Cyclopedia of Trial Practice*, vol. 1, 2d ed. In Wright, *Handbook of the Law of Federal Courts* (C. Wright, St. Paul, MN: West Publishing Company, 1970).

order must be made by motion except in a hearing or trial. An application to the court must be in writing and must state the grounds and the relief or the order sought. The rules vary from state to state, so a paralegal should always determine whether a *brief* or *memorandum of law* (discussed later in this chapter) and supporting affidavits are necessary to support the motion. A motion for summary judgment should always be supported by a brief.

If the motion is modified, however, counsel may request to modify it by hand for the judge's signature, making certain that all copies—especially the one served on opposing counsel—contain the changes. Otherwise, an order must be prepared for later submission to the court.

Several sample motion forms and orders are included in this chapter that you may adapt to comply with your local rules and state statutes. These can be adapted to your attorney's particular style. These forms are intended to be used as guidelines, not to be chiseled in stone. Your office may have a form file made up of prior motions that your attorney may prefer you use as a guide. Be sure to check with your attorney if you wish to change the format of a particular motion. Be prepared to show your attorney why the change would be an improvement. Some of the sample forms for the federal district courts may be used in the form that they are given, but, as always in using forms, be sure to check the local district court rules for compliance.

• Purposes of Motions

Motions have several purposes:

1. To obtain judicial relief, such as dismissal of the action, exclusion of evidence, or a new trial.
2. To narrow the issues for trial.
3. To establish a record for appeal.

A motion may involve any one of these purposes or a combination of them. The first of these purposes is to give the moving party the opportunity to obtain relief without the expense of a lengthy trial. The second serves to clarify and redefine the lawsuit for trial. The third serves to allow questions of law to be raised that must be decided by the judge. If the judge's decision on these questions is appealed, the motion establishes the fact that an issue was raised in a proper and timely manner, thereby preserving the right to have the issue heard on appeal.

• Structure of Motions

Motions consist of four essential features:

1. The *notice* to all appearing parties that the motion is being made.
2. The *brief* of law and legal argument in support of the motion, that is, the evidence supporting the motion.
3. The *service* of the motion, supporting brief and affidavits upon opposing counsel.
4. The proposed order.

Form 6.1

Notice of Motion

IN THE UNITED STATES DISTRICT COURT
NORTHERN DISTRICT OF GEORGIA
ATLANTA DIVISION

ELTON D. THORN AND LYDIA A. THORN,))) Plaintiffs,) v.)) WAVERLY CORPORATION, et al.,)) Defendants.)	CIVIL ACTION FILE NO. C90–4458

NOTICE OF MOTION

TO: Tammy Griner
Griner & Associates
Attorney for Plaintiffs
One Hundred Building
Suite 2009
Atlanta, Georgia 30303

Please take notice that the undersigned will bring the above action for hearing before this Court at 9:30 a.m., on the 12th day of April, 1992, or as soon thereafter as counsel can be heard.

Goede & Fulks

By: Darryl F. Goede
Attorneys for Defendants

Geode & Fulks
101 Marietta Tower
Suite 1700
Atlanta, Georgia 30303
(404) 351–0020

Notice of Motion

A *notice of motion* (Form 6.1) must be prepared to inform the opponent that a motion is being filed. The notice must state the date, time, and place of the hearing. Even though the court rules require that this information be given in the caption, underneath the case number and document title, it is also set forth in the first paragraph of the notice. The motion must be served at least 15 days before the hearing, with an additional 5 days for mailing.[2]

---

[2]Rule 7(b), *Federal Rules of Civil Procedure.*

Memorandum of Law

A *memorandum of law,* also referred to as a memorandum of points and *authorities,* must be filed with every motion. *Points* are the argument, and *authorities* are the citations to the law. There are three parts to a memorandum: statements of law, fact, and argument which are explained below. Courts tend to favor shorter memos. Many clerks will not file a motion exceeding 15 pages until the attorney obtains another court order permitting filing.

A brief citation to the law and explanation of how the law applies to the case is generally sufficient. A short description of the key issues in the case is usually all that is necessary, since most law and motion matters concern other issues, such as whether interrogatories have been answered.

The memorandum of law should be attached to the motion and served upon counsel for all parties.

Statements of Law
Statements of law set forth the law on the issues being addressed. Citations to appropriate legal authorities must follow legal statements. Primary authorities, such as court opinions and law journal articles, are favored. Secondary sources, such as digests and summaries, are disfavored.

Statements of Fact
Statements of fact set forth the facts as supported by references to evidence. The type of evidence depends upon the type of motion. For example, the attorney's statement in the memorandum that requests for production were answered on a particular date must be supported by evidence. The evidence may be a certificate of service, or it may be an affidavit by the attorney that the requests were answered.

Statement of Argument
The argument portion of the memorandum of points and authorities consists of (1) a statement of the issues presented by the case, (2) the applicable rule of law, (3) the application of the rule to the specific facts of the case, and (4) the conclusion. The drafter argues that the facts of the case are either consistent with facts in other cases that held in his favor or inconsistent with cases holding against him. Argumentative statements need not be supported, because they are advocating an application of the cited law to the facts cited.[3]

Drafting the Memorandum and Checking Citations
You can be of great assistance to your attorney by writing the rough draft of the memorandum. Be careful and meticulous. Check each citation twice while you are still in the library to save a return trip. Checking citations is a tedious but important task. Keep track of where you have located information in the books. This will make it will be easier to retrace your steps if you misplace a citation. (See Chapter 10 for more information on citations.) Although you should find a

---

[3]Susan Bennett Luten, *California Civil Litigation* (St. Paul, MN: West Publishing Company, 1989), p. 244–245.

good instructional book to help you with the details of drafting written by experienced attorneys,[4] here are a few basic pointers:[5]

- Make your memo short, using simple and direct language.
- Set forth a brief statement of fact relevant to the motion and the law and evidence upon which it is based.
- Summarize the legal arguments if the motion exceeds the number of pages set forth in your local rules.
- Check your local rules to see if there is a requirement for a table of contents or a table of authorities.
- Make sure your memorandum does not exceed the number of pages set forth in your local rules.
- Make a brief citation to the law and explain how the law applies to the case.
- Describe the main issues in the case briefly.
- Explain how this situation compares with accepted legal principles.

Service upon Opposing Counsel

When the motion, supporting brief, and affidavits are filed with the court, opposing counsel should be served with a copy not less than five days before the date of the hearing on the motion. A certificate of service is filed with the motion.[6] Be sure to check your state codes, since requirements may vary. A responsive affidavit or memorandum may be filed by the adverse party.

Preparation of Accompanying Order

It is customary for the party filing the motion to prepare an *order* (Form 6.2) for the judge's signature to be filed with the motion and accompanying briefs and affidavits. Prevailing counsel should ask that the court sign the order on the spot. This allows counsel to serve it on opposing counsel before leaving the hearing.

You may be assigned to prepare the order in advance to help expedite the process, as well as to monitor compliance by other parties. If the motion is granted without modification, the court may sign the proposed order filed with the moving papers, or counsel may take two copies to the hearing. One copy will be kept by the court, and the other will be served.

An order prepared after the hearing is usually submitted to the opposition to sign "approved as to form" before it is submitted to court. Check your local rules, since many now require that all orders be "approved as to form" by all counsel before being submitted to the court for signature. While the signature of the opposing counsel indicates that she has reviewed the order and that it conforms to the order of the court at the hearing or the tentative rule, it is still compared to the court's minute book records by the clerk. After approval by the

---

[4]See Morris L. Cohen, Robert C. Berring, and Kent C. Olson, *How to Find the Law*, 9th ed. (St. Paul, MN: West Publishing Company, 1989).

[5]Luten, *California Civil Litigation*, pp. 243–245.

[6]Rule 6(d), *Federal Rules of Civil Procedure*.

IN THE UNITED STATES DISTRICT COURT
NORTHERN DISTRICT OF GEORGIA
ATLANTA DIVISION

ELTON D. THORN and	)	
LYDIA A. THORN,	)	
	)	CIVIL ACTION
Plaintiffs,	)	
v.	)	FILE NO. C90–4458
	)	
WAVERLY CORPORATION, et al.,	)	
	)	
Defendants.	)	

ORDER

Plaintiffs' Motion for Summary Judgment has been read and considered. Let the Defendants show cause before the undersigned in the United States District Court of the Northern District of Georgia, Atlanta Division, Room 1310, at 2 p.m. on the 18th day of August, 1992, THEN AND THERE TO BE HEARD, why said Motion should not be granted, and why the Court should not grant judgment in his favor and why this Complaint should not be dismissed.

This 4th day of August, 1992.

Judge, United States District Court

---

clerk, the original is kept for the court's files, and the copies are returned to the submitting party.

The submitting party then serves the order, which is attached to a document entitled "Notice of Entry of Order," and served on all parties. The date of service of the notice of entry is the date from which time is calculated for any act required by the order.

• Supporting Affidavits

An *affidavit* is a written statement or declaration sworn to or affirmed under oath. It frequently accompanies a motion. All affidavits must be made based on personal knowledge; that is, the affiant must swear only to the facts within his personal knowledge. Affidavits must set forth such facts as would be admissible in evidence and should show that the affiant is competent to testify to the matters stated in the affidavit.

Certified or sworn copies of all papers or parts of papers referred to in the affidavit must be attached to the affidavit or served with it. Affidavits may be supplemented or opposed by depositions, answers to interrogatories, or further affidavits.

Where affidavits are submitted in support of a motion for summary judgment, the adverse party's response must set forth specific facts showing that

Form 6.3

**Affidavit in Support of
Summary Judgment**

IN THE UNITED STATES DISTRICT COURT
NORTHERN DISTRICT OF GEORGIA
ATLANTA DIVISION

ELTON D. THORN and	)	
LYDIA A. THORN,	)	
Plaintiffs,	)	CIVIL ACTION
v.	)	FILE NO. C90–4458
	)	
WAVERLY CORPORATION, et al.,	)	
Defendants.	)	

AFFIDAVIT OF LAUREN PANNELL
IN SUPPORT OF MOTION FOR SUMMARY JUDGMENT OF PLAINTIFFS

Personally appeared LAUREN PANNELL on behalf of ELTON D. THORN and LYDIA A. THORN, Plaintiffs in the above-styled action, who being duly sworn says:

I reside at 1654 Liholiho Street, Apartment No. 14, Acworth, Georgia. I am employed as a secretary for the WAVERLY CORPORATION.

This Affidavit is given on the basis of the affiant having knowledge pertaining to the above-styled action, and more particularly to a Motion for Summary Judgment on behalf of Plaintiffs, ELTON D. THORN and LYDIA A. THORN.

Plaintiffs' records reflect the accounts of WAVERLY CORPORATION at 1220 Third Street, Marietta, Georgia, show a deficiency of $9,800. I have checked the records for this account, and they are true and correct as stated.

Defendant WAVERLY CORPORATION has not paid the $9,800 due for the services furnished to the account of Defendant's business, THE WAVERLY RESTAURANT, through January 31, 1992, which account is the subject of the above-styled action, and said amount is still due and owing.

_____
Lauren Pannell, Affiant

(notarial clause)

there is a genuine issue for trial. He may not rest merely upon the allegations or denials of his pleadings.

If the adverse party does not present by affidavit facts essential to justify his opposition, the court may: (1) refuse the application for judgment; (2) order a continuance to permit affidavits to be obtained, depositions to be taken, or discovery to be had; or (3) make another order as is just.

If it can be proven that the affidavits presented with the motion are presented in bad faith or solely for the purpose of delay, the court will order the initiating party to pay to the other party the amount of the reasonable expenses. These expenses include those incurred by the filing of the affidavits as well as reasonable attorney's fees. Any offending party or attorney may be adjudged guilty of contempt for these actions. A sample *affidavit in support of motion for summary judgment* is shown in Form 6.3.

IN THE SUPERIOR COURT OF CLAYTON COUNTY
STATE OF GEORGIA

MARLENE BARTON,   )
)
    Plaintiff,   )
)
v.   )   CIVIL ACTION
)
)   FILE NO. 89–173
)
TODD RUDNER, M.D.,   )
)
    Defendant.   )

PLAINTIFF'S MOTION FOR JUDGMENT
ON THE PLEADINGS

Plaintiff MARLENE BARTON moves the court pursuant to Section 12(c) of the Civil Practice Act to enter judgment in his favor in the above-styled action on the ground that the answer of Defendant TODD RUDNER, M.D., admits the allegations of the complaint and shows that plaintiff is entitled to the relief sought in his complaint.

This 19th day of August, 1989.

Respectfully submitted,

Tammy Griner
Attorney for Plaintiffs

Griner & Associates
One Hundred Building
Suite 2009
Atlanta, Georgia 30303
(404) 565–7285

• Motion for Judgment on the Pleadings

A *motion for judgment on the pleadings* (Form 6.4) is based on the premise that the pleadings in and of themselves allow a judgment. In other words, the motion argues that there is sufficient information in the pleadings for the judge to render a judgment without it being necessary to take up any more of the court's time. An order for this motion is shown in Form 6.5.

• Motion for Summary Judgment

A motion for summary judgment (Form 6.6) is based on the argument that since there is no genuine issue of material fact, the party moving for summary judgment is entitled to prevail as a matter of law.

Form 6.5

**Order for Judgment
on the Pleadings**

IN THE SUPERIOR COURT OF CLAYTON COUNTY
STATE OF GEORGIA

MARLENE BARTON,   )
)
    Plaintiff,   )
)
v.   )   CIVIL ACTION
)
)   FILE NO. 88–173
)
TODD RUDNER, M.D.   )
)
    Defendant.   )

ORDER

Plaintiff MARLENE BARTON having moved the court for an order for judgment on the pleadings, and it appearing from the face of the pleadings that plaintiff is entitled to the relief sought in her complaint, it is ORDERED, that Plaintiff MARLENE BARTON have judgment against Defendant TODD RUDNER, M.D., in the sum of $95,000 and her costs in this action.

This 12th day of December, 1990.

Judge, Superior Court of Clayton County, Georgia

If the pleadings and discovery documents on file in the lawsuit, and the affidavits which accompany the motion, show conclusively that there is no genuine issue as to any material fact and that the moving party is entitled to a judgment as a matter of law, summary judgment is appropriate. A summary judgment may be rendered on the *issue of liability* alone, although there is a genuine issue as to the amount of damages.

Rule 56 of the *Federal Rules of Civil Procedure* provides for summary judgment, but check your state statutes as well. According to Rule 56, the plaintiff may move for summary judgment at any time after the expiration of 20 days from the commencement of the lawsuit or after service of a motion for summary judgment by the adverse party. However, a defending party may move for summary judgment at any time. The motion must be served at least 10 days before the hearing. The adverse party may serve opposing affidavits at any time prior to the hearing.

• Motion for More Definite Statement

A motion for more definite statement (Form 6.7) is usually based on the claim that the present form of the complaint is vague and uncertain so that the defendant is unable to prepare a responsive pleading. According to Rule 12(e) of *Federal Rules of Civil Procedure*, the opponent must be provided with sufficient facts to determine the claim or defense and have the opportunity to respond.

IN THE UNITED STATES DISTRICT COURT
NORTHERN DISTRICT OF GEORGIA
ATLANTA DIVISION

ELTON D. THORN and	)	
LYDIA A. THORN,	)	
	)	CIVIL ACTION
Plaintiffs,	)	
v.	)	FILE NO. C90–4458
	)	
WAVERLY CORPORATION, et al.,	)	
	)	
Defendants.	)	

PLAINTIFFS' MOTION FOR SUMMARY JUDGMENT

COMES NOW Plaintiffs ELTON D. THORN and LYDIA A. THORN and moves this Honorable Court as follows:

That it enter, pursuant to Rule 56 of the Federal Rules of Civil Procedure (28 U.S.C.A. § 156) a summary judgment in Plaintiffs' favor for the relief demanded in its Complaint on the ground that there is no genuine issue as to any material fact and that Plaintiffs are entitled to a judgment as a matter of law.

If summary judgment is not rendered in Plaintiffs' favor upon the whole case or for all the relief asked and a trial is necessary, that the Court, at the hearing on the motion, by examining the pleadings and evidence before it and by interrogating counsel, ascertain what material facts are actually and in good faith controverted, and there upon make an order specifying the facts that appear without substantial controversy and directing such further proceedings in the action as are just.

This motion is based upon:

(a) The pleadings, interrogatories, requests for admissions, on file with this Honorable Court in this action;

(b) The deposition of Celena Bullard on file with this Court; and

(c) The supporting affidavits of Kim Turner and Paula Turner attached hereto and incorporated herein by reference.

Tammy Griner
Attorney for Plaintiffs

Griner & Associates
One Hundred Building
Suite 2009
Atlanta, Georgia 30303
(404) 565–7265

• Motion to Strike

A motion to strike (Form 6.8) serves as a vehicle to clean up the pleadings and make sure that they are to the point, and free of ambiguous and useless rhetoric. Under Rule 12(f) of *Federal Rules of Civil Procedure*, the court may order that any

CERTIFICATE OF SERVICE

This is to certify that I have this day served a copy of the within and foregoing Plaintiffs' Motion for Summary Judgment upon counsel for Defendants:

> Darryl F. Goede
> Goede & Fulks
> 101 Marietta Tower
> Suite 1700
> Atlanta, Georgia 30303

by depositing a copy in the United States mail in a properly addressed envelope with sufficient postage affixed thereto.

This 3rd day of August, 1992.

> Tammy Griner
> Attorney for Plaintiffs

Griner & Associates
One Hundred Place
Suite 2009
Atlanta, Georgia 30303
(404) 565–7265

---

insufficient defense or any redundant, immaterial, impertinent, or scandalous matter be stricken from any pleading.

• Motion to Dismiss

Probably the most common motion is the motion to dismiss (Form 6.9), which requests the court to reject (dismiss) the complaint based on any one of the following reasons:[7]

1. Lack of jurisdiction over the subject matter.
2. Lack of jurisdiction over the person.
3. Improper venue.
4. Insufficiency of process.
5. Insufficiency of service of process.
6. Failure to state a claim upon which relief can be granted.

If the plaintiff can amend the complaint to eliminate the basis for dismissal, then the case may proceed.

Some states, such as California, use a *demurrer* for this same purpose. A demurrer is a pleading objecting to defects appearing on the face of the complaint and creates *issues of law* only. A demurrer must be filed within 30 days.

---

[7]Rule 12(b), *Federal Rules of Civil Procedure.*

IN THE UNITED STATES DISTRICT COURT
NORTHERN DISTRICT OF GEORGIA
ATLANTA DIVISION

ELTON D. THORN AND LYDIA A. THORN,	)))	
Plaintiffs,	))	CIVIL ACTION
v.	))	FILE NO. C90–4458
WAVERLY CORPORATION, et al.,	))	
Defendants.	)	
and		
CHARLES R. BURNETT and LILLIAN K. BURNETT,	)))	
Plaintiffs,	))	CIVIL ACTION
v.	))	FILE NO. C90–4490
ROBERTSLOON CORPORATION, et al.,	))	
Defendants.	)	

DEFENDANTS WAVERLY CORPORATION
AND ROBERTSLOON CORPORATION'S MOTION FOR A
MORE DEFINITE STATEMENT

Come now Defendants WAVERLY CORPORATION and ROBERTSLOON CORPO-
RATION and move this Court, pursuant to Rule 12(e) of the Federal Rules of Civil Procedure, to require that Plaintiffs ELTON D. THORN, LYDIA A. THORN, CHARLES R.
BURNETT and LILLIAN K. BURNETT state, in their amended pleadings, the time, place
and content of the alleged fraudulent concealment as well as the identity of persons participating in the alleged fraud and what was obtained by the alleged fraud so as to allow
defendants to reasonably frame a responsive pleading.

Respectfully submitted,

Darryl F. Goede
Attorney for Defendants

Goede & Fulks
101 Marietta Tower
Suite 1700
Atlanta, Georgia 30303
(404) 351–0020

Form 6.8

Motion to Strike

IN THE SUPERIOR COURT OF CLAYTON COUNTY
STATE OF GEORGIA

SANDRA KOREY,	)	
	)	
Plaintiff,	)	
	)	
v.	)	CIVIL ACTION
	)	
STEVEN REIFF,	)	FILE NO. 91–783
	)	
Defendant.	)	
	)	
	)	

PLAINTIFF'S MOTION TO STRIKE
PORTIONS OF DEFENDANT'S
ANSWER AND CROSS-COMPLAINT

Comes now Plaintiff SANDRA KOREY and moves the court, pursuant to Section § 12(f) of the Georgia Civil Practice Act [*Ga. Code Ann.* 81A-112(f)] for an order striking from Defendant STEVEN REIFF'S Answer and Cross-Complaint in the above-entitled case Defendant's prayers (c) and (d) on the ground that the award of such relief to Defendant is contrary to Georgia law.

This 25th day of October, 1991.

Respectfully submitted,

Tammy Griner
Attorney for Plaintiff

Griner & Associates
One Hundred Building
Suite 2009
Atlanta, Georgia 30303
(404) 565–7265

A motion to dismiss is not the same as a motion for summary judgment, even when it is based on the same reason—that the complaint does not state a claim for which relief can be granted. A motion for summary judgment seeks a judgment and a motion to dismiss seeks to have the matter dismissed entirely. Both motions may request a ruling on the entire case.

Frequently a memorandum of law is prepared for a motion to dismiss. You may be asked to do some research in order to prepare this memorandum. You may also have to prepare a draft of the order for the judge to sign, but check with your attorney first.

• Stipulations

A *stipulation* (Form 6.10) is a material condition, requirement, or article in an agreement between opposing litigants that certain facts are true or that certain

IN THE UNITED STATES DISTRICT COURT
NORTHERN DISTRICT OF GEORGIA
ATLANTA DIVISION

ELTON D. THORN AND LYDIA A. THORN,	)))	CIVIL ACTION
Plaintiffs,	))	
v.	))	FILE NO. C90–4458
WAVERLY CORPORATION, et al.,	))	
Defendants.	)	

and

CHARLES R. BURNETT and LILLIAN K. BURNETT,	)))	
Plaintiffs,	))	CIVIL ACTION
v.	))	FILE NO. C90–4490
ROBERTSLOON CORPORATION, et al.,	))	
Defendants.	)	

DEFENDANTS WAVERLY CORPORATION AND
ROBERTSLOON CORPORATION'S MOTION TO
DISMISS PLAINTIFFS' COMPLAINTS

Come now Defendants WAVERLY CORPORATION and ROBERTSLOON CORPO-
RATION and move the Court, pursuant to Rule 12(e) and 41(b) of the Federal Rules of Civil
Procedure for an order dismissing Plaintiffs ELTON D. THORN, LYDIA A. THORN,
CHARLES R. BURNETT and LILLIAN K. BURNETT's Complaint for failure to comply
with the order of this Court, dated September 12, 1990, requiring them to make a more
definite statement as to the allegations of their amended Complaints. In the alternative,
Defendants move the Court for whatever order it deems just under the circumstances.

Respectfully submitted,

Darryl F. Goede
Attorney for Defendants

Goede & Fulks
101 Marietta Tower
Suite 1700
Atlanta, Georgia 30303
(404) 351–0020

Form 6.10

**Stipulation for Extension
of Time**

IN THE UNITED STATES DISTRICT COURT
NORTHERN DISTRICT OF GEORGIA
ATLANTA DIVISION

ELTON D. THORN AND LYDIA A. THORN,))) Plaintiffs,) v.)) WAVERLY CORPORATION, et al.,)) Defendants.)	CIVIL ACTION FILE NO. C90–4458

STIPULATION FOR EXTENSION OF TIME

It is stipulated among counsel for Plaintiffs and Defendants in the above-styled action that Plaintiffs, ELTON D. THORN and LYDIA A. THORN, shall have an extension of time through and including March 2, 1991, to move, plead, answer, or otherwise respond to Defendants' pleading in this action.

DATED: January 15, 1991.

Griner & Associates

Tammy Griner
Attorney for Plaintiffs

Griner & Associates
One Hundred Building
Suite 2009
Atlanta, Georgia 30303
(404) 566-7265

Goede & Fulks

Darryl F. Goede
Attorneys for Defendants

Goede & Fulks
101 Marietta Tower
Suite 1700
Atlanta, Georgia 30303
(404) 351-0020

acts may take place. In a judicial proceeding, stipulations by the parties or their attorneys facilitate and expedite the trial by dispensing with the need to prove certain factual issues formally.

Stipulations are also used to modify or amend filed pleadings upon agreement of counsel—for example, an admission of certain facts. Of course, stipulations and proposed amended pleadings should be mailed to other counsel of record, if any.

IN THE UNITED STATES DISTRICT COURT
NORTHERN DISTRICT OF GEORGIA
ATLANTA DIVISION

ELTON D. THORN and	)	
LYDIA A. THORN,	)	
	)	CIVIL ACTION
Plaintiffs,	)	
v.	)	FILE NO. C90–4458
	)	
WAVERLY CORPORATION, et al.,	)	
	)	
Defendants.	)	

NOTICE OF HEARING

Plaintiffs ELTON D. THORN and LYDIA A. THORN's Motion for Summary Judgment will be heard at 2 p.m. on the 16th day of August, 1992, in the United States District Court for the Northern District of Georgia, Atlanta Division.

DATED: August 3, 1992.

Tammy Griner
Attorney for Plaintiffs

Griner & Associates
One Hundred Building
Suite 2009
Atlanta, Georgia 30303
(404) 565–7265

An order should accompany the stipulation. The moving party should provide the order for the court. This enables the judge to sign the order during the hearing and allows counsel to serve it on opposing counsel before leaving the hearing (see "Structure of Motions" earlier in this chapter).

• Notices

According to Rule 3 of the *Federal Rules of Civil Procedure,* an application to the court for an order shall be made by a motion, which must be made in writing if it is not made during a hearing or trial. If the motion is stated in a written *notice of the hearing of the motion* (Form 6.11), the requirement of writing is fulfilled. Therefore, motions filed in the federal court can be accompanied by a written notice of the hearing. This may be in the form of a *notice of order to show cause hearing* (used in California), or a *rule NISI* (Form 6.12) (used in Georgia), or a form similar to the standard one of a *notice of motion* (refer again to Form 6.1). Be sure to check your local court rules for applicable provisions regarding notices filed in the federal court. For notices filed in the state courts, check your state code and local procedural rules.

Form 6.12

Rule NISI

IN THE UNITED STATES DISTRICT COURT
NORTHERN DISTRICT OF GEORGIA
ATLANTA DIVISION

JOANN DRESDON,	)	
	)	CIVIL ACTION
Plaintiff,	)	
v.	)	FILE NO. C91–358
	)	
JON DRESDON,	)	
	)	
Defendant.	)	

RULE NISI

TO: Jon Dresdon, Defendant herein, by and through his attorney of record, Gino Vincent, Vincent & Price, 230 West Fifth Street, Atlanta, Georgia 30301.

You are hereby ordered to be and appear before the Honorable Corneill Stephens, Judge of the United States District Court of the Northern District of Georgia, Atlanta Division, Room 872, on the 14th day of April, 1992, then and there to be heard and show causes why the Motion annexed here should not be granted.

This 30th day of March, 1992.

Judge, United States District Court

Often the motion may require a supporting brief and/or affidavits. A notice of motion is not required under the *Federal Rules of Civil Procedure* unless local rules differ. Of course, the attorney should make this determination.

• Summary

Your role in motion practice will depend upon the amount of responsibility delegated to you by your attorney. Whether your attorney gives you significant responsibility in preparing motions will ultimately depend upon how much knowledge about motions and motion procedure you have and how much ability you have demonstrated in drafting motions. Again, the forms you use should be guidelines and not taken verbatim. You may or may not have an opportunity to prepare a memorandum of law in support of the motion. Usually, this is a task delegated to associates or law clerks.

The primary motions that you will most frequently come in contact with are motions for summary judgment, motion to dismiss and the various notices and stipulations. Remember that briefs and motions go hand in hand, and that orders must be prepared in advance for the judge's signature.

Getting Results from Pretrial Investigations

7

• Introduction

Pretrial investigation is one of the tools used by attorneys for the effective preparation of a lawsuit for settlement or trial. It involves gathering information formally and informally. To do your part as a paralegal, you need to be methodical and organized. This chapter gives you techniques, procedures, forms, and checklists to help you organize your investigation and teach you how to follow through and ensure the accuracy of the information you gather. In addition, this chapter discusses how to interview witnesses and take witness statements. A brief overview of the rules of evidence is given to help you in your investigation.

• Purpose and Scope of Pretrial Investigation

Investigation entails far more than *discovery*, which is a formal procedure governed by court rules and sanctions in which opposing counsel exchange information in the lawsuit (see Chapter 8). Investigation involves many informal procedures as well as formal ones for the major purposes of:

- Obtaining relevant facts.
- Gathering and preserving evidence to be used at trial.
- Obtaining impeachment material that might be used to impeach a witness or a party to the action.
- Eliciting admissions.
- Locating potential witnesses.
- Locating additional leads to additional evidence.

Investigation is certainly one of the most critical phases in the progress of the lawsuit. Since it often requires considerable time, your attorney may request your assistance in various ways. For example, you may be asked to visit the scene of an automobile accident to diagram the layout of the street lanes and the traffic flow. Another one of your tasks may be to conduct interviews with and obtain statements from all witnesses in an automobile negligence action. Your interviewees may include the investigating police officer, ambulance driver, and medical technicians, towing truck operator, doctor, and any attending nurses. In addition, you may have to investigate the events prior to and subsequent to the accident, take photographs of the vehicles, or obtain essential public reports regarding the accident.

In a breach of contract action, you may have to get witness statements from persons who witnessed the execution of the contract, and those who could attest to the breach of contract. Likewise, in a fraud suit, you may need to interview witnesses to the events surrounding the fraud. In a malpractice action, you may interview former patients of the defendant doctor, or the hospital employees. In a divorce action, witnesses as to the income of the parties may be relevant.

The nature of the your investigative assignments will be as varied as the different individual clients your firm represents. Some examples follow:

- Locating missing persons, such as heirs, witnesses, property owners, and parties to litigation.
- Locating assets for purposes of enforcing and collecting judgments.
- Investigating various aspects of a negligence action.
- Investigating the circumstances surrounding a questionable workers compensation claim.
- Investigating a routine aspect of a criminal matter.
- Locating and gathering facts, documents, and evidence for a lawsuit.
- Conducting a general background and character investigation of an individual.

Of course, numerous other investigative assignments are possible. (In addition, your attorney may hire a private investigator for some portions of the investigation.) Although the examples given in this chapter are mostly tort-related, they illustrate a methodology of fact-gathering or investigation that can be adapted to the particular case on which you are working.

Also included in this chapter are numerous checklists and forms to help you in recording and documenting relevant information. If you commonly investigate certain types of cases or frequently use certain types of information, you should develop your own checklists and forms. In addition to ensuring against the omission of important information, they can be a tremendous time-saver, because you can submit them instead of preparing a lengthy memorandum, or attach them to a short memorandum.

• Investigative Methods to Save You Time and Trouble

Here is a step-by-step procedure that will help your investigation be successful.

- **Step 1:** Determine the scope of the investigation.

- **Step 2:** Conduct your preliminary investigation from your office.

- **Step 3:** Conduct your investigation in a timely manner.

- **Step 4:** Gather and review relevant facts and basic documents carefully.

- **Step 5:** Identify basic principles of law.

- **Step 6:** Visit the scene of the accident or incident immediately.

- **Step 7:** Make contacts and establish credibility in the community.

- **Step 8:** Interview all witnesses and obtain statements.

- **Step 9:** Obtain and preserve evidence properly.

- **Step 10:** Document all information, including conversations.

- **Step 11:** Revise your plan if necessary.

- **Step 12:** Seek help from professional experts when necessary.

- **Step 13:** Report your progress to your attorney.

Here is an explanation of each of these steps, which may vary in order depending upon the details of your assignment.

- **Step 1:   Determine the scope of the investigation.**

You need to know the scope and limits of the investigation in order to develop a tentative, flexible plan. When you are first given the assignment, take specific notes, listen carefully, and ask questions regarding portions of your assignment that are unclear to you. Ask the following questions if your attorney does not cover them:

1. What information, pleadings, depositions, interrogatories, or other documents are available for review?
2. What specific investigative tasks are you to undertake?
3. How the information will be used, e.g., to impeach a witness, to enter into evidence?
4. What are the physical and geographic limits of your assignment?
5. How much time do you have to complete the investigation?
6. What interim reports will your attorney need?
7. Are there any specific witnesses or other persons that your attorney expects you to contact or interview?
8. Are you authorized to take photographs, if necessary?
9. Has any previous investigation been done on the subject assignment? If so, obtain a copy of any previous investigative report.
10. What leads, sources, or other evidence does your attorney already have?
11. Are you to obtain any witness statements or affidavits?
12. What are the known basic facts that are relevant to the assignment?
13. What expenditures are you authorized to make to obtain documents and other information?
14. What specific public records are you to search?
15. What relevant points of law should you be familiar with prior to undertaking the investigative assignment?
16. Are you authorized to obtain the assistance of a professional investigator, if necessary?
17. Are you authorized to contact the client to obtain information relevant to your assignment?

Exhibit 7.1

**Checklist for Developing
an Investigative Plan**

- General areas to cover in your investigation.
- Specific witnesses to interview and the location of these witnesses.
- Known leads to explore.
- Sources to use.
- Places to visit to conduct your investigation and the best time to visit these places.
- Materials you will need to conduct the investigation.
- Parts of your investigation you can conduct by telephone in the office.
- Maps or other directions you will need to locate particular people and places.
- Problems you must identify.
- Specific steps to take.
- Your immediate and final goals and priorities.

18. Are you expected to tape record any interviews with witnesses or other persons who have knowledge to matters relevant to your assignment?
19. How does your attorney want the information you obtain documented, e.g., report or memo?
20. Is any of the information that you have been given by your attorney strictly confidential? (It is always best to assume all information is confidential.)
21. What documents or records are you to obtain, e.g., copies of judgments or public records?

After you have been given all the information available and necessary to conduct your investigative assignment, develop a preliminary plan to serve as a blueprint. Exhibit 7.1 presents a checklist that will assist you in developing your plan:

• **Step 2:   Conduct your preliminary investigation from your office.**

In most cases you can conduct most of your preliminary investigation from your office. Your greatest asset will be the telephone. Use the telephone to:

1. Make appointments where possible with witnesses to be interviewed.
2. Conduct a preliminary oral interview with known witnesses to determine in advance whether a potential witness may be helpful to you. (This step will often save you from wasting time by conducting an interview that will not be useful.)
3. Obtain directions to places you plan to visit.
4. Obtain relevant information or facts.
5. Obtain preliminary leads.
6. Determine sources of information.
7. Make preliminary contacts to discover unknown witnesses.
8. Contact the client to obtain necessary information.
9. Order or obtain documents by mail where feasible.

Exhibit 7.2

Checklist of Investigation Matters to Act on Promptly

○ Photographs to take (for example, a person's scarred face in a malpractice action arising from plastic surgery, or the scene of an accident or other relevant occurrence).

○ Witnesses to interview or obtain statements while their recollection of the events is still fresh in their minds.

○ Evidence to preserve before it disappears (for example, documents in a fraud action or a surgical instrument in a medical malpractice action).

○ People to contact before the opposing counsel coaches them.

○ Assessment of property damages to obtain.

○ Documents to locate before they are unavailable or lost (for example, a partnership agreement in a breach of contract action or a memo regarding a fraud action).

○ Specific notations or records you should make (for example, measurements of skid marks resulting from an automobile accident, or the condition of the nursing home where a malpractice action arose.)

○ Leads to pursue immediately.

○ Matters to act upon so that your attorney may advise the client immediately (for example, examining property to assess damage that needs to be repaired immediately or obtaining repair estimates).

○ Information and facts to gather immediately from the client to avoid delays in your investigation (for example, documents relating to an airplane crash, or income tax returns in a divorce or dissolution of marriage matter).

• Step 3: Conduct your investigation in a timely manner.

Many crucial areas of your investigation must be conducted immediately. Some of the matters that you should act on promptly are shown in the checklist in Exhibit 7.2.

• Step 4: Gather and review relevant facts and basic documents carefully.

Most of the basic facts about your investigative assignment will probably be given to you by your attorney, who will have obtained them from the client. Therefore, it is helpful to establish a rapport with the client so that you may verify or clarify any facts where necessary. Some attorneys prefer to maintain communication with the client exclusively themselves, but if you can obtain permission to communicate directly with the client, do so.

If you have not personally conducted the initial interview with the client in which basic information was obtained, be sure you understand the information given to you by the interviewer. Do not assume that the facts the interviewer gives you are correct. Verify those facts with the client or other reliable sources. Review the interviewer's report or notes meticulously to identify inconsistencies or unclear areas or to determine what new facts may exist. Update the interviewer's report by contacting the client for further information.

Your next step is to gather all relevant documents necessary for conducting your investigation. The checklist in Exhibit 7.3 includes some of the basic documents and information regarding the matter that you should obtain, if available.

Exhibit 7.3
•
Checklist of
Basic Documents and
Information to Obtain

- All relevant client files.
- Client authorizations for release of information, medical or hospital records, or other related documents.
- Depositions, interrogatories, or other relevant documents.
- Previous witnesses' statements or investigative reports.
- Reports, memos, or notes of any client interviews.
- Photographs, pictures, or diagrams that have been made.
- Public records previously obtained.
- Any relevant attorney's notes.
- Names, addresses, and telephone numbers of witnesses, relatives, neighbors, or other persons having knowledge of the matter.
- Police, accident, or investigative reports.
- Tape recordings previously taken.
- Related newspaper or magazine articles.

After you have gathered all of the relevant facts and basic documents that are available, review them carefully. This review will help you determine how to conduct your investigation. Leads and sources may be revealed. Often related depositions or answers to interrogatories will help you. Your attorney may want you to verify and cross-check some of the facts uncovered in your investigation. Becoming familiar with the contents of these documents will often enable you to recognize conflicts that will need clarification in future depositions or interrogatories.

• Step 5:   Identify basic principles of law.

Research the relevant basic principles of law to conduct your investigative assignment. For example, if the matter is a personal injury action, you may need to be familiar with the last clear chance doctrine (see Chapter 3). If the matter is a criminal action involving the possession of narcotics, you should have a basic understanding of search and seizure laws. If you have difficulty in finding the basic principles of law, refer to encyclopedic works. If you still have questions, ask your attorney.

In addition, you should have some basic understanding of the rules of evidence and how to preserve evidence properly (discussed more thoroughly later in this chapter). Become familiar with civil procedure, the various discovery documents, and their use in litigation proceedings (see Chapter 8).

Often you will need to understand the strategy and trial techniques that your attorney plans to use at trial. Perhaps you can attend strategy meetings conducted by the trial attorney to help show you how to structure your investigative assignment.

As the investigation progresses, consult with your attorney to ensure that you are proceeding correctly. Make sure that you are not going off on a tangent and wasting valuable time. It is always better to ask questions as they arise. Get further direction when you need it. Your attorney would prefer that you check first rather than expend valuable time pursuing useless leads or unreliable sources, so check back with your attorney frequently.

• Step 6: Visit the scene of the accident/incident immediately.

In a negligence action, you should visit the scene of the accident immediately, before you begin any of the other portions of your investigation. If possible and where necessary, conduct an on-the-scene investigation. For example, in the case of a chemical explosion at an industrial plant, you can gather some of your most valuable information on the scene. Take enough people with you to assist you in interviewing all the witnesses while they are still available. Use a tape recorder to save time in interviewing witnesses and to preserve their testimony while it is still clear in their minds. Of course, ask the witness's permission to use the recorder.

It is important to gather statements from everyone, including those persons who state that they have no knowledge of the accident. You may want to use their statement to that effect later for impeachment purposes. In some states, Georgia, for instance, inconsistent statements can be used as substantive evidence. Some of the key persons may be those who appear to be in charge and who were closest to the scene of the accident. When you return to the office, make notes while your observations are still clear in your mind. At the same time, make notations of items of information to be followed up or clarified later.

Even when it is unnecessary for you to conduct an on-the-scene investigation, it still is imperative that you visit the scene promptly. Often you will discover skid marks, obstructions to vision that have not been removed, or other pertinent evidence that may disappear later. In a product liability action, evidence must be collected immediately.

If it is feasible and safe, you may want to visit the scene at approximately the same time or under the same conditions that the accident occurred, especially if photographs are being taken to account for sunlight, shadows, road conditions, and other factors.

Take the following materials with you: measuring tape, compass, sketch pad, chalk, and camera. Make diagrams of the area and record all possible relevant measurements and directions. Make notations of bumps, holes, or indentations in the roadway or street. Note traffic signs and light signals. Indicate hills and slight or gradual elevations in the street. Take color photographs where they might be helpful, using colored chalk to highlight directions, pavements, or gouge marks.

In the case of an accident in a bakery, for example, you would diagram the related area, take measurements where necessary, note the condition of the lighting, heating and air conditioning systems; get samples of any materials involved, such as glass. You would talk to the employees, asking specific questions about what happened prior to, during, and after the accident, what the injured was wearing at the time of the accident, and so on. You would also take pictures from all angles of the related work area.

On the other hand, if you are visiting the hospital where an alleged malpractice incident took place, you will have different considerations to keep in mind to conduct your investigation. For example, if a baby was injured in delivery by forceps, you have an extensive investigation to conduct. But you may not be allowed to conduct it by the hospital. In any event, you must be careful to check back with your attorney so that you do not make any ethical errors that may damage the outcome of the case. Many documents and items, for example, will have to be requested through the legal process.

• Step 7:   Make contacts and establish credibility in the community.

Some of your initial contacts may not be persons from whom you will wish to obtain statements, but these persons may lead you to known witnesses. Make contacts and develop sources of information that will aid you not only in this investigation, but also in future investigations. The only way to do this is by getting out in the field. By befriending a neighbor, a gas station attendant, or perhaps a real estate salesperson, you may be able to locate persons whom you might not otherwise find. Approach people with a friendly but casual attitude. People are more likely to offer information if they understand your purpose. Sometimes by relating some basic facts to them, you will spark their interest or refresh their memory. You will more likely earn their cooperation by being forthright, honest, and sincere. Be sure to thank them for their assistance.

After you have gathered, organized, and segregated the relevant facts and materials that you have obtained from the client, conduct a thorough review of this information. Often you will uncover numerous leads or possible sources of information or evidence.

Evidence is defined as proof that establishes the point in question. There are two types of evidence: physical and testimonial. Of course, not all evidence is admissible. Your attorney will determine whether the evidence you get can be used at trial. This is another reason for obtaining guidance from your attorney to make sure that you are proceeding in the right direction. (Evidence is discussed further under "Rules of Evidence" later in this chapter.)

You must be willing to work hard, sometimes following many futile leads until you find a productive one. Trial and error coupled with common sense will be your best approach. Through experience in the field, you will develop your own techniques. Often you will not know what you are looking for, so the best approach is to "leave no stone unturned." Of course, your time schedule may often prevent you from being as thorough as you would like. In that case, determine what are your best leads and pursue them first.

Your sources of information are sometimes limited only by your ingenuity and imagination (see discussion later in this chapter). Again, you should develop your own personal sources of information and network of contacts. This will take some time at first, but will save you considerable time and trouble in the future.

• Step 8:   Interview all witnesses and obtain statements.

One of the most important aspects of your investigative assignment is the interviewing of nonparty witnesses. Not only should you interview friendly witnesses, but you should interview both neutral and hostile witnesses. You may find that what you thought was a hostile witness becomes a favorable witness during the interviewing. Do not shy away from interviewing hostile witnesses. Remember, too, that hostility may be a basis for impeachment.

In addition, you may be able to discover other witnesses or gather other useful information through interviews of any type of witness. Obtain a statement from every pertinent witness even if he or she has no direct knowledge of the matter under investigation. The statement may be a basis for impeachment later. (This subject will be discussed more thoroughly later on.)

One of the keys to conducting a thorough investigation is to develop an inquisitive attitude. Never make any assumptions. They will lead you down the wrong path. Check and double-check your information. Never become so excited about the information you discover that you neglect to verify it through reliable sources. For example, often the views of some witnesses are prejudiced. Therefore, one of the key principles to remember is to trust no one but yourself. Organize your information and put your theories to the test. Again, openness and receptivity to new information are an absolute necessity.

You should avoid coloring the information you receive with your own prejudices or feelings. Do not fill in the gaps in your information with assumptions. Be precise and accurate in your perception of the facts and reality.

Be inquisitive about things that may seem to be very basic. For example, a paralegal was given an investigative assignment in a negligence case wherein his office represented the plaintiff, who was injured in an automobile accident. He was to locate a number of key X-ray films. The radiology department of a major hospital had informed the opposing counsel that it had sent the X-ray films to his supervising attorney's office. However, they were never received. Defendant's counsel planned to attack the credibility of the plaintiff's case by presenting evidence that the plaintiff's attorney had received the X-ray films, and therefore the defendant scheduled the deposition of the acting supervisor of the radiology department.

The paralegal was instructed by the supervising attorney to find out exactly what had happened to those X-rays prior to the scheduled deposition. He interviewed the acting supervisor, questioning the details of their X-ray filing procedures, and their transmittal and recording procedures. By asking what appeared to be numerous basic questions about their routine procedures, he discovered the presence of a transmittal log that the radiology department personnel had used to record the X-ray films that they sent out.

Also, the paralegal discovered that there was a temporary changeover in personnel when the regular supervisor was out on sick leave during the time the X-ray films were allegedly transmitted to his supervising attorney's office. When he examined the log, he discovered that there were no X-ray films recorded as having been sent to his attorney's office. Consequently, the acting supervisor then admitted that although he had informed the opposing counsel's office that the X-ray films had been sent to the plaintiff's attorney's office, he now realized that he had been mistaken.

When the defendant's counsel arrived to take the acting supervisor's deposition the next week, he told him he had been mistaken in informing him that he had sent the X-ray films to the plaintiff's attorney. As a result of this admission the defendant's counsel informed the plaintiff's attorney that he was canceling the deposition and that he would not raise the issue at trial. It was a job well done, but it could not have been accomplished without the open and inquisitive attitude of the investigating paralegal.

• **Step 9: Obtain and preserve evidence properly.**

When you obtain physical custody of evidence, handle the evidence properly to preserve it for trial. You have to use the correct procedures to guard its admis-

Exhibit 7.4

Checklist of Investigative Information Obtained Daily

- Date, place, and relevant circumstances of your investigation.
- Persons you contacted.
- Witnesses you interviewed, and where you conducted the interviews.
- Witness statements you obtained.
- Information and documents you obtained.
- General background of the witness.
- Your appraisal of the witness.
- Evidence you obtained, how you obtained it, and its relative value.
- New leads or sources of information you discovered.
- Ideas you had that you may want to investigate in the future.
- Pertinent observations you made.
- Other relevant information.

sibility. In other words, the circumstances under which the evidence is obtained may be relevant to its admissibility at trial. Telephone your attorney immediately to find out how to handle the evidence properly. In fact, it might be better to refrain from taking physical possession of any evidence prior to contacting your attorney.

• Step 10: Document all information.

As your investigation progresses, it is important that you carefully document your progress and the information you receive. Exhibit 7.4 presents a checklist of notations to make at the end of each day of your investigation.

Documenting the progress of your investigation will jog your memory in recalling relevant information and will often prevent you from duplicating your efforts.

• Step 11: Revise your plan if necessary.

After your investigation has significantly progressed, review your preliminary plan to determine whether you need to revise it. Often you will find that your investigation, especially if it is a complicated one, will take an entirely new direction. If this is the case, revise your skeletal plan accordingly. Do not spend much time doing this revision, because your basic motive is to complete your investigation quickly. However, a revised plan will enable you to conduct a more efficient investigation.

• Step 12: Seek help from professional experts when necessary.

Often you will find it impossible to conduct the entire investigation yourself due to lack of time or ability. Recognize your limitations and seek additional assistance when necessary. A professional investigator has numerous advantages over a paralegal:

1. The investigator has more reliable sources of information built up with experience.

2. The investigator has the opportunity to conduct the investigation at irregular hours.

3. The investigator is more qualified to conduct criminal investigations that often involve being exposed to dangerous situations.

4. The investigator has more specialized education and training in investigative techniques.

You may decide to suggest to your attorney that a professional investigator be hired. However, you can still offer assistance, not only in briefing the investigator on the background of the matter, but also in coordinating the investigation. In many instances, there may still be other portions of the investigation that you will have to do yourself. You can monitor the investigation to save valuable time by working closely with the investigator.

Often you may need to seek assistance from professional experts such as engineers, accountants, chemists, or economists. Contact the administrative personnel in colleges and universities, who may be able to refer you to available experts on their staff. Also, you may get names of experts from other attorneys who handle similar cases. You should solicit their opinions of the expert's qualifications and expertise. In addition, Lawyers Cooperative Publishing Company has published a widely used reference book, *Lawyer's Desk Reference*,[1] which contains a list of experts in designated areas. (See also Chapter 9 for sources of medical experts.) An on-line database of experts is also available if you have access to a computer and modem. Contact AimsPlus, Inc., Richardson, Texas or Teletrieves Systems, Inc., Mt. Vernon, Washington.

• Step 13: Report your progress.

Periodically, let your attorney know the progress of your investigation. One of the main reasons for doing this is that it is imperative that you receive proper legal guidance and direction. Your attorney has the total perspective of the case and the particular strategy for litigating the case. Also, your attorney knows and is aware of the practical aspects of the case and the client's position. By reporting your progress periodically to your attorney, you can get the guidance you need to accomplish your investigative assignment.

Throughout your investigation, keep alert for the necessity for further discovery proceedings. For example, if after interviewing a witness, you believe the witness's deposition would be beneficial to the case, suggest this. Likewise, when reviewing relevant documents, if you think it would be supportive of your client's position to produce these documents through discovery, say so.

• Rules of Evidence

Become familiar with the rules of evidence. They will act as a guidepost in your investigation and also in your preparation during the discovery process. Gathering evidence can be one of your most interesting paralegal tasks.

---

[1]Harry M. Philo, Dean A. Robb, and Richard M. Goodman (Englewood Cliffs, N.J.: Prentice Hall, Inc., 1989), 9th ed.

144   Chapter 7

What Is Evidence?

Everything that you may find relating to the lawsuit is not necessarily evidence. The law determines what information can be presented as evidence at trial. In the federal court system, the *Federal Rules of Evidence* are used. Many states have adopted the *Federal Rules of Evidence* or designed their rules in a similar fashion. Check with the applicable court rules of the court of jurisdiction.

The primary purpose of evidence is to be used in the trial of a lawsuit to determine whether the plaintiff has presented the necessary proof to win his case. Without rules of evidence, untrue information could be entered to support a case.

Direct versus Circumstantial Evidence

Circumstantial evidence allows the inference that a certain matter has occurred or exists. On the other hand, *direct evidence* results from a direct observation and proves the contention that a certain matter has occurred or exists.

Evidence Admissible in Court

To be admissible in court, evidence must first be *relevant*. According to Section 401 of the *Federal Rules of Evidence,* for evidence to be relevant, it must (1) have material consequence to the determination of the action, and (2) be inclined to prove or rebut a significant fact.

Relevant evidence is not the primary key to whether evidence is admissible, however. It also must have *probative value;* that is, the anticipated value of what it professes to prove must outweigh any potential harm that may result from its admission.

Many types of *privileged communications* exist, such as attorney-client, physician-patient, husband-wife, priest-penitent, and social worker-client. The court highly respects these privileged communications and limits their relevancy. Seldom are these privileges overcome by other rules of evidence. As a paralegal, you should have a good understanding of these privileges. Also, become familiar with your local rules on this subject.

Testimony of Witnesses

Here is a good overview of the rules affecting the testimony of a witness:

1. The testimony of witnesses must be based on first-hand knowledge.[2]
2. Laypersons are allowed to give opinions on speed, weight, height, or distance or repeated observations to identify a specific signature or voice, or opinions as to the sanity of a person they know.
3. Highly specialized, educated experts are permitted to give opinions on matters at issue that relate to their field.[3]
4. An opinion on the character and conduct of a witness is admissible.[4]

---

[2]*Federal Rules of Evidence,* §602.
[3]Ibid., §702.
[4]Ibid., §607, 610.

5. Prior statements of a witness must be used to attack the witness's credibility.

6. Any witness may be examined for the ability to observe, record, recollect, or narrate. Numerous factors may influence the witness's abilities such as mental capacity, intelligence, distractions, distance from the event observed, lighting conditions, weather conditions, influence of drugs or alcohol, and others.

7. *Hearsay* is a repetition of a statement made by another and given by the witness while testifying at trial or hearing offered in evidence to prove the matter stated. Because hearsay is generally inadmissible, you should try to find the original source for needed evidence.

There are, however, some important exceptions to the hearsay rule. These are found in the *Federal Rules of Evidence* beginning with Rule 7801(d). A brief explanation follows:

Statements That Are Not Hearsay

A statement is not hearsay if it is a prior statement by the witness. If a statement made by the witness at the trial or hearing contains any of the following components, it is subject to cross-examination:

- The statement is inconsistent with the witness's testimony and was given under oath subject to the penalty of perjury at a trial, hearing, or other proceeding, or in a deposition.

- The statement is consistent with the witness's testimony and is offered to rebut an express or implied charge against the witness of recent fabrication or improper influence or motive.

- The statement is one of identification of a person made after perceiving the person.

A statement is also not hearsay if it is an admission by the party-opponent. An opponent may make an admission against a person who previously makes a statement against himself. For example, "Joe admitted in court today that he intended to breach his contract with Bella Corporation, and he said the same thing to me on January 4, 1991."

Statements Excluded from the Hearsay Rules

The following are excluded from the hearsay rule, even though the witness is available as a witness:

1. *Present sense impression.* A statement describing or explaining an event or condition made while the witness was perceiving the event or condition, or immediately thereafter. For example, "Jane said, 'Dr. Rademaker looked drunk to me before he went into the operating room.'"

2. *Excited utterance.* A statement relating to a startling event or condition made while the witness was under the stress of excitement caused by the event or condition. For example, "My wife said, 'Watch out! There is a child on a bicycle.'"

3. *Then-existing mental, emotional, physical condition.* A statement of the witness's then existing state of mind, emotion, sensation, or physical condition, such as intent, plan, motive, design, mental feeling, pain, and bodily health, but

not including a statement of memory or belief to prove the fact remembered or believed unless it relates to the execution, revocation, identification, or terms of witness's will. For example, "Ms. Pittman said, " 'I had this knee problem before I slipped and fell in that grocery store.' "

4. *Statements for purposes of medical diagnosis or treatment.* Statements describing medical history, or past or present symptoms, pain, or sensations, or the inception or general character of the cause of a problem insofar it is reasonably pertinent to diagnosis or treatment. For example, "Kim Turner told me (doctor), 'My chest has hurt me for months.' "

5. *Recorded recollection.* A statement recorded concerning a matter about which a witness once had knowledge, but which he is now unable to recollect. If admitted, the memorandum or record may be read into evidence, but it may not itself be received as an exhibit unless offered by an adverse party. For example, if you take a statement from a potential witness who later cannot remember what she said, the recorded statement can be read into evidence.

6. *Records of regularly conducted activity.* Records kept in the course of a regularly conducted business activity are admissible. For example, a daily ledger of a convenience store may be admitted into evidence.

7. *Absence of entry in records kept in accordance with the provisions of paragraph (6).* Evidence that a matter is not included in the records kept in the regular course of business in an attempt to show that this proves the nonoccurrence or nonexistence of the matter. For example, if daily ledgers were not kept by a convenience store and should have been, evidence showing the nonexistence of such records is admissible.

8. *Public records and reports.* Records and reports of public offices or agencies indicating related activities of the office or agency, except for criminal matters, or in civil actions and proceedings and against the government in criminal cases, are admissible.

9. *Other records.* Records or data compilations, in any form, of births, baptismal, fetal deaths, deaths, marriages, religious organizations, family genealogical or related records, real estate property documents, statements from ancient documents, market reports, commercial publications, and published treatises.

10. *Reputation concerning character, personal or family history, boundaries or general history.* Statements concerning family history, boundaries, or a person's character are admissible. Statements as to proof of matters of personal family or general history, or boundaries, essential to the judgment are admissible if the same would be provable by evidence of reputation.

11. *Absence of public record or entry.* Evidence that a matter is not included in the public records is admissible.

12. *Judgment of previous conviction.* Court judgments are admissible if offered to prove any fact essential to sustain the judgment.

13. *Unavailable witness.* If a witness is unavailable, either deceased or unavailable through reasonable efforts, refuses to testify or is protected from testifying, or is unable to remember, some hearsay evidence is admissible.

Researching Evidentiary Issues

Under the direction of your attorney, you may need to research a particular issue concerning evidentiary matters. Although you may want to consult your law librarian, the following is a partial list of the books on evidence:

Federal Rules of Evidence

McCormick on Evidence

Graham's Federal Rules of Evidence

Wigmore on Evidence

• Finding Leads and Sources

Finding leads and sources of information is really a task of organization and know-how. You need to learn what types of information you can get from various agencies or organizations. Build a database or record of these various agencies. Also note particular information that you might need in future cases. Most sources can be divided into three categories: (1) accessible leads; (2) more difficult leads; and (3) city, state, and federal government agencies and organizations.

Accessible Leads

Accessible leads include the client, the neighborhood, medical records, the telephone book, directories, and newspapers.

Client

The client is obviously the starting point for most basic information and relevant documents. Reviewing the client's files and documents will often reveal numerous leads and sources of information, and possible evidence. If at any time during your investigation you need further clarification, talk directly to the client. Often he can fill in the gaps of information that he may have forgotten to include in his interview, or that he felt were not important.

Neighborhood

A neighborhood canvas can be conducted for various investigative purposes. For example, in a negligence action, visit the neighborhood near the scene of the accident to uncover such information as:

1. Visiting friends and relatives, salespersons, delivery persons, utility workers, and business customers who may have been in the area at the time of the accident.
2. Business or service facilities, such as laundromats that may have been visited by neighbors at the time of the accident.
3. Public carriers that may have traveled in the vicinity of the accident at that time.

When you are unable to determine the names of witnesses who may have been in the area, try to obtain descriptions of them. Visit the neighborhood at the same time of day that the accident occurred so that you are more likely to be able to interview persons who regularly travel through the area at that particular time.

If you want to obtain general information about either a witness, plaintiff, defendant, or a missing person, canvas the neighborhood to obtain the following information:

1. Age and physical description.
2. Personal habits, hobbies, or pastimes.
3. Occupation, employer, or place of business.
4. General reputation.
5. Background, including information relating to criminal activities.
6. Institutions where the subject conducts her financial business.
7. Friends and relatives that usually visit her home.
8. Political activities.
9. Membership in any clubs or organizations.
10. Church or school attended by the members of her family.
11. General descriptions and information about her family.
12. A description of her automobile.
13. Any previous conversations that she may have had with neighbors that revealed relevant information or potential leads.

Medical Records and Bills

The medical records and medical bills of anyone other than your client usually must be obtained through discovery or subpoena. The decision of *Canfield v. Sandock* somewhat limits the defense attorney's discovery. This decision lets the burden of discovery fall upon the attorney who is requesting records through a request for production and subpoena *duces tecum.* Attorneys who attempt to subpoena the plaintiff's entire medical history from a medical provider must show how it relates to the present litigation. For example, you may have to limit your request for production to just the records that the medical provider maintains regarding the plaintiff's past and present alleged condition.

Often the plaintiff's attorney may be agreeable to having the plaintiff sign a medical authorization, which is a release to the medical provider for all of his records. This means less paperwork and the medical provider usually feels more at ease in providing the records when there is an authorization.

Telephone Book

Because the telephone book is one of the most accessible books of information, you may frequently overlook its value. For instance, by calling a currently listed number, you can sometimes obtain a forwarding number. In some instances, the telephone information operator will give you addresses, although most telephone companies will no longer give out this information. However, some will release it to an out-of-state caller.

Remember that you may review telephone books from prior years by visiting your local telephone company or library. Most local telephone companies retain old telephone books on file for several years. By searching these outdated books, you may often locate a previously listed telephone number that is now is unlisted and an accompanying address. An old address may be a starting point from which to trace a current address through the post office.

City and Suburban Directories

Most cities (and many suburbs) have *directories* that are usually found in the local public library. These directories list names, telephone numbers, and addresses of residents. They frequently list occupations, places of employment, and spouses' names as well. Most libraries retain directories from previous years. Some of these directories give reverse information. For example, if you know the street name and number, you can usually find who lives there, keeping in mind that the information outdates itself very quickly because of the transient U.S. population. Many law firm libraries purchase these huge directories.

Newspapers

Most newspaper publishers retain copies of their newspapers for only 30 days, but most local public libraries retain microfilm or microfiche copies of prior editions of local newspapers dating back years. By reviewing newspaper articles regarding an automobile accident, for example, you may find names of reporters who were at the scene and took pertinent notes that were not included in their news articles, as well as names of other potential witnesses. Be sure to check both city and local neighborhood newspapers.

More Difficult Leads

Some more difficult leads may be well worth the effort of tracking. Examples follow:

Employment Records

Employment records are difficult to gather without discovery procedures. However, sometimes city and suburban directories list a person's employer. You can always go back several years to track the employment record.

Television Videotapes

With the arrival of videotapes, many television stations have changed their policies about retaining their news stories. Call them to find out what their policy is and how long they retain their news stories so that you can obtain a copy of a videotape if permitted and should you need it. With mobile news units and on-the-scene news telecasts, television personnel are often among the first to reach the accident scene. If you are unable to visit the television station before the videotape is disposed of, perhaps you will be able to obtain an interview with the TV personnel who visited the scene and who made personal observations. Realize, of course, that the media is often reluctant to release information.

Emergency Vehicles at the Scene

Emergency vehicles include not only ambulance drivers and their radio personnel but also fire department personnel, paramedic squads, towing truck operators, Special Weapons and Tactics squads (SWAT), and investigating police department officers. Always ask personnel if written records are available. Interview all investigating police officers who were at the scene, even though you may have their written reports. Often in discussing the particular circumstances and events regarding the accident, they recall personal observations not included in their written report. (See "Questions to Ask the Investigating Police Officer" later in this chapter.) Also interview other emergency room personnel, attending nurses, and nurses' aides who may have had conversations with the patient or may have overheard the patient talking with other persons.

Free-Lance Photographers
Free-lance photographers frequently monitor the local police radio circuit and are sometimes the first on the scene of an accident in an attempt to solicit business. They can often be primary witnesses and may supply photographs.

Employers
Although most employers are reluctant to release any information regarding their employees to outside persons, attempt to talk to them. Some employers might give you information or possible leads. Also, if you can interview any of the person's fellow employees, you may be able to obtain information from them that they learned through previous conversations they have had with the person. They may not realize the significance of the information they have.

Relatives
Although most relatives are reluctant to disclose information, you sometimes find a hostile relative who will be cooperative. At least make an attempt to pursue these sources, even though they are more remote possibilities.

Adversary
Although you must never rule out the possibility of obtaining information from the opposition, either by informal request or by discovery, unless specifically directed by your attorney, the opposing counsel should never be contacted. Check with other attorneys who have been previously involved in the case to obtain information.

Newspaper Advertisement
Do not eliminate the possibility of locating a plaintiff, defendant, a potential unidentified witness, or missing person through a newspaper advertisement. Although this is a remote possibility, it is worth a try. Place the ad in the personal or miscellaneous column of the local newspaper, soliciting a request for identification of the party, potential witnesses, or other related information. A nominal reward will probably increase the likelihood of receiving a response.

Credit Bureau
Credit bureaus or private agencies normally charge a fee for information. Often they give information to selected companies or subscribers. They retain invaluable sources of information, including an individual's financial background, present and previous addresses, employers, and any litigation in which he may be or has been involved, and other miscellaneous information. Verify and double-check any information you receive from this particular agency.

City, State, and Federal Government Organizations
Some public organizations of the city, state, or nation can provide valuable information.

   County Courthouse.   There are numerous records located in the county courthouse that vary from state to state but usually include:

   1. Trade name registrations.
   2. Partnerships and limited partnerships records.

3. Military records.
4. Civil lawsuits indexed by both plaintiff and defendant.
5. Deeds and property books.
6. Mechanic's liens.
7. UCC or financing statements.
8. General execution or judgment docket.
9. Marriage records.
10. Probate records.
11. Criminal records.

(See "Public Record Searches" later in this chapter.)

Driver's License Information. In most states general information regarding driver's licenses is available. Usually information concerning a person's driving record is not available unless an attorney requests the information due to pending litigation. Check with the Department of Motor Vehicles, the Department of Transportation, or related agency in your state to find out how to obtain this information.

County and Local Agencies. County and local agencies vary from county to county and from city to city. Some cities have organized departments that may be new or even experimental in nature. A visit to the city hall would be beneficial in determining what services are available to you. (See Appendix L for a listing of county and local agencies found in most parts of the United States.)

Public Libraries. A trip to the local public library and a consultation with the reference librarian will often reveal sources of important information. A handy guide to sources of business information is *Business Information Sources*.[5] The business reference section of the library contains most of these publications.

State Agencies. Because the names of these departments will vary from state to state, the names listed are merely for purposes of identification (see Appendix K). Some states have laws similar to the U.S. Freedom of Information Act[6] that is applicable to state government agencies. Check your state's statutes to determine if similar laws are applicable to the release of public information.

Federal Agencies. Generally speaking, federal agencies will provide you only with public information pursuant to the U.S. Freedom of Information Act. However, in rare circumstances, they may provide you with other information. For example, such agencies as the Social Security Office, the Internal Revenue Service, and the Federal Bureau of Investigation may cooperate with you if you can prove to them you have a legitimate reason for locating a person, as in the case of a missing heir. Another reason why a federal agency might cooperate with you would be if a mutual interest exists—that is, if you and the agency can exchange information.

This is not to suggest that an agency will always assist you under such circumstances, but there is a possibility that it will. The Privacy Act of 1974[7]

---

[5]Lorna Daniels, *Business Information Sources* (Berkeley: University of California Press, 1976).
[6]*U.S. Code*, Title 5, §552.
[7]*U.S. Code*, Title 5, §552a.

governing the release of information to individuals is of primary concern to these agencies. The U.S. Freedom of Information Act of 1966 is a key to much of the information held by the federal agencies. Most of these agencies have a Freedom of Information Office. They usually have a nominal charge for searching and copying documents.

A list and brief description of some of the major federal agencies that might offer you information and assistance relating to general litigation matters can be found in Appendix J. This list is not all-inclusive. However, you may obtain, free-of-charge, a *Directory of Federal Consumer Offices* published by the Office Consumer Affairs from the Consumer Information Center, Pueblo, Colorado 81009, which lists several other federal agencies that might be helpful. Another book that is available from your local bookstore is *Information U.S.A.*[8]

Federal/State Courthouses.   The federal courthouse maintains a civil and criminal index in addition to a bankruptcy index. The state courts maintain alphabetical cross-indexes that allow you to look up the name of plaintiff or defendant. A quick check of the plaintiff and defendant indexes will reference the file numbers. You may request any file on record to review. A search of a prior bankruptcy of an individual, of course, may reveal numerous leads. Files that are several years old are usually stored, but may be available by special request.

• Step-by-Step Procedure for Investigating a Negligence Action

Although the following steps are not all-inclusive, they will serve as a guideline for conducting your investigation of a negligence matter. Be open to pursue any leads that you get along the way and flexible enough to alter your plan as you see fit.

- **Step 1:**   Obtain copies of all client documents, tax returns, and pleadings regarding the action, including notes from all interviews.

- **Step 2:**   Obtain signed authorizations for release of medical records, including X-ray films and wage information from the client (send for this information immediately).

- **Step 3:**   Obtain a copy of police report(s).

- **Step 4:**   Interview police investigating officer(s).

- **Step 5:**   Obtain a copy of reported testimony of traffic court hearing.

- **Step 6:**   Visit the scene of the accident promptly. Measure and diagram related area and resultant skid marks, if any. Take professional colored photographs of the accident scene, automobiles, property damage, and visible injuries of the client.

- **Step 7:**   Obtain traffic time-cycle or traffic density report, if relevant.

---

[8]Matthew Lesko, *Information U.S.A.* (New York: Viking Penguin Books, 1986).

- **Step 8:** Obtain copy of death certificate, where applicable.

- **Step 9:** Obtain driver's license record and automobile registration on defendant's automobile.

- **Step 10:** Obtain driving record of plaintiff.

- **Step 11:** Obtain estimates of property damage.

- **Step 12:** Locate and preserve all available evidence.

- **Step 13:** Interview all witnesses and obtain statements, including negative statements.

- **Step 14:** Canvass neighborhood and surrounding businesses where accident occurred.

- **Step 15:** Retain copies of local newspapers that reported the accident.

- **Step 16:** Watch local news stations for television reports of accident. If the TV station reports the accident, contact the television station immediately to obtain copy of videotape.

- **Step 17:** Pre-interview doctors, radiologists, and other assisting medical personnel.

- **Step 18:** Obtain certified copy of weather report from the National Weather Service.

- **Step 19:** Order survey by licensed surveyor or engineer's drawing of accident.

- **Step 20:** Obtain aerial photographs and topographical maps, if necessary.

• Interviewing Witnesses

Interviewing witnesses prior to trial has several advantages. The most beneficial is that if you are fortunate enough to be able to interview a witness before the opposing counsel coaches him, you may elicit valuable information that you might not otherwise be able to obtain. Also, you may sometimes obtain information that will enable you to better prepare for trial. Use the checklist in Exhibit 7.5 to help you interview witnesses in a negligence action and make sure that you cover everything. You may also use this checklist as a guide for developing checklists for other types of matters.

Use the following list of suggested techniques as a guide to developing your individual procedures.

1. *Be the first to interview the witness.* As soon as you discover an important potential witness, interview her as quickly as possible. There are numerous reasons for doing this. The most obvious is that you can interview her prior to

Exhibit 7.5

Summary Checklist for Interviewing Witnesses in a Negligence Action

- Date of interview.
- Full name, address, county, and telephone number.
- Occupation, employer, and business address, county, and telephone number.
- Age and sex of witness.
- Other known witnesses observed at accident scene.
- Service or business vehicles observed at accident scene.
- Date, time, and location, including county and city of occurrence.
- Weather condition at time of occurrence.
- Location of parties at accident scene.
- Location of other witnesses at accident scene.
- Ability of witness to observe.
- First attraction by witness to occurrence.
- Damages to personal or real property of parties.
- Time of arrival of emergency vehicles.
- Personal injuries to parties.
- Comments, quotations, or statements by parties.
- Comments, quotations, or statements by other witnesses.
- Physical condition of accident scene (e.g., holes in road or obstructions).
- Physical impairments of witnesses and participants, such as intoxication or vision or hearing deficits.
- Ability to identify physical evidence.
- Ability to identify parties.
- Ability to identify photographs.
- Ability to identify vehicles.
- Distance and speed of vehicles observed by witness.
- Location of vehicles prior to accident.
- Location of vehicles subsequent to accident.
- Any personal, financial, or other business interests in case.
- Information regarding character of parties or witnesses or other facts to impeach.
- Any statement given to adverse party—oral ( ), negative ( ), written ( ), recorded ( ).
- Availability to testify in court trial.

her being coached by opposing counsel. Another obvious advantage is that her recollection of events and circumstances usually will be clearer, and you can often obtain relevant information before it is forgotten. Be sure to obtain a statement from her even if she claims to have no knowledge of the matter. This will make it more difficult for her to change her story at a later time and to become a witness for the opposition.

2. *Contact the potential witness in advance.* Often by contacting the potential witness in advance, you can accomplish two things: (1) After informally talking with the potential witness, you may determine that he would not be a useful witness; and (2) should you decide that he would be a potentially valuable witness, you may be able to set the stage for a friendlier interview and to prepare more properly for the interview. However, if you suspect that the potential key

witness might be hostile and might try to avoid an interview, then it will be better not to forewarn him. Don't give him an opportunity to talk to anyone else before the interview, or before he attempts to avoid the interview.

After you have affirmed that the witness's testimony could be very important, it is important to meet the potential witness in person. This personal assessment will allow you to assess what kind of impression he will make on a jury if the litigation extends that far.

3. *Interview the witness in a conducive atmosphere.* Your interview will be more successful if you are able to interview the witness in an atmosphere where she feels at ease and has no distractions. You may find a witness more relaxed if you interview her at her own home. However, in some instances, it will be more advantageous to interview the witness at her place of work. This, of course, will depend on several things, such as whether the potential witness has valuable information at her place of work that would not be available at her home, or whether you suspect that she would prefer being interviewed at work.

In your pre-interview with a potential witness, you can often determine from your conversation where it would be more beneficial to conduct the interview. Unfortunately, this is not always possible. However, if she has a harried job that might distract her during the interview, such as is in a manufacturing plant, then attempt to conduct the interview somewhere else.

It is always better to interview the witness alone, without any other persons present who may influence or affect her conversation with you. Spouses can often be detrimental influences, because they may try to tell the witness what to say or correct the witness, consequently making the witness either embarrassed or uncomfortable.

4. *Be friendly but firm with the witness.* Begin the interview on an informal note so that the witness will be more comfortable and relaxed. Start with friendly small talk. As the interview progresses, be direct, and control the interview so that you can cover all relevant points. However, if the witness is vacillating and evasive in his responses, make him see the purpose of the interview. Tell him that you need his cooperation. You may be able to appeal to his basic human desire to be helpful.

5. *Quiz the witness about additional sources and leads.* Ask the witness if he saw anyone else who might lead you to additional sources. Ask the question in different ways to probe the witness's mind. Get a description of any other witnesses from him.

6. *Listen to his entire conversation to sort out relevant material.* Most people take considerable time to express themselves. Sometimes you may have to listen to a long-winded explanation to pick out one important fact. Be patient. If you interrupt the witness's conversation, or if you are rude, you may lose his cooperation. It is up to you to sort the relevant information in your notes. You can ask questions intermittently to redirect the conversation, or to fill in the gaps of important information.

7. *Be careful not to lead the witness.* Leading the witness (where the answer is contained in the phrasing of the question) can sometimes have the advantage of catching her offguard when she has made a conflicting statement. It is usually more beneficial, though, to ask direct questions of the witness that will elicit her impression of the critical facts. Direct questions elicit more informative answers. For example, consider this leading question: "When the plaintiff was speeding on the freeway, did he slow down when he reached the intersection?" The

established premise is that the car was speeding. Therefore, if the witness answers the question with a positive response, you would assume that (1) the plaintiff's car was speeding, and (2) he slowed down when he reached the intersection. However, the witness might not mean to agree with the first assumption, that the plaintiff was speeding. She might not have heard the whole question, or she might decide that it is not important to correct your assumption that the plaintiff was speeding. Therefore, it would be better to ask the question in two parts: (1) "Was the plaintiff speeding on the freeway?" and (2) "Did the plaintiff slow down at the intersection?"

8. *Evaluate the witness's credibility and demeanor.* During the interview, interject questions and comments that will elicit information relating to the witness's background and any biases he may have. This will enable you to objectively evaluate the witness's believability and demeanor, that is, his likely effect on the stand. This, of course, is important in determining whether the witness's testimony is valuable. If his testimony is inconsistent and unbelievable, he might even endanger your client's position.

At the end of the interview, document your impressions of the witness. This will be one of the determinants for your attorney's decision whether to use this witness at trial, whether to enter his statement into evidence, or whether his testimony would be subject to impeachment by the opposition. Remember that people overreact to extraordinary events, downplay embarrassing or unfavorable facts, and sometimes even invent facts. Be alert for these possibilities if the witness's story seems unlikely.

9. *Encourage the witness to describe the scene by making a diagram or identifying photographs.* Clarify first whether the witness actually saw or heard the accident. Then determine whether any subsequent descriptions are based on what the witness actually saw or heard.

Most people can better explain themselves by drawing a rough diagram or picture. This is an especially good technique to use in questioning a witness about an automobile accident. Her personal pictorial version of the accident can often reveal facts that support your client's position. Ask her to identify pertinent areas in her diagram and note the position of particular persons and vehicles involved before and after the collision.

Show the witness photographs of the accident area, and ask her to identify the position of the vehicles, the point of impact, if observed. Also have her pinpoint the location of the injured parties subsequent to the accident, and any other relevant information she can illustrate or recall from viewing the photographs.

10. *Get a statement from the witness.* This is the ideal time to get a statement from a witness. Prepare the statement and read it back to the witness and get him to sign it. The next section of this chapter will deal with obtaining an effective statement.

• Witness Statements

To obtain witness statements that will be admissible at trial, it is important that you study your local statutes regarding admissibility of *ex parte* statements, which are those prepared for, in behalf of, or on the application of, one party only. Work closely with your attorney to develop standard procedures to ensure the completeness and authenticity of the statements you prepare. Although your attorney may frequently use *ex parte* statements for impeachment purposes, some states give them probative weight.

Be aware that under the attorney work product rule, the other side may request your prepared witness statement. Your attorney may prefer that you draft a memo containing your "mental impressions" instead of preparing a written statement for the witness to sign or recording a statement. Always check with your attorney to see the preferred method.

Some pointers on obtaining an effective witness statement follow:

1. *Obtain the witness's cooperation.* Although many witnesses will talk freely with you during the interview, they are usually reluctant to sign a statement. It may appear to them as a legal instrument with unknown ramifications. By using another word for the term "statement," such as "accident report," you might obtain a more favorable reaction. (It appears that most witnesses expect accident investigators and attorneys to make "accident reports.")

Often you can obtain the witness's cooperation by telling him that his statement will increase the possibility of settling the controversy without it being necessary to go to court.

2. *Use the witness's own words in the statement.* The obvious advantage to using the witness's own words is that it will be more difficult for her to deny having said something at a later time. If the witness would prefer to write out the statement in her own handwriting, then let her do so. This, of course, may be more time-consuming, but it may be worth the extra time to gain the witness's cooperation. Also, be sure to have the witness initial any corrections made in the statement, because this will prove the fact that the witness read the statement before signing. It will also enhance its impeachment value.

3. *Do not include names of other witnesses in the statement.* You can prevent embarrassment to your attorney by not including the names of other witnesses in the statement, since those witnesses might not be available for trial. In addition, including other names can confuse a jury. Make any notations regarding other witnesses in your file, however, so that you can relate the information to your attorney.

4. *Obtain a negative statement when the witness claims no knowledge.* If the witness claims to have no knowledge of the matter, document this in a statement, often called a *negative statement,* to prevent his later changing his testimony to reveal damaging facts. The negative statement may impeach his change of testimony. It may prove more valuable than a comprehensive statement of facts.

5. *Include a disaffirmance of other relevant facts in the statement.* At the conclusion of the interview, ask a closing question such as, "Mr. Reiff, can you think of anything else you know about this case that we have not discussed and incorporated into your statement?" The response to this question is a *disaffirmance,* similar to a negative statement.

6. *Have the witness sign the statement.* Have the witness read the completed statement and initial each page. It is best to have her sign at the bottom of the last page, but, as mentioned, many witnesses prove reluctant to sign the statement. For this reason, on the last page you should write the following: "I have read the foregoing statement consisting of _____pages, and it is true and correct to the best of my knowledge and belief." Then the witness can simply write the word "yes" or "O.K.," which many find less objectionable. If possible, have the statement notarized.

7. *Avoid giving the witness a copy of the statement.* The primary reason for not giving the witness a copy of his statement is that doing so may remove it from the protective shield of the attorney's work product. You also want to prevent the possibility of the witness giving the opposition a copy of the statement. An exception to this rule occurs when the statement is favorable to your case; by giving the witness a copy, you make him less likely to give the opposition a contradictory statement.

Because this is a situation where attorneys may disagree, you should discuss your attorney's policy in advance. If your attorney prefers not to give witnesses copies, and the witness absolutely insists on receiving a copy of his statement, tactfully tell him that you will inform your attorney of his request and get back to him.

8. *Avoid using joint or multiparty statements.* In all cases avoid making joint or multiparty statements, because witnesses tend to influence one another. Such statements are difficult to use for the purpose of impeachment. However, if you are unable to obtain individual statements, then, of course, this type of statement would be better than none at all.

9. *Obtain an affidavit statement for key witnesses.* When you interview certain witnesses, such as the aged or infirm, obtain their statements in affidavit form. However, in some states affidavits under such circumstances may not be admissible. Check your statutes or ask your attorney for the specific requirements of your state.

After you have completed interviewing the witness, determine whether to prepare the statement immediately for the witness's signature, or, if you have a cooperative witness, prepare it later and return it to the witness for her signature. In most instances, especially where you are obtaining a short statement from a witness out of the office, it is preferable to immediately prepare a handwritten statement for her signature. (Refer again to the checklist in Exhibit 7.5.) Of course, if you need a more formally prepared statement for trial later, she will most likely reexecute the statement. However, do not delay obtaining the executed statement, because the witness may change her mind about signing it, or you may be unable to locate her later.

If you believe that requesting personal background information would alienate the witness and possibly make her reluctant to give you any statement, obtain a short declarative statement setting out the particular circumstances surrounding the occurrence that she witnessed. If your attorney later determines that this particular witness would be a valuable witness, he can always take her deposition later, or have you conduct a more thorough second interview at a later date.

Entitle the statement "Statement of (name of witness)" or similar words, date the statement, and indicate the city and state where it was taken. Be sure to number each page. If you prepare the statement by handwriting it, write as legibly as time permits. The checklist in Exhibit 7.6 suggests the main categories of information that should be included in preparing a witness statement in a negligence action. It is best to relate the events chronologically and in detail. Some of the detailed subcategories of information in Exhibit 7.6 may be excluded if they are irrelevant to the particular matter. Also, this checklist is not all-inclusive, so a situation may call for additional information.

Exhibit 7.6

**General Witness
Information**

Identification of Witness

○ Name.

○ Address (prior address).

○ Age.

○ Telephone number.

○ Occupation and current place of employment (prior jobs).

○ Marital status.

○ Names of children or other relatives living in the same county or judicial district as the witness.

○ Relation of witness to any parties involved in the accident.

○ Any financial or personal interest the witness has in the litigation regarding the accident (include negative statements, if applicable).

Information Regarding Taking of Statement

○ Name of the party taking statement.

○ Date of the statement.

○ Time statement was taken.

○ Location where statement was taken.

Events Prior to Accident

○ Location of the witness.

○ Time witness was at the scene of the accident.

○ Names of other witnesses who were near the scene prior to the accident.

○ Location of other witnesses who were near the scene prior to the accident.

○ What the other witnesses were doing prior to the accident.

○ What the other persons who were near the scene were doing prior to the accident.

○ Brief description of the scene prior to the accident, including:

  Location of other vehicles, animals, or other objects.

  Status of traffic light signals, if known.

  Descriptions of any obstructions to vehicles involved.

  Density of traffic.

○ Estimated distances and speeds of involved vehicles.

○ Brief description of weather.

○ Any specific observations regarding the vehicles or parties involved, e.g., reckless driving or intoxication.

○ Number of other persons who were passengers in the involved vehicles.

Occurrence of the Accident

○ Time the accident happened.

○ First attraction of attention of witness to collision.

○ Did the witness actually see the accident or did he or she just hear it and react.

○ Details of inspection made by witness.

○ What specific sounds or noises the witness heard, e.g., horns or explosions.

○ Where the accident actually happened.

○ Where the vehicles were located when the accident happened.

○ Where other persons were located when the accident happened.

Exhibit 7.6

Continued

Events Subsequent to Accident
○ Description of the position of vehicles after the accident (include a rough hand-drawn diagram, if possible).
○ Location of persons who were injured in the accident.
○ Descriptions of visible injuries of persons involved.
○ Time of arrival of emergency vehicles, including police, ambulance, fire, and paramedical vehicles.
○ Events that took place after the arrival of emergency vehicles.
○ Approximate length of time the emergency vehicles were at the scene.
○ Descriptions of conversations of the persons involved and other witnesses.
○ The presence of any reporters, television news people, doctors, attorneys, photographers, and others, including any persons who took statements.

What the Witness Does Not Know
○ What the witness did not see or hear.
○ Any facts or information that the witness is not aware of, such as the time of the accident, other witnesses, other parties, other cars involved, statements made by the parties and unheard by the witness.

Opinion and Conclusion
○ Witness's opinion as to who was at fault.
○ The basis and facts supporting the witness's opinion.

• Questions to Ask the Investigating Police Officer

In addition to the questions in Exhibit 7.6, use the following special questions when interviewing the investigating police officer(s). Again, these questions are not all-inclusive. Ask other relevant questions as the situation and the circumstances dictate.

1. Were there any traffic violations made by either of the parties?
2. If so, were there any traffic citations issued to either party?
3. What are the names of the parties who received traffic citations, the specific citations, and the number of each citation?
4. Were there any witnesses to the accident other than those listed on the official traffic report regarding this accident?
5. If so, please state the name and address, if known, or give a brief description of each.
6. Were there any comments or discussions among the parties or specific quotations made by the individual parties relating to the accident or its cause? If so, what were they?
7. Were any obstructions to the vision of the parties or the vehicles of the parties removed from the scene of the accident? If so, please describe.
8. Did ambulances or other emergency vehicles appear at the scene of the accident? If so, when did the ambulance arrive, and when did it depart? What people did it transport?

9. Were there towing trucks that removed any vehicles from the scene of the accident? If so, what is the name of the towing company, and what specific vehicles were removed from the scene of the accident?

10. Was there any evidence of intoxication by either of the parties involved in the subject accident?

11. Were there any admissions of prior drinking by either of the parties involved in the subject accident?

12. Were there any physical disabilities that are evident to you in either of the drivers involved in the accident?

13. What was the exact position of the vehicles immediately subsequent to the accident that you observed?

14. Were there any skid marks as a result of the accident? If so, what were the lengths and locations of the skid marks?

15. What would you estimate as the approximate speed of both vehicles immediately prior to the accident?

16. Can you give a more specific description of the weather and visibility conditions at the time of the accident other than the information given in your written accident report?

17. What do you estimate was the point on the highway or street where the vehicles collided?

18. What injuries to the parties did you notice?

19. What were your general observations regarding the injuries to the parties involved in the accident?

20. Did you inquire of either party as to his or her condition and/or injuries? (e.g., "How do you feel?") If so, what was the response?

21. Is there any other information not included in your written report regarding the accident that you can add?

22. Have you made any other reports or diagrams or drawings relating to the subject accident other than the official traffic report? If so, where did you submit these reports and/or diagrams or drawings?

23. To your knowledge, did the police department take any photographs?

24. If photographs were taken, what were they taken of?

25. When were these photographs taken?

26. Where are these photographs located now?

• Public Record Searches

Forms 7.1 and 7.2 are for the exclusive purpose of assisting you in conducting your investigation by searching public records. Form 7.1 is a basic form for recording information abstracted from litigation records found at the various courthouses. Use it to record the court, date of filing, style of the case, civil action file number, and the amount of damages sought in the suit. Of course, a similar form may be used for criminal lawsuits.

Form 7.2 is for researching prior litigation of a particular party, either a plaintiff or a defendant in individual courthouses. Often you will have to go

Form 7.1

Litigation Record

Court	Case No.	Date of Filing	Plaintiff*	Defendant*	Amount of of Suit
					$
					$
					$
					$
					$
					$
					$
					$
					$
					$
					$
					$
					$
					$
					$
					$

*Circle Our Client

Paralegal: _____

Date Completed: _____

Form 7.2

Prior Litigation Search

Court_____ County_____

Name of Party	19___		19___		19___		19___	
	Pl	Df	Pl	Df	Pl	Df	Pl	Df

through numerous plaintiff and defendant indexes, usually referred to as *court docket books*, computerized records, or microfiche. Keep track of what docket books you have searched and exactly where you are in your search at any particular time. There are two docket books or computer logs for a particular year in some courthouses. For example, for 1991, you may have to search two docket books for both the plaintiff and defendant because each docket book may contain only a six-month period, making a total of four books to be searched for the entire year.

Use both the two upper and lower portions of the square to insert your checkmarks under both the plaintiff and the defendant columns for the year 1991. Use the upper portion of the square for the six-month period, January through June, and the lower portion of the square for the latter portion of the year, July through December 1991. You probably will not want to use this form if you just have one or two parties to research.

If you have to research a time period of more than three or four years, or if you have more than three or four parties to research, you will find that this form will aid you in recording your progress to ensure that no docket book is left unsearched. This will also serve as a record for the file to show that you have conducted a thorough and accurate investigation.

• Automobile Accidents (Personal Injury)

Information gleaned from pretrial investigation and client interviews is often similar in personal injury actions involving automobiles. Thus, it is easy to systematize your organization of this information. The following forms will assist you in doing this.

On the Accident Fact Sheet (Form 7.3) you can record the general facts surrounding the accident, including the witness's names and addresses. (For recording further information regarding witnesses, see Exhibit 7.6.) Also, this form provides for recording information regarding the names and addresses of the insurance companies for both sides. Note the adjuster's name and telephone numbers, because you and your attorney will refer to them often. Keep this form stapled to the inside of the folder or in another convenient place, because you will use it often.

When you conduct your investigation at the scene of the accident, carefully note the relevant information you obtain on The Accident Scene Investigation Report (Form 7.4). Although much of the information may seem insignificant at the time of your investigation, you will frequently discover that you need this information as the case progresses. Obtain it when you are first investigating the accident to save yourself from having to return for a subsequent investigation.

Again, do not hesitate to ask questions at the accident scene in order to obtain this information. Bring a camera, a tape measure, and some chalk with you.

The information included on the Information on Vehicle form (Form 7.5) will be helpful throughout the litigation process. Although most of this information is general, some of it, such as the defects in the vehicle of a defendant, may not be uncovered until the formal process of discovery. Therefore, fill in as much information as possible in your pretrial investigation, and add the remaining information as it is discovered.

Use the Automobile Property Damage Report on Vehicle form (Form 7.6) to record information that is necessary for settlement negotiations or for preparing for

Accident Fact Sheet

Client Name & Matter: _____ File No.:_____

Responsible Attorney(s):_____ Date:_____

Date of Accident: _____ Time of Accident: _____ _____.m.

Location of Accident:_____

_____

Description of Accident: _____

_____

_____

Investigating Police Officer:_____ Badge No.:_____

Driver Vehicle #1 (name & address): _____

_____ Phone No.: _____

Driver Vehicle #2 (name & address): _____

_____ Phone No.: _____

Injured Party #1 (name & address): _____

_____

Injured Party #2 (name & address): _____

_____

Witness #1 (name & address): _____

_____ Phone No.: _____

Witness #2 (name & address): _____

_____ Phone No.: _____

Dates Statements Given : Driver Vehicle #1 _____ Driver Vehicle #2 _____

Injured Party #1_____ Injured Party #2_____

Witness #1 _____ Witness #2 _____

Client's Insurance Company (name & address):_____

_____ Adjuster: _____ Phone No.:_____

Adverse Party's Insurance Company (name & address): _____

_____ Adjuster: _____ Phone No.:_____

Our Client Is (   ) Plaintiff   (   ) Defendant   (   ) Other in This Matter.

Notes: _____

_____

Investigator:_____

Form 7.4

Accident Scene Investigation Report

Client Name & Matter: _____ File No.: _____

Responsible Attorney(s): _____ Date: _____

Name of Investigator: _____

Date Of Investigation: _____ Time of Day: _____ _____.m.

Date Of Accident: _____ Time of Day: _____ _____.m.

If Scene Investigation is Made at Approximately the Same Time of Day as Accident, Note Mail Delivery and Other Commercial and Delivery Vehicles in the Area as Well as Personal Vehicles Traveling Through the Area: _____

_____

_____

Description of Immediate Surrounding Area: ☐ residential ☐ school ☐ vacant land ☐ commercial ☐ industrial ☐ business ☐ park ☐ shopping center ☐ combination (residential, commercial, and/or industrial) ☐ other: _____

_____

Description of Accident Area (detailed diagram description on attached sheet):

Intersection: ☐ yes ☐ no ☐ major ☐ minor

Type of highway: ☐ interstate ☐ state ☐ main thoroughfare ☐ city street ☐ secondary road ☐ county road ☐ other: _____

Width of street or road: _____ ft. _____ in.

Number of lanes: _____ Width of lines: _____ ft. _____ in.

Describe lines dividing lanes: _____

If divided highway, describe median: _____

Condition of road: _____

Type of road surface : ☐ dirt ☐ concrete ☐ asphalt ☐ gravel ☐ other: _____

Location of hills: _____

Location of curves: _____

Traffic signs and/or signals: ☐ signs ☐ signals ☐ both

Describe position of traffic signs and/or signals: _____

_____

Posted speed limit: _____ m.p.h.

Length of skid marks: _____ ft. _____ in.

Visibility: ☐ good ☐ bad ☐ day ☐ night ☐ dusk ☐ dawn

Weather: ☐ fog ☐ drizzle ☐ light rain ☐ heavy rain ☐ clear ☐ sunny ☐ cloudy ☐ sleet ☐ snow ☐ other: _____

Client Name & Matter: _____ File No.:_____

Responsible Attorney(s):_____ Date:_____

Year: _____ Make: _____ Model: _____ Color: _____ Weight: _____

No. Cylinders: _____ Horsepower: _____ Manufacturer's I.D. No.: _____

Tag No.: _____ State Where Tag Issued: _____ County: _____

Transmission: ☐ automatic ☐ manual standard ☐ 4-speed ☐ 5-speed ☐ _____

Brakes: ☐ power ☐ disc ☐ power disc Steering: ☐ power ☐ standard

Defects of Vehicle: Brakes_____ Lights_____

Motor_____ Seat Belts _____

Steering _____ Tires _____ Windshield Wipers_____

Other _____

Previous Condition of Vehicle: _____

Condition of Vehicle After Accident: _____

Present Location of Vehicle: _____

Registered Owner of Vehicle (name & address): _____

_____ Phone No.:_____

Legal Owner of Vehicle (name & address): _____

_____ Phone No.:_____

Driver at Time of Accident (name & address): _____

_____ Phone No.:_____

Driver's Relation to Owner: _____ Was He/She Driving With Permission:_____

Driver's Destination and Purpose at Time of Accident: _____

Is This a "Company" Car?: _____ Was It Being Used Within Scope of Employment?:_____

Amount of Insurance: Liability $ _____ P.D. $ _____ Med. $_____

Comprehensive $ _____ Collision $ _____ Uninsured Motor Veh. $ _____

No Fault $ _____ Other _____ $_____ Amount of Deductible $_____

Other Passengers:

Name	Address	Seat Location in Vehicle
(1)		
(2)		
(3)		
(4)		
(5)		

Notes: _____

Investigator: _____

Form 7.6

Automobile Property Damage Report on Vehicle of ( ) Plaintiff ( ) Defendant

Client Name & Matter: _____ File No.:_____

Responsible Attorney(s):_____ Date:_____

Our Client Is ☐ Plaintiff   ☐ Defendant   ☐ Other in this matter.

Date of Accident: _____ Time of Accident: _____ _____.m.

Vehicle Damaged: Year_____ Make _____ Model _____

Driver of Vehicle Damaged (name & address):_____

_____ Phone No.: _____

Owner of Vehicle Damaged (name & address): _____

_____ Phone No.: _____

Date Vehicle Purchased: _____ Amount: $ _____ New/Used (circle one)

Seller (name & address): _____

_____ Phone No.: _____

Odometer Mileage on Date of Accident:_____ No. Prior Accidents:_____

Description of Damage Done in Prior Accidents: _____

_____

Location of This Accident: _____

_____

Description of Damage This Accident: _____

_____

Repair Estimates This Accident:

Name and Address of Estimator		Amount
(1)_____	_____	$_____
(2)_____	_____	$_____
(3)_____	_____	$_____

Repairer:_____ Actual Cost of Repairs: $_____

Loss of Use From _____ To _____ at $ _____ Per_____ = $_____

Alleged Values: Before Accident $_____ After $_____ = Loss $_____

Collision Claim Against _____ For $_____

Subrogation: ☐ Yes ☐ No Date Notified:_____ Total Claim: $_____

Notes: _____

_____

Investigator: _____

trial. Be diligent in reminding the client to obtain the necessary repair estimates requested by your attorney as soon as possible and *before* any decision is made regarding repairs. Have the client give the copies of the estimates to you so that you may attach them to this form for review by your attorney. Also, remind that client to give you any valuations of the vehicle before and after the accident as your attorney instructs. During your interview with the client or subsequent conversations, obtain information concerning prior vehicle damage as well.

• Summary

Investigation involves the gathering of facts and information about a specific incident (as opposed to research into case or statutory law). It must be done in a methodical and organized manner. Facts must be checked and rechecked. Timing is especially important to obtain evidence and witness's statements while still fresh. Handling and preserving evidence must follow the *Federal Rules of Evidence* and your state statutes. The importance of making sure the attorney knows what you are doing and that you get proper direction cannot be over-emphasized. When questions arise, be sure to ask them rather than make assumptions. Investigation is a challenge that requires persistence and diligence.

8

Excelling in Discovery

• Introduction

Discovery is one of the most active phases in litigation, and it is an area in which a paralegal is used extensively. To ensure your success as a litigation paralegal, you should learn everything you can about discovery and develop some efficient techniques. The purpose of this chapter is to help you understand the process of discovery and give you some practical step-by-step procedures for handling many of its various aspects. Some of these tasks are drafting interrogatories and requests for admissions, digesting (or summarizing) depositions, and preparing objections to discovery and motions to compel discovery. In addition, this chapter will include ways to respond to discovery documents presented by the adverse parties.

• Purposes of Discovery

Discovery is the process by which opposing counsel exchange information in accordance with court rules or by court order. Federal and state law govern discovery procedures. Through discovery, parties can obtain information unavailable from their own independent investigation. The parties request and exchange relevant information in hope of narrowing the issues and forming the basis of the lawsuit for each side. Years ago parties would often surprise the opposition with certain information, but now the rules of discovery prevent such tactics.

If the discovery process reveals no basis for the lawsuit, a summary judgment or a voluntary dismissal may occur before the trial goes any further. This saves considerable time and effort. Discovery may also lead to a settlement of the lawsuit prior to an expensive trial. If the lawsuit is to continue, triable issues become clearer through discovery, allowing both parties to properly prepare in advance of trial to support their positions.

Discovery also serves to reveal inconsistencies in witnesses' testimony and to preserve evidence. For example, if a witness is unavailable for trial, the deposition is entered as evidence at trial. Therefore, the purposes of discovery are:

1. To narrow the legal and factual issues, thus saving the client both time and legal fees at trial.
2. To obtain basic and factual information for purposes of preparing the case for trial.

3. To ascertain the opposing party's contentions.

4. To ascertain the identity of the opposition's witnesses, including expert witnesses.

5. To ascertain, locate, and preserve demonstrative evidence and testimony.

6. To determine or prove the amount and the type of damages (i.e., injury), whether to person, property, or rights.

7. To impeach the witness should his answers be inconsistent with his testimony at trial.

8. To eliminate the element of "surprise," particularly with respect to evidence or witnesses at trial.

9. To hasten settlement.

10. To "narrow the issues" by supporting various kinds of motions (e.g., motions to strike and pretrial orders).

Five discovery devices are commonly used in the process of discovery:

1. *Written interrogatories.* Written questions in which one party in a lawsuit requests the other party to answer in writing under oath. Interrogatories are sent to parties only.

2. *Requests for production of documents and things for inspection.* Written requests for the other party to produce certain written documents and things for inspection.

3. *Requests for admissions.* Written requests for the other party to acknowledge certain facts or the authenticity of certain documents. These facts will then not have to be proven at trial.

4. *Depositions.* Written record of a formal procedure whereby a party or witness answers questions under oath prior to trial. The questions may be submitted to the deponent either orally or in writing, but the deponent (testifying party) does not usually know the questions in advance although many introductory questions are routine.

5. *Physical or mental examinations.* When the physical or mental condition of a person involved in the lawsuit is at issue, the adverse party may require that an impartial doctor examine that person.

• Rules of Discovery

The following is a descriptive list of the rules regarding discovery set forth in the *Federal Rules of Civil Procedure* (as amended in 1987) discussed in this chapter. Check your state statutes and procedural rules for actions filed in the state courts.

Rule 26: General Provision Regarding Discovery

Rule 26(a): Discovery methods

Rule 26(b) (1): Scope of discovery

Rule 26(b) (2): Insurance agreements discoverable

Rule 26(b) (3): Trial preparation materials

Rule 26(b) (4): Experts

Rule 26(c): Protective orders

Rule 26(d): Sequence and timing of discovery

Rule 26(e): Supplementation of responses

Rule 27: Depositions Before Action or Pending Appeals

Rule 27(a): Before action

Rule 27(b): Pending appeal

Rule 27(c): Perpetuation by action

Rule 28: Persons Before Whom Depositions May Be Taken

Rule 28(a): Within the United States

Rule 28(b): In foreign countries

Rule 28(c): Disqualification for interest

Rule 29: Stipulations Regarding Discovery Procedure

Rule 30: Depositions upon Oral Depositions

Rule 30(a): When depositions may be taken

Rule 30(b) (5): Notice of Depositions accompanied by request for production

Rule 30(b) (6): Deposing corporation, partnership, association or government entity

Rule 30(c): Examination and cross-examination; record of examination; oath, objections

Rule 30(d): Motion to terminate or limit examination

Rule 30(e): Submission to witness; changes, signing

Rule 30(f): Certification and filing by officer; exhibits; copies; notice of filing

Rule 30(g): Failure to attend or to serve subpoenas; expenses

Rule 31: Depositions upon Written Questions

Rule 31(a): Serving questions; notice

Rule 31(b): Officer to take responses and prepare record

Rule 31(c): Notice of filing

Rule 32: Use of Depositions in Court Proceedings

Rule 32(a): Use of depositions

Rule 32(b): Objections to admissibility

Rule 32(c): (Abrogated July 1, 1975)

Rule 32(d): Effect of errors and irregularities in depositions

Rule 33: Interrogatories to Parties

Rule 33(a): Availability; procedures for use

Rule 33(b): Scope; use at trial

Rule 33(c): Option to produce business records

Rule 34: Production of Documents and Things and Entry upon Land for Inspection and Other Purposes

Rule 34(a): Scope

Rule 34(b): Procedure

Rule 34(c): Persons not parties

Rule 35: Physical and Mental Examination of Persons

Rule 35(a): Order for examination

Rule 35(b): Report of examining physician or psychologist

Rule 36: Requests for Admissions

Rule 36(a): Request for admission—Procedure

Rule 36(b): Effect of admission

Rule 37: Failure to Make Discovery: Sanctions

Rule 37(a): Motion for order compelling discovery

Rule 37(b): Failure to comply with order

Rule 37(c): Expenses on failure to admit

Rule 37(d): Failure of party to attend at own deposition or serve answers to interrogatories or respond to request for inspection

Rule 37(e): Subpoena of person in foreign country (abrogated April 29, 1988)

Rule 37(f): Expenses against United States (repealed October 1, 1981)

Rule 37(g): Failure to participate in the framing of a discovery plan

Rule 45: Subpoenas

Rule 45(a): For attendance of witnesses

Rule 45(b): For production of documentary evidence

Rule 45(c): Service

Rule 45(d): Subpoena for taking depositions; place of examination

Rule 45(e): Subpoena for a hearing or trial

Rule 45(f): Contempt

• Common Paralegal Discovery Tasks

Again, paralegals probably perform discovery tasks more than any other paralegal duties. It is important to learn to handle these tasks efficiently. Don't be shy about asking your colleagues to share their "tricks of the trade." If you are a paralegal supervisor or legal assistant manager, encourage your paralegal team to support each other. Although the technical aspects of the work may be different, the methods of doing the tasks are similar, and you can share them. Your duties in discovery may vary from firm to firm, but most paralegals perform similar tasks.

The most common discovery tasks are:

1. Drafting interrogatories.
2. Researching answers to interrogatories and drafting responses.
3. Drafting requests for admissions.
4. Researching answers to admissions and drafting responses.
5. Preparing requests for production of documents or notices to produce.
6. Gathering, comparing, coding, date-stamping, listing, and organizing documents.

7. Entering, sorting, supervising, and handling the management of documents and communications with the attorneys.

8. Preparing subpoenas and subpoenas *duces tecum*.

9. Reviewing depositions, and organizing and compiling information contained in depositions in the form of deposition digests, indexes, and summaries.

• Drafting Interrogatories

Written interrogatories are one means of obtaining basic information about the opposing party, his or her version of the accident, transaction, or occurrence, and the existence of items of evidence. Questions concerning the identity of witnesses, the existence of documents and other tangible evidence, the nature and extent of the loss, and the method of calculating damages can be answered through discovery.

In other words, interrogatories help establish dates and facts and identify relevant documents and individuals who have knowledge of the facts relating to a certain case. Interrogatories are also used to further explore a party's legal contentions and allegations. They are particularly useful when the attorney has questions that may require the opposing party to research, gather background information, give extremely complex answers, or compile data not previously available. Further answers to interrogatories may establish that the opponent lacks certain evidence. You should check whether your state court rules allow discovery of any question, not privileged, that is relevant to the subject matter involved.

The following step-by-step procedure will help you prepare interrogatories easily:

• Step 1:   Know what you want to accomplish.

In various types of actions you may have different objectives in preparing interrogatories. For example, in a breach of contract case in which your office represents the defendant, you will need to know the specific events prior to and after the alleged breach, the specific parties allegedly involved and their alleged actions, the context of any communications between the parties, the alleged amount of damages, the location of documents and evidence relating to the breach, and the basis for the plaintiff's calculations of damages.

In a personal injury action, by contrast, you will want to know the basis for the plaintiff's claim. This will include the details and facts surrounding the alleged wrongdoing of the defendant, the witnesses, if any, and the basis for the alleged damages. You also need to ascertain the physical and mental condition of the plaintiff before and after the alleged accident. The circumstances surrounding the occurrence of the accident—such as driving while intoxicated or defects in the plaintiff's vehicle prior to the accident—and the basis for the specific allegations made by plaintiff in the complaint are important as well.

• Step 2:   Organize your questions into basic areas.

After you determine your objectives, arrange the portions of inquiry of the case into the following categories:

1. Liability.
2. Damages.
3. Basic information needed.
4. Documents.
5. Names of witnesses.
6. Defenses.

Then divide each area into subparts, and develop a skeletal outline of your questions.

As an illustration, in drafting interrogatories to a defendant in a personal injury action, the headings in your outline might include the specific elements necessary to establish a *prima facie* case, the defenses and basic information needed. For example:

1. Jurisdictional issues.
2. Duty of care owed by defendant.
3. Breach of duty by defendant.
4. The violation of a statute (negligence per se).
5. Damages to defendant.
6. Proximate cause.
7. Defenses raised by defendant.
8. Documents and basic information.
9. Witnesses for defendant.

As another illustration, in a products liability case wherein your office represents the defendant, the headings might include the following:

1. Witnesses to alleged accident.
2. Statements taken or given relating to alleged accident.
3. Information regarding plaintiff's purchase and use of the product.
4. Warranties or representations allegedly made by defendant.
5. Test reports and warnings given the defendant.
6. Alleged physical damages to plaintiff.
7. Alleged emotional and mental damages to plaintiff.
8. Documents supporting plaintiff's damages.

• Step 3: Review the pleadings and discovery documents.

Before you begin to draft interrogatories, carefully review the pleadings and discovery documents previously filed in the action. Examine them to determine specific information needed to assist the attorney in properly representing the client. Take notes and outline the specific areas of the case that are unclear and that need further clarification.

• Step 4: Cite rules

The first paragraph of the interrogatories should cite the state procedural rule, statute or, if the action is in the federal district court, Rule 33 of the *Federal Rules of Civil Procedure* under which interrogatories are governed. For example:

Plaintiffs, Georgia Conrad and Eula Conrad, and pursuant to Rule 33 of the *Federal Rules of Civil Procedure* (or to Georgia Civil Practice Act § 33[1]) serve upon Defendant James L. Bowen, Jr., the following Interrogatories and require this Defendant to answer them as provided by law, and that these answers be served upon the undersigned attorney within the time[2] required by law. If the whole of a question is unknown, so state and answer the part known.

The second paragraph should include wording regarding the rules set forth in *Hickman v. Taylor*,[3] (i.e., that the answers must include information known to the agents of the party, including her attorney, as well as the party herself.) For example:

These Interrogatories include in addition to Defendant, her employees, agents, servants, representatives, private investigators or others who are in a position to or who have obtained information for or on behalf of Defendant.

The third paragraph usually sets forth the statutory requirement pursuant to federal or state statute for supplemental answers to interrogatories. For example:

These Interrogatories are continuing and require supplemental answers if Defendant or her attorneys obtain further information between the time the answers are served and the time of trial. Any supplemental answers are to be filed and served upon counsel for Plaintiff within thirty (30) days of receipt of such additional information, or by the date of the trial in this matter, whichever is sooner.

• Step 5:   Include definitions and abbreviations.

To avoid confusion in drafting complicated interrogatories and to save repeating and redefining certain words and phrases, include a precise set of definitions or abbreviations at the beginning of the interrogatories. For example:

(a) As used herein, "person" shall mean the full name, current or last-known residence address (designating which).

(b) Any reference to these Interrogatories to the singular person, place, thing, or entity, including, but not limited to partnership, corporation, firm, proprietorship, association, governmental body, shall include the plural, as well as the singular, and the feminine gender, as well as masculine.

(c) As used herein, "ARM" shall mean the "Association of Retail Merchants."

(d) As used herein, the term "the collision" shall mean that certain collision between the automobiles of the plaintiff and defendant, that occurred on the first day of June 1988, at the intersection of First Street and Broad Street in Cleveland, Ohio.

• Step 6:   Draft introductory interrogatories.[4]

If the interrogatories you are preparing are for an individual, use the following introductory form:

---

[1]*Ga. Code Ann.* § 81A-133

[2]Specify the number of days, etc.

[3]*Hickman v. Taylor*, 329 U.S. 495 (1947).

[4]See *Bender's Forms of Discovery* (New York: Matthew Bender Publishing Co., 1992) for additional forms.

INTERROGATORIES

1.

State:

(a) Your full name and any other names you have used in the past, and the period during that you were known by each such name.

(b) Your date of birth, birthplace, and Social Security number.

(c) Your profession or employer and title or occupation, and any other offices you hold and the name of any corporation or other organizational entity for which you are an officer, director, or agent.

(d) Your residence address and any past residence addresses you have had within the past 10 years, and the period during which you lived at each such residence.

(e) Your marital status; and if married, the date of your marriage, and your present spouse's name.

(f) The date of any previous marriages, and the names of any previous spouses.

2.

List the present employees, agents, servants or representatives of defendant who are familiar with any aspect of this case, their titles and addresses, and the particular aspect of which they would have knowledge.

If the interrogatories you are preparing are for a corporation, use the following introductory form:

INTERROGATORIES

1.

State:

(a) The name of the officer or agent answering these Interrogatories.

(b) The title and duties of such person.

(c) The length of employment for this person with the corporation and his present position.

2.

List the present employees, agents, servants or representatives of defendant who are familiar with any aspect of this case, their titles and addresses, and the particular aspect of which they would have knowledge.

3.

Who is the present agent, employee, or representative most familiar with the particular aspects listed in the answer to the preceding interrogatories?

• Step 7:   Divide the paragraphs of the pleadings into sections.

If your office represents the defendant, Nancy Lewis, an excellent way to begin is to photocopy the complaint and divide each allegation in the complaint into sections. Of course, if your office represents the plaintiff, then you would begin drafting the interrogatories with the answer. This causes the responding party to give more definite responses.

4.

On May 16, 1988, at approximately 5:30 P.M., the Defendant Nancy Lewis was the operator of a certain automobile owned by Defendant, Scientific Wagons, Inc. This automobile was being driven in a negligent fashion in a southerly direction along Vinings Road, Franklin County, Montana, behind Plaintiff, Becky L. Peters, so as to cause Defendant's automobile to collide into the back of the automobile of Plaintiff.

Now develop individual interrogatories on each section. Dividing the allegations of the complaint into separate parts will cause the responding party to give more specific responses. Use the following formula, which covers all aspects of the allegations: **5(W) + H,** or:

1. Who?
2. What?
3. When?
4. Where?
5. Why?
6. How?

Taking the preceding example, you might draft the following questions to the plaintiff:

Who?

1. In reference to Paragraph 4 of Plaintiff's Complaint, specify in detail (including, but not limited to, names, dates, places, documents, and manner and substance of all communications, written and oral) all facts upon which you rely to support the basis of Plaintiff's allegation that "on May 16, 1988, at approximately 5:30 P.M., the Defendant Nancy Lewis was the operator of a certain automobile owned by Defendant Scientific Wagons, Inc."

What?

2. In reference to Paragraph 4 of Plaintiff's Complaint, describe the vehicle allegedly driven by Plaintiff, Becky L. Peters, on May 16, 1988, stating make, model, vehicle tag number, number of cylinders, color and condition immediately prior to and subsequent to the alleged accident.

When?

3. In reference to Paragraph 4 of Plaintiff's Complaint, list the names, addresses and ages of each person who you allege was traveling with the Plaintiff in the vehicle driven by Plaintiff at the time of the alleged accident.

Where?

4. In reference to Paragraph 4 of Plaintiff's Complaint, state the exact location of Plaintiff's vehicle immediately prior to and subsequent to the alleged accident.

Why?

5. Immediately prior to the alleged accident referred to in Paragraph 4 of Plaintiff's Complaint, did Plaintiff observe or have knowledge of any traffic signals and, if so, what were they?

How?

6. In reference to Paragraph 4 of Plaintiff's Complaint, specify in detail (including, but not limited to, names, dates, places, documents, and manner and substance of all communications, written and oral) all facts upon which you rely to support the basis of Plaintiff's allegations that "this automobile was being driven in a negligent fashion in a southerly direction along Vinings Road, Franklin County, Montana, behind Plaintiff Becky L. Peters so as to cause Defendant's automobile to collide into the backside of the automobile of Plaintiff."

Of course, there are numerous additional interrogatories that you may draft.

• Step 8:   Ask general interrogatories regarding the last pleading filed by the party.

If your office is representing the defendant, refer to the last pleading filed by the plaintiff in the beginning of the Interrogatories:

To Plaintiff:
Specify in detail (including, but not limited to, names, dates, places, documents, and manner and substance of all communications, written and oral) all facts upon which you rely to support the basis of the allegations in **Paragraph 2, of Count I of Plaintiff's complaint** that:
"This Defendant is without knowledge or information sufficient to form a belief as to accuracy of the allegation of Paragraph 7 of Plaintiff's Complaint."

If your office is representing the plaintiff, and the last pleading filed by defendant is the answer, the interrogatory might read as follows:

To Defendant:
Please state each and every (a) fact upon that you rely and (b) statute, rule, provision, case, authority or law upon which you rely to support your contention in the **Sixth Defense of Defendant's Answer** that:
"Plaintiff failed to exercise ordinary care for her own protection and such failure occasioned her injury and damage, if any, and therefore she is not entitled to recover in this case."

• Step 9:   Ask interrogatories regarding the basic areas of the action.

After you have finished the general interrogatories, draft interrogatories regarding the basic areas of the action as outlined in Step 2. Now apply the formula discussed in Step 7, **5 (W) + H,** by asking each question in the formula regarding the crucial areas of the case, as noted in Step 2, such as what is the exact amount of damages to plaintiff's property? Attacking the crucial areas from all angles will make your interrogatories more comprehensive.

• Step 10: Ask concluding interrogatories.

The concluding Interrogatories may regard the identification of:
(a) Those persons who assisted in answering the interrogatories.
(b) Those persons whom the responding party intends to call as witnesses and experts at trial.
(c) Those persons who have any information or may have made statements regarding the case.

Some examples follow:

(a) Identify each person who assisted the plaintiff in the preparation of the answers to these Interrogatories by:

(i) Providing the person's name, address, telephone number, title and occupation; and

(ii) Stating the number of each answer to each interrogatory with which the person assisted you.

Witnesses:
(a) Identify all other individuals plaintiff may call to testify by providing the name, address, telephone number, occupation and title of each.

Expert Witnesses:
(a) Identify each person whom the Plaintiff expects to call as an expert witness at trial; and

(i) provide the name, address, telephone number, occupation and title of each; and

(ii) state the substance of the facts and opinions to which the expert is expected to testify and a summary of the grounds for each opinion.

(iii) Identify all other individuals who may have knowledge or provide information pertinent to the claims presented by plaintiff or the defense raised by any defendant in this case.

(b) To your knowledge, have any of these persons made any statements, either written or oral, concerning this action?

(i) If so, provide the name, address, telephone number, occupation and title of each individual and the nature of the statement.

(ii) If so, provide the location and name of the custodian of the statements.

(iii) Will you voluntarily furnish a copy of any such oral or written statement?

Identify all witnesses to the facts alleged in Plaintiff's Complaint by providing the name, address, telephone number, occupation and title of each witness.

Some of these questions may not be discoverable under some state statutes, so be sure to check.

• Step 11: End the interrogatories with signature and certificate of service.

After you have completed the interrogatories, prepare a signatory line for the attorney's signature, the attorney's state bar number (if required in your state), and include the firm name, address, and telephone number (including zip code and area code). Pursuant to the *Federal Rules of Civil Procedures* and most state statutes, you should also include a Certificate of Service.

• Step 12: Review the interrogatories.

Before you present the interrogatories to the attorney, review them carefully for errors, omissions, and ways in which you can improve them. Remember, they should be clear and concise.

Finally, count the total number of interrogatories. If the total is beyond the statutory limit, ask the attorney which interrogatories could be eliminated. Many states limit the number of interrogatories to 50, including subparts. Check your state statute and local court rules. The attorney may want to ask some of the questions in a deposition instead of as interrogatories to avoid objections that they are burdensome and excessive.

To prepare comprehensive interrogatories, use the following pointers:

1. *Be precise.* Each interrogatory should be short, clearly stated, and precise to avoid confusing the responding party and therefore eliciting incorrect information. Also, a broadly stated interrogatory affords grounds for objections. For example, an interrogatory requesting "all" information the responding party has about the accident is too broad.

2. *Make sure interrogatories are calculated to lead to the discovery of admissible evidence.* The primary standard for deciding whether interrogatories are objectionable is whether they are calculated to lead to the discovery of admissible evidence. Generally, objectionable interrogatories are beyond the scope of discovery and therefore irrelevant. This objection prevents opposing counsel from a "fishing expedition," looking for unrelated information through discovery.

3. *Avoid excessive and irrelevant interrogatories.* Another frequent objection to interrogatories is that they are burdensome, oppressive, or repetitious. Some federal district courts have taken the position that interrogatories "should be relatively few and related to the *important facts of the case* rather than very numerous and concerned with never-ending details"[5] (emphasis added.) Therefore, make sure each interrogatory you draft is calculated to lead to the discovery of admissible and necessary evidence.

4. *Ask for opinions or contentions that relate to fact or the application of law to fact.* Under Rule 33(b) of the *Federal Rules of Civil Procedure*, and some state procedural statutes, you are permitted to ask interrogatories calling for opinions or contentions that relate to fact or the application of law to fact. If you are drafting interrogatories in a state court, you should review your state's rules to determine if this procedure is permissible in your state.

5. *Gear "canned" interrogatories to your case.* While it is useful to prepare basic forms of interrogatories, you should tailor the basic form precisely to fit the particular case. "Canned" or form interrogatories are models that can serve as a guide to drafting a set of interrogatories specifically suited to your case.

6. *Do not ask complicated or ambiguous questions.* Keep your Interrogatories simple and use commonly understood words. Frame your questions to avoid "yes" or "no" responses and to prevent objections. Use subsections if necessary. However, too many subsections can become confusing.

7. *Ask several different questions about crucial areas of the case.* In crucial areas of the case, where it is imperative that you obtain specific information, frame the same question in various ways. Doing so may tend to dissuade opposing counsel from (a) making objections to specific interrogatories or (b) attempting to sustain objections to *all* interrogatories.

8. *Include definitions and rules.* To avoid confusion in drafting complicated interrogatories, and to save repeating and redefining certain words and phrases, include a precise set of definitions and abbreviations at the beginning of the interrogatories.

Additionally, include an explanation of the rules set forth in *Hickman v. Taylor*[6] (i.e., that the answers must include information known to the agents of the party, including his attorney, as well as to the party himself.)

---

[5]*Ball v. Paramount Pictures, Incorporated,* 4 F.R.D., 194, 195 (W.D. Pa. 1944).

[6]*Hickman v. Taylor,* 329 U.S. 495 (1947).

Form 8.1

Certificate of Service

Of Counsel:

Lee & Ashmore
5400 Candler Building
Atlanta, Georgia 30303

(404) 258-8097

CERTIFICATE OF SERVICE

I, John M. Schwartz, do hereby certify that I have this date served a copy of the within and foregoing PLAINTIFF'S FIRST SET OF CONTINUING INTERROGATORIES to Defendant James W. Bruno, M.D., upon counsel for Defendant:

> Ms. Jill Bonner
> Bonner & Goldberger
> Suite 1498
> 250 Piedmont Avenue, N.E.
> Atlanta, Georgia 30303

by depositing same in the United States Mail,* properly addressed with sufficient postage affixed thereto to insure delivery.

This 12th day of October, 1992.

_____
John M. Schwartz
Attorney for Plaintiffs

---

*If express or hand delivered, change language accordingly.

9. *Always ask one or more summary interrogatories.* To prevent the responding party from introducing additional evidence at trial, it is imperative that you ask summary questions: For example:

(a) Does the respondent have any other relevant information relating to the subject of this lawsuit in any way whatsoever not set forth in his answers to Interrogatories Nos. 1 to 20 contained hereinabove?

(b) In preparing the answers to these Interrogatories, have you contacted all persons whom you know who might have information regarding the lawsuit?

(c) List the names, addresses and capacities of all persons who assisted you in obtaining answers to these Interrogatories, indicating the particular answer with which each person assisted you.

• Raising Objections to Interrogatories

It is important to understand the general basis for allowable objections to discovery so that when you draft discovery requests, you can frame them to avoid objections. Although most states pattern their state procedural rules after the

Federal Rules of Civil Procedure, refer to your state statutes for specific rules regarding your state. However, your best guide to understanding the underlying principles and scope of discovery is Rule 26(b) of the *Federal Rules of Civil Procedure.* The Rule states:

> Parties may obtain discovery regarding any matter, not privileged, that is relevant to the subject matter involved in the pending action, whether it relates to the claim or defense of the party, including the existence, description, nature, custody, conditions and location of any books, documents, or other tangible things and the identity and location of persons having knowledge of any discoverable matter. It is not ground for objection that the information sought will be inadmissible at the trial if the information sought appears reasonably calculated to lead to the discovery of admissible evidence.

To obtain a ruling on objections, Rule 33(a) requires the party submitting the interrogatories to move for an order under Rule 37(a) to compel discovery or motion for protective order. Word your objections to discovery to indicate the deficient portions of the requests. You must specifically explain why the cited parts are improper. Blanket objections usually fail. The five most common objections are:

1. The information sought is privileged.[7]

OBJECTION. This Interrogatory calls for information that is privileged by nature of the relationship between certain parties (e.g., attorney-client or physician-patient).

2. The information sought is not relevant to the case.

OBJECTION. This Interrogatory calls for information that is irrelevant to the subject matter of this action and that is not calculated to lead to the discovery of admissible evidence.

3. The information sought is attorney work product.

OBJECTION. This Interrogatory calls for information prepared in anticipation of trial and does not show the necessary need for this information or the discovering party's inability to obtain the substantial equivalent.

4. The information sought is too broad, vague, and extensive.

OBJECTION. The information sought in this Interrogatory is too broad, vague, extensive and general, and places an unreasonable burden on the respondent.

5. The information sought is information that was obtained from nonwitness experts specifically retained in anticipation of litigation or preparation for trial. Proof must be shown of exceptional circumstances that prevent the party seeking discovery to obtain facts or opinions from other sources.

OBJECTION. This Interrogatory calls for information regarding nonwitness experts specially retained in anticipation and in preparation for trial. The necessary showing of exceptional circumstances under which it is impracticable for the party seeking discovery to obtain facts or opinions on the same subject by other means has not been made.

---

[7]Privileges vary from state to state.

In any discovery document, you should:

1. Be clear and concise in making your objection.
2. Pinpoint the specific reasons for your objection.
3. Make sure your objection can be substantiated (do your case research).
4. Make sure your objection is allowable under either state or federal rules, whichever are applicable.

If you are in doubt about any of these points, check with your attorney.

Impact of Filing Objections

Objections act as a protective device for the client. If they succeed, they save him from answering the specific questions or requests contained in the interrogatories, requests for admissions, and requests for production of documents. They attempt to prevent the opposing party from prying into matters irrelevant to the case. All questions and requests not successfully objected to must be answered according to the state or federal rules governing discovery, whichever is applicable.

• Answers to Interrogatories

Answers to interrogatories should be responsive, nonevasive, and complete. However, do not give any more information than necessary. Avoid using the phrase "incorporated by reference" in an answer unless using it will prevent unnecessarily long, complex, and repetitious answers. "Incorporated by reference" is a phrase used to refer to another document, usually an exhibit, which then becomes a part of the main document. To illustrate: "This complaint incorporates by reference Exhibit A, a contract between the parties dated November 10, 1988." means the contract is now part of the complaint. If you must use this phrase, be sure to refer to pertinent parts of the document specifically. Do not refer to a lengthy deposition without specifying the particular portions or pages where the information may be located.

Rule 33(c) of the *Federal Rules of Civil Procedure* provides that you may refer to the business records of the respondent when preparing an answer to a discovery request. For example:

> The information sought in Interrogatory No. 12 may be obtained by a search of the Plaintiff's business records, which records will be provided to the Defendant.

Form 8.2 is a response to a request for production of documents, an opposition to a request for production of attorney's work product.

• Requests for Production

In requests for production, which are titled "Requests for Production of Documents and Things," one party requests the other party to produce certain physical evidence ("documents and things") and allow the requesting party to in-

Form 8.2

**Opposition to Request for
Production of Attorney's
Work Product**

IN THE SUPERIOR COURT OF SHASTA COUNTY
STATE OF CALIFORNIA

LYNDA KAY PITTMAN,)
    Plaintiff,)
v.)   CIVIL ACTION FILE NO. 891
)
)
DAVID ROMER,)
    Defendant.)

PLAINTIFF'S OPPOSITION TO REQUEST FOR
PRODUCTION OF ATTORNEY'S WORK PRODUCT

COMES NOW the Plaintiff, LYNDA KAY PITTMAN, by and through her attorney, JOHN H. HOUSE, of NICHOLS & HOUSE, and objects to the Request for Production filed on November 24, 1988, by Defendant, DAVID ROMER, for Dr. Bonner's expert report in that our research concerning the defective tire is Plaintiff's work product, and we have paid large amounts of money for Dr. Bonner's expertise and research. As a matter of law, Defendant DAVID ROMER is not entitled to our private work product, although counsel is entitled to take the deposition of Dr. Bonner.

WHEREFORE, Plaintiff, LYNDA KAY PITTMAN, prays that she be relieved of any duty to produce said expert report listed in Defendant's Request for Production dated November 24, 1988.

THIS 15th day of December, 1988.

_____

LINDA SUIT

800 Jones Building
Redding, California 96001

---

spect them. This includes the testing of certain things such as relevant formulas, products, inventions, materials, machinery, or other items involved in the litigation. The purpose is to make evidence available to both sides to assess its value and avoid surprise at trial. The requesting party can use this opportunity not only to locate evidence that may be damaging to the other side, but also to discover evidence that supports its own side. For example, if the plaintiff in a discrimination case requests the production of the business records of the defendant, her employer, she may find prior memos and office correspondence previously unknown to her that support her case.

The physical evidence requested in a request for production can include land and buildings to be made available for inspection. Thus, one request is titled "Requests for Production of Documents and Things and Entry Upon Land for Inspection and Other Purposes." In the federal district courts all these requests are governed by Rule 34 of the *Federal Rules of Civil Procedure*. Although many states have adopted statutes similar to the federal rules, always check for specific rules regarding your state. Rule 34 includes the following:

writings, drawings, graphs, telephone records, and other data compilations from which the information can be obtained, translated, if necessary, by the respondent through detection devices into reasonable usable form, or to inspect and copy, test, or sample any tangible things that constitute or contain matter with the scope of Rules 26(b) and which are in the possession, custody or control of the party upon whom the request is served; or (2) to permit entry upon designated land or other property in the possession or control of the party upon whom the request is served for the purpose of inspection and measuring, surveying, photographing, testing, or sampling the property or any designated object or operation thereon, within the scope of Rule 26(b).

Computer data banks and usable printers are now included as well.

Consider this example of a request for production: Plaintiff Linden was a chemist for a pharmaceutical company where he invented a particular drug that his former employer company claims it invented. A request for production could enable plaintiff's counsel or expert to make an independent analysis of the drug on site. As another example, in a quiet title action in which the plaintiff is trying to clear his title to certain property, the defendant could make a request to enter upon the land to have the property surveyed to protect his interest in particular portions of the property.

Many attorneys abuse this rule by making excessive and burdensome requests. Often they use canned requests for production in an attempt to avoid forgetting any item permissible to request—even items not necessary to their case. The result can be burdensome, oppressive, or unduly disruptive requests. For example, access to observe the intricate operations of a computer factory might disturb day-to-day operations.

Excluded from this rule are trade secrets and privileged and work-product information. Also, a "fishing expedition," in which irrelevant information is requested in the hope that it might turn up some relevant evidence, is not allowed under this rule.

To sum up, the *Federal Rules of Civil Procedure* provide that any party may serve on any other party a request to produce specific items of evidence for inspection, copying, or testing. They also allow any party to permit any other party to enter upon designated land or other property of the responding party to inspect, measure, survey, photograph, or test or sample the property or any designated objects on the property.

Procedure for Requests for Production

The responding party is allowed 30 days to respond to the request for production under Rule 34. If the request is served with the summons and complaint, then the responding party is allowed 45 days to respond. The party making the request for production may ask the court for an order shortening the time. The responding party may file a written response within the required time period, stating, in regard to each request, that inspection and related activities will be complied with or giving grounds for objection. The party must specify any part of an item where the objection is to one party only.

The responding party is required to produce the requested documents as they are kept in the usual course of business or to organize and label the documents to correspond with the categories in the request.

Inspection, Copying, and Testing

Usually inspection is made at the office of the counsel representing the party who has custody or control of the documents and things. The party who has made the request must, if requested, pay the reasonable cost of having the copies of documents or photographs made. With photographs, the negatives are usually provided to the requesting party, and the owner or custodian of the negatives retains the originals. In any event, the custodian should keep either the negatives or the photographs to protect himself.

Because of the dangers of damage or loss, the custodian of the articles to be tested is usually reluctant to give up temporary possession. Both parties will usually work together to determine an amicable solution to this problem. If this cannot be accomplished, then it may be necessary to resort to the court through the medium of a motion to compel, and a protective order (both of which are discussed later in this chapter), after which the judge will usually set guidelines for testing or inspection.

Introductory Paragraph

First, prepare the introductory paragraph that sets forth the appropriate provisions of either your state statute or the U.S. Code. An example follows:

> You are hereby requested, pursuant to Rule 34 of the *Federal Rules of Civil Procedure,* to produce and permit the Plaintiff MARY GRACE DIEHL or persons acting in her behalf, to inspect and copy the documents in your possession or control designated hereinafter. The production, inspection, copying, and all acts necessarily related thereto shall take place at the offices of Plaintiff's counsel of record, Rory Cheyenne, 6330 Church Street, Riverdale, Georgia 30274, commencing at 10:00 a.m., February 9, 1990, and continuing from day to day thereafter until the inspection, copying and related acts are completed by Plaintiff.

Provision for Supplemental Documents

Next, prepare a paragraph providing for supplemental documents as follows:

> This request is continuing, and if, at a time after Defendant Mary C. Pugh has produced the requested documents or otherwise responded thereto, further documents (called for in these requests but not previously produced) come into your possession and control, then you are requested to further respond and to produce these documents at this location within thirty (30) days from receipt by you of such documents, and in all events prior to the time of pretrial conference, or, if none, trial.

Keys to Preparing Thorough Requests for Production

There are basically two keys to preparing thorough requests for production: (1) determine which items you want, and (2) describe specifically which items you want. To determine which items you want in the particular case, consult with your attorney. This discussion with the attorney will cause him or her to think through the strategies to be used in the case. Consequently, the attorney will be able to give you a better perspective of the case, enabling you to better determine the items you should request.

Again, review the documents and pleadings in the case, and if interrogatories have not been presented to the opposing party, discuss the idea of interrogatories with the attorney prior to preparing the requests. Interrogatories may (1) reveal documents and things that the responding party has that relate to the subject of the litigation, and (2) enable you to better describe the particular documents and things to request.

The second key to preparing thorough requests is to describe the items requested precisely. A simple way to describe documents and things is to refer to the other party's pleadings—complaint, answer, etc.; or discovery documents—answers to interrogatories, depositions, etc. For example:

> All correspondence, communications, memoranda, documents and other tangible evidence relating in any way to Defendant's contention in Paragraph 21 of the Twelfth Defense of Defendant's Answer to Plaintiff's Complaint in this action.

A more specific method of describing documents is by identifying each document as follows:

1. Type (e.g., agreement).
2. Title.
3. Date.
4. Originator.
5. Addressee.
6. Number of pages.

Another way to describe documents and things specifically is by categorizing the documents. In the following example, the documents are categorized by specific theories: the execution of the contract, breach of the contract, and damages.

> All correspondence, communications, memoranda, documents, and other tangible evidence pertaining to (a) the alleged contract between the parties referred to in Paragraph 3 of the Complaint and underlying this action, (b) Defendant's alleged breaches of this contract, and (c) the damages allegedly suffered by Plaintiff.

In the following request, the documents are named specifically:

> Any and all copies of the income tax returns filed by you, individually or jointly with any other persons with federal and state governments for the years 1988, 1989, 1990, and 1991.

• Requests for Admissions

Requests for admissions are written requests asking a party to a lawsuit to do any of the following:

1. Admit or deny the truth of certain facts.
2. Admit or deny the truth of certain opinions of fact, or of the application of law to fact.
3. Admit or deny the genuineness of certain documents.

Parties may serve written requests for admissions under Rule 36 of *The Federal Rules of Civil Procedure*. The purpose is to define and limit the issues of the case and related areas of proof. This reduces the time needed for discovery and investigation and often the number of witnesses needed for trial. Those requests admitted are no longer at issue. Possibly, the case may be settled as a result of certain admissions, summary judgment may be made, or the need for a trial may be eliminated. Generally, requests for admissions aid the forward movement of a case and make the process more efficient.

Requests for admissions are different from interrogatories or depositions in that they do not request information, but rather a confirmation of the validity (or invalidity) of previously discovered information. Requests for admissions are used during the discovery period after the answer is filed. Check your state statutes for requirements.

It is imperative that you carefully draft your requests for admission so that they are effective and accomplish the purposes of discovery. If the responding party denies them, but your attorney can later prove that the admissions set forth in the requests are true, then your client may be awarded the cost of proving the facts set out in the requests.

To assist you in drafting clear requests, here are ten suggestions:

1. Review cases involving objections to requests for admission to become familiar with the basic grounds for objections to them.

2. List the documents for which you wish admissions of genuineness at the beginning of your requests, indicating that you have attached a copy of the document to the requests. If possible, identify each document by:

1. Type (e.g., contract).
2. Title.
3. Date.
4. Originator.
5. Addressee.
6. Number of pages.

An example follows:

That each of the following documents, exhibited with the Complaint, is genuine:
a. The "Purchase Order" dated December 15, 1988, a copy of which is attached to Plaintiff's Complaint as Exhibit "A" (hereinafter "Purchase Order").
b. The "Guaranty Agreement" dated December 15, 1988, a copy of which is attached to Plaintiff's Complaint as Exhibit "B" (hereinafter "Guaranty Agreement").

3. It is a good practice not to use the phrase "incorporated by reference" in your requests to include previously cited requests, documents, or information in any other documents. Unless the document is an exhibit, do not refer to a request by number only. For example, do not say, "as stated in Request No. 8," without repeating Request No. 8. However, it is acceptable to refer to a document previously set out for identification in the beginning of the same request to save repetition. Your primary rule is to make sure your language is clear, and that there can be no misunderstanding as to which documents you are referring to.

For example:

Wrong: Defendant Paula Turner executed the Guaranty Agreement referred to in Interrogatory No. 14.

Right: Defendant Paula Turner executed the Guaranty Agreement dated January 4, 1989, identified in Request No. A-1 hereinabove.

4. Divide requests into subparts and use only one subpart in each request. The reason for doing this is to prevent the responding party from denying the entire request when only a portion of the request is subject to denial. In the following example, if one of the dates were incorrect, then the entire request

could be denied by the responding party. Therefore, in the example, you would divide the request into six subparts and draft a separate request for each.

> **Wrong:** Plaintiff Vanessa Stogsdill made an oral demand to Defendant Steve Reiff as Buyer, on March 2, 1989, and on March 15, 1989, for payment of principal and interest due and outstanding under the terms of this Purchase Order.
>
> **Right:**
> a. Plaintiff Vanessa Stogsdill made an oral demand to defendant Steve Reiff as Buyer for payment of principal due and outstanding under the terms of this Purchase Order.
>
> b. Plaintiff Vanessa Stogsdill made an oral demand to Defendant Steve Reiff as Buyer for payment of interest due and outstanding under the terms of this Purchase Order.
>
> c. Plaintiff Vanessa Stogsdill made an oral demand to Defendant Steve Reiff as Buyer on March 2, 1989, for payment of principal due and outstanding under terms of this Purchase Order.
>
> d. Plaintiff Vanessa Stogsdill made an oral demand to Defendant Steve Reiff as Buyer on March 2, 1989, for payment of interest due and outstanding under the terms of this Purchase Order.
>
> e. Plaintiff Vanessa Stogsdill made an oral demand to Defendant Steve Reiff as Buyer on March 15, 1989, for payment of principal due and outstanding under the terms of this Purchase Order.
>
> f. Plaintiff Vanessa Stogsdill made an oral demand to Defendant Steve Reiff as Buyer on March 15, 1989, for payment of interest due and outstanding under the terms of this Purchase Order.

5. Make each request specific, clear, and precise. Avoid wordiness.

> **Wrong:** Defendant Gary Wall, as stated as a guarantor of the Note, that he executed concurrently with the Guaranty referenced hereinabove, as more specifically stated in the Complaint filed herein in this matter, failed to make a timely quarterly payment of interest on the appropriate date, September 30, 1989, on this Note, referred to hereinabove, as agreed to and as stated hereinabove.
>
> **Right:** Defendant Gary Wall, as a guarantor of this "Note," or in any other capacity, failed to make the quarterly payment of interest on the outstanding principal balance due September 30, 1989, on this "Note."

The problem is obvious with the first example. It is wordy and confusing. Rewrite where necessary to delete unnecessary words and to improve clarity.

6. Ask several requests in a crucial area in different ways to avoid a denial by the responding party on the basis that your request was not entirely correct. For example:

> a. Maker, Jones Corporation, Inc., failed to make the quarterly payment of interest due October 30, 1988, on the outstanding principal balance on this "Note."
>
> b. Harper Jones, Jr., as a guarantor of this "Note," or in any other capacity, failed to make the quarterly payment of interest due October 30, 1988, on the outstanding principal balance on this "Note."
>
> c. Defendant Peter Brown, as a guarantor of this "Note," or in any other capacity, failed to make the quarterly payment of interest due October 30, 1988, on the outstanding principal balance on this "Note."
>
> d. Neither Maker, Jones Corporation, Inc., Harper Jones, Jr., nor Peter Brown, as principals or guarantors of this "Note," made the quarterly payment of interest due October 30, 1988, on this "Note."
>
> e. No person, firm, corporation or other entity has made the quarterly payment of interest due October 30, 1988, on the outstanding principal balance on this "Note."

trant party be stricken;[11] that whole pleadings be stricken;[12] or that judgment be rendered in favor of the discovering party.[13] These orders are for more drastic misconduct, such as total lack of response to requests and subsequent violation of the order to compel.

    3. Contempt citations for violations of court orders or flagrant misconduct.[14]

    4. Monetary sanctions (e.g., losing party pays expenses of motion to winning party) for overall lack of cooperation and failure to obey orders.[15]

    You may assist your attorney to compel discovery in one or more of the following ways:

- Analyzing responses.
- Researching validity of objections or responses.
- Preparing briefs in support of a motion to compel.
- Preparing a motion to compel.

Analyzing Responses

In a complex case, analyze the objections to determine their validity. For example, in a negligence action wherein the plaintiff sued a manufacturer to recover damages for injuries sustained by the plaintiff, the defendant sent interrogatories to the plaintiff requesting information regarding medical treatment, damages sustained, manufacturer's warranties and warnings received.

    One of the four main objections by the plaintiff was that the information sought had been provided in prior depositions, interrogatories, medical reports, records or bills. The paralegal was asked to determine whether information sought by the defendant (client) was actually in the prior discovery documents. This information was used to prepare the motion to compel.

Researching Validity of Objections or Responses

Your research in most instances will be done to prove the validity of the objection (e.g., attorney-client privilege or work product). Depending upon the complexity of the case, your research may involve simple statutory law or complex case law. For example, if the grounds for objection are physician-patient privilege, you may have to research whether the applicable statutes make it a valid objection. Or if the grounds for objection are attorney work product involving a witness's statement, you may review numerous cases to determine if the particular circumstances surrounding the taking of the statement in question tend to prove the assertion that it was prepared in anticipation of trial.

Preparing Briefs in Support of Motion to Compel

To determine if a brief is required to support the motion to compel, consult your attorney first, then check the pertinent local court rules. In a complex case, a

---

[11]Ibid., Rule 37(b)(2)(B).

[12]Ibid., Rule 37(b)(2)(C).

[13]Ibid., Rule 37(b)(2)(C).

[14]Ibid., Rule 37(b)(2)(D).

[15]Ibid., Rule 37(b)(2)(E).

supporting brief will clarify the facts for the judge. The memorandum of law should summarize the facts, the nature of the objections, the argument and a summary. The argument should delineate the contentions of the discovering party and the supporting case and statutory law. (see Chapter 10).

Preparing a Motion to Compel

The following discussion is based upon Rule 37(a) of the *Federal Rules of Civil Procedure*. Check your state statutes and procedural rules for actions filed in state courts. Here is a step-by-step procedure for preparing a motion to compel discovery.

• Step 1: Determine the proper court.

An application for an order or motion to compel discovery must be made in the court where the action is pending. On matters relating to a deposition of a party or a nonparty, it may also be made in the court in the district where the deposition is being taken.

• Step 2: Prepare the introductory paragraph.

The introductory paragraph should contain the particular rule that applies, that is, Rule 37(a) (Federal District Court), and the introduction of the parties. For example:

> The defendant R. K. DRUG COMPANY moves the Court pursuant to Section 37(a) of the *Federal Rules of Civil Procedure* for an Order compelling Plaintiff SHELLEY JONES to respond fully and completely in writing, under oath, to its First Interrogatories to the Plaintiff of the following grounds, to wit:
>
> 1.
>
> On the 14th day of February, 1988, Defendant R. K. DRUG COMPANY filed with this Court and Served its First Interrogatories Propounded to Plaintiff upon Plaintiff SHELLEY JONES.
>
> 2.
>
> Plaintiff SHELLEY JONES has not filed any Answer to these Interrogatories.

• Step 3: Prepare the concluding "prayer" in which the action wanted is specified.

An example follows:

> WHEREFORE Defendant R. K. DRUG COMPANY prays that an Order be issued requiring Plaintiff SHELLEY JONES to respond fully and completely to Defendant R. K. DRUG COMPANY's First Interrogatories Propounded to Plaintiff, SHELLEY JONES, and for the imposition of sanctions against Plaintiff SHELLEY JONES, including Defendant's attorney's fees incurred herein.

In a motion to impose sanctions, the prayer might read as follows:

> WHEREFORE, Defendant R. K. DRUG COMPANY prays that an Order be duly issued, pursuant to Sections 37(b) and 37(b)(2)(C) of the *Federal Rules of Civil Procedure,* striking out Plaintiff SHELLEY JONES' pleadings or rendering a default judgment against Plaintiff SHELLEY JONES, and that Plaintiff or her attorney be required to pay the reasonable expenses, including attorney's fees caused by the failure to answer.

IN THE SUPERIOR COURT OF SHELBY COUNTY
STATE OF TENNESSEE

Shelley Jones, Plaintiff,	)))	Civil Action
v.	))	File No. B-97335
R.K. Drug Company Defendant.	)))	

MOTION TO COMPEL DISCOVERY

COMES NOW the Defendant, R.K. DRUG COMPANY, and moves the Court pursuant to Section 37(a) of the Federal Rules of Civil Procedure, for an Order compelling Plaintiff, SHELLEY JONES, to respond fully and completely in writing, under oath, to its First Interrogatories, to Plaintiff on the following grounds, to wit:

1.

On the 14th day of February, 1988, Defendant, R.K. DRUG COMPANY, filed with this Court and served its First Interrogatories Propounded to Plaintiff upon Plaintiff, SHELLEY JONES.

2.

Plaintiff, SHELLEY JONES, has not filed any Answer to these Interrogatories.

WHEREFORE, Defendant, R.K. DRUG COMPANY, prays that an Order issue requiring Plaintiff, SHELLEY JONES, to respond fully and completely to Defendant, R.K. DRUG COMPANY's First Interrogatories Propounded to Plaintiff, SHELLEY JONES, and for the imposition of sanctions against Plaintiff, SHELLEY JONES to include Defendant R.K. DRUG COMPANY's attorney's fees incurred herein.

This 19th day of March, 1988.

Respectfully submitted,

_____

Gordon Duffin
Attorney for Defendant

1801 Century Park East
Memphis, Tennessee
(901) 658-8080   (Certificate of Service)

• **Step 4:   Conclude with signature line and certificate of service.**

Refer again to Form 8.1 to see a certificate of service.

An example of the completed motion to compel is shown in Form 8.3.

If a motion to compel discovery is granted as a result of unanswered requests for admissions, under Rule 37 of the *Federal Rules of Civil Procedure,* the court may require either the party, deponent, or attorney whose conduct necessitated the motion to pay the moving party the reasonable expenses incurred in obtaining the order, including attorney's fees.[16]

On the other hand, if the motion to compel is denied, the court may require the moving party, or the attorney advising the motion, or both of them, to pay to the party who opposed the motion the reasonable expenses incurred in opposing the motion, including attorney's fees. If the motion is granted in part and denied in part, the court may apportion the reasonable expenses incurred in relation to the motion among the parties and persons.

• Protective Orders

A motion for protective order differs from an objection to discovery, which may be filed based on specific grounds, such as attorney-client privilege or work product. The discovering party may respond by moving for an order to compel discovery. If the order to compel discovery is granted, the responding party may move for a *protective order* to protect the party from embarrassment, oppression, undue burden or expense. A party may also move for a protective order against producing confidential documents, such as trade secrets. The protective order may stipulate that such documents be disclosed only to counsel or to certain other persons.

The court may also issue a protective order when the period for discovery has expired or will expire before the statutory period for answering a particular discovery document has expired. Paralegals should be aware that a discovery period is limited by statute, and in order to extend it, it will usually be necessary to get the permission of the court. Because this is a legal procedure that is sometimes unsuccessful, paralegals should take care to enter the discovery period limits of all their cases in their tickler system. Under Rule 26(c) of the *Federal Rules of Civil Procedure,* protective orders may provide that:

1. The discovery not be had. For example:

Interrogatory No. 6 need not be answered because it is irrelevant.

2. The discovery be had only on specified terms and conditions, including a designation of time or place. For example:

Deposition is to take place at deponent's office.

3. The discovery be had only by a method of discovery other than that selected by the party seeking discovery. For example, if the discovering party requests that an oral deposition be taken of a deponent who is severely ill, the court might order that written interrogatories be served instead.

4. Certain matters not be inquired into, or that the scope of discovery be limited to certain matters. For example, if the discovering party has previously spent a large amount of time on irrelevant matters in prior discovery, the court might order that discovery be limited to certain issues.

---

[16]Ibid., Rule 37(a)(4).

5. Discovery be conducted with no one present except the persons designated by the court. For example, if the discovering party desires to inquire into highly personal matters, the court might order that only certain persons be present at the deposition.

6. A sealed deposition sealed be opened only by order of the court. Thus, in the foregoing example, the court might order the deposition to be sealed and opened only by order of the court (called *in camera* inspection).

7. A trade secret or other confidential research, development, or commercial information not be disclosed or be disclosed only in a designated way.

8. The parties simultaneously file specified documents or information enclosed in sealed envelopes to be opened as directed by the court (at a specified time in front of only specified persons).

• Depositions and Deposition Digests

One of your primary tasks as a litigation paralegal will be to schedule depositions and to summarize, or *digest*, depositions. A *deposition* is a formal procedure in which a person answers questions under oath. The person giving the testimony, whether he or she is a party, witness, or an expert, is called a *deponent*. Depositions allow the counsel for both sides to gather factual information from the written testimony of the parties, witnesses, and experts. This information helps them determine their strategy. Also, counsel may spot inconsistencies or weaknesses in testimony that allow impeachment of a witness or expert.[17] For example, if the deponent says that it was rainy at the time of accident, and at trial says it was a sunny day, the difference in testimony may serve to throw doubt on the reliability of the deponent's trial testimony. The transcribed deposition may or may not be entered into the record for trial. It can be offered as evidence at trial in the case of a deceased or absentee witness.

Scope of a Deposition

Depositions allow counsel to depose persons besides the parties, such as experts, document record custodians, witnesses, bystanders, neighbors who may serve as character witnesses, and others. The scope of the deposition, examination, and cross-examination, is covered by Rule 30(c) of the *Federal Rules of Evidence*. Rule 26(b) covers all other aspects of depositions. Always check state statutes as well.

Types of Depositions

There are three types of depositions:

1. Depositions on oral exam.
2. Depositions on written questions.
3. Depositions taken before the action is commenced.

---

[17]Ibid., Rule 32.

Depositions on oral exam are the most common type of deposition used. Governed by Rule 30 of the *Federal Rules of Civil Procedure,* these depositions are most like the actual trial in that the deponent takes an oath, and questions and answers are exchanged, although there is no jury or judge.

Depositions on written questions are infrequently used. Under Rule 31, this device is most often used to gather information on matters not in dispute and on documents from a person other than a party. The person is read direct questions from one party and cross-questions from the other party, who answers the questions orally in the presence of a person authorized to administer oaths. For example, under Rule 31, written questions about the authenticity of medical records may be asked of a records custodian.

Depositions taken before the action is commenced is governed by Rule 27 and is primarily used to preserve testimony that may be unavailable later—for example, in the case of a terminally ill witness or a witness who will later be out of the country. Rule 27 contains rather strict requirements.

Paralegal's Role in Depositions

Although paralegals cannot take a deposition or actively participate in them, they can:

1. Assist in assessing and identifying potential witnesses.
2. Conduct a preliminary interview of the client deponent (does not apply to adverse parties).
3. Schedule the deposition.
4. Draft key questions for the attorney to ask at the deposition.
5. Prepare the client or expert for testifying at the deposition.
6. Gather information and prepare exhibits.
7. Take notes during the deposition.
8. Review the deposition for inconsistencies, omitted questions, and specific information.
9. Observe the deponent during trial.
10. Assist the attorney in various ways during the deposition.

Assist in Assessing and Identifying Potential Witnesses

Although your attorney will make the ultimate decision about whom to depose, you can assist your attorney by providing information and facts that might help identify potential witnesses. First, you must be familiar with the facts of the case and the pleadings. One key document will be the opponent's answers to interrogatories.

You also may provide some strategic analysis of prospective witnesses based on your perceptions of the case and information you have gathered. Be alert for any hostile witnesses who may hurt the case. Keep good notes on any observations you have of potential witnesses for future use by your attorney.

Conduct a Preliminary Interview

If the attorney is unsure whether or not to take a particular person's deposition, she may ask you to interview the potential witness to determine whether he has knowledge of the facts relevant to and supportive of the client's case. In this particular type of interview, it is imperative that you understand the specific facts the attorney wants to establish. For example, if you represent the plaintiff in a personal injury action, you may be requested to interview the physician who treated your client immediately following an accident. In this situation, the attorney wants to know whether your client, the plaintiff in a personal injury case, made any specific complaints regarding his injuries to the doctor. If he did make such complaints, which would help prove your client's case, then the attorney may decide to subpoena the doctor for the deposition. On the other hand, if you find that the client did not make any relevant statement to the doctor, you will have saved not only your attorney's time, but also the doctor's time. Additionally, the client will save legal fees.

Schedule the Deposition

Here is a step-by-step procedure for scheduling a deposition:

- **Step 1:** **Check the date and time legally allowed for the deposition, and confirm deponent's deposition date and time.**

Make sure that the deposition is not scheduled within 30 days of service of the summons and complaint pursuant to Rule 30(a) or your local court rules. Check with your attorney, the client if he is to be present, and the attorneys for the parties. If your attorney instructs you, check with the person who is being deposed if it is your attorney's client or the attorney for the person being deposed.

You may be requested to contact the deponent to make arrangements for the deposition. The deponent may be a client who has previously spoken with the attorney concerning the deposition, an expert witness, or a nonparty witness such as a character witness or eyewitness. Make certain all parties are aware of the specific time, date, and place of the deposition. Keep notes of contacts made to schedule the deposition so that if a change is made in the deposition schedule, you will know whom to contact.

Because depositions of some nonparties, such as physicians or psychologists, may be particularly difficult to arrange because of their busy schedules, give ample notice by contacting the deponent as soon as possible about the deposition. It is always best to serve a notice of deposition on the deponent. If the deponent is served and does not appear, sanctions may apply. If the deposition is rescheduled, serve another, revised notice on the deponent. Physicians will frequently request that the deposition be conducted in their office and will normally charge a fee for their time (see Step 6).

- **Step 2:** **Arrange for the site of the deposition.**

The deposition may be held in the firm's or opposing counsel's conference room, a hotel conference room, a room at the courthouse, or another mutually agreeable site. Remember that the plaintiff may be required to attend a deposition in the jurisdiction where the action was brought. Other persons may be deposed in the jurisdiction where they live and work. Sometimes doctors' depositions are scheduled at their offices. Check to see that the arrangements are suitable, with proper facilities, including power outlets and convenient access to necessary facilities.

- **Step 3: Arrange for the court reporter to be present or for some other method of recording.**

A court reporter must also be scheduled for the deposition. If possible, try to use the same court reporter throughout all discovery proceedings, particularly in large and complex cases. Familiarity with the terminology and facts of a case can improve the reporter's accuracy and efficiency. This also enables you to design and implement a uniform system for marking and indexing exhibits to depositions. Always confirm the date, time, and location of the deposition with the court reporter the morning of the scheduled deposition.

- **Step 4: Prepare witness fee checks, if requested.**

Check with your attorney to see if any witness fee checks need to be prepared for the deposition. Check relevant statutes to determine the amount of the fee and whether a mileage fee check is applicable. Be sure to allow plenty of time to obtain the check from your accounting or bookkeeping department.

- **Step 5: Calendar the deposition date.**

Finally, enter the deposition date on your attorney's desk and pocket calendar or in the firm's tickler system. Inform the receptionist if the deposition is scheduled to be held in a particular conference room.

- **Step 6: Prepare notices to take depositions.**

It is important to prepare notices to take depositions to ensure that the deposition is a matter of record. If the deposition date changes, then prepare an "Amended Notice to Take Deposition." You need to keep all discovery dates in mind. For example, in federal court all discovery depositions must be taken by the discovery end date. The one exception is evidentiary depositions, which are allowed after the discovery cut-off date.

Draft Key Questions

While the attorney has the primary responsibility for finalizing the questions for the deposition, you may be requested to draft outlines of suggested questions. To prepare such questions, review the pleadings, discovery documents, notes, and other information in the client's file. Learn the basic facts of the case and the purpose of the deposition. Understanding your attorney's strategy for the deposition will help you tailor the questions to the specific points your attorney wants to cover.

Prepare Client or Expert

The attorney will normally discuss the deposition with the client and may instruct you to talk with the client as well and remind him of the basic instructions. Exhibit 8.1 presents a checklist of these basic instructions.

Explaining the deposition procedure to the client will help eliminate some of his nervousness resulting from a fear of the unknown. Assure him that all deponents are nervous, and remind him that it will be easier if he relaxes and acts naturally. Explain the basic purpose of the deposition to him, for example, that it will aid discovery. Remind the client that the attorney will be there if needed, and that he may consult with the attorney during the deposition, if

Exhibit 8.1

Checklist for
Preparing Your Client
for a Deposition

○ Dress neatly and cleanly; no flashy clothes.

○ Tell the truth at all times. (Be careful about prior claims.)

○ Answer the questions directly, giving short answers; then stop talking. Never volunteer any information.

○ Be courteous at all times and do not lose your temper.

○ Don't memorize.

○ If you are asked whether you discussed your testimony with your attorney, say of course you did.

○ If you don't understand a question, ask that it be repeated or explained.

○ If you made a mistake, correct it as soon as possible.

○ Don't look at your attorney for help when asked a question.

○ Pause to allow time for your attorney to make objections.

Source: Charles E. Robbins, *Attorney's Master Guide To Expediting Top-Dollar Case Settlements* (Englewood Cliffs, NJ: Executive Reports Corporation, 1977), p. 509.

necessary. However, the client should be aware that too many consultations may tend to put the opposing counsel on guard or make the veracity of the client's testimony suspect.

Rehearse the deposition questions with the client, if necessary. Explain to the client that personal questions referring to his residence, name and aliases, marital status, children, relatives, employment history, and medical history are normally asked for specific purposes. For example, the determination of the deponent's relatives may alert counsel to potential jurors who are related to the deponent. Also an inquiry into the deponent's past residences and aliases might be helpful to counsel in establishing or refuting damages. Of course, many questions are directed to the deponent for purposes of impeaching his testimony. You should also tell the client, "If your attorney states an objection, stop talking and do not complete your answer unless your attorney so directs."

Gather Information and Prepare Exhibits

To prepare for conducting the deposition properly, the attorney frequently needs a summary of relevant information and exhibits. For example, in a personal injury action, the attorney may need a compilation of damages, such as medical and miscellaneous expenses. Your previous record keeping is valuable here. Use the various forms and checklists shown throughout this book to prepare information in an accessible form for the attorney's convenience.

Prepare exhibits and evidence as you would prepare them for trial, making sure that the copies are legible for identification by the court reporter (see Chapter 12). Do not damage original exhibits or evidence by stapling or cutting without your attorney's permission.

Take Notes During Deposition

Paralegals may attend depositions for the purpose of observation, training, notetaking, and offering assistance to the attorney. Because there is usually insufficient time to take complete notes during the deposition, outline the testimony of the deponent, jotting down the main points. If you think of a question that the attorney did not ask that may be important, write the question on a piece of paper and inconspicuously hand it to the attorney when there is a pause in the questioning. A well-founded question is worth the interruption.

Review Deposition

When the court reporter returns the deposition, the attorney may request you to review it for errors, inconsistencies, and omissions prior to the deponent's review. Omitted questions may be asked in future interrogatories, depositions, or at trial. The attorney may also ask you to extract specific information from the deposition, such as the amount of medical expenses. Inconsistencies can be used to impeach the opposing party's testimony. For instance, on page 10 the deponent may state that he has never been involved in another civil action, but on page 54, he may indicate that he sued a woman whose automobile collided with the back of his.

Observe Deponent

If the deponent is a witness for the opposite party, observe her during the deposition to detect any obvious signs of extraordinary nervousness, such as facial expressions or fidgeting. These signs may indicate that the deponent is not being fully truthful. If you feel that the deponent is lying, tell the attorney during the recess.

Assist Attorney

During the deposition the attorney may request you to leave the room to obtain particular information or to make a telephone call for her. Your assistance enables the attorney to better concentrate on taking the deposition.

Deposition Digests

A deposition digest is a condensation or summary of the actual deposition. It usually includes a line-by-line description of the highlights of the deposition, including the page and line number, together with a brief summary of one or more pages. Deposition digests help the attorney review the deposition more quickly and make it easier to find a particular part of the deposition. They are usually typed in an organized linear format with most of the text written in a brief style, often with abbreviations.

For trial attorneys, digesting depositions is an important task that is ideally suited for delegation to an accomplished paralegal. Any reader who has spent endless hours indexing and summarizing depositions can well understand why the attorney would want to delegate this task to someone else. It can be a burdensome and tedious job, but the results can prove invaluable at trial during the examination of a witness. Of course, your attorney must trust your ability to bring all important facts into the summary before he or she will assign you this task.

The How, Why, and When of Deposition Digests

Whether a deposition is taken for discovery or evidentiary purposes, or both, the litigating attorney should have a summary of it if she wants to use it to best advantage. A deposition is usually taken months or years before trial, often by an attorney other than the one who ultimately tries the case, in which case the

litigating attorney may have difficulty finding the portions she wants. Sometimes the deposition is simply too long to permit rapid location of desired portions testimony, even if the attorney prepared it herself and is familiar with it.
Whatever the circumstances, a deposition digest should always be prepared.
More complex cases may require more detailed digests and an index, as will be
discussed later in this chapter.

For a deposition to be used effectively at the trial, the attorney must know not
only its substance, but also have a reference to the exact location of pertinent
testimony, by page and line number. Trial attorneys are familiar with the courtroom
spectacle of judge and jury waiting impatiently while the embarrassed attorney
hurriedly thumbs through a deposition to locate a choice quotation of impeaching
testimony. By the time she finds it, the threat of her cross-examination has been
broken and the impact of the impeaching testimony seriously diminished. This
failure can be avoided by summarizing and indexing the deposition before trial.

Traditionally, most attorneys have prepared their own summaries or digests, and it probably makes sense in many cases for the attorney to jot down a
summary of a short deposition transcript rather than delegate the work to someone else less familiar with the case. The growing trend, however, is for the
attorney to involve the paralegal from the inception of the case, and thus the
paralegal is completely familiar with the case and will be better able to prepare
a workable summary. More and more paralegals are attending depositions to
take notes for reference to use until the actual transcript is received and to
observe and take notes on the demeanor of the deponent in preparation for trial.

Deposition summarizing requires a well-organized and analytical mind far
more than a substantive knowledge of the law, thus, the professional caliber of
the legal work on the case will not suffer from a non-attorney (a paralegal)
preparing the digest. This permits the attorney's time to be spent more profit-
ably. Regardless of whether the paralegal attends the deposition, there are several ways the attorney may finally assign a particular deposition for summary to
the paralegal:

1. If the paralegal is extremely competent in summarizing depositions, the
attorney can merely give the transcript to the paralegal with an instruction to
summarize. The paralegal makes an evaluation on which summary method to
use based on the complexity and length of the deposition.

2. If the paralegal is somewhat experienced in summarizing depositions and is
already familiar with the case or has prepared digests for cases with similar issues
and fact situations, the attorney will need only to consult briefly with the paralegal
and help him or her decide on the summary method.

3. If the paralegal has limited experience and is unfamiliar with the case, the
attorney can give a brief, oral outline of the facts or have the paralegal read the
pleadings and memos in the file before summarizing, and indicate to the paralegal which areas of questioning are particularly important.

In cases involving complex litigation, the deposition should be summarized
as soon as the transcript is received, so that need for further discovery can be
determined and satisfied. In other cases, such as personal injury cases, firms
often delay preparations until trial is imminent. The likelihood of settlement
makes early preparations a waste of effort and money. These firms sometimes do
not even order a copy of the deposition transcript until it comes clear the case
will not be settled. This approach overlooks the fact that early preparation of
summaries often promotes settlement by encouraging litigants to view realisti-

cally the strengths and weaknesses of their case. On the other hand, a digest that is prepared after all discovery has been completed may be more significant, because the attorney can then better evaluate the deposition testimony and have the substance of the testimony fresh in mind when he tries the case.

It is customary to draft the deposition digest by using the first person singular and omitting personal pronouns, "I", "we", "he", "she", and "they". For example, if the deponent states,

> My sister and I were walking on Main Street when we heard an awful screech of tires, and we saw this red car plow into the rear of the pickup. We saw all this glass flying all over the place,

the deposition digest might read,

> Pedestrian Smith observed accident on Main Street; heard tires screech; observed red car hit rear of pickup; saw flying glass.

While it takes significant time to summarize such sentences, the attorney time saved in review of the deposition will give him the opportunity to spend time in other areas. Five methods of digesting a deposition transcript are:

1. Simple case short deposition.
2. Index.
3. Chronological summary or line-by-line summary.
4. Narrative summary.
5. Summary by category.

We will discuss each of these methods, using, in most cases, as an example a maritime personal injury case in which a paralegal has summarized plaintiff Lewis's deposition for defendant Smith Company's attorneys. After consulting with the trial attorney, the paralegal has noted all statements relating to plaintiff's version of the accident and his damages. Any statements or admissions that could bear on Smith Company's liability—that is, working conditions, plaintiff's prior experience with similar cargo operations, or possible defects in work method—are also noted.

This deposition has been digested without reference to other information in the file, as is quite often the actual practice. It is useful to insert notes in the summary where statements reflect on other information already developed, particularly where discrepancies exist. For example, it could be noted if additional witnesses not named by the deponent were named in answers to interrogatories, or if the medical records revealed treatment not discussed in the testimony. Comments might also be made where particular statements have a bearing on liability and where certain statements suggest the need for further investigation or discovery, including additional interrogatories.

Simple Case, Short Deposition

In a simple case there are usually few depositions and none are lengthy. Summaries need be no more than factual statements from the transcript, with page and line reference. Many deposition transcripts contain a blank page entitled, "Personal Notes" that is designed for this purpose (see Form 8.4). When filled in by the attorney or paralegal, the page provides a rough chronological summary of the deposition in which asterisks are used to signal important statements.

Form 8.4
•
Example of a
Short Deposition in a
Simple Case

PAGE	LINE	PERSONAL NOTES
5	8	Visibility poor. Fog on highway.
6	10-16	Speed "about 35-40" when first saw plaintiff.
6	22-25	Plaintiff's vehicle 30-40 yards in front when first saw it. Defendant applied brakes immediately "hard".
9	2	Read statement taken by police and signed it.
9	5*	Never told police plaintiff's tail-light not on.
11	7-10	Refreshed recollection before depo. by reading over statement he gave to Ins. Co. two days after acc. [MOVE TO COMPEL PRODUCTION]

Source: Reprinted with permission of the National Association of Legal Assistants, Inc., 1601 S. Main, Suite 300, Tulsa, OK 74119. This material appeared in an article entitled "The Legal Assistant and Preparing Deposition Summaries" by Lana J. Clark, CLA, published in the October 1986 issue of FACTS & FINDINGS.

Thus, in a simple personal injury case, the attorney or paralegal might, after the deposition is taken, fill in the summary page as shown in Form 8.4.

Index

An index (Form 8.5) is the easiest to prepare and least detailed summary method. The main subjects are listed by pages. It can be used alone, or to provide access to both the chronological summary (discussed next) and the deposition transcript itself. The combination is especially useful if the chronological summary is lengthy, or particular subjects appear at many different pages of the transcript.

Form 8.5

Index to Deposition

SMITH CO./LEWIS
D/A: 3/3/84
SHIP: S.S. SEAWORTHY

INDEX TO DEPOSITION OF PLAINTIFF 4/22/85

Subject	Pages
Circumstances of Injury	
Accident scene & location	4, 5, 26
Cargo and gear	6, 7, 9, 10, 11, 17
Exhibit	38
How accident occurred	9, 10, 11, 13, 18, 29
Description of dunnage	10, 11, 30, 32
Notice and complaints	11, 23, 27
Work method	7, 8, 9, 17, 29, 30, 32
Injury	
Description	3, 4
Disability	14, 19, 27, 34
Residuals	15, 20, 23, 24, 34
Treatment	15, 20, 21, 23, 27, 28
Plaintiff's Gang	
Hatch tenders	5, 28
Identification	3, 4, 5
Location	6, 29, 30
Supervisory personnel	13
Witness to accident	12, 19
Work partner	4, 22
Work History	
Current work	25, 26, 35
Lost time, this accident	14, 21, 24, 34, 35
Prior to injury	16, 25, 35
Vacations	26
Expenses	25
Prior Suits	21

Source: Reprinted with permission of the National Association of Legal Assistants, Inc., 1601 S. Main, Suite 300, Tulsa, OK 74119. This material appeared in an article entitled "The Legal Assistant and Preparing Deposition Summaries" by Lana J. Clark, CLA, published in the October 1986 issue of FACTS & FINDINGS.

If the index is the only summary to be prepared, you can make a handwritten list of subjects and annotate the page references while reading through the transcript. If the index is to be used as an adjunct to the more detailed chronological summary, you will, of course, have to wait until it is more easily prepared after the chronological summary is prepared.

Chronological Summary

The chronological summary (Form 8.6) covers the subjects of the deposition page by page, in the order they appear in the transcript. Citations are to page and line; major topics are underlined for easier visual reference, and asterisks signal important statements. The paralegal can easily dictate the summary. Because the statements are taken chronologically from the deposition, there is no time spent collating subject references. As previously discussed, an index such

SMITH CO./LEWIS
D/a: 3/3/84
SHIP: S.S. SEAWORTHY

Deposition of Plaintiff 4/22/85

Page	Lines	Contents
3	3-12	Address: 1234 Shady Lane - for past 8 years. Married 15 years, wife May
	17-21	Description of injury: Injuries to left ankle and/or foot
4	1	Membership gang No. 15, frontman
	4-14	Work partner: Bob Strong. Have been 20 years on and off. Are social acquaintances as well.
	16-18	Lewis is a registered longshoreman, Class A Work No. 235423.
	19-25	Has had no injuries to left leg prior or subsequent to this injury.
	27	Arrived at work D/A 6 p.m. Night shift
5	1-3	Vessel berth: 111, Long Beach
	4-14	Shed lights were on and visibility on the apron was reading strength at time of acc., which was 1:30 a.m., 3/3
	17-21	There were no frontmen save plaintiff and his partner

Source: Reprinted with permission of the National Association of Legal Assistants, Inc., 1601 S. Main, Suite 300, Tulsa, OK 74119. This material appeared in an article entitled "The Legal Assistant and Preparing Deposition Summaries" by Lana J. Clark, CLA published in the October 1986 issue of FACTS & FINDINGS.

as the one shown in Form 8.5 may be prepared as an adjunct to a lengthy chronological summary.

Narrative Summary

Unlike the other summaries, the narrative (Form 8.7) is only a report on the testimony rather than an actual reference tool. It is, therefore, most useful for status reports or case evaluations and is usually not the only summary prepared except, for example, when the deposition is of a minor witness and the time needed to prepare a more detailed summary is not warranted.

If the narrative is the only summary needed, it can be prepared from notes or dictation after the deposition has been reviewed for its highlights. If a chronological or categorized summary has been already prepared, it can be used to provide the information for the narrative.

Summary by Category

The summary by category (Form 8.8) is the most detailed and time-consuming, but it is especially valuable when a deposition is lengthy and complex. There are several ways to prepare a summary by category:

1. The paralegal can first dictate a detailed index or chronological summary. Once that is transcribed, statements about particular objects can be brought together either by "cut-and-paste" method or by dictation from the summary. (The example in Form 8.8 was prepared from a chronological summary.)

Form 8.7

Narrative Summary

SMITH CO./LEWIS
D/A: 3/3/84
SHIP: S.S. SEAWORTHY

Deposition of Plaintiff 4/22/85

Circumstances of injury: This injury occurred when two steel coils were discharged to the front from the vessel, S.S. Seaworthy. A piece of dunnage, estimated to be a 4x4, was lodged between the two coils. The dunnage was released as the coils were lowered to the dock, and it fell into plaintiff's work area. As plaintiff stepped forward to unhook the bridle from the cargo, he stepped on the dunnage and sustained an injury to his left ankle.

Working Conditions: Plaintiff testified that at the time of the accident the front area was well lit, and that there was no grease, oil, or other unusual substance on the dock surface.

Work Method: The coils were lifted out of the hatch by means of a crane using wire bridles. No more than two coils were taken out at a time. Plaintiff testified that the coils lay side-by-side during the lift with their hollow centers in a horizontal position. It was plaintiff's job to unsling the coils once they were brought over the apron to the dock.

Notice and complaints: Plaintiff stated it is not unusual to find dunnage lodged in this kind of cargo, but that normally it is insignificant, "just like trash." He did not see any dunnage the evening of the accident, however. There was nothing unusual with respect to either the cargo or the equipment, and no complaints were made by any personnel with respect to the operation.

Source: Reprinted with permission of the National Association of Legal Assistants, Inc., 1601 S. Main, Suite 300, Tulsa, OK 74119. This material appeared in an article entitled "The Legal Assistant and Preparing Deposition Summaries" by Lana J. Clark, CLA, published in the October 1986 issue of FACTS & FINDINGS.

2. The paralegal can label sheets of paper with headings for each subject to be covered and write statements on the appropriate pages while reading through the deposition.

3. The transcript can first be photocopied in its entirety, then all statements pertaining to a given subject be cut from the copy and pasted together to make the summary. Parts of the transcript may have to be duplicated more than once if they pertain to more than one category.

The time and expense of the last method usually make it impractical for all but the largest cases or the most complex depositions. By bringing together statements from several volumes of testimony, it can become a useful tool for the impeachment of a witness at trial, because it provides quick access to full quotations on a given subject.

Basic Guidelines for Deposition Digests

Digesting depositions is often the primary function of the litigation paralegal. At times this task is tedious, especially when the testimony is repetitious, but an accurate digest is extremely important to the attorney. Concentration is essential to ensure accuracy. Beware of becoming lax as a result of boredom. Keep in mind that your attorney will be able to present a better case with a well-prepared, accurate, and thorough digest. At trial the digest can be the focal point of the attorney's attention, and the court's attention as well.

At first, digesting depositions may seem awkward, but with experience you will learn to work through them more quickly. Here is the order in which to approach the task:

SMITH CO./LEWIS
D/A: 3/3/84
SHIP: S.S. SEAWORTHY

Deposition of Plaintiff 4/22/85

Subject and Statements	Page	Lines
CIRCUMSTANCES OF INJURY:		
Cargo: steel coils	6	10-28
Approximately 4 ft. high, 2 1/2 ft. wide, weighing 2 1/2 to 7 tons.		
Diameter varies		
Coils were bands of metal sheathing wrapped spool-fashion and hollow centers.	10	17-22
Gear: Shoreside-based mobile crane	7	2-11
Operator: Unknown longshoreman (not a member of plaintiff's gang)	8	15-28
Work Method: The coils were lifted by the crane, using a woven wire strap, 4" wide and 30' long having an eye at each end.	9	1-8
One eye was passed through the center of the coil and attached to the blacksmith on the gear. (See sketch-Exhibit A)	10	15-28
Accident scene and location: The vessel was moored at Berth 111, Long Beach.	5	1-3
The shed lights were on, and visibility on the apron were reading strength at the time of the accident.	5	4-13
How accident occurred: "The load was being lowered...on the dock, and I steeped forward to unhook the sling. As the spreader bar and hooks are being lowered down to me, I stepped forward on a piece of dunnage and twisted my ankle and fell.	9	20-28
Description of dunnage: Estimates the dunnage was 4x4" and 2' long.	10	8-16
When asked whether dunnage is unusual he responded: "There's always a few loose pieces of dunnage...in between the hollow of the coils...that...are not removed by the hold men."	11	15-21

INJURY

(The remainder of the summary would proceed in the above manner using the subject headings listed in the index.)

Source: Reprinted with permission of the National Association of Legal Assistants, Inc., 1601 S. Main, Suite 300, Tulsa, OK 74119. This material appeared in an article entitled "The Legal Assistant and Preparing Deposition Summaries" by Lana J. Clark, CLA, published in the October 1986 issue of FACTS & FINDINGS.

1. On a photocopy of the deposition, highlight the important questions and answers with a yellow marker.

2. Prepare deposition digest.

3. Prepare general index.

4. Prepare a word index for all depositions and documents, answers to interrogatories and admissions, etc., for use at trial.

The key to preparing an effective digest is to make it brief by condensing each page of testimony to no more than one or two short sentences. More sentences might be necessary for technical depositions. Although some attorneys use slightly different methods for digesting depositions, here are some basic guidelines. You will develop your own shortcuts depending upon the nature of the litigation in which your attorney is involved and your own paralegal tasks. Be aware also that there are many types of sophisticated computer software designed specifically for digesting depositions, and many firms and independent consultants specialize in this area (see Chapters 12 and 13).

• Step 1: Become thoroughly familiar with the facts of the case.

Before you begin looking at the depositions, read all the documents in the file and discuss the case with the attorneys involved, if possible. Ask questions about any facts and issues you don't understand. Determine what the defenses and legal theories are. Take thorough notes. Go over the complete file and read all the notes that the attorney has made in interviews and for other preparation. Look at any evidence available. Ask your attorney for the questions used in the deposition, and ask what specific topics are of prime importance to the case.

• Step 2: Determine what form of digest your attorney prefers and what information should be included in the digest.

Ask your attorney what type of digest and what type of index is desired. In particular, ask if there is a specific style preferred for the digest and, if so, get samples of a similar digest. For example, your attorney may prefer a topical heading style and may even wish to give you the specific heading topics. If this is the first digest that you have done for this attorney, be sure to obtain a sample digest to follow. Also ask if there should be a particular emphasis on certain items of testimony.

Try to ask all your questions during the initial conversation with your attorney. Waiting until later to ask questions may find you at a loss when your attorney is unavailable.

As you probably already know, most attorneys are very particular about small details, such as the placement of commas (the rules of grammar permit some variation) and the use of underlining. You should get specific guidance on such details. Ask whether a paraphrased or ellipsis format is preferred. Also ask the attorney how and by whom the digest will be used. If it is to be used only by those who are very familiar with the case, it can be less detailed. Perhaps you need only to prepare an index, as was shown in Form 8.5. If, on the other hand, the digest is to be used by clients, co-counsel, or others outside the firm, a more complete and detailed summary may be needed, perhaps with an index as an adjunct to it. Other questions you might ask the attorney before preparing the digest are (1) how many digests are needed, (2) should they be cross-indexed, and (3) how much time should you spend on them.

You should discuss with your attorney what information in addition to the testimony of the witness should be included in the digest. For instance, some attorneys prefer to include certain extraneous information such as the names of those present at the deposition, objections made by counsel, or general colloquy between counsel.

Conversations between counsel may be summarized in some situations, as in, "Colloquy between counsel re: continuation of deposition." It may not be necessary to even summarize such conversations where no major objection, stipulation, or decision is involved. You should, however, make a note of any refusal by a witness to answer a question or an instruction by his attorney to answer, as in, "Jones instructed not to answer because of attorney-client privilege." Of course, you must be able to determine what testimony is important enough to be included. For instance, the educational or occupational background of a witness may not be important—unless he is an expert witness, in which case it is extremely important.

• Step 3.   Make a quick review of the deposition.

While it may seem a waste of time, skimming the deposition first will allow you to get a better feel for the breadth of the deposition, its importance to the case, and its place in the whole picture of the position your attorney represents. This cursory review will enable you to determine the scope of the deposition and the significance of certain issues. This way you can more easily spot the relevant parts of the deposition. Highlight them with a yellow marker. Jot down topical headings that are suggested by this quick review and add others as you make your more detailed review.

• Step 4:   Draft an outline.

After you have completed your quick review of the deposition, draft a topical outline or tentative table of contents, listing the topics in the sequential order from the deposition. Take the topical headings you have noted and arrange them in the order they appear in the deposition. For example:

Personal history

Education

Employment history

Medical history

Prior injuries and accidents

It may be necessary to repeat headings as they appear.

• Step 5:   Make a plan.

Preparing an organized plan for digesting the deposition will help you maintain continuity in your digest and ensure that all topics are covered. Making a time schedule is also a good idea to prevent you from spending too much time on one area.

• Step 6:   Prepare the digest.

You may dictate the digest, or you may compose it on a computer. As mentioned earlier, specialized software is available for this purpose. You may also choose to use a popular word processing software.

Note the identifying client and attorney information at the top of the page in Forms 8.5 through 8.8. Making captions or headings in the digest, as shown in Forms 8.7 and 8.8, will help the attorney locate specific portions of the deposition easily.

In a complex case you may have several depositions to digest. Keep the attorney informed of your progress so that he can (1) review them in preparation for trial, (2) send copies to co-counsel, and (3) determine if you are going to be able to complete them in time and, if not, obtain additional assistance.

As discussed earlier, it is best to use the first person singular, but to omit the personal pronoun ''I.'' For example, suppose the deponent stated,

Form 8.9

**Table of Contents for
Deposition Digest**

Client Name & Matter: R.H. Lewis v. M.L. White _____ File No.: 455L-179

Responsible Attorney(s): K. Overstreet/S. Ames _____ Date: 12/20/89

Deposition of: _____ Russell H. Lewis _____

Date(s) Taken: _____ December 5 & 6, 1989 _____

I reviewed Specification No. 1058-X on April 14, 1989, and noted the required service changes to the aircraft manufactured by Boeing Aircraft Corporation, but I was unable to make the changes.

You would draft the following sentence:

Reviewed Specification No. 1058-X, dtd. 4/14/89, w/reqd changes for Boeing aircraft; did not make changes.

• Step 7: Prepare table of contents for digest.

After you have completed your digest, you should prepare a table of contents (Form 8.9), which identifies the particular subjects and incidents referenced in the deposition. The description and page numbers are given to provide quick access to the contents of the deposition.

Exhibit Index

It is also helpful to prepare an exhibit index (Form 8.11) so your attorney can immediately identify the exhibits referenced in the depositions.

• Motions for Physical and Mental Examinations

If good cause can be shown, an adverse party is permitted to require the other party to submit to a physical and mental examination by an independent medical examiner. (Rule 35 of the *Federal Rules of Civil Procedure* and parallel state rules.) For example, in a medical malpractice action, this independent medical examination enables the other party to ascertain the actual mental or physical injuries and thus prevent fraudulent claims. In a paternity action, for example, the blood type of the child may be ascertained. In a negligence or automobile accident, physical injuries may be ascertained, as well as the potential for recovery of the injured party.

An examination is allowed under Rule 35(a) when two tests are met: (1) the alleged condition is in dispute, and (2) good cause exists to require the examination. *Good cause* is defined as a legitimate need to confirm the injury or to discover information that is apt to affect the case. The court interprets the term very strictly to prevent its abuse, and the intrusion into the privacy of the person subject to examination. Motions for medical examinations will be denied if the information can be acquired through other means. Personal injury cases require medical examinations more frequently. While most attorneys are cooperative regarding such exams, a motion for a court order may be required if an informal request is rejected or ignored.

• Summary

The process of discovery is a cumbersome one at times. A lot of paper is exchanged and a significant amount of information passes between the parties. Your role as a paralegal is to facilitate the exchange of this information in an organized fashion. You will be expected to know the whereabouts of all these documents and information so that you may respond to any requests your attorney may have at any time. In addition, you are likely to be called upon to prepare deposition digests, which are of immense value to your attorney. Your role in the discovery phase of litigation is key to the success of the outcome of the litigation. Be diligent, persistent, and organized, always questioning any inconsistencies.

9

Handling Medical Discovery

• Introduction[1]

A significant investment of money is usually required to pursue medical negligence claims, which are typically handled on a contingency basis. You may therefore be asked to assist your attorney in determining whether a case is meritorious. Everything you have learned about discovery applies here, but medical discovery involves some additional tasks.

In this chapter medical discovery is broken down into four phases:

1. Information gathering
2. Organizing and Reviewing Information
3. Selecting experts Witnesses
4. Preparing Clients and Expert Witnesses

We will use obstetrical negligence claims as our main example. Most medical negligence or medical malpractice cases that receive verdicts for large amounts of money are in this field. Specifically, they usually involve injury to or death of the *neonate* (babies one-month-old or less) as a result of negligence on the part of the delivering obstetrician. Occasionally, a claim involves injury or death to the mother. All medical negligence claims have much in common, so most of the information relating to these cases can be generalized to all types of medical negligence.

Because you will be dealing with many professionals in the medical discovery process, your manner must be highly professional at all times. The technical aspect of your job on a medical malpractice case will be an ongoing learning experience. Care must be taken to take good notes and double-check any questionable items. The medical terminology should prove a challenge in itself, but with good resource books, you will do fine.

• Phase 1: Information Gathering

The information gathering phase is subdivided into:

1. Conducting the initial client interview.
2. Obtaining pertinent medical records and documents.

---

[1] Todd W. Rudner, M.D., The Keenan Ashman Firm, Atlanta, Georgia, co-authored this chapter.

3. Organizing medical records.
4. Initial review of medical records.
5. Deciding whether the case is meritorious.

Initial Client Interview

In conducting client interviews, remember that any forms that you use are to serve as a guide and not as a control over the interview. Do not pay so much attention to the form that you forget to listen to the client so that you can direct your further questions based on the information that you receive from the client. Frequently, you will receive information from telephone calls from clients or referring attorneys as well. There are five vital questions you must have answered by the end of this initial contact:

- Referral source.
- Date of injury or death.
- Institution at which injury or death occurred.
- Client's contentions as to nature of alleged negligence.
- Present status regarding damages.

After analyzing this information, your attorney may make a decision not to take the case for any of the following reasons:

1. Statute problems.
2. Case is in the low range of damage awards, and your firm deals only with the high range.
3. Your firm has no experience with this type of case.

If your attorney has any question as to whether the case has merit, get the records needed to make a decision. Of course, if a referring attorney is calling, have the records forwarded to you for review. The following information is essential before proceeding with a medical negligence claim:

- Full name (maiden and married).
- Present address.
- Phone numbers.
- Date of birth.
- Social security number.
- Referred by whom.
- Previous attorneys who have reviewed case and their reactions.
- Name of injured or deceased party.
- Date of injury or death.

Since these cases almost always involve tragic outcomes to clients' loved ones, initial interviews can be difficult and somewhat emotional. However, the facts must be elicited. The more information that you can get on the first interview, the easier it will be to determine whether the case is worth pursuing.

First, you need to obtain a complete medical history with the following components:

- Past medical history.
- Family history.
- Obstetrical history.
- History regarding present claim.

Past Medical History

The past medical history can be very revealing. Prepare a checklist of items to ask the prospective client about, including:

- Hypertension (high blood pressure).
- Diabetes (insulin-dependent, diet-controlled, or requiring oral medication).
- Birth defects.
- Heart disease.
- Sexually transmitted diseases (herpes genitalis, genital warts, syphilis, gonorrhea, cytomegalovirus, or AIDS).

Family History

Information concerning the family history may be relevant to the prospective client's health or injuries. Inquire about such items as:

- Congenital or birth defects.
- Twins.
- Diabetes or gestational diabetes.

Obstetrical History

You need to establish your client's *gravidity* (how many times she has been pregnant, including the present pregnancy) and *parity* (how many times she gave birth). This information is typically subdivided into four parts, each represented by a number as follows:

G4 P 1 - 1 - 1 - 2

The number after "G" indicates how many times the woman has been pregnant, including a present pregnancy. The first number after "P" indicates the number of full-term births; the second, the number of pre-term births; the third, the number of abortions; and the fourth, the number of live births.

Thus, in this example, a woman presently pregnant has a history of one abortion, one previous live birth of a pre-term gestation, and one previous full-term live birth.

History Regarding Present Claim

An obstetrical claim must obtain a complete history of the prenatal period, labor and delivery period, initial neonatal course, and subsequent neonatal course. *Prenatal Period.* Your first step is to gather information about the pregnancy, that is, the period before labor and delivery. This would include the following:

- Complications.
  - Pregnancy-induced hypertension.
  - Gestational diabetes.
  - Infections.
  - Premature labor.

- Dates and results of examinations.
  - Ultrasound examinations.
  - Physical examinations.
- Status of fetus during pregnancy.
  - Movements.
  - Fetal heart tones.
  - Alpha-fetoprotein.

Labor and Delivery Period.   Your second step is to establish the events of the labor and delivery that are the subject of the present claim. This would include information on whether the client had a cesarean section, and if so, whether it was an emergency procedure or an elective one. If she had a spontaneous vaginal delivery, was it forceps-assisted, and if so, what were the indications for such assistance?

You also need to find out her hours in labor and results of any fetal monitoring, external or internal. Note any comments by nurses.

Initial Neonatal Course.   Your third step is to gather information on the initial neonatal period:

- The estimated gestational age of the neonate at birth.
- Results of APGARs.
- Whether the neonate was taken to the nursery or neonatal intensive care, and why.

Also find out the condition of neonate until hospital discharge, noting, for example, date of onset of any seizures, and so on. If the baby was transferred to another facility, note why.

Subsequent Neonatal Course.   Finally, gather information on the subsequent development of the injured neonate. If mother is the injured party, rather than the neonate, the same information is required. Always ask the client what her contentions are as to the breaches of standard care. Many times this information has no bearing whatsoever on actual breaches of standard of care, but clients should be invited to thoroughly voice their opinions.

Obtaining Medical Records and Documents

Experience will help you to determine what records you will need. However, in general, for obstetrical cases you will need the following:

- Labor and delivery flowsheet.
- Discharge summary.
- Prenatal visits flowsheet (submitted by the doctor when patient is admitted to the hospital for labor and delivery).
- Operative report (if cesarean section was performed).

For non-Obstetrical cases, you will need:

- Ambulance report sheet.
- Emergency Room (ER) sheet.
- Discharge summary.
- History and physical examination records.

Form 9.1

Health Care Authorization Form

HEALTH CARE RECORDS AUTHORIZATION FORM

TO: (Name of physician or medical care facility)

    Please allow my attorneys, _____ , or their representatives, to examine and copy any and all records you have in your possession in regard to the treatment, care and/or confinement of the undersigned.

_____

(Patient)

_____

(Address)

_____

(City/State/Zip)

Birthdate: _____

Subscribed and sworn to this

_____ day of _____ , 19____.

_____

Notary Public

My commission expires:

_____

    Three key documents that you must have in order to obtain records from any physician, hospital, or medical facility are the health care authorization form (release) (Form 9.1), the obstetrical intake sheet (Form 9.2), and the developmental questionnaire (Form 9.3). Health care authorization forms should be signed by the client but not dated, because you may need to request follow-up records at a later date, and many hospitals will not provide records if requested more than 30 days from the date of authorization. Exhibits 9.1 and 9.2 show letters that would accompany this form. Always include a paragraph in the cover letter requesting a certified copy of the complete chart. When requesting records regarding an obstetrical claim, specifically ask for the fetal heart monitor strips.

    You can fill in the obstetrical intake sheet and developmental questionnaire during the client interview, or allow the client to take it home and send it back. Many times the client will include information when at home that she forgot to tell you during the initial interview. Be sure to obtain a complete list of the names and addresses of all treating physicians, including the prenatal-care doctor, delivering doctor, pediatrician, neurologist, and others.

Following up on Requests

Allow two weeks for a response before following up your requests with a phone call to the medical records department of the hospital or the office of the private

I. GENERAL

Client Name _____

Address _____

Phone Number work _____

                 home _____

                 SS# _____

Referred to this firm by _____

Other names used when hospitalized/doctor's office: _____

_____

Present Problem with Child _____

_____

_____

_____

If the child is deceased, what was the doctor's explanation: _____

_____

_____

II. MATERNAL HISTORY

Age of mother at delivery _____

Age now _____

D.O.B. _____

Prior children (state age & sex) _____

_____

_____

Length of time in labor _____

Prior method of delivery _____

EDC _____

Delivering Doctor _____

Hospital _____

Diabetes? _____

Any complications _____

_____

Miscarriages (dates and reason) _____

_____

Birth control devices used (dates) _____

_____

_____

Past weight control problems: _____

_____

Weight before pregnancy _____

Weight at time of delivery _____

High Blood Pressure _____

_____

Past venereal disease _____

_____

Any past diseases _____

_____

Any vaginal complications of any kind _____

_____

Any prior surgery _____

_____

Form 9.2

Continued

III. PATERNAL HISTORY
Age of father at delivery _____

Father's name _____

Father's address _____

Where employed _____

Phone number _____

Any children with birth defects _____
_____

Venereal disease _____
_____

Prior marriages _____

Children by prior marriage _____
_____

Any past disease _____
_____

IV. MATERNAL FAMILY HISTORY
Any early deaths or health complications _____
_____
_____

Diabetes in family _____
_____

High Blood Pressure _____
_____
_____

Instance of venereal disease _____
_____

Instance of heart attack or stroke _____

V. PATERNAL FAMILY HISTORY
Any early deaths or health complications _____
_____
_____

Diabetes in family _____
_____

High Blood Pressure _____
_____
_____

Instance of venereal disease _____
_____

Instance of heart attack or stroke _____

VI. CHOICE OF DOCTOR
Source of referral _____
_____

Knowledge of doctor's qualifications _____
_____

VII. PRENATAL DOCTOR VISITS
When first told was pregnant and where _____
_____

Date of first visit to delivering doctor/address _____
_____

Prior to the delivery, approximately how often would you visit the doctor _____
_____
_____

When visited, would you visit the doctor or someone else _____

_____

Did anything unusual occur during the doctor visits _____

_____

_____

Was an ultrasound done _____

Was an amniocentesis done _____

Did the doctor consistently tell you the same due date _____

_____

Did you have any bleeding during the prenatal time period _____

_____

VIII. DELIVERY
Type of delivery (vaginal/C-section) _____
Date & Time arrived at hospital _____
Time baby delivered _____
Time in labor _____
Weight of baby _____
Describe any unusual occurrences during labor and delivery _____

_____

_____

What did the doctor say about the condition of the baby _____

_____

_____

Was a monitor used (if so, type) _____
How long was monitor on _____
When did the membranes rupture _____
Contractions _____
Were forceps used _____
Any pressure placed on the abdomen _____
How long was head out _____
Could you see the delivery _____
Was husband present _____
IX. NURSERY
Did anything unusual occur in the nursery _____

_____

_____

Source: Reprinted with the permission of The Keenan Ashman Firm, which specializes in medical malpractice, Atlanta and Savannah, Georgia.

physician. If you have received no response within another week after the phone call, send another letter and make another phone call. If after a reasonable period of time, you still do not receive a response, talk to your attorney about preparing a motion to compel discovery.

It is best to tell clients that it will take at least two months to complete an initial review. This does not include obtaining any expert opinions, but involves

Form 9.3

**Developmental
Questionnaire**

DEVELOPMENTAL QUESTIONNAIRE

Dear Parent:

Please find listed below certain questions which we request you to answer regarding the status of your child's development, treatment and certain family information. Should you have any questions, please don't hesitate to give us a call:

Please list the names and *complete addresses* of other professionals who have worked with you and your family. If more space is needed, please use the back of page.

Pediatrician _____

Family doctor _____

Neurologist _____

Orthopedist _____

Ear, nose and throat _____

Ophthalmologist _____
    (eye specialist)

Surgeon _____

Dentist _____

Psychiatrist _____

Psychologist _____

Audiologist _____

Speech therapist _____

Occupational therapist _____

Physical therapist _____

Social worker _____

Dietician/nutritionist _____

Osteopath _____

Chiropractor _____

Health Department (nurse) _____

Child Guidance Clinic _____

Mental Health Clinic _____

Department of Social _____
Services

Other (please specify) _____

Note below if any of the child's relatives have had any of the following conditions. (For example, brother, aunt, cousin.)

Convulsions _____

Cerebral Palsy _____

Hearing Loss _____

Mental Retardation _____

Speech Problems _____

School Difficulties _____

Muscular Weakness _____

Deformities _____

Severe Visual Impairment _____

Alcoholism _____

Emotional Problems _____

Other _____

Describe any of the above.

CHILD'S DEVELOPMENT
FEEDING:
For his/her age, is your child: _____average _____underweight _____overweight.
Has the child had frequent or severe problems with ____ diarrhea ____ constipation?
What eating problems or unusual food habits does child have?
Does child take vitamins or other supplements? _____If so, what?
Has child had any problems with chewing? _____with teeth? _____with
swallowing?_____
What concerns do you have about your child's diet?
LANGUAGE AND HEARING:
Do you feel your child hears? _____well _____poorly _____not at all_____
inconsistently _____uncertain
Does your child communicate mostly by: _____gestures _____words _____crying
At what age did your child: (write "not yet" when appropriate):
_____make single sounds _____used words
_____combine words in short sentences
Did your child begin to use words and then stop? _____Yes _____No
What concerns do you have about your child's speech, language or hearing?
MOTOR SKILLS:
At what age did your child: (write "not yet" when appropriate)
_____smile _____roll over _____sit without support
_____crawl _____pull to standing _____walk alone
_____bladder trained _____bowel trained
What concerns do you have about your child's motor development?
BEHAVIOR:
Do parents agree on methods of discipline? _____Yes _____No If "No", describe.
What methods are used? _____
Are you having any problems with your child's behavior? _____ If so, describe.
Who generally disciplines child?_____
Is anybody else (e.g., school, sitter) having problems with your child's behavior? ____
If so, describe.
What do you like best about your child?
What do you feel is your child's main problem?
What do you feel caused your child's problem?
What have you been told by doctors, teachers and/or others about your child's problem?
What do you expect or hope to have happen as a result of an evaluation at the Center for
Development and Learning?
Children with developmental problems often act like children younger than they are.
What age level do you think best describes the current behavior of your child?
Do you have concerns about your other children? _____If yes, please explain.

Source: Reprinted with the permission of The Keenan Ashman Firm, which specializes in medical malpractice, Atlanta and Savannah, Georgia.

only obtaining all the records and doing an initial assessment. If the case passes this first investigative stage, then you typically obtain an expert physician's or nurse's opinion which may take another one to two months (discussed later in this chapter).

• Organizing and Reviewing Information

Chapter 8 gives numerous tips for organizing discovery documents, and the principles are the same for medical cases. Your primary concern should be

Exhibit 9.1

Sample Letter Requesting Hospital Records

---

11 October 1991

Medical Records Department
Medical Center
Atlanta, GA 30363

RE: Ida Blake
Date of Death: 6/15/90

Dear Ladies/Gentlemen:

Enclosed is a Health Care Authorization Form executed by our client, John Blake and Lynda Blake, mother and father of Ida Blake, deceased. This form authorizes you to release to this office the following medical records:

a. Autopsy report.
b. Admission summary including history and physical.
c. Emergency room report.
d. Discharge summary.

Please include the above documents from the most recent admission up to the time of death.

We would appreciate you sending a letter of certification stating that these are a true and correct copy of Ida Blake's medical records. If there is a charge for compliance with this request, please send your statement along with the records, and we will remit upon receipt. If you have any questions or require additional information, please do not hesitate to contact me. Thank you for your cooperation and assistance.

Sincerely,

Amelia Hansen
Legal Assistant

---

accessibility and maintenance of the integrity of the documents. Do not mark on original documents. Use Post-It® notes. In medical discovery, you should be sure to include the following documents:

- Depositions Digests and Abstracts
- Fact notebooks
- Trial notebooks
- Deposition digests
- Curriculum vitae
- Articles and books published by defendant(s)
- Expert witnesses (on both sides)
- Memos listing every pertinent comment by defendant(s) and expert witnesses.
- Direct-exam questions for experts.
- Developing databases of documents on the computer will speed the organizing process (see Chapter 14).

Exhibit 9.1

Continued

Medical Records Department
Medical Center
Atlanta, GA 30363

RE: Ida Blake
Date of Death: 6/15/90

Dear Ladies/Gentlemen:

Enclosed is a Health Care Authorization Form executed by our clients, John Blake and Lynda Blake, mother and father of Ida Blake, deceased. This form authorizes you to release to this office the following medical records:

> a. Autopsy Report:
> b. Admission Summary including history and physical;
> c. Emergency Room Report; and
> d. Discharge Summary.

Please include the above documents from the most recent admission up to the time of death.

We would appreciate your sending a letter of certification stating that these are true and correct copies of Ida Blake's medical records. If there is a charge for compliance with this request, please send your statement along with the records, and we will remit upon receipt. If you have any questions or require additional information, please do not hesitate to contact me. Thank you for your cooperation and assistance.

Sincerely,

Kathy Allen
Legal Assistant

Flowsheets

A flowsheet is probably the most important first step in organizing medical information. The sample flowsheet in Exhibit 9.3 reflects the order in which most hospitals organize their charts. It includes many records that are not pertinent to every case, such as autopsy reports, and it excludes certain other records that you may handle, but it provides a guideline to assist you in organizing most records. If you categorize the type of document (e.g., report), you can include it under a general subheading, such as "Radiological Reports" or "Laboratory Reports," for example.

Initial Review of Records

After the records are received and organized, you should make an initial review of them. The *timeline chart* (Exhibit 9.4) will assist you in this task. Its goal is to condense the entire medical record in a two- or three-page memo. On it you document the major changes in therapy, status of the patient, dates of transfer, and so on. There are many formats possible—you can document nursing actions, physician actions, tests ordered, whatever is relevant. Remember, however, the simpler memos are preferred. Another variation is shown in Exhibit 9.5.

13 May 1992

George Peacock, M.D.
1654 Liholiho St., Apt. 24
Honolulu, Hawaii 92822

RE: Ida Blake
DOB: 14 February 1960

Dear Dr. Peacock:

Enclosed is a Health Care Authorization Form executed by our clients, John Blake and Lynda Blake. This form authorizes you to release to this office the entire contents of Ida Blake's medical records file maintained in your office. This includes copies of reports and consultations you have received from other health care providers as well as your own office notes.

Georgia law requires that your office provide us with certification to the effect that these are the entire contents of your medical records file on same name. Usually, a letter to that effect on your letterhead is sufficient.

If there is a charge for compliance with this request, please enclose your statement with the medical records, and we will remit upon receipt.

Thank you for your cooperation and assistance.

Sincerely,

Kathy Allen
Legal Assistant

MEDICAL RECORD AUTHORIZATION FORM

TO: (Name of physician or medical care facility)

RE: Patient: _____

        Address: _____

        City/State/Zip: _____

        Birthdate: _____

        Date(s) of Treatment: _____

Enclosed is a Health Care Authorization form signed by the above person.

Please send us your medical records regarding treatment rendered to this person during the above period of time, indicating your diagnosis, treatment, and prognosis of the conditions treated.

Please send an itemized statement of your services rendered for this patient, including lab and related fees. A self-addressed stamped envelope is enclosed for your prompt reply.

Please feel free to bill us for this information and your services related to the preparation of this report.

Thank you for your prompt assistance in this matter.

Very truly yours,

Exhibit 9.3

Sample Flowsheet Checklist

- *Face Sheet*—Admission date and time are important.
- *Emergency Room Admission*—Initial impressions, tests performed, and initial complaints.
- *Emergency Room Treatment Records*
- *Ambulance Trip Report*—A good source of information on the initial condition of the patient.
- *Discharge Summary*—A good overview source.
- *History and Physical Report*
- *Progress Notes*
- *Physician's Order Sheets*
- *Consultation Reports*
- *Nursing Assessment*
- *Nursing Admission Summary*
- *Nurses' Notes*—Compare with physician's progress notes, and note late entries.
- *Intake and Output*—Oral and intravenous fluid intake record and urine output; important in cases of heart failure, kidney failure, etc.
- *Graphics*—Nursing records of vital signs (blood pressure, temperature, respiratory rate).
- *IV Fluid Record*
- *IV Flow Sheet*
- *Bedside Care Flow Sheet*
- *Nutritional Progress Notes*
- *Nursing Care Plan*—Will list medical problems and nursing actions.
- *Medication Sheets*
- *Pharmacy Department Report*
- *Preoperative Nursing Assessment Record*
- *Operating Room Nursing Record*
- *Operation Report*
- *Pre-Anesthesia Evaluation*
- *Anesthesia Record*
- *Post-Anesthesia Recovery Room Record*
- *Radiological Reports*
- *Laboratory Reports*—Note date and time received. Cultures can take several days or weeks for final reports. Be sure to get periodic updates.
- *Microbiology Reports*
- *Pathology Reports*
- *Tissue Reports*
- *Nursing Discharge Summary, Patient/Family Education*
- *Consents*
- *Authorizations*
- *Medical Examiner's Report*
- *Autopsy*

Exhibit 9.4

Timeline Chart

17 April 1991	18 April 1991	18 April 1991
Admitted to Holy Cross Hospital - 4:30 PM. Left pupil noted to be dilated, unresponsive to light. Left hemiplegia noted, with Babinski sign on the left. CT scan revealed large subcortical infarct. Moved to ICU - 8:30 PM.	Echocardiogram revealed vegetations on aortic valve. Heparin started at 8:30 AM. Initial bolus of 10,000 units ordered by Dr. X. Nurse Y, an LPN, administered 100,000 units bolus at 10:00 AM - incident report charted by nursing supervisor, Nurse Fix-It.	Dr. X notified, Antithrombin III started at 11:00 AM. Patient's blood pressure dropped to 60/0 per Dinemapp. Three units whole blood ordered to be infused rapidly. Patient pronounced dead at 11:18 AM after resuscitative efforts unsuccessful. Autopsy revealed large retroperitoneal hemorrhage.

Exhibit 9.5

Variation of Timeline Chart

DATE	PROGRESS NOTES	NURSES NOTES	LABS	ACTION TAKEN
1/2/87	Admitted for premature labor - 11:31 PM - Cx every 3 minutes, strong, dilation 4 cm, station 0	External monitor applied at 11:30 PM - rate 140s, accelerations good long-term variability	Hb - 10.3 grams PT, PTT - WNL	Terbutaline ordered by Dr. P. - administered 11:45 PM

Breaches in Standard of Care

The *standard of care* is what any reasonable physician would do in a similar situation. The standard of care is a national standard and not confined to one locality. For example, because one hospital has 40 beds and another has 400 does not mean that a different standard is applicable. (This subject will be discussed further later in this book.) Some specialties actually define the standard of care. One example is the American College of Obstetricians and Gynecologists, which frequently prints various manuals and technical bulletins on the standard of care.[2]

An integral part of any initial workup of a potential claim must include enumeration and description of the damages resulting from *breaches* of the standard of care, or areas where the defendant(s) failed to apply the standard of care. Damages should be of a permanent and disabling nature. Often the permanency of an injury cannot be established until several months or more following the injury. However, an expert can often be obtained to testify as to all aspects of the damages to include permanency.

Prepare a memorandum listing the breaches of the standard of care (Exhibit 9.6) of each potential defendant. This is helpful in choosing appropriate experts. A separate column can be included as to which expert specialty would best address each specific breach.

Medical records can often be contradictory. The contradictions may be very subtle. However, an easy test to discover breaches is to compare the nurse's notes with the physician's progress notes. Also note times on laboratory sheets

[2]These can be obtained by writing A.C.O.G. Distribution Center, P.O. Box 91180, Washington, D.C. 20090-1180.

Exhibit 9–6

Memorandum Listing
Breaches of the
Standard of Care

MEMORANDUM

FROM: Kathy Allen
TO: File
RE: List of Defendants/Breaches/Experts Needed
FILE: *Lynda Pittman v. Bonita Valley Hospital*
DATE: May 13, 1992

DEFENDANT	BREACHES	EXPERT NEEDED
J.W. Bruno (dentist)	Postponed treatment of #13 due to patient's lack of insurance.	dentist/oral surgeon
D. Duffin (oral/maxillofacial surgeon)	Failed to obtain Panorex view of maxilla.	dentist/oral surgeon
J. Sadlier (surgeon)	Failed to more aggressively treat with surgery after spiked temps on broad spectrum of anitibiotics.	Specialist in infectious disease or general surgeon
La Veuda Phillips (ophthalmologist)	Failed to conduct adequate eye examination.	ophthalmologist

("time collected") to see if a test was actually ordered at the time the doctor contends. Look for the times the doctor was notified by the nurse, and what the nurse charted as to the doctor's response or lack thereof.

Another useful memorandum used during the first phase of review lists the times the nurses notified the doctor, what the doctor was told, when the doctor was actually present, and what the doctor's specific actions were. This can help in distinguishing whether the nurses and the employer hospital breached the standard of care and should be included as defendants in the suit.

Medical Reference Books and Journals

In preparing your initial workup, you will probably need the help of various medical reference books and journals.

The *Index Medicus,* found in any medical library, will help you locate the material you need. It is printed monthly and lists hundreds of journals by topic (e.g., breast cancer) and subtopic (e.g., estrogen receptors in breast cancer), as well as by author. It has been largely supplanted by modern computer search programs such as *Paperchase*[3] and *Medline*.[4] However, the old-fashioned way of manual research can often uncover articles that are not found in the computer programs. Using both systems will help you conduct a more thorough literature search.

---

[3]For information on the *Paperchase* service, contact Paperchase, Longwood Galleria, 350 Longwood Ave., Boston, MA 02115.

[4]*Medline* is available in over 200 libraries and is the world's leading bibliographic computer database of medical information.

As you know, the bibliography section at the end of a scholarly article lists the references and sources used. This can be an invaluable shortcut to a review of a specific area in the medical literature.

A list of recommended literature sources follows:

General
Stedman's Medical Dictionary Illustrated, 25th ed. (Baltimore: Williams & Wilkins, 1990).
Dorland's Illustrated Medical Dictionary (Philadelphia: W. B. Saunders, 1988).
T.R. Harrison, ed., *Harrison's Principles of Internal Medicine,* 12th ed. (New York: McGraw-Hill, 1991).
David C. Sabiston, Jr., *Textbook of Surgery* (Philadelphia: W. B. Saunders, 1991).
Robert Berkow, ed., *The Merck Manual,* 14th ed. (Rahway, NJ: Merck Sharp & Dohme Research Laboratories, 1982).

Journals:
New England Journal of Medicine and *Annals of Internal Medicine.*
ANATOMY
Gray, H. and Williams, P. L., *Gray's Anatomy,* 37th ed. (Edinburgh: Churchill Livingstone, 1989).
R.M.H. McMinn and R.T. Hutchings, *Color Atlas of Human Anatomy* (Chicago: Year Book Medical Publishers, 1977).
OBSTETRICS
Cunningham, F.G. MacDonald, P.C., and Gant, N.F., eds., *Williams Obstetrics,* 18th ed. (Norwalk, CT: Appleton & Lange, 1989).
Robert Percival and Eardley Lancelot Holland, *Holland & Brews Manual of Obstetrics.* (Edinburg: Churchill Livingston, 1980).

Journal: *American Journal of Obstetrics and Gynecology*
PEDIATRICS
Richard E. Behrman and Victor C. Vaughan, III, *Nelson Textbook of Pediatrics,* 14th ed. (Philadelphia: W. B. Saunders, 1991).

Journals:
Journal of Perinatology Pediatrics American Journal of Childhood Diseases
NEONATOLOGY
Gordon B. Avery, *Neonatology: Pathophysiology and Management of the Newborn,* 3d ed. (Philadelphia: J. B. Lippincott, 1987).
PHARMACOTHERAPEUTICS
PDR®—*Physician's Desk Reference,* 45th ed. (Oradell, NJ: Medical Economics Data, 1991).
Alfred Goodman, Louis S. Goodman, and Alfred Gilman. *Goodman and Gilman's The Pharmacological Basis of Therapeutics,* 6th ed. (New York: MacMillan, 1980).
American Medical Association, *AMA Drug Evaluations* (Chicago: American Medication Association, 1983-).

• Phase 3: Selecting Expert Witnesses

Preparing a memorandum on breaches of the standard of care (Exhibit 9.6) will help you provide your attorney with the information he or she needs to decide on the expert witnesses needed. In addition to building your own expert file, you can contact the following services that provide the names of experts:

Technical Advisory Service for Attorneys (TASA)
1166 DeKalb Pike, Blue Bell, PA 19422-1844
(1-800-523-2319)

The Medical Quality Foundation
104 Elden Street, Herndon, VA 22070
(1-800-336-0332)

Medical Witnesses
P.O. Box 800, Riverside, CT 06878
(1-800-431-1777)

Medical Advisors, Inc.
2133 Arch Street, Philadelphia, PA 19103
(1-800-666-7045)

Medi-Legal Services
P.O. Box 1464, El Cajon, CA 92022-1464
(1-800-343-2135)

Speaking to the Expert

Be prepared with all the basic information on your case when calling a busy potential expert physician. He or she will be greatly frustrated if you are unable to answer simple questions about the file. Also, since many experts are hesitant to cooperate with a "cold call," it is wise to have a referral name of an attorney who has used them in the past or with whom they are familiar.

Be sure to organize your thoughts before calling, and have an idea of the specific areas you want the expert to address. Ask the expert about charges for reviewing the file, deposition time, and trial time. Also ask what the estimated cost is for the initial review of the file and send this amount as a retainer.

You will gain more information from the expert who has agreed to review the case if you can speak to him or her after the review rather than relying on a written report. Indicate that you would prefer a telephone call rather than a written memo. Have the file handy when the expert calls, and be sure all of the areas you are interested in are covered.

Composing the Expert Package

Once an expert is chosen, you should assemble a package of information to send her. In your cover letter include a list of enclosed medical records. To expedite the expert's review, enclose a summary of the case and a list of specific questions. Be sure that you do not state what the firm is hiring the expert to prove. For example, the letter should not say, "We will pay you $500 to prove there was negligence." Instead, the message should read, "Here are the facts. Please evaluate the situation." A sample cover letter is provided in Exhibit 9.7.

Checking Board-Certification Status

To determine the board certification status of medical doctors, two sources are widely used: *Marquis' Who's Who*, which publishes a three-volume listing every

Exhibit 9.7

May 13, 1992

VIA FEDERAL EXPRESS

Expert Physician
Hospital/office address

RE: Client name

Dear Dr. _____ :

Thank you for agreeing to review the above-captioned file, per our telephone conversation on August 8, 1991. I am enclosing the following medical records for your review:

A Prenatal records;

B Labor and delivery records;

C Fetal heart monitor strips;

D Initial Neonatal records; and

E Subsequent records of child.

Briefly, this case involves a 29-year-old white female (at time of delivery), G3 P0–0–2–0, with history of miscarriage at 2 months in 1981, and an ectopic pregnancy in 1988. Prenatal course complicated by mild to moderate preeclampsia in the last trimester. Admitted to Haudin Hospital in Newbud, Georgia, on December 9, 1989, at 12:22 PM, 3 days prior to her EDC. Admission BP 170/104, treated with magnesium sulfate. Developed failure to progress in labor with cervix 2 cm dilated at 1 PM, and 3 cm at 2 PM until delivery at 6:00 PM. Station remained at -2 from admission to delivery.

External monitor revealed variable decelerations to 60, which responded to positional change and oxygen. Beat-to-beat variability appeared adequate. Internal monitor placed at 1:50 PM showed variable and late decelerations continuing over the next 4 to 5 hours, with decreased variability and no progress in labor. Emergency C-section ordered at 5:30 PM, delivery at 6:00 PM of a 6 pound male infant, APGARs 1/1. Complete placental abruption noted. Initial Ph 6.9.

Infant required mechanical ventilation and developed seizures several hours after birth. Transferred to Colombo, Georgia, on December 12, 1989. Patient currently requires gastrostomy feedings, has a spastic quadriparesis and seizure disorder due to hypoxic static encephalopathy.

We are interested in your opinions on any aspect of this case: specifically on when the hypoxic damage began, when the damage was irreversible, and when a C-section should have been ordered in the face of failure to progress and evidence of fetal distress on the strips. Also, since this woman was at high risk of placental abruption and required magnesium sulfate for control of her preeclampsia, should she have been taken directly to the operating room?

I am enclosing check no. 1156 for $850 for retainer, as discussed. I understand you bill $250 per hour for review. Please send us your bill should you spend additional time on this file, and we will remit upon receipt.

Once again, thank you for agreeing to review this tragic case. The statute of limitations on this matter runs only for the next several months, and we appreciate your attention to this matter. Please give me a call at your earliest possible convenience to discuss your opinions. Our toll-free number is 1–800–687–2021. I look forward to hearing from you.

With warm regards,

Sincerely,

Kathy Allen
Legal Assistant

two years, and the toll-free service of the Computer Databank of Board-Certified Physicians, 1-800-776-CERT. You may call this number to obtain information on all board-certified physicians in the United States. If a physician has been certified within the last six months, however, his or her name may not appear in the databank.

• Phase 4: Preparing Clients and Expert Witnesses

Paralegals are often entrusted with the task of getting the client and/or the expert witness ready for the deposition. Many clients have distorted views of what is involved in giving a deposition. Often they get these views from television or other people they know who have had certain experiences in depositions. It is important that you clarify their misunderstandings and answer all their questions. If you don't know the answer, you can always find out.

Describe the atmosphere of the deposition to the client. Tell him not to be intimidated by appearances. Include appropriate suggestions as to dress and demeanor. You will find that a sample deposition video describing the proceedings is very helpful in allaying client concerns. There are many such videos on the market.

Meet with the client at least one week prior to the scheduled deposition. At this time review in detail the facts of the case, including dates, times, nurses' and doctors' comments, and so forth. Clients appreciate tips on general strategies in answering questions. Often it is difficult to find the balance between volunteering too much information and saying enough to make the key points of the case. It is helpful to role-play to make this distinction finer for the client.

You should have a candid discussion with the client about the necessity of telling the truth. The client should be comfortable with her version of the truth. It is unwise and illegal to fabricate answers. It is imperative to identify potential problem areas from which the other side can easily score "points".

Preparing Expert Witness for Deposition

Prior to the expert witness's deposition, it is beneficial to meet with her to review the facts and get her opinions on the case. It is crucial that you be aware of precisely what the expert is going to say. Emphasize what the potential problem areas are from a medical-legal perspective, and discuss how the expert is going to tackle these areas.

Preparing for Opposing Expert's Deposition

When preparing for the opposing expert's deposition, it is beneficial to review any available prior deposition testimony to get a feel for his style. A thorough review of any publications authored by him can also provide potential areas for your attorney to score points. For example, it is certainly questionable when an expert has published a particular opinion in a scholarly journal, then gives the opposite opinion in his deposition to support the opposition's contentions in this case. A very useful tool for the attorney is to have such contradictions typed on a cover sheet and highlighted on a copy of the literature attached to the cover sheet. You can also do the same for other questions and areas the attorney will be covering, that is, have the question typed on one sheet and attach it to the highlighted copy of the literature.

Documenting Your Assessment of Experts

After the deposition of an expert (yours or the opposition's), it is helpful to immediately prepare a memo regarding your subjective feelings about what type of witness the expert will make.

• Summary

Medical discovery tasks are more technical and require more precision than other discovery tasks. Most likely, you are untrained in the medical field, unless you are a nurse paralegal or have other medical experience. Because of this, you must learn a lot of medical terminology on the job. You also need to learn the way in which physicians and hospitals operate. Try to collect this information and related forms in a file to save yourself from repetitious research. Also, remember that in working with doctors and hospital administrative personnel, you need to be especially careful to maintain a professional demeanor at all times. Beware of overstepping your knowledge or expertise and making assumptions. Always clear questionable items in advance with your attorney. Finally, keep thorough notes on all conversations and put your notes in memorandum to file form.

How to Expedite Your Legal Research

10

• Introduction

When the paralegal profession began, it seldom included training in complex legal research. Even when advanced legal research classes were added to the paralegal program in the 1970s, they were primarily introductory in nature, and the prevailing sentiment was that legal research should be left to the law clerks — that nonlawyers lacked the necessary skills. Since then, however, competent paralegals who frequently took on the task of legal research have proved this theory wrong. Moreover, law clerks and associates move on to other clients and other work, while the paralegal who stays in his or her position year after year can become extremely proficient in the tasks of a particular specialty and the type of research the firm performs. Now even the more traditional, prominent firms that were most hesitant to let paralegals do their research have changed their policy, provided the paralegal in question seems capable and conscientious. Often a paralegal has to be assertive to get the chance to prove his or her competence. Then the important thing is for the paralegal to check back with the attorney should any doubt or question arise. You can spend a lot of time spinning your wheels in the law library if you don't know what you are doing.

If you are an experienced paralegal and have no legal research training, a course at a local law school or college, or even an intensive seminar, can help you. With training and access to some of the excellent books that exist on the subject, you should learn quickly. Most of your learning, however, will take place through trial and error in the law library.

• General Approach to Legal Research

You must always approach each legal research task as unique and one in which you are bound to learn as you go along. Like going down a strange highway, you will see some familiar milestones, but essentially you are always treading on new territory. Questions will arise you had not thought of at the time your attorney gave you the assignment. Note them as you go along to ask later at an appropriate time.

This chapter is designed to help you stay on target and not double-track or go around in circles. Accuracy in recordkeeping and noting citations will help you more than anything. This chapter includes a chart that will give you an instant picture of where you have been in your research path, as well as some proven procedures. Even though they may seem time-consuming to use, they will save you more time in the end. With experience, you may develop your own research techniques using index cards and other tools, such as computerized research systems. In general, the following principles should help you save time and be more efficient:

1. *Understand the assignment.* The first step in any research assignment is to make sure that you understand the necessary facts and issues you are to research. When your attorney gives you the research problem, ask questions about any parts of the assignment that are unclear. Ask your attorney if he or she wants copies of the statutes, cases, or *Shepardized* cases, meaning those that have been checked in *Shepard's Citations,* a set of books setting forth the history and subsequent treatment of a published opinion.

Find out if you are to do statutory or case research. *Statutory research* generally involves looking up state or local statutes, whereas *case research* involves researching a particular issue for precedent and Shepardizing the cases you find. Always ask your attorney how much time you will be allowed for the assignment and how detailed you should get. Overkill is easy to do in legal research.

2. *Define the issues.* Immediately after you are given the assignment, write down the issues as you understand them. Make notes of any questions you did not think of during the discussion with your attorney. Make notes on any explanatory information that your attorney gave you while it is still fresh in your mind—do not trust your memory.

3. *Review relevant pleadings and documents.* In most paralegal assignments, you should review all relevant pleadings and documents in the file to get a better perspective of the client's problem. From this review you will gather facts that could affect the manner in which you conduct your research. It also will help you know what documents your attorney may want to request to properly prepare the case.

4. *Develop a research plan.* Although it takes time to draft a flexible research plan, it will save more time than it takes. The blueprint of your plan will depend on the assignment. Beware of the temptation to just jump in and do the assignment. Without a plan you are likely to flounder at some point and may duplicate your research steps.

5. *Use a research guide chart.* To save valuable time in keeping track of your progress and to prevent duplicating your efforts, use the simple-to-use research guide chart shown in Exhibit 10–1. This will allow you to see at a glance where you have been in the law books and where you need to go. It is easy to forget whether you checked a particular set of books. We explain how to use this chart later, under "Research Guide for Keeping Track of Progress."

6. *Keep a list of cases and statutes reviewed.* On a separate piece of paper, note the citations of the cases and the statutes that you have reviewed, making certain that you copy them correctly. An inaccurate citation could cause you to waste valuable time retracing your steps. Check off each case or statute after you review it. Also, this list will serve as a double-check when you Shepardize the pertinent cases you find.

7. *Take brief excerpts from cases and/or statutes.* First, read the headnotes at the beginning of the case in the National Reporter System (discussed later in this chapter under "Computerized Research Systems") to determine if the case covers the issues relevant to your case. Use West's key number system to track similar cases and spot relevant issues easily. If a brief scan of the headnotes does

Exhibit 10.1
•
Research Guide

Topics, Subjects, Words, Phrases, etc.	State Code	State Reports	State App. Rpts.	State Ency.	State Session Laws	Black's	State Digest	Regional Digest	Regional Rptr.	Federal Rptr.	Federal Supp.	C.J.—C.J.S.	Am. Jur.—Am. J.2d	A.L.R., 2d, 3d	Restatements	U.S.C.A.	Adm. & Exe. Pub.	Periodicals	Words & Phrases	Atty. Gen. Ops.	Law Review	Shepard's
Automobile																						
Liability																						
Negligence																						
Last Clear Chance																						
Assumption of the Risk																						
Contributory Negligence																						
Streets & Highways																						
Vehicles																						
Probable Cause																						

Research Assignment: _____   Paralegal: _____

Client Name & Matter: _____   File No.: _____

Responsible Attorney(s): _____   Date: _____   Date Due: _____

not indicate any relevant points of law, then do not waste your time reading the case unless your attorney has specifically requested you to do so. As you review each case or statute, take excerpts summarizing the points of law. If there are cases you are unsure about whether to review, note them. You can always go back to them if you need to later in your research.

8. *Keep your attorney informed of your progress.* As your research progresses, check with your attorney periodically to get feedback on what you have researched. Attorneys want to be informed; they are more likely to be troubled by a lack of contact. Attorneys always have to be cognizant of what is going on in their cases because of all the time deadlines and the potential for malpractice. A quick call or a brief update will often suffice. Take the initiative; don't make your attorney track you down.

9. *Review your notes before completing your assignment.* After you have completed your research, review your notes as set forth in your memorandum to be certain all portions are covered. Check off each issue on your list. Go back over your research to make sure you have recorded citations properly.

• Step-by-Step Procedure for Developing a Research Plan

A concrete research plan will save you many hours in the library and will enable your research to progress smoothly. Of course, the exact sequence of your research plan will depend upon the particular case on which you are working. As an example, assume you are requested to research the landlord's liability to a tenant for damages and personal injuries as the result of an accident involving the tenant's minor child walking through a glass door. The following step-by-step procedure predicated on this example case will serve as a general guide for developing a research plan for any case. As you finish each step and discover cases and statutes, add them to your master list.

• Step 1:   Begin by checking the index to the state code.

By checking the index to the state code, you will be able to determine what specific code sections might fall under the following headings: negligence, sliding glass doors, glass, landlord-tenant, attractive nuisance, contributory negligence, children, minors, lessee/lessor products liability, merchantability, and so forth. Of course, you may not locate any cases under some of these headings, but you should check all topics or words and phrases you can possibly think of. Remember that different books index the statutes and cases in many different ways, and indexes may vary from publisher to publisher and from book to book.

• Step 2:   Review the state statutes and annotations.

If your state code is *annotated,* meaning it lists cases that interpret the statutes, note the relevant cases. Often these cases lead to additional cases that might be helpful.

• Step 3:   Review state and general legal encyclopedias.

Many states have encyclopedias interpreting the particular state's laws. If you are unable to locate the information you need in your state encyclopedia or your state does not have such an encyclopedia, refer to the general legal encyclopedias, *Corpus Juris (C.J.)*, *Corpus Juris Secundum (C.J.S.)*, *American Jurisprudence (Am.Jur.)*, and *American Jurisprudence 2d. (Am.Jur.2d)*.

• Step 4: Review digests.

A *digest* is a composite of summaries of the facts and holdings of a case indexed under particular points of law referencing to the source. Digests can save valuable time in locating pertinent case law. West Publishing Company has digests for a single state or territory (e.g., *Illinois Digest*), a group of neighboring states (e.g., *Southern Digest*), a single court or systems of courts (e.g., *Federal Digest*), and for all courts (e.g., *First Centennial Digest*.) Always begin your research in the digests with the local digest, that is, the state digest.

• Step 5: Review applicable cases in the state reports, federal court reports, and regional reports.

After you have located numerous cases, make a quick review of them, starting with the cases in the forum state. Consult the state reports and appellate reports before reviewing the cases in the neighboring states and in the federal courts. If you do not have a case *on point* ("on all fours," meaning a precedent that fully supports the case being researched), in the forum state or in a neighboring state, refer to a case in the appropriate federal circuit in which the forum state is located. For example, if you have a case within the jurisdiction of the state of Georgia, and you cannot locate a case on point in Georgia, look for a case in a neighboring state, such as Alabama, in the *Southern Reporter (So.)* or *Southern Reporter 2d. (So.2d)*.

If you cannot find a case on point in a neighboring state, consult the *Federal Reporter* series for a case in the circuit in which the state is located, which in this case would be the Fifth Circuit. Examine the cases to determine if the particular cases you found in the Fifth Circuit originated in the state of Georgia. If not, another state in the Fifth Circuit would be an excellent authority. To determine what states are located in each regional reporter, that is, the *Southern Reporter* or *Southern Reporter 2d.*, refer to the binder of any reporter in that series.

• Step 6: Consult your attorney.

This is an excellent time to take a break from your research and report to the attorney on your progress. The purpose is to avoid progressing in the wrong direction and wasting valuable time.

• Step 7: Shepardize the relevant cases.

Shepard's Citations is used to check on the validity of the statutes and cases that a lawyer wishes to cite as authority. Because the law is fluid, changing by legislative or judicial action, the prudent lawyer Shepardizes every authority. As mentioned earlier, the history and subsequent treatment of a published opinion can be found in *Shepard's Citations*. It covers all states and units of the National Reporter series and a special Labor Law Citator. By checking *Shepard's Citations*, you can determine whether a case was affirmed or reversed, whether it has been used as a precedent in many other cases, and whether it has been overruled in a subsequent case. Tips on efficient Shepardizing are presented near the end of this chapter.

Often, by Shepardizing the cases you have located in your state code and regional reporters, you will uncover additional cases in your jurisdiction. Again, do exhaustive research in the forum state or region before researching cases in other regions. For example, if the forum state is Georgia, research the annotated state code, *Georgia Digest, Southern Digest,* and *Southern Reporter* before researching in other states.

Both LEXIS and WESTLAW have online databases designed specifically for the purpose of verifying the accuracy and validity of citations. These databases do not provide the breadth of information available in *Shepard's,* but focus specifically on developments in the same type of litigation and cases that have a precedential impact on the decision being verified. Called *Auto-Cite* on LEXIS and *Insta-Cite* on WESTLAW, these systems operate similarly to Shepard's in that the researcher simply types in the citation to a case. The resulting display includes the name of the case, any parallel citations, and the names and citations of relevant cases, with the effect of each subsequent decisions noted. Even if there are no subsequent developments in a case or later decisions affecting its authority, Auto-Cite and Insta-Cite are a simple and trustworthy means of verifying the accuracy of citations and of finding parallel citations. This subject is discussed further under "Computerized Research Systems" in this chapter.

• Step 8: Consult the federal code.

If you are working with a case in the federal courts, consult the federal statutes, that is, the *United States Code Annotated* and relevant federal legislation such as *slip laws* (legislative enactments that are separately and promptly published after their passage in pamphlet or in single sheet format) and *session laws,* which are normally published on a periodic basis in pamphlet format, throughout the legislative session. At the end of the session they are bound, in the order of their enactment, into a more permanent form.

• Step 9: Review *American law reports annotated.*

Next, consult the *American Law Reports Annotated* (*A.L.R., A.L.R.2d.* and *A.L.R.3d*), which is, according to the publisher, a compilation of annotations, each a complete and detailed treatise on a practical point of current law, preceded by a report in full of a modern case from a state or federal appellate court involving the problem annotated.

• Step 10: Consult treatises, restatements, uniform state laws, dictionaries, words and phrases, and attorney general opinions.

Textbooks and treatises are secondary authorities covering a particular subject in narrative form and giving footnote references to primary and other authorities. They are important in that they restate and synthesize decisions and statutes, summarize historical developments, analyze and explain apparent discrepancies and inconsistencies, predict future changes, and provide practical guidance for the conduct of legal business by the legal profession and the lay public. Since they are secondary authorities, it is imperative that you always check their primary references of cases and statutes.

Restatements of the Law, prepared under the auspices of the American Law Institute, have become one of the most frequently cited, widely respected, and yet controversial secondary legal authorities. They are a unique form of legal literature, covering only ten specific fields of law: agency, conflict of laws, contracts, foreign relations law, judgments, property, restitution, security, torts, and trusts.

Uniform state laws originate from the national Conference of Commissioners on Uniform State Laws, which was formed in 1892. The Conference meets annually to draft, promulgate and promote uniform laws, which the states can then adopt as proposed, or modify, or reject, as they see fit.

Dictionaries, such as *Black's Law Dictionary*, are secondary authorities, as are attorney general opinions. There are two types of attorney general opinions: First are the opinions by the Attorney General, head of the Department of Justice and chief law officer of the Federal Government, on legal matters concerning the United States and advice and opinions to the President and to the heads of the executive departments of the Government; second are the opinions issued by the attorney general who is the chief law officer of the state, who gives advice and opinions to the governor and to executive and administrative departments or agencies.

Another secondary authority is the set of books entitled *Words and Phrases*, in which you can locate particular cases easily through certain words and phrases.

• Step 11: Check periodical literature.

Finally, check legal periodical literature, which includes law school reviews and special-interest periodicals such as periodicals of bar organizations, professional societies, symposiums, annual survey and special-subject periodicals, *United States Law Week* (which contains slip decisions of the U.S. Supreme Court), slip laws of Congress, and other information about development in the courts, both federal and state, in Congress, and in federal administrative agencies.

• Step 12: Check administrative and executive publications.

If your research problem involves a matter concerning administrative and executive government agencies, consult the administrative and executive publications such as the rules and regulations of the federal administrative agencies like the Nuclear Regulatory Commission.

Be aware of time constraints at all times when doing your research. Keep track of your library time and exactly what you do so that when you prepare your time sheets, they will correctly reflect what you did. The attorney then can prepare a more accurate, thorough bill for the client. Be careful not to overkill or underkill your assignment. Even young law associates frequently do one or the other, and your attorney will spot it in a moment. Ask questions if you are unsure about how thorough your research should be.

• Research Guide for Keeping Track of Progress

To use the handy research guide shown in Exhibit 10–1, insert all topics, subjects, and phrases that lead you to relevant cases. For example, if you are researching an automobile accident you might insert the following words in the "Word and Phrases" column: automobile, liability, negligence, last clear chance, assumption of the risk, contributory negligence, streets and highways, vehicles, probable cause. Then as you research each topic, subject, word or phrase in each book (*State Code, Regional Reporter*, etc.), place a check in the appropriate box.

This research guide will help prevent you from duplicating and will enable you quickly to determine which books or words and phrases have or have not been researched. It will also enable you to stop your research and return to it later. Note code sections or key numbers in the box, or use the note section of the research guide sheets to make notes on a particular item. The research guide also serves as a record for the attorney to review and then insert in the file for purposes of allocating and substantiating your billable research time.

• Computerized Research Systems

Following is a description of popular computerized research systems.[1]

> The two major computerized legal research services, West Publishing Company's WESTLAW and Mead Data Central's LEXIS, have revolutionized the ways in which case research is conducted. Both services allow access to the full texts of judicial opinions, and permit researchers to retrieve all cases with any specified terms or combinations of terms. One can also search for opinions by a particular judge or cases involving specified parties, to mention only two of numerous possibilities.
>
> Although both services offer far more than just cases, with extensive databases of statutes, administrative materials, and secondary sources, court decisions remain their primary focus. Both WESTLAW and LEXIS contain full texts of opinions from the federal courts and from all 50 states. Cases available online include not only those published in official reports and commercial reporters such as West's National Reporter System, but "slip opinions" obtained from the courts and inaccessible through traditional printed resources.
>
> In this section we briefly discuss WESTLAW and LEXIS capabilities for case-finding. The systems differ in coverage and in search techniques, as well as in concept and design. WESTLAW's concept is full text plus providing an additionally enhanced online database, whereas LEXIS is just data. The specific methods of searching in each system can best be learned through the extensive training programs and tutorial materials developed expressly for that purpose.* Instead of teaching computerized legal research, this section surveys its possibilities and limitations.

---

[1]Reprinted with permission from Morris L. Cohen, Robert C. Berring, Kent C. Olson, *How to Find the Law*, 9th ed., (St. Paul, MN: West Publishing Company, 1989).

*The basic instructional materials for the two systems are *Discovering WESTLAW* (West,1991); *WESTLAW Reference Manual*, 4th ed. (West, 1990); Nancy Johnson, Robert Berring, Thomas Woxland, *Winning Research Skills*, (West, 1991), which provides an integrated overview of both manual and WESTLAW legal research; K. M. Carrick, *Lexis: A Legal Research Manual* (Mead Data Central, 1989); and *Learning LEXIS* (Mead Data Central, 1989). The first five chapters of W. Harrington, *The Dow Jones-Irwin Lawyer's Guide to Online Data Bases* (Dow Jones-Irwin, 1987), provides an interesting and readable introduction to online research and a comparative explanation of searching procedures on both systems.

Case Databases

The first decision an online researcher must make is the choice of database in which to search. In both WESTLAW and LEXIS, one can search the decisions of a particular state of a particular court, or can use databases which combine the decisions either of all 50 states or of all federal courts. Whether to limit research to a particular jurisdiction depends on a variety of factors, such as the nature and purpose of the research, the amount of available time and money, and the value of precedent from other jurisdictions.

The decisions available to any particular state are basically the same in either WESTLAW or LEXIS, although one system may have more extensive retrospective coverage and one may have quicker access to recent opinions. The major difference in the cases appearing in the two systems is that LEXIS documents consist simply of opinions as received from the courts, while WESTLAW includes (for cases published in West reporters) the West editorial enhancements: synopses, headnotes and en-hanced, corrected opinions.

As part of their display of a case, both systems provide citations to any pub-lished versions, whether in official reports, West reporters, and other reporters. One can retrieve the citation from the computer and then go to one of these printed resources for further examination. The computer may be used for checking, but be sure to cite the published source. Until recently, a case that was available online but was not otherwise published was referred to as a "slip opinion" (the same term used to designate the original document issued by the court). In 1988, however, both WESTLAW and LEXIS instituted systems by which cases found only online can be cited. Each case is assigned a unique citation, which is used until a published citation is available. Before a United States Court of Appeals case is printed in the *Federal Reporter,* for example, it can be cited as "1989 WL 4339 (D.C.Cir.)" or "1989 U.S.App. LEXIS 973."

Search Strategies

Both WESTLAW and LEXIS enable the user to search the full text of opinions for any words or phrases he or she believes may appear in relevant cases. This alone would be an immense aid in situations where digests and other printed indexes are not specific enough or are not organized in a way to meet particular research needs. More importantly, the systems permit the use of Boolean searching techniques, which make it possible to retrieve documents containing two or more words or phrases in specified combinations. For example, one can retrieve all cases containing the words "damages" and "shrubbery," or all cases where those two words appear within five or ten words of each other. Instead of functioning as a simple concor-dance to every word in every opinion, the systems thus allow a unique and complex set of search criteria to be created for any research issue. On WESTLAW one can also retrieve documents containing words in the same sentence or the same paragraph.

This ability to combine two search terms means that one can automatically limit retrieval to cases containing each of several essential elements, instead of scanning several columns or pages of a digest or an annotation for cases with particular facts. It also means that one can combine two concerns in a way not possible in most printed resources. An attorney working on the *Fisher v. Lowe* litigation, for example, might have to choose whether to research issues of tree damages or issues of no-fault insurance, since even a case directly on point might be indexed under one but not the other. Online, however, both issues can be combined in one search to retrieve any cases directly on point.

When searching opinions for a relevant fact or issue, one must try to frame a search request to include any words or phrases that judges would use to express the concept. For printed indexes and digests, an editor ensures that all references to a particular subject can be found in one place. All cases on attorneys, for example, would be listed under "attorneys." Because a full-text only database has no intervening editor, however, the user must search not just for "attorney," but also for other terms a judge might use instead, such as "counsel," "lawyers," or "pettifogger." The art of framing successful search requests can be learned only through a familiarity both with the legal terminology of the subject area and the potentials of the computer system. Preliminary planning of a search by analysis of the problem and careful selection of search words and connectors is essential.

The inclusion in WESTLAW's databases of West synopses and headnotes lends some standardization, since these editorial additions may contain descriptive terms which are normally used by which may not be employed by a particular judge. In addition, West Digest topics and key numbers can be used in WESTLAW searches, either alone or in combination with words or phrases in opinions. The researcher can thus use a topic or key number to limit retrieval to a particular subject matter and keywords to specify fact situations within that subject. This is particularly valuable in areas such as constitutional law or securities regulation where all cases would be classified similarly, but the descriptive language used by the court may vary widely.

An aspect of online searching that can be extremely valuable is the use of document *fields* (in WESTLAW) or *segments* (in LEXIS). Fields or segments are specified parts of a case, such as the names of the parties, or the judge writing the opinion, or the date of decision. A search request limited to a particular field or segment can retrieve, for example, all cases involving a specific corporation or decided after a certain date. It would be a lengthy and tedious process manually to find all opinions written by a particular judge. Online databases can easily retrieve a complete list of judge's opinions, and allow the researcher to combine that request with other search terms to find a judge's opinions on particular issues. In WESTLAW, one can use the "synopsis" field to search only for words appearing in the paragraphs added by West to summarize each case's facts and holding, and can thus retrieve a smaller body of cases more precisely on point.

Integrating Manual and Computerized Research

Although many law library resources, such as reporters and digests, are expensive to acquire, they do not cost more money each time they are used by a researcher. Under most circumstances, on the other hand, the cost of WESTLAW or LEXIS is based on the amount of use. While almost all law schools have arrangements that allow use of the services at a flat, discounted rate, other users incur a fee each time they go online. The key to efficient use of the services is to remember that they are generally case-finding tools and not case reporters. The terminal should be used to frame searches, skim highlights, and obtain citations. Unless a case is not available in print, the efficient researcher then looks for decisions in the standard reporters. Carelessness in searching or reading whole cases online can become very expensive.

There are important reasons other than financial constraints for not relying exclusively on computerized research. There are many research situations where the benefit of a publisher's editorial work in organizing and analyzing case is indispensable. A digest or annotation can arrange cases by precise issue addressed and disregard the occasionally discursive aside, while the computer cannot distinguish between holding and incidental dictum. The computer has no way of distinguishing the most important and influential cases in an area of law, but a treatise or law review article will focus its discussion on such cases. Finally, although both WESTLAW and LEXIS are expanding the scope of their databases and adding older cases, there are many opinions which are not online and which can be found only through manual research techniques.

WESTLAW and LEXIS can undoubtedly achieve results impossible through manual research. They add great flexibility and incredible speed to the process of case finding. They are not foolproof, however, and many miss essential cases simply because the courts' vocabulary or phrasing does not precisely match the search request. The computerized systems are most effective when used a part of a carefully developed research strategy integrating a number of different approaches. Computers can never eliminate of the most important research steps, *reading* relevant cases retrieved by either manual or electronic methods. One must read a case to analyze its reasoning and to determine on what precedent it relies.

• Checking Citations

Often when a brief is prepared by the attorney, the citation has been improperly copied—due to the attorney's haste, the typist's mistake, or for any number of other reasons. The plaintiff's or defendant's name may also be misspelled. The attorney may request you to check the citations in the brief (and name spellings) after it is typed before filing the brief with the court. You should also make sure the spacing in the citation is typed properly. Check all statistics, case cites, and statements of fact; but in particular, check case cites to make sure not only that they are accurate but that they are written in the proper form. Use the *Maroon Book*[2] or *A Uniform System of Citation*, more commonly known as the *Harvard's Citator*[3] if in any doubt about the proper preparation of citations. An incorrect citation could irritate the judge and cause embarrassment to the attorney and the firm.

When you are under pressure to check citations, you may not have enough time to go back to the original case. The following four methods will help:

Method 1: Under the "Table of Cases" located in the last volume or last two volumes of either your state digest (e.g., *Mississippi Digest*) or your regional digest (e.g., *Southern Digest*), you may look up the case either under the plaintiff's name or the defendant's name. For example, in the case *Jones v. Brown,* simply look under "Jones" or "Brown." A reference will be given to the citation of the case. Check it carefully.

Method 2: Refer to the list of cases at the beginning of the *American Court Reports* (e.g., *Georgia Reports, Georgia Court of Appeals,* the *Federal Supplement,* or any other relevant book that you may be using). The *Federal Reporter* or the *Federal Supplement* has the cases listed by circuit (e.g., Fifth Circuit).

Method 3: Some states, such as Georgia, have a book referred to as the "blue and white book". If you refer to either the official or unofficial citation in this book, you can check the cross-citation. For example, in the above case, *Jones v. Brown,* 234 Ga. 35, 99 S.E.2d 201, you may refer to the official cite (the first citation) in the blue and white book, that is, 234 Ga. 35, and find the unofficial citation, 99 S.E.2d 201.

---

[2]The *Maroon Book* is published by the Lawyers Co-operative Publishing Company and Mead Data Central, Inc. It was launched by students at the University of Chicago Law School.
[3]*A Uniform System of Citation* has been published since 1926 by a consortium of law reviews led by Harvard and Columbia law schools.

If the official citation is incorrect, then the unofficial citation will also be incorrect. Whenever both citations do not match the citation in the brief, you should question the entire citation and use another method to determine the correct citation.

Method 4: *Shepard's Citations* publishes citators for every set of official reports and every unit of the National Reporter System. If a case has more than one citation, it can be Shepardized in more than one citator. The citator volume in each set provides the official cite, the unofficial cite and the date in proper citation form.

• Sheylardizing

Shepard's Citations, Inc. provides an excellent pamphlet, "How to Use *Shepard's Citations*," giving precise instructions on Shepardizing. You may obtain a copy by writing Shepard's Citations, Inc., Colorado Springs, Colorado 80901. Here are a few additional tips on Shepardizing.

1. Type the abbreviations used in *Shepard's Citations* denoting the history of the case and the treatment of the case on a 3 × 5 inch index card for easy reference, for example, "a" (affirmed), "cc" (connected case), "d" (distinguished), and so on. If you prefer, you may photocopy the abbreviations from the front pages of any *Shepard's Citator* and tape them on an index card.

2. When Shepardizing, always refer to the relevant headnote number first. For example, if you have located a headnote on a specific point of law in a particular case, which is on point, such as headnote No. 2 in 25 F.2d 209, then check all the cases with headnote No. 2 first. In the following example, wherein cases are denoted under the case being Shepardized you would check only the cases checked, that is, 1 F.S. 301 and 98 So.2d 45.

> *25 F.2d 209*
> 1 F.S. 301
> 24 Ga. App. 98
> 98 So.2d 45

3. List the cases you want to Shepardize on a separate piece of paper. Below the underlined case, list only the cases with the appropriate headnote. After you have completed Shepardizing all the cases, cross off each case after you review it. However, be sure you can still read each case citation that is crossed off in case you need to return later to research other cases with different headnotes. In the above example, that case would be 24 Ga. App. 98.

• Summary

Legal research is a skill that can be acquired, but it must be done diligently and thoroughly. There is no such thing as "casual research." Cases are often won or lost according to the quality of the research job. When you do research, leave "no stone unturned" and be meticulous. Your attorney must be able to rely on your research completely. If you concentrate, stay focused, and keep track of where you have been and where you are going, you will do a good job.

Assisting in Negotiations, Pretrial Conferences, and Settlement

11
—•—

• Introduction

The vast majority of cases are settled prior to trial. They may be settled during various stages of litigation, but many are literally settled on the courthouse steps. A few cases are settled during appeal.

Numerous factors cause parties to settle. Usually, they decide to settle to save time, money, and additional hassle and inconvenience. Some settle because they are uncertain they will win as the progress of the case reveals new factors. Others simply wish to avoid the ordeal of a trial.

Factors to be considered in settling are the amount of damages, ability of the defendant to pay, insurance coverage, ease with which liability and damages can be proven, nature of the injury (permanency, horror factor, disability), sympathy the jury is expected to feel for plaintiff, whether the plaintiff needs to be paid right away or can hold out through trial, amounts of verdicts in similar cases in the same area, respective abilities of attorneys, attitude of the judge, and desire of either party for vindication, among others.[1]

Although the paralegal cannot conduct negotiations, because it may be construed as giving legal advice, you may play a key role in the settlement process. First you might be responsible for gathering and organizing information needed for drafting the necessary settlement documents. Then you might prepare this information for use by your attorney in negotiating with the other side for settlement purposes. Finally, you might actually draft the settlement documents. At all times, you should be alert to key information that your attorney can use in negotiations. In some instances, you may negotiate a settlement under the attorney's direction. In many small cases, such as personal injury matters, negotiating may be an everyday occurrence for the paralegal. The key phrase here is "under the attorney's direction," so that you are not in danger of practicing law without a license.

Your attorney must counsel you on the ethics of settlement. For example, the client, not the attorney (or the paralegal), makes the decision to accept settlement. You may not make settlement offers, accept offers, or give advice to the client on whether or not to accept a settlement.

---

[1]James W. H. McCord, *The Litigation Paralegal* (St. Paul, MN: West Publishing Company, 1988), p. 371.

Caution must be used at all times when discussing a case with an adverse attorney or paralegal. When preparing settlement documents, be careful not to reveal information that may harm your client's case. Always make sure your attorney reviews any documents that are presented to the opposing side. Client's confidential information must always be protected. Always check with your attorney when in doubt.

This chapter will give you various techniques for assisting your attorney in preparing for negotiations, pretrial conferences, and settlement. Your tasks may include preparing or reviewing any of the following documents:

1. Pretrial statement.
2. Documentary evidence.
3. Settlement precis.
4. Settlement brochure.
5. Settlement distribution statement.
6. Settlement agreement.
7. Releases.
8. Dismissals.

• Doing Your Homework Prior to Settlement

At all times prior to trial, you should be preparing for settlement. That is, whether or not the file is in settlement, your files and documents should be in impeccable order to allow your attorney to negotiate whenever the opportunity arises. In all your trial preparation, keep in mind that settlement may be imminent.

A part of preparing for settlement may be to evaluate the opposing side's proposal. Therefore, you should be aware of both sides of the case and be prepared to defend your position. Key factors in settlement negotiations involve liability, damages, insurance coverage, nature of the injury, and case law supporting your client's position, among others.

• Information Needed for Settlement Documents

Three types of settlement documents are the brochure, précis, and letter. A *settlement précis* is different from a *settlement brochure* in that it is more of a summary or abstract, whereas a settlement brochure is more lengthy and comprehensive. A *settlement letter* is very brief, usually only one page in length. To prepare a settlement letter, précis, or brochure, you will have to compile a compendium of information concerning the party before and after the injury, including:

Personal

1. Age.
2. Education.
3. Occupation.
4. Income.

5. Benefits.
6. Career potential.
7. Hobbies.
8. Interests.
9. Lifestyle.
10. Religion.
11. Personal character, values, and reputation.

Medical History

1. Prior injuries, lawsuits, and medical history that may affect the injuries received from the current accident.
2. Injuries sustained in the accident.
3. Diagnosis and prognosis.
4. Post-accident impediments such as shock, unconsciousness, and embarrassment (these often explain statements or actions inconsistent with allegations of injuries).[2]
5. Unwillingness to admit disability.
6. Causal relationship between alleged wrong and injury.
7. Treatment required (emergency, surgery, tests, hospital care, home care, checkups, other medical consultations).
8. Progressive stages of healing. hideous nature of injury or effects, temporary injuries and disability.
9. Permanent injuries, disfigurement, disabilities, psychological, and emotional injury.
10. Effect on personality and happiness.
11. Need for future medical care (nursing care, prosthetic devices).
12. Pain and suffering (at time of injury, during medical treatment, permanent).
13. Former life expectancy.
14. Life expectancy because of injuries.
15. Occupational implications of injuries.
16. Disabilities and impairments.
17. Effect on hobbies, interests, and home life.
18. All out-of-pocket expenses for medical bills, travel for treatment, and prosthetic devices.
19. Projection of future medical care and related out-of-pocket expenses.

Collect all the items (bills, medical reports, witness statements, etc.) necessary to prove or disprove these factors. Consider if the injured party has the following "three strikes" against him: has not seen a doctor, has not lost work, has not used home remedies.[3] In addition to the party's medical condition, his economic factors need to be considered. A thorough investigation to collect evidence to

---

[2]J. Jeans, *Trial Advocacy*, pp. 398–403 (West Publishing Co., St. Paul, 1975).
[3]Ibid., p. 411.

prove these losses must be conducted. For example, the following items affecting the injured party's economic condition need to be considered: (See Forms 11.6 and 11.7.)

1. *Income.* The party's income before the injury, the loss of income after the injury, and the loss of future income must all be considered.

2. *Personal and real property.* The value of personal and real property before and after the injury; replacement cost; loss of business prior to and subsequent to the injury, including future projected losses; loss of business reputation and image; loss of future opportunity; loss of rental of property; loss of good employees and the replacement costs to find new employees; and how the allegations affect these losses must all be considered.

3. *Research and investigation.* In addition to legal research, you can compile statistics on juries and verdicts rendered by judges in the forum jurisdiction. Check the microfiche at the local library to find newspaper and magazine articles on particular cases that may be similar or of interest.

Similar to preparing for trial, your investigation should include researching expert witnesses, opposing counsel, the settlement record of the relevant insurance company, actuarial tables, cost-of-living statistics, inflation factors, career potential of the injured, and any other information pertinent to the facts of the particular case. Be sure to keep a cost ledger of the estimated costs of the opposing counsel. Your firm's accounting department should enable you to determine the cost of your firm's involvement in the case easily.

• Settlement Precis

Although the settlement brochure is usually prepared in larger cases, a settlement precis, or summary, is often used in smaller cases. The primary difference between these two tools is their scope and size. Both are presented by one attorney to the opposing side and to the insurance company for the purpose of settling the case.

While it is true that lawyers must be concerned with ethics as well as the economic value of a case, they must take the size of the case into consideration. Obviously a case with a potential settlement value of less than $1,000 cannot be handled in the same fashion as one with a settlement value ten or twenty or a hundred times that much. The client is concerned with the net amount of the settlement, and the lawyer who diverts a substantial percentage of that settlement into expenses for photographs, plats, and so on when the potential of the case does not deserve it, is guilty of dissipating billable time and the client's money.

But the smaller case has the same need of effective presentation as the larger one. Some format should be adopted that will have the advantages of a persuasive disclosure without the attendant expense of time and money in its preparation. The use of a settlement precis seeks to meet that need. Its primary purpose is to present the claim in as persuasive a fashion as possible. It has six main sections:

- Identity of the plaintiff.
- Facts of the case.
- Theory of liability.

- Medical damages.
- Expenses.
- Analysis of evaluation.

The preparation of such a precis will precipitate two secondary advantages: It will discipline the lawyer to analyze liability, marshall evidence, and appraise the case; and it will provide a dress rehearsal for trial in the event efforts at settlement are fruitless. (See Exhibit 11.1 for an illustration of a settlement précis.)

• Settlement Brochure

In some instances, the parties may agree to mediate the dispute. Mediation is a formal process although it does not technically involve the courts. A settlement brochure may be part of the settlement "package." In other instances, a settlement package may be used in the process of mediation. If you are involved in mediation of a lawsuit, you should determine how the process is regulated and how it can apply to the particular case.

A settlement brochure concerns two areas, liability and damages. It is a compilation of factual information and materials, including photographs, written descriptions of the injured party's condition and lifestyle, her income prior to and subsequent to the alleged injury, and other descriptive information. It should also describe the accident or occurrence in a dramatic narrative, giving details of the injured party's suffering, and the burden the party carries or will carry in the future as a result of the accident—including monetary losses or expenses. It should paint a convincing picture of the injured party in a pathetic condition, attempting to evoke an emotional and sympathetic response from the defense.

While the purpose of a settlement brochure is to be persuasive and helpful to the parties in negotiating a settlement, it should not be used to puff up a weak case or bolster the small case beyond its proportions. In other words, it should not be used to deceive defensive counsel. Work closely with your attorney to present the case in its most favorable light. Be creative, but never distort the facts. The following techniques will help you prepare the specific portions of the settlement brochure: (See Exhibit 11.2 for a sample settlement brochure.)

1. *Portrait of the injured party.* The main ingredients of the pictorial narrative of the injured party follow:

- Educational background.
- Employment credentials and qualifications.
- Personal background.
- Summary statement of the injured party's "bleak" future as a result of the accident.

2. *Income statement.* This can be presented in several ways, depending upon the injured party's employment or profession. A simple statement of the injured's income before and after the alleged accident will suffice; however, a breakdown of her income figures by year would be more impressive. Discuss with your attorney what approach to use. That may include copies of federal and state income tax returns for the relevant years in this portion of the brochure.

Form 11.1

Social History—Sharon Williams was born July 10th, 1980, the fourth of four children born to John and Virginia Williams. The family lives at 2305 Grand Vista, Columbia, Missouri. Mr. Williams is employed as a machinist at Eagle Air Craft Co., a position he had held for six years.

Sharon is a student in the second grade of Middleton Grade School. She is a member of Girl Scout Troop 378 and is a member of the YMCA girl's swimming team.

Medical History—Sharon had a normal prenatal history and a normal birth. She had been attended by Dr. Grant Fry, a pediatrician, from birth. She has suffered from her childhood diseases of chicken pox and measles. She has never suffered any disabilities in her lower limbs and has never sustained any injuries to her legs, back or spine. Dr. Fry's medical report is attached.

Facts of Accident—On April 5, 1987, Sharon was enroute from her home to school. The attached police report confirms that the day was clear and warm and the streets were dry. Sharon was by herself and crossing Grand Avenue at its intersection with Washington Street moving westwardly from the southeast to the southwest corner approximately six feet south of the south curb line and within the designated crosswalk. Grand Avenue is forty feet wide with two lanes of traffic moving in each direction. It is straight and level and surfaced with asphalt. There were no cars parked within sixty feet of the intersection. A sign located one hundred feet south of the intersection on Grand had a legend "Caution Children." Police report confirming the description of the scene of the accident is attached.

Sharon was struck by the north bound automobile of defendant at a point five feet from the center line. The attached photographs show the following:

Photo 1 skid marks ten feet long, blood on street.

Photo 2 damage to left head light.

Sharon states that when she left the southeast corner of the intersection the light was in her favor. She never looked at the light again. She walked at a normal pace until she was hit. She was looking forward and never saw or heard the defendant's automobile. The accident occurred at 8:35 A.M. The school is two blocks away and convenes at 8:45 A.M.

A statement taken from the defendant, a copy of which is attached, acknowledges that he didn't see the plaintiff until she was fifteen feet from him and that his automobile came to a stop twenty feet after impact.

Theories of Recovery

1. That defendant violated a red light;
2. That defendant failed to keep a lookout; and
3. That defendant failed to exercise the highest degree of care to bring his automobile to a stop or slacken speed after plaintiff came into a position of immediate danger.

The proof of the first theory is supported by plaintiff's testimony that when she left the curb the light was green for westbound traffic. By reason of the plaintiff's age the court may not permit her to testify. In that event, the defendant's failure to keep a lookout could be submitted as an alternate theory of recovery. Defendant has acknowledged that he didn't see plaintiff until he was fifteen feet away from her and she was already in his path. This would place Sharon at least twelve feet from the curb. The court will judicially notice that the pace of walk is approximately two or three miles an hour or 2.9 to 4.4 feet per second. (*Wofford v. St. Louis Public Service Co., Mo.,* 252 S.W.2d 529.) Sharon was in the street and visible to defendant for almost three seconds before the accident. At defendant's acknowledged speed of twenty five miles per hour, he was traveling at approximately thirty six feet per second or was approximately one hundred feet away when he should have seen Sharon. He was further alerted by the warning sign as he approached the intersection.

By reason of her age, it is questionable whether Sharon would be held responsible for her own actions. *Malott v. Harvey,* 199 Mo.App. 615, 204 S.W.940; *Quirk v. Metropolitan St. Ry. Co.,* 200 Mo.App. 585, 210 S.W. 103.

In the event Sharon could be held accountable for not maintaining a proper lookout a third theory of recovery is available: defendant's failure to stop or slacken after plaintiff came into a position of immediate danger. By defendant's admission he came to a stop twenty feet after the impact and he did not attempt evasive action until he was fifteen feet from Sharon, therefore his overall stopping distance was thirty five feet. A jury could find that by reason of Sharon's obliviousness that she was in immediate danger as she approached the path of the vehicle and when defendant's automobile was more than the thirty five feet that was available to bring his vehicle to a stop.

The skid marks indicate that no slackening took place until the defendant's vehicle was within ten feet of the impact. The damage to the automobile indicates it was the left front headlight that struck Sharon. Sharon was within two feet of safety beyond the path of the car when she was struck. Moving at 4.4 feet per second, in one half second she would have escaped injury. From this the jury could assume that a failure to slacken at an earlier time was the proximate cause of the injury.

Medical

The police report states that Sharon was "bleeding about the face and mouth" complaining of "pain in the right hip." She was taken by police cruiser to Welfare Hospital where it was discovered that she had suffered the loss of a front upper left tooth that was permanent, a laceration of the lip necessitating six stitches and a bruise of the right hip. Portions of the hospital record are attached. She was examined by her pediatrician Dr. Fry who referred her to Dr. William Jones a dentist for examination. He confirms the loss of the permanent tooth and outlines the dental prostheses that will be needed throughout her growth stage and into adulthood. His report is attached. The stitches were removed after six days by Dr. Fry leaving a hairline scar one-fourth long near the upper lip.

Expenses

Emergency room Welfare Hospital	$265.00
Dr. Grant Fry	$125.00
Dr. William Jones	$ 80.00
Anticipated treatment	$860.00

Analysis of Evaluation

Actual out of pocket expenses total $470.00 with anticipated costs for dental prosthetic devices throughout Sharon's growth period adding $860.00 for a total of $1330.00. The loss of the tooth is permanent and will necessitate special prophylactic care to maintain the prosthetic devices that must be employed. The scar above the lip is discernible and will be permanent.

It is anticipated that a jury verdict could fall within the $6,000 to $7,000 range. If the case could be settled without further legal procedure I would recommend a settlement of $6,500.

3. *Health statement.* This should describe in detail the injured party's health before the accident. Of course, if you can show that the plaintiff enjoyed good health prior to the accident and had no prior disabilities, the statement will be more effective. However, if the injured party had a prior disability or injury, it is imperative that you mention this in the brochure since omission may tend to create suspicions in the mind of the defense counsel. Moreover, your attorney

Appendum 11.2:

Settlement Brochure

IN THE UNITED STATES DISTRICT COURT
FOR THE NORTHERN DISTRICT OF GEORGIA
ATLANTA DIVISION

WILLIAM COLE,	§	
Plaintiff,	§	
	§	
v.	§	CIVIL ACTION
	§	FILE NO. 89-101
DAVID SIMPSON,	§	
Defendant.	§	

Roger R. Taylor
Taylor & Taylor
999 Fifth Street
Atlanta, Ga 30308
(404) 223–4577

(A family portrait showing William Cole before the accident)

PORTRAIT OF WILLIAM COLE

William Cole lived a very normal life. William was born in an average family with a modest income, but his determination and fortitude enabled him to work his way through college and graduate school. His education enabled him to obtain a position as a junior executive with a major corporation, Blackstone, Inc. William was 40 years old.

Again, William's determination and persistence made him quickly advance on the corporate ladder, becoming a vice-president within 11 years, grossing an annual income of $80,000.

William was a family man. With his busy work schedule, he still managed to spend every weekend with his family in his newly purchased beachfront home. William was an avid swimmer. He had just completed his scuba diving course and was about to take his test for his license. He planned to travel around the world with his family to explore the oceans.

Now William's active life has come to a standstill. His two boys cannot understand why their Daddy can't play baseball or soccer with them. His wife, Betty, spends all her waking hours waiting on William who now lies in bed day after day just staring at the ceiling. William gets more depressed as each day goes by.

WILLIAM COLE
A Successful Man

William Cole was earning $80,000 annually with liberal fringe benefits: company car, expense account, access to the company's condominium in New York, four weeks paid vacation each year, and many other benefits.

William was soon to be the president of Blackstone, Inc. He was informed by the Board of Directors that it was almost certain that he would be president when Mr. Blackstone retired, a mere two years away. His salary would have been $125,000 a year as president.

WILLIAM COLE
A Picture of Perfect Health

William Cole was a picture of perfect health before his tragic accident. He led a busy work schedule and an active physical life, practicing scuba diving every weekend, jogging daily with his wife, playing tennis and exercising at the YMCA. He enjoyed excellent health.
(Photograph of William in his scuba diving outfit)

THE TRAGIC DAY

As usual, William arose early to run his regular five miles through his neighborhood on the 4th day of January 1989. He put on his running clothes and headed out of the door after ten minutes of warm-up.

While William was peacefully jogging down the street, he noticed a white Cadillac speeding towards him. He was jogging facing the traffic. The automobile was driven by a young man on his way to Georgia Tech, a local college. William gracefully moved over closer to the side of the road. All of a sudden the driver lost control of the car, and the car swerved off the shoulder of the road and hit William.

The young man got out of the car to assist William. He said, "I'm so sorry. I shouldn't have been driving so fast. I was half asleep."

David Simpson said he was half asleep, and now William will suffer the rest of his life, hopelessly paralyzed—now a paraplegic.

THE SUFFERING

As a result of this tragic accident, William cole's life has completely changed: it has come to a standstill, a complete standstill. Not only has his professional life come to a halt, but also his personal life—in fact, all of his life has stopped.

Every day William stares at the ceiling of his bedroom, counting the cracks in the ceiling just to amuse himself. An intelligent man—wasted. He tries to move, but every time he does, he hurts, very badly. His lovely and patient wife must watch William closely and tend to his every need. A bed pan is always by his side. He is withering away. Every day he loses more weight because he can't eat.

William is depressed. He misses the active live he lived. He misses making love to his wife. He longs for the feel of fresh air and sunshine. He only has memories to live with now. His children still clamor for his fatherly attention—to tussle in the grass with him, to tackle him in a football game. But William can no longer do that. William tries to snap himself out of his depression, but the complete lack of activity is a new experience for him. His life has stopped.

(Photographs of William in his hospital bed, being tended to by his wife)

ITEMIZATION OF LOSSES, EXPENSES AND DAMAGES CLAIMED
As of August 26, 1989

Medical Expenses		
Arthur Kadish, M.D.	$ 9,879.00	
Monrad G. Majewski, M.D.	5,443.08	
Joseph P. Lovercamp, M.D.	4,333.89	
Gregory H. Henderson, M.D.	4,231.00	
Spencer A. Proffitt, M.D.	2,981.00	
Total:		$26,867.97
Hospital expenses		
Paradise Valley Hospital	$28,981.45	
St. Mary's Hospital	14,999.22	
Mercy Hospital	8,448.03	
St. Francis Xavier Hospital	4,028.33	
Chula Vista Hospital	3,289.00	
Total:		$59,746.03

Appendum 11.2

Continued

Medical Supplies, Pharmaceutical, Etc.		
Hospital bed rental	$ 2,345.11	
Pharmaceutical	981.00	
Wheelchair	454.81	
Bedside equipment	189.44	
Miscellaneous supplies	222.45	
Total		$ 4,192.81
Loss of Income		
From January 4, 1989 to date		39,919.32
Physical and Mental Pain and Suffering		
Loss of use of entire lower half of body		
Loss of motor and sensory control		
Loss of control of bladder, bowels		
Loss of ability to engage in social activities		
Loss of consortium		
Total		$ 2,000,000.00

FUTURE EXPENSES AND LOSSES

Future Medical Expenses		
Daily nursing care* (30 Years)	$ 360,000.00	
Physicians and medical care	430,000.00	
Medical supplies	89,400.00	
Hospital expenses	1,440,000.00	
Total:		$ 2,319,400.00
Future Loss of Income		
$55,000 per year for 2 years	$ 110,000.00	
$95,000 per year for 30 years	2,850,000.00	
Total:		$ 2,960,000.00
Future Physical and Mental		
Pain and Suffering		
Loss of use of entire lower half of body		
Loss of motor and sensory control		
Loss of control of bladder, bowels		
Loss of ability to engage in social activities		
Loss of consortium		
Total:		$ 9,000,000.00
GRAND TOTAL:		$16,410,126.13

*Daily nursing care necessary because Mrs. Cole must now return to work. (Estimated at $12,000 per year for 30 years.)

may want to present a particular legal theory relevant to a preexisting condition to support a claim that the condition was aggravated.

4. *Tragic-accident narrative.* A chronological description of the specific details of the accident should include the time, date, place, persons involved, particular events prior to and subsequent to the accident, proximate cause of the accident (without stating legal conclusions), and any other relevant information. The tragic-accident narrative may be slanted dramatically to capture the sympathy of the reader but never at the expense of the truth or in a way that is not supported by evidence.

5. *Results of tragic accident.* The statement portraying the results of the alleged accident should include a graphic description of the injured party's injuries and disabilities that he presently suffers and that he will continue to suffer as a result of the accident. It may also include any medical opinions or any prognosis

regarding the party's medical condition. Again, while it is essential that you present a sympathetic picture of the injured party's condition. do not exaggerate it.

6. *Itemization of losses, expenses, and damages claimed.* To prepare the itemization of present and future losses and expenses (e.g., medical, hospital, and personal expenses), review all the injured party's bills, receipts, invoices, check stubs, income tax returns, payroll records, and other related records so that you can compute the expenses accurately.

To prepare the statement of present and future damages, such as physical and mental pain and suffering, and loss of consortium, you should ask your attorney at what amounts to assess these exemplary damages. Your attorney may want to consult an expert to place a monetary value on these particular damages.

Recheck your figures for accuracy. An incorrect figure could be embarrassing to your attorney and may tend to cast doubt on the legitimacy of the injured party's claim.

7. *The caveat.* Include a statement similar to the following:

> The information contained in this brochure is furnished solely for the benefit of certain persons and is prepared for settlement purposes only. The statements contained herein are not to be considered as evidence or admission.

Without such a caveat, the other party may seek to introduce the information contained within the settlement as evidence at trial. Your attorney may also want to include other caveats in this portion of the settlement brochure.

8. *Additional items.* There are a few additional items that may be included in the settlement brochure depending upon the circumstances of the particular incident. For example, if the alleged incident is an automobile accident, you might include photographs of the scene of the accident, the party's injuries, (e.g., a picture of the injured party in a wheelchair or in braces), or the injured party's family. A map or diagram of the accident scene, a copy of the accident report, or any other relevant reports may also be included. Since each case merits different treatment, exercise judgment and discretion in preparing each individual statement.

• Settlement Negotiations Checklist

The settlement negotiations checklist shown in Exhibit Form 11.3 was prepared by two successful attorneys and is a good basis for your attorney to use in evaluating a case for settlement and recording settlement proposals. You can assist by recording and computing the amount of damages and other general information on this form prior to the case evaluation. Most personal injury attorneys realize the importance of preparing a settlement distribution statement to substantiate the financial disbursements of the settlement proceeds.

• Settlement Distribution Statement

The settlement distribution statement (Exhibit 11.4) can be prepared in various ways; however, it is imperative that all the expenses and disbursements be accurately noted in the statement to clarify the distribution of the proceeds for

Exhibit 11.3

Settlement Negotiations Checklist

☐ Case Evaluation (See Damage Section) (Consider Liability)   Totals
   ☐ Add Provable Damages
      ☐ Special $ _____
      ☐ Property   _____
      ☐ Other _____   _____
           Actual Damages   _____
      ☐ General   _____
      ☐ Other   _____
   ☐ Gross Case Value Considering Actual & General $ _____
   ☐ Add to or Reduce Gross Value by Variable Factors
      ☐ Prior Injuries   _____
      Comments _____
      _____
      _____

      ☐ Other Miscellaneous Factors—Party Impression   _____
      Comments _____
      _____
      _____

      ☐ Experience of (Plaintiff-Defendant) Attorney   _____
      Firm _____
      File Handled by _____
      Legal Ability _____
      Years of Experience _____
      Courtroom Experience _____
☐ Total Value Case $ _____
☐ Settlement Conversation Record
   Negotiation Date By—Conference, Telephone or Mail   *Amount Offered by Party*
   _____
   _____

Source: Thomas W. Elliott and Agnes M. Elliott, *Tort Resume: For Use in Prosecution and Defense of All Damage Claims* (Copyright, 1965), p. 26.

the client and to prevent future disputes about the settlement disbursements. In some states the attorney's contingency fee is not taken out of the gross proceeds, but only after subtraction of costs.

• Settlement Agreement

Preparing settlement agreements is an area in which you can save your attorney considerable time. In time, you should be able to develop a good form file that will help you expedite this process. Also, using word processing and even software form programs to record standard paragraphs will speed the preparation.

Make sure the settlement agreement does not contain any inconsistencies by checking the chronology of events, and make sure that the order of particular items mentioned is consistent throughout the document.

Your attorney may wish you to review the settlement agreement for numerous other reasons. Make your review thorough, and ask your attorney about any provisions in the agreement that you do not understand. Your attorney would

Exhibit 11.4

**Settlement Distribution
Statement**

Sam Sears v. Albert Lussier
Civil Action No. C-12349
Gwinnett County Superior Court
Gwinnett County, Georgia

Gross Settlement:		$55,000.00
Less Contingency Fee (1/3 of gross proceeds)*		18,333.32
Subtotal:		$36,666.68
Less Expenses:		
William G. Downs, M.D. (medical report)	$50.00	
Darryl Roberts (photographer)	85.00	
Gwinnett Co. Police Dept. (accident report)	3.00	
Notary Fees	5.00	
Long Distance Telephone Charges	43.54	
Crawford Long Hospital (x-ray films)	69.23	
Ready Blueprint Company		
(prints of x-ray films)	41.93	
Court costs	50.00	
Photocopies	12.00	
		359.70
Net Proceeds Due Client:		$36,306.98

*Pursuant to agreement, dated August 16, 1988, between Strauss & Simpson, Attorneys at Law, and Sam Sears

certainly prefer that you spot these problems rather than have the client or any of the other parties involved do so.

• Pretrial Conferences

If settlement negotiations fail, then the next step may be the pretrial conference. Pretrial conferences are heavily regulated by the court, and you should be sure to check both your state code and your local court rules. If the case is in federal court, then check the *Federal Rules of Civil Procedure*. Rule 16 provides for a pretrial conference for consideration of one or more of the following purposes. (Some state courts require pretrial conferences, while in other states they may have to be specially requested.) The participants at any conference under this rule may consider and take action with respect to:

1. The formulation and simplification of the issues, including the elimination of frivolous claims or defenses.
2. The necessity or desirability of amendments to the pleadings.
3. The possibility of obtaining admissions of fact and admissions as to the genuiness or admissibility of documents to avoid unnecessary proof, stipulations regarding the authenticity of documents, and advance rulings from the court on the admissibility of evidence.
4. The avoidance of unnecessary proof and of cumulative evidence.

5. The identification of witnesses and documents, the need (and schedule) for filing and exchanging pretrial briefs, and the date or dates for further conference and for trial.
6. The advisability of referring matters to a magistrate or master.
7. The possibility of settlement or the use of extrajudicial procedures to resolve the dispute.
8. The form and substance of the pretrial order.
9. The disposition of pending motions.
10. The need for adopting special procedures for managing potentially difficult or protracted actions that may involve complex issues, multiple parties, difficult legal questions, or unusual proof problems.
11. Such other matters as may aid in the disposition of the action.

Lawyers and the judiciary are well aware of the importance of solid preparation for the pretrial conference. While most of the attorney's preparation is focused on strategy and productive bargaining, you can assist your attorney by preparing and gathering the necessary documents for her to take to the pretrial conference or settlement conference. Your input will help your attorney present the case to the judge and the opposing party in the most favorable manner possible. You can also offer input into the strategy of the case since you have worked very closely on the case and may have gained some valuable insights.

Pretrial Order

The court may make a *pretrial order* that recites the action taken at the conference, the amendments allowed to the pleadings, and the agreements made by the parties as to any of the matters considered. The pretrial order also limits the issues for trial to those not disposed of by admissions or agreements of counsel. The order, when entered, controls the subsequent course of the action, unless modified at the trial to prevent manifest injustice. It specifically supersedes all previous pleadings.

Pretrial Calendar

The court may establish a *pretrial calendar* by rule on which actions may be placed for considerations enumerated above. The court may confine the calendar to jury or non-jury actions.

Pretrial Statement

The information included in a *pretrial statement* will vary according to the nature of the action. A personal injury action will be used as an example in this discussion. It is suggested that a copy of the pretrial statement be given to the judge or examiner if requested. Sometimes courts will allow you to file the pretrial statement with the court. Your attorney will decide whether to file the statement. Generally speaking, the pretrial statement in personal injury cases should include the following items:[4]

---

[4]Charles E. Robbins, *Attorney's Master Guide to Expediting Top-Dollar Case Settlements* (Englewood Cliffs, NJ: Executive Reports Corporation, 1977), pp. 609–610.

1. Acts of negligence claimed.
2. Specific regulations, statutes or ordinances alleged to have been violated.
3. A statement that the doctrine of *res ipsa loquitur* is relied upon (if applicable.)[5]
4. A detailed list of permanent personal injuries claimed, including the nature and extent.
5. The age of plaintiff.
6. The life expectancy of plaintiff, if permanent injury is claimed.[6]
7. The life expectancy of plaintiff's spouse, if permanent loss of consortium is claimed.[7]
8. An itemized statement of all special damages, such as medical, hospital, and nursing expenses, with the amount noted and to whom paid.
9. A detailed statement of loss of earnings claimed, including loss of future earnings.
10. A detailed list of all property damage.
11. Names of witnesses and area of testimony, including experts.[8]

Preparing Documentary Evidence and Exhibits for Pretrial

At the pretrial hearing, many courts allow counsel to produce all documentary evidence (or copies) and other exhibits to be introduced at the trial. In personal injury actions, the court usually requests that the documents and exhibits presented include at least the following:[9]

1. All bills and statements supporting claims for special damages.
2. All photographs and X-ray films intended to be offered at trial.
3. All medical and X-ray reports intended to be offered at trial.
4. If permanent injuries are claimed, medical support documented by the physician's report, deposition, or affidavit.
5. Blown-up plat, map, or diagram of place where accident occurred.
6. Drawing, diagram, or photograph of instrument alleged to have caused accident.
7. Documentary support for any loss of earnings claimed.
   a. If plaintiff is self-employed, copies of federal income tax returns for the years (usually three) prior to injury and for period of claimed loss.

[5]*Res ipsa loquitur* means "the thing speaks for itself." It is a doctrine in negligence law wherein the court holds that no further proof of negligence is needed other than the incident itself.
[6]See an actuarial or mortality table, or consult an insurance agent or bank trust officer for this information.
[7]*Consortium* is the duties and obligations which, by marriage, the husband and wife take upon themselves toward each other.
[8]See Chapter 7.
[9]Robbins, *Attorney's Master Guide*, pp. 610–611.

b. If plaintiff is salaried, copies of withholding statements, or a statement from his employer as to earnings for three years prior to injury and for the period of claimed loss.

• Releases

A *release* is a document by which one or more executing parties relinquishes all or certain claims against one or more specified parties. The purpose of a release is to protect the specified party or parties against future litigation or claims of the other party arising from the same factual situation.

These are two categories of releases: general and specific. A *general release* is designed to eliminate all possible claims, whereas a *specific release* is designed to eliminate only certain specific claims set forth in the release. A release may be general in language but refer only to particular claims.

The Uniform Tort-Feasor Act that has been adopted in numerous states provides a formula for computing the settlement on a pro-rata basis among *joint tort-feasors*. This type of release is frequently used in antitrust litigation.

Mutual releases are used when both parties have claims. For example, when a defendant has filed a counterclaim or cross-complaint against the plaintiff, a mutual release could be executed ensuring the plaintiff that the defendant releases the plaintiff and counter-defendant from "any and all claims arising out of the defendant and counter-plaintiff's claims."

In some instances, an *indemnity agreement* may be included in a release. This is usually entitled, "A Release and Indemnity Agreement," and is for the collateral purpose of indemnifying certain parties, their heirs, executors, agents, administrators, and so on, from any and all liability arising out of the parties' incident (e.g., an automobile accident).

In some instances, a *covenant not to sue* is executed by the party entitled to recovery under alleged cause of action. A covenant not to sue does not have the same effect as the release, since it is *prospective* (that is, it regards the future), whereas a release covers something that has already happened, such as a civil action that has already been filed.

Because of the serious consequences of an improperly drafted release, it is imperative that your attorney do the major part of the drafting.

• Stipulation and Order for Dismissal

Rule 41(a) (1) of the *Federal Rules of Civil Procedure* provides that a dismissal may be entered by plaintiff without order of court (1) by filing a notice of dismissal at any time before service by the adverse party of an answer or of a motion for summary judgment, whichever first occurs; or (2) by filing a *stipulation for dismissal* (Exhibit 11.5) signed by all parties who have appeared in the action. Unless it is stated otherwise in the notice of dismissal or stipulation, the dismissal is *without prejudice*, meaning that the party may file a subsequent action on the same issue or issues in the former action. In a dismissal *with prejudice* the party may *not* file any further action based on the issue or issues in the former action. A dismissal should reflect which party will pay court costs. A notice of dismissal filed by a plaintiff who has previously dismissed in any court of the United States or of any state an action based on or including the same claim is considered an adjudication upon the merits.

IN THE UNITED STATES DISTRICT
COURT FOR THE
WESTERN DISTRICT OF CALIFORNIA
SOUTHERN DIVISION

MARLENE BARTON

§

    Plaintiff,   §   CIVIL ACTION,

§   FILE NO. 92-1489

v.   §

JAY MACHAMER,   §

§

    Defendant.   §

STIPULATION FOR DISMISSAL

The above-styled action, having been fully compromised and settled,

NOW THEREFORE, it is hereby stipulated and agreed by and between the parties hereto that this action may be and is hereby dismissed with prejudice and without further costs to any of the parties.

IT IS FURTHER STIPULATED AND AGREED by and between the parties that either party, without notice to the other, may cause judgment of dismissal with prejudice to be entered herein, and that Plaintiff will pay all costs in these proceedings.

                                Conrad & Conrad
                                (Name of Firm)
           By: James Conrad
                  Attorney for Plaintiff

92 Lake Shore Dr.
St. Petersberg, FL 33707

                        Hoover Espirito & Sellers
                            (Name of Firm)
           By: Joseph Espirito
                 Attorney for Defendant

873 West Wicuca Blvd.
Jacksonville, FL 33700

An action may also be dismissed by order of the court pursuant to Rule 41(a)(2). However, if a counterclaim has been pleaded by a defendant prior to the service upon him of the plaintiff's motion to dismiss, the action shall not be dismissed against the defendant's objection unless the counterclaim can remain pending for independent adjudication by the court. Under this rule, the action is considered dismissed "without prejudice" unless otherwise stated.

After a settlement has been reached, and the releases, indemnity and settlement agreement are executed, a stipulation and *order for dismissal* (Exhibit 11.6) must be filed if the dispute is the subject of a lawsuit. In some states, an order may be entered into "settling, discontinuing and ending" the action. Check your state statutes and procedural rules for the particular prerequisites for dismissal of civil actions in your state.

Form 11.6

Order for Dismissal

IN THE UNITED STATES DISTRICT COURT
FOR THE NORTHERN DISTRICT OF NEW YORK
CENTRAL DIVISION

Justine Jeffries,	)	
	)	
	)	
Plaintiff,	)	CIVIL ACTION
	)	
v.	)	
	)	FILE NO. 92-48964
	)	
Darlene Johnson,	)	
	)	
	)	
Defendant.	)	

ORDER FOR DISMISSAL

It appearing that the parties consent hereto, therefore it is
ORDERED that the above-entitled action be dismissed without prejudice after payment of all costs in these proceedings by Plaintiff.
SO ORDERED, this 30th day of Oct., 1992.

_____
Judge, United States District Court
for the Northern District of New York
Central Division

• Summary

The paralegal's role in the negotiation, pretrial, and settlement processes is an ancilliary one. Primarily, you should concentrate on gathering information, assembling it in the proper package, and ensuring its accuracy. Often, numerous documents are involved in this stage of litigation, and you must be careful that they are kept intact and in order. Your diligence will be one of the most needed skills by your attorney. Whether your cases reaches settlement or not, you must always be prepared for settlement. Be alert for anything that you may need to bring to your attorney's attention that might help in the negotiation, pretrial, and settlement processes.

Assisting in Trial Preparation

• Introduction

The paralegal's involvement in preparing for trial varies according to the attorney's ability to delegate and the degree of trust he or she has in the paralegal. This chapter will give you ideas and practical tools on how you can assist your attorney prepare for trial. If you find things in this chapter that you are not doing, be assertive and suggest to your attorney that you do them. You can, for example, to evaluate prospective jurors through background searches, prepare drafts of jury instructions, and prepare case summaries and case evaluation sheets. One key task is to organize the trial book to enable your attorney to retrieve facts, information, and testimony easily. You also need to know how to prepare exhibits.

Your goal is to help your attorney get organized and prepare for trial, and you need to work closely with your attorney to make sure that you get the proper guidance to do things correctly. You also should be aware of the limitations you have as a paralegal in preparing for trials so that you do not overstep your authority.

• Preparing Witnesses for Trial

Your attorney is actually the one who prepares witnesses for trial, but you may be able to help. Ethical considerations are of utmost importance here.

Lay Witness

Your attorney will normally meet with the lay witness to discuss the presentation of testimony for trial in detail. You may assist your attorney by helping the witness understand the part the witness will play. Preparing the witness for trial is similar to preparing the client for his deposition (see Chapter 8). Do not under any circumstances answer any question in a way that may be construed as giving legal advice. The best advice is, "If in doubt, ask your attorney."

Once discovery is completed, you can prepare drafts of whatever petitions or orders are necessary to place the case on the trial list. At that time, accumulate all information necessary to prepare a pretrial memorandum. Arrange all medical records and reports, bills, photographs and other such items in an appropriate order with a list of these so they can be supplied to the court or counsel quickly when called for.

Expert Witness

Your contact with the expert witness will not be as direct as the attorney's. You can, however, do the following:

1. Find out if the expert witness will need anything for trial, such as a follow-up examination of the injured plaintiff.
2. Check with the expert witness to see if the data in the file are accurate and current.
3. Ask the expert witness to provide you with a curriculum vitae setting forth his or her credentials.
4. Ask the expert witness if he or she has appeared as an expert for any case in the past or given his or her deposition.
5. Assist your attorney in locating and contracting expert and other witnesses.[1]
6. Make preliminary arrangements for the witnesses to appear at trial.
7. Assist in preparing correspondence to witnesses regarding their interviews with your attorney and documents your attorney may need in preparation for trial or to be used as exhibits at trial.
8. Assist in preparing the necessary subpoenas and subpoenas *duces tecum*.[2]
9. Communicate with the witness by telephone or personally, if necessary, concerning these and related matters.
10. Assist your attorney and the expert witness in obtaining physical evidence the expert needs to conduct tests and inspections.
11. Gather information from the expert witness regarding qualifications and credentials (e.g., schooling, date and state of their professional licenses, specialized training, experience, including military service, company affiliations, memberships in professional associations, publications, professional honors received, etc.). Most of this information may be found in the curriculum vitae.
12. Assemble any materials, research materials, treatises, articles, etc., that your attorney or the expert witness might want to use in the presentation at trial.
13. Obtain, assemble, prepare, and document any other evidence that your attorney believes necessary for trial.

The final interview of the expert and the preparation of any pretrial motions or of the pretrial memorandum must, of course, be handled by the attorney.[3]

---

[1]See Chapters 7 and 9.

[2]A subpoena *duces tecum* directs the witness who is required to appear to testify to bring certain documents or other things to be presented to the court at the time of his testimony. Most subpoenas and subpoenas *duces tecum* are preprinted by the courts.

[3]Dudley Hughes, "Employment of Paralegals in Trial Preparation," *Forum* 1146 (1976).

How to Locate Expert Witnesses

Over a period of time, each attorney develops his or her own bank of expert witnesses. This is usually done through contacts with other attorneys and experts. There are several databanks of experts available, including *WESTLAW*, as well as many private databanks. In addition, the firm usually receives brochures and flyers from services that provide the names of experts. (See Chapter 9.)

In addition, a good source of experts is colleges and universities. Finding an expert is tough—an art in itself. Be sure you can get opinions based on clinical knowledge or standard of care in medical malpractice actions. Make sure that the expert has an excellent reputation, is highly published, well respected, and not just out to make money. Be aware that highly valued experts are protected by the attorneys who use them. Often an attorney may get one expert who is not well known to prepare an affidavit and then use another, more reputed expert for trial.

When you call the expert, you may be instructed by your attorney to brief the expert on the case. Later the attorney will fill him or her in on the details. Be sure to say who referred you when you first call. Of course, get the curriculum vitae.

Using Focus Groups to Prepare Witnesses

Many firms are now using *focus groups* to prepare witnesses for trial. People in the focus group act as parties, jurors, and other witnesses in a mock trial, to give the witness an idea of what it will be like in court. This mock trial also gives the attorney some good practice. More importantly, it gives the attorney the opportunity to test the potential reaction of a jury to the witness's testimony.

Videotaping Witnesses

You also can have a witness videotaped to spot any nervous habits that might detract from his testimony. While your attorney may want to coach the witness on how to present his testimony, do not under any circumstances tell the witness what to say.

Subpoenas for Witnesses

Some witnesses will need a subpoena to miss time from their work. If the witness is a friendly one, you can talk with her about the date that she is to testify. But always follow this up with a formal subpoena. Subpoena all witnesses that your attorney designates. Check your local rules and procedures to guide you in preparing the subpoenas. You may have a sheriff, process server, or anyone over the age of 18 serve the subpoena. In most states, marshals no longer serve subpoenas. The subpoena must be personally served. When the return of service is complete, it must be filed with the court. Check Rule 45 of *The Federal Rules of Civil Procedure* and your state statutes for the rules governing the service of subpoenas.

• Evaluating Prospective Jurors

Although often there is too little time for in-depth research on all prospective jurors, you may be requested to conduct a general background investigation on them. Jury commissions in some jurisdictions may provide attorneys with information derived from computer printouts containing the name, address, age, sex, and occupation of each member of the jury's panel. Potential jurors who have been subpoenaed by the court are included on the jury panel list prepared by the court, and a smaller jury pool is chosen before the trial.

The primary purpose of the background investigation is to assist your attorney in preparing questions for *voir dire,* which is the preliminary oral examination of a prospective juror conducted by the attorneys to all parties prior to the actual trial. A thorough background investigation may give your attorney information to use in eliminating jurors from the panel through *challenges.* There are two types of challenges: challenges for cause and peremptory challenges. A juror may be *challenged for cause* when it can be shown that he probably could not render an impartial judgment. A *peremptory challenge* may be executed against juror without any reason given. Challenges for cause are unlimited in number; peremptory challenges are usually limited in number.

Since it is the attorney's responsibility to use this background information for the purpose of gaining insight into how a juror will perform, discussion will be omitted on the rationale for the necessity for various information. Instead we will focus on how to obtain this information. Some cities have private jury services that keep files on people who have served on juries, proving information such as the nature and outcome of the juror's previous cases as well as the juror's vital statistics. If you do not have such services in your community, or if you wish to obtain additional information on the jury panel, the suggestions that follow may be beneficial to you in obtaining information. Remember, never contact the jury candidate himself. Such contact is highly improper and could be considered an attempt to influence the juror's vote.

Also, you should not conduct such a thorough investigation of the jury candidate that she would discover the investigation. For example, you would not want to contact her neighbors or friends. Your investigation should be merely a surface investigation to obtain general vital statistics. Caution should always be exercised. Most of your investigation should be limited to searching public records. Much of the following information will be provided to you on juror questionnaires:

1. Name and any aliases.
2. Age.
3. Sex.
4. Race.
5. Occupation.
6. Residence, including city.
7. Income class.
8. Religion.
9. Previous litigation experience as a party or a juror.
10. Health.
11. Marital status.
12. Children.
13. Political affiliations.
14. Professional associations.

15. Friends.
16. Relatives.
17. Financial interest in case.
18. Relation or indebtedness to attorneys, witnesses, and/or parties in the case.
19. Prejudices.

To locate this information, use the following sources:

1. Telephone book.
2. City directory.
3. Newspapers.
4. Voter registration records.
5. County courthouse.
6. Federal courthouse.
7. Bureau of Vital Statistics.

Additionally, if you work in a large firm, you might circulate the jury panel list to all employees. Often one of the other attorneys, paralegals, or secretaries may know something about the potential juror.

After you have gathered all the pertinent information on the potential jurors, organize it in a memorandum or in a chart for your attorney, or use a form like Exhibit 12.1.

• Assisting with Jury Instructions

Giving instructions to the jury is one of the most crucial stages of the trial proceedings. A *charge* is an instruction to the jury on the law, given by the judge after the closing argument. A *request to charge,* or a *point for charge,* may be prepared by counsel for either party.

Standard civil jury instructions are used by some states and are changed only where an attorney can substantiate the reason for a change.

The judge's charge to the jury consists of:

1. The judge's review of the evidence.
2. An explanation of the burden of proof, that is, which side has the burden of proving the allegations at issue.
3. A statement of the applicable law.
4. Instructions for applying the law to the facts of the case.

The judge's review of the evidence is not binding on the jury; however, the statement of the applicable law is. Jury instructions are prepared by each attorney and submitted to the judge for consideration before the judge instructs the jury. Jury instructions are statements of the law and the proposed instructions for applying the law to the facts of the case.

Samples of Jury Instructions

If your attorney asks you to assist in preparing jury instructions, be sure to check with your local and state statutes. An example of a proposed jury instruction in

Exhibit 12.1

Prospective Juror Evaluation Form

Client Name & Matter: _____ File No.: _____

Responsible Attorney(s): _____ Date: _____

Name:_____

Aliases, if any:_____

Home Address:_____

_____ Phone No.:_____

Sex:_____ Race:_____ Age:_____ Birthdate:_____ Birthplace:_____

Present Employer (name & address): _____

_____ Phone No.:_____

Job Title: _____ Supervisor: _____ Date of Employment:_____

No. Yrs. on Job:_____ Salary at Date Employed:$ _____Present Salary:$_____

For other previous employment; see reverse.

Marital Status: _____No. of Marriages: _____No. of Children:_____

Spouse's Name: _____ No. Years Married to this Spouse:_____

Spouse's Address: _____

Spouse's Sex:_____ Race: _____ Age: _____ Birthdate: _____Birthplace: _____

Spouse's Present Employer (name & address):_____

_____ Phone No.:_____

Spouse's Job Title: _____ Supervisor: _____ Date of Employment:_____

No. Yrs. on Job:_____ Salary at Date Employed:$ _____Present Salary:$_____

For previous employment, see reverse.

Professional Associations:_____

Political Affiliations/Community Organizations: _____

Religion: _____ Health: _____ Financial Interest in Case: $_____

Relation to or Indebtedness to Attorneys, Witnesses, and/or Parties: _____

Friends: _____ Relatives: _____

Previous Litigation Experience as a Party in a Suit or as a Juror:_____

_____ Prejudices:_____

Notes: _____

_____

_____

_____

_____

an automobile negligence action for a case filed in Georgia is shown in Exhibit 12.2.

• Preparing and Evaluating Cases

Pretrial memoranda, case summaries, case evaluation sheets, settlement brochures, pretrial order, and trial books all serve a distinct purpose in bringing the case to fruition. Much of the information needed for trial preparation is already available and already drafted within the case file. For example, a *mediation summary* is nothing more than a settlement demand package.

Exhibit 12.2

Sample Jury Instructions

1. Proximate Cause: Definition

Proximate cause is that which, in the natural and continuous sequence, unbroken by other causes, produces an event, and without which the event would not have occurred. Proximate cause is that which is nearest in the order of responsible causes, as distinguished from remote: that which stands last in causation, not necessarily in time or place, but in causal relation.

2. Proximate Cause: Concurrent Negligence
(Joint Proximate Cause)

Where concurrent causes operate directly in bringing about an injury there can be a recovery against one or all of the responsible parties. The mere fact that the injury would not have been sustained had only one of the acts of negligence occurred will not of itself operate to define and limit the other act as constituting the proximate cause: For if all acts of negligence contributed directly and concurrently in bringing about the injury, they together constitute the proximate cause. (*Tallman v. Green,* 74 Ga. App. 731, 734).

In other words, the proximate cause of an injury may be two separate and distinct acts of negligence of different persons acting concurrent acts of negligence operated in bringing about an injury, the person injured may recover, from either or both of the persons responsible, compensation for the entire loss. (*Milton Bradley Co., et al., v. Cooper,* 79 Ga. App. 302, 307)

If you find the defendant or his agent negligent in at least one respect and that this negligence, joined together with the negligence of a third person, proximately caused the collision, then it is not necessary for you to determine whether the defendant (or his agent) or a third person was more at fault as the plaintiff would be entitled to recover against either his full damages.

After the jury instructions have been finalized by your attorney, insert them in the trial book, properly indexed. Some courts provide a standard instruction book of jury instructions for civil actions. You may prepare a form book of standard charges that are frequently used by the attorneys in your office. An indexed loose-leaf notebook or binder will assist you in methodically organizing these charges and will save you time in assisting your attorney prepare for trial.

Case Summary

The *case summary* is similar to a trial preparation report wherein all the pertinent information is assembled and condensed in a readable form for your attorney to use when preparing for trial or for settlement negotiation. Depending upon the particular type of case on that you are working, organize the relevant information regarding the case in a concise report. A sample format from a civil action prepared by the defense of a personal injury claim from an asbestos worker is shown in Exhibit 12.3. You may wish to use this as a guideline; however, you will need to tailor the format to include the particular facts and issues involved in the case on which you are working.

Case Evaluation Sheet

The *case evaluation sheet* (Exhibit 12.4) is a more detailed synopsis of the pertinent aspects of the case to be considered in evaluating the status of the case. It may be used both for purposes of settlement negotiations and in preparation for trial.

Exhibit 12.3

●

James Walter Goodman— Case Summary

Born:	1918, Savannah, Georgia
Died:	October 6, 1986
Dependents:	Wife: Susan Anne Goodman
	Route #2
	Atlanta, Georgia 30318
	Married: March 14, 1956
Previous Marriage:	Carolyn Sneed
	Divorced 1958, Marietta, Georgia
Military History:	U.S. Navy, Chief
Medical History:	Dr. William J. Jones was his physician for about 16 years. Dr. G. Braun was his physician the past five years. His general health from 1962 to 1985 was good.

3/2/65: Automobile accident which injured his left shoulder.

4/5/82: Complete physical by Dr. G. Braun. Health—Good

8/9/82: Admitted to the hospital with the flu. In January 1984 his first symptoms appeared. Suffered weakness, shortness of breath. He was admitted to South Cobb Hospital one month later for treatment of pneumonia. He was x-rayed on 10/11/82. X-ray report showed pleural calcification and mild chronic lung changes. There was no mentioned of interstitial fibrons, but mesothelioma was not ruled out.

Exploratory surgery revealed a bronchogenic carcinoma of the left lower lobe a pulmonary resection (left lower lobectomy) was done. Post-operative radiation to the chest wall and lower esophagus as begun as the tumor was in close contact with these areas.

Final Diagnosis:

Asbestosis in the left pleural space. Dr. McLaughlin's progress notes show a history of fiberglass exposure, no mention of asbestos.

Worker's Compensation:	Previous case settled for $21,000. Lew Insulations. Paid by Zep Insurance Company.
Social Security:	No information regarding social security benefits.
Life Insurance:	$75,000 paid by Smith Mutual Life Insurance Company.
Medical Expenses:	Medicine and drugs $ 2,245.45
	Medical Supplies 1,195.21
	Misc. Doctors 23,000.00
	$26,400.66
Defenses:	Assumption of risk—Claimant smoked two packs of cigarettes a day from 1974 until his death.

Employment History:	Annual Salary	Date	Employer
	$ 6,400.00	1962-1974	North Insulation Company
	8,940.00	1975-1979	United Brothers, Inc.
	11,871.00	1980-1985	Lew Insulations

Lost Wages:	Total Earnings (1974-1985)—$171,915.00
Products Used:	Toyla Block Pipe Covering, Two shot cement and asbestos cloth.
Possible Witnesses:	1. Paul Warren—Foreman, North Insulation Company
	9 Outer Road, Norwalk, CN 06854
	2. Robert C. Butler—Coworker, North Insulation Company
	890 Ridgewood Road, Atlanta, GA 30318
	3. Roy Newell—Supervisor, United Brothers, Inc.
	4618 Newman Road, Covington, GA 30209
Expert Witnesses:	1. Dr. William La Lane, Charleston, SC
	2. Dr. Wilfred Spaeth, Marietta, GA
	3. Dr. Fernando Whitney, Riverdale, GA
	4. Dr. Robert McLaughlin, Atlanta, GA
	5. Dr. G. Braun, Atlanta, GA

Exhibit 12.4

Case Evaluation Sheet

1. Name _____
2. Age_____
    When? _____
    Where? _____
3. Address _____
    Own home? _____
    How Long? _____
    Previous Address _____
    _____
4. Occupation_____
    Where? _____
    What capacity? _____
    Previous duties _____
    How long? _____
    Salary_____
    Previous employment _____
        (a) Why terminated?_____
        (b) Salary _____
    Duties after injury_____
    Present status _____
5. Education:
    Where? _____
    What years? _____
    What degrees obtained? _____
6. Married? _____
    How long? _____
    Where? _____
    Maiden name_____
    Divorced? _____
    When?_____
7. Spouse:
    Name _____
    Age_____
    Address _____
    _____
    Occupation:
        Where? _____
        What capacity? _____
        How long? _____
        Salary_____
        Previous employment _____
    Divorced? _____

Exhibit 12.4

Continued

8. Children:

   Name _____

   Age _____

   Address _____

   _____

   Occupation _____

     Where? _____

     What capacity? _____

   Married? _____

9. Describe accident:

   Generally _____

   _____

   _____

   Specially:

     Time (hour & date) _____

     Place _____

     Weather _____

     Speed _____

     Distances _____

     Circumstances _____

     Destination _____

     Previous whereabouts _____

     Companions _____

     Familiarity of surroundings _____

10. Witnesses:

   Names _____

   _____

   _____

   _____

   Addresses _____

   _____

   _____

   _____

   _____

   Employees _____

   _____

   _____

   _____

11. Photographs:

   Of what _____

   _____

   Where? _____

   Who has? _____

The assigned paralegal completes the case evaluation sheet with all the information except the client's name or other identifying information. Then several attorneys hold a roundtable discussion of the value and merits of the case. The attorneys are not informed as to which party the firm represents. Then each attorney evaluates the liabilities of the case, both for defendant and plaintiff, and denotes a monetary valuation. If the case is going to trial, the attorneys will discuss specific issues and how they would prove them, and suggest additional information or facts needed to prepare the case for trial properly. Of course, the case evaluation form may be used for other purposes, such as compiling a case summary or a checklist of necessary information.

Settlement Brochure

The *settlement brochure* is a formal composite of the pertinent aspects of the case prepared for negotiation and settlement purposes. It often contains photographs and/or diagrams to support the position of the parties. If your state courts use a mediation procedure, then much of the information will already be available for preparation of a settlement brochure (see Chapter 11).

Pretrial Order

To summarize the issues and expected proof in a lawsuit, most federal district courts now require that a *pretrial order* be prepared by all counsel prior to trial and after discovery is completed. The courts usually have a prescribed format for a pretrial order (see Chapter 11).

Trial Book

The *trial notebook* is a collection of the various items that your attorney will need at trial. It serves as a composite reference and guide for your attorney and frequently is the main source of information and guidance.

Here are concrete suggestions on what to include in the trial book and how to organize it meticulously to help your attorney win cases.[5]

1. Allow yourself plenty of time to prepare the trial book so your attorney can use it well in advance of and in preparation for trial.
2. Work closely with your attorney to make the trial book flexible so that you can add to, eliminate, or consolidate items in the book as your attorney instructs you. An 8 1/2″ × 11″ loose-leaf binder will allow you to do this.
3. Organize items in folders first, then divide into sections in the trial book (e.g., correspondence, memoranda, exhibits, notes, etc).
4. Use colored tabs as dividers to make the separate categories in the book easily identifiable. Use highlighter pens to mark specific items. Exhibit 12.5 is a checklist of suggested items to include in the trial book. Remember that each case varies and may require that items be added or deleted. Use this skeletal outline as a starting point.

---

[5]Contributions were made to this section by Connie Coe, litigation paralegal.

Exhibit 12.5

**Checklist for Contents
of Trial Book**

Client Name & Matter: _____ File No.: _____
Responsible Attorney(s): _____ Date: _____
√ Check When *Completed*

ITEM

- 1. Preparation agenda
- 2. Table of contents
- 3. General information
- 4. Case memoranda
- 5. Police reports and statements
- 6. Pleadings and pretrial order
- 7. Motions
- 8. Evaluations of prospective jurors, *voir dire,* and notes
- 9. Case summaries
- 10. Analysis of the issues and outlines of proof
- 11. List of witnesses
- 12. Witness files—expert, plaintiff's, and defendant's witnesses
- 13. Witness depositions digests
- 14. Outlines of testimony
- 15. Notes for opening statement
- 16. Notes for cross-examination
- 17. Index of discovery
- 18. Material to be used at trial
- 19. Notes and briefs on law and evidence, and trial motions
- 20. Jury instructions
- 21. Notes for final argument
- 22. List of exhibits and exhibit file
- 23. Trial agenda
- 24. "To do" list
- 25. Medical brief (if applicable)
- 26. Technical notes
- 27. Master index/cross-index

---

5. Become familiar with the facts of the case and the legal issues involved so that you can assist your attorney by drafting the analysis of the issues and the outlines of proof.

6. Determine what are the issues and how you can go about proving them. It is important that you work closely with your attorney to prepare these items in the trial book. You may prepare the initial draft to save time.

7. Keep a running index of items to go into the final trial book as the case progresses. Make duplicates to prevent loss of documents.

Now we will discuss each item on the checklist in Exhibit 12.2.

1. *Preparation agenda.* A list of things that must be done to assemble and prepare the trial book. This is not a list of things to do for trial. Essentially, it contains notations on the items and documents to be inserted into the trial book. More than anything, it gets you started.

2. *Table of contents.* Should be completed, with page numbers, after all the items are in the trial notebook in the right order.

3. *General information.* All important names, addresses, phone numbers, fax numbers, beeper numbers, and hotels/motels. Include the following:

- Courthouse, judge, clerks, bailiff, sheriff, and record.
- The firm's staff: attorneys, paralegals, couriers, and others.
- Client.
- Witnesses.
- Expert witnesses.
- Opponent's firm, staff, witnesses, and experts.
- Carryout food services if needed.
- Taxicab services, if needed.

4. *Case memoranda.* All the main memoranda prepared by the firm regarding the facts of the case, inserted in chronological order.

5. *Police reports and statements.* If the case is a personal injury automobile case, insert all police reports and statements.

6. *Pleadings and pretrial order.* Organize all major pleadings and amendments, including the complaint, answer, interrogatories, request for admission, and motions in a separate binder. They will be too voluminous to fit in the trial notebook, and presumably they will have already been kept in a binder throughout the progress of the case. Index them in chronological order. Tab and color-code each as to plaintiff and defendant. Key sections should be highlighted. Include the pretrial order in this section also. Summaries of this pleadings may be inserted in place of the pleadings if your attorney so desires.

7. *Motions.* Any remaining pretrial motions with supporting authorities may be inserted in this section, but keep them in a separate binder and indexed in chronological order. Be prepared with authorities to oppose any likely last-minute motions by the opposition.

8. *Evaluations of prospective jurors, voir dire, and notes.* Evaluations of prospective jurors, motions, the file and case evaluation sheet, the witness files, and the preparation of exhibits for trial. Prepare a jury chart to indicate the number or name of each juror, as well as your attorney's notes on suitability. Then have a blank chart ready to insert the actual names of jurors selected to hear the case.

Make notes on the description of the jury according to sex, approximate age, race, and any other information you have, such as marital status, number of children, and occupation. Your attorney may want you to take notes from day to day as to the jurors' reactions to certain testimony. You can add these to the notebook during trial, indexing them by day and indicating what testimony was heard.

9. *Case summaries.* As explained previously, the case summaries give the factual and legal issues in narrative form. The facts are set forth in chronological order first, and then the legal issues are defined.

10. *Analysis of the issues and outlines of proof.* This section contains a master chronology of events referenced to exhibits and deposition testimony. In addition, it contains *outlines of proof,* which are issues of facts and evidence along with the source of proof of that evidence. For example, in a breach of contract action, the execution of the contract would be the fact to be proved. The source might be a page in the deposition of the witness to the execution of the contract where she stated that she witnessed the execution. Using the pretrial order, arrange the issues of fact or statement from the contentions of your client on individual pages. Insert several blank pages of paper between each issue or statement. Then, with the assistance of your attorney, note the source of anticipated proof for each. For example, you might note, "Live testimony of John Gilman; deposition testimony of Dr. Roy Evans; defendant Correl's answer for Interrogatory No. 21."

11. *List of witnesses.* A master list of witnesses in the order of presentation, along with telephone number, address (home and work), and age.

12. *Witness files—expert, plaintiff's, and defendant's witnesses.* Separate and organize the witnesses into three categories: expert, plaintiff's, and defendant's witnesses. Make separate color tabs for each. Put each potential witness in the notebook in alphabetical order. Include a sheet on each witness summarizing identifying information and relevant points that need to be brought out from that witness's testimony. Place questioning lists in each witness's section. If the witness was deposed prior to trial, these questions may already be prepared and may just need some revisions or additions. Behind each witness's tab, insert all pertinent information about the witness:

- Address and phone number.
- Age.
- Deposition summaries and cross references to other deposition digests.
- References implicating witnesses from documents and depositions.
- Interview notes.
- Outline of testimony.
- Outline of direct and/or cross-examination.
- Date of service of subpoena.
- Exhibits to be introduced through the witness.
- Anticipated evidentiary problems with legal authority.

13. *Witness deposition digests.* These will provide the attorney with a quick reference form to previous testimony during examination and cross-examination. Organize them in alphabetical order. Then highlight the most relevant points for the plaintiff's case in one color and the most relevant points for the defense in another color. Also include a "key" to your color system behind your alphabetical listing of the digests. Number the digests on the list, and then use tabs for easy reference.

Many times expert witness depositions will be videotaped. Index these along with all the other deposition digests as discussed above, and organize the tapes in a separate box. Also, you will need to call the court to make arrangements to allow the videotapes into the courthouse without going through the x-ray security equipment as this can erase the tape.

14. *Outlines of testimony.* These should include excerpts from depositions, interrogatories, requests for admissions, interviews, and so forth.

15. *Notes for opening statement.* Your attorney may wish to prepare notes or an outline for the opening statement. During trial, your attorney may want you to take detailed notes of the opposing counsel's opening statement for use or reference during trial. File these, tab them, and list them in the table of contents.

16. *Notes for cross-examination.* Drafted questions and notes for cross-examination may be collected under this section.

17. *Index of discovery.* A complete index of the pleadings and depositions should be inserted here for easy reference by your attorney at trial. The exact location of each document should be indicated on this list.

18. *Material to be used at trial.* Any other material, illustrations, visual aids such as maps, graphs, or charts, or other documents should be listed here and their location indicated. Include a list of all physical equipment you will need to ensure the availability of: flipchart, chalkboard, maps of accident scene, magic markers and highlighters, tape recorders, television, VCR, or other equipment.

19. *Notes and briefs on law and evidence, and trial motions.* These items along with other trial memorandum that may arise during trial, and the legal authority supporting their position, should be separated by issue. Cases and other supporting documents should be included. Also, it may be helpful to do an index of the main cases to be used as support and then summarize briefly the issues in each case. Indicate how these cases are similar and differing from the issues in your case.

20. *Jury instructions.* Depending upon local statutes and procedures, attorneys normally submit the jury instructions to the judge before trial, or at the beginning of the trial, or after the testimony is closed and prior to the final summation. Include a copy of these in this section, one to a page. Also include a section for opposing counsel's instructions, as well as the court's if it issues its own instructions. Make a notation on the jury instruction as to whether it was accepted, rejected, or modified.

21. *Notes for final argument.* Your attorney can synthesize her final argument in this section, making notes and points to emphasize.

22. *List of exhibits and exhibit file.* A complete indexed list of all exhibits in order of introduction should be prepared, indicating the date of the exhibit, a description, including number of pages, size (e.g., poster, photograph), what the exhibit entails, its significance, case file number, or witness number needed for introduction, and a brief statement of authorities on its admissibility. Collect the exhibits in a compendium form in a separate binder labeled "Exhibits," and tab them. This will usually include many documents and will therefore not fit in the trial book itself.

You will also need to call the court about exhibit stickers and place some extras in the trial notebook in a plastic "ziplock" loose-leaf enclosure, just in case a document is added as an exhibit unexpectedly. Determine the number of copies of each exhibit needed, because when an exhibit is entered, you must give copies to the court and all other counsel.

23. *Trial agenda.* This is your attorney's own blueprint for trial. It should be a complete outline of the things your attorney plans to do at the trial and the order in which to do them.

24. *"To Do" list.* The final section of the trial book should be a page for a "To Do" list, wherein your attorney can note things that come up at trial that have to be done. You can assist your attorney by compiling a list of notes made at trial at the completion of each trial day.

25. *Medical brief (if applicable).* If the case involves medical issues, insert all briefs and memoranda relevant here. Medical reports and diagrams may also be inserted as well as current medical literature. Include a quick reference summary of specific incidence rates, percentages, numbers of deaths, etc., and highlight pertinent passages.

26. *Technical notes.* If the case involves a technical problem, lengthy technical documents and data should be accumulated in this section for easy reference by your attorney.

27. *Master index/cross-index.* After you complete the organization of the trial book, prepare a master index and cross-index by names, topics, issues of law, etc. If you are able to attend trial with your attorney, reinsert items into the trial book as they are returned.

• Preparing Organized Witness Files

A file should be opened by you on every witness involved in the litigation proceedings in any way whatsoever, regardless of whether the witness will testify at trial. This includes the adversary's known witnesses, although some of this information may be unobtainable. (For recording general information regarding witnesses, see Chapter 7.) Your attorney will give you information to insert in this file and will expect you to keep up with it.

The witness file should include:

1. General and personal background information (e.g., name, age, residence, employment, etc.).
2. Witness's statement.
3. Outline of witness's testimony and your attorney's notes for direct and cross-examination.
4. Excerpts of testimony from depositions, interrogatories, requests for admissions, interviews, etc.
5. A list of exhibits relating to witness's testimony to be introduced into evidence at trial.
6. Copies of witness's subpoena or *subpoena duces tecum.*
7. Attorney's and paralegal's notes regarding their impressions of the witness.
8. Any other relevant information or documents.

Make a separate exhibit list. Prepare and number all the original exhibits for trial, separating them from the witness files. Put a copy of the exhibit list in the pertinent witness file. Do not put the original exhibits in the witness file (these will be discussed shortly).

Insert an identifying label on each witness file and indicate the telephone numbers at which the witness may be reached. Make dividers and tabs for each category of information listed above. A loose-leaf notebook is preferable.

• Preparing Exhibits for Trial

You can organize and index the exhibits for your attorney before trial. The exhibit index may include:

1. A summary of its contents.
2. The document number of whatever numbering system is used.
3. The location of the document in storage file.
4. The purpose for which the document may be used at trial.

The categories counsel selects to organize and index the documents will depend on the requirements of the case. The simplest is by the name of the item. A cross-index or cross-indexes by topics or by witnesses who will be using the documents might be a helpful tool. In simple cases, the keying of the documents into the witness sheets can serve as a cross-index.

The thumbnail abstract of the contents of the documents takes time to prepare but can be invaluable for voluminous documents. At a glance you can get the gist of the document without having to retrieve it.

You may use copies of documents to be used as exhibits where necessary; however, when possible use the originals. Some courts now accept photocopies, but check the court rules and procedural statutes in the forum state.

Here are eight helpful rules for handling documents in litigation:

1. **Don't** mark or mutilate originals.
2. **Do** work with copies of important documents.
3. **Don't** file original documents with depositions.
4. **Do** stipulate for the substitution of copies.
5. **Do** safeguard important documents in a safe.
6. **Do** obtain original documents from the client, not copies.
7. **Do** insist that the opponent produce original documents, not copies in discovery.
8. **Do** indicate the source of each document. A simple way is to write the source on a slip of paper and attach it by paper clip. Do not staple.

• Additional Ways to Be Helpful at Trial

Many paralegals attend the trials of the cases on which they have been working. This opportunity can be an extremely valuable one for you. Not only can you see the results of your hard work on the case but also, you can also see one of the most important parts of the litigation process. Watching your attorney as an advocate will show you how the relevant issues are tried and proven.

Since the trial procedure is a complicated process, you should understand the basic rules of evidence and the various steps in the trial procedure, for example, the opening argument, direct and cross-examination, redirect examination, and closing argument. Your attendance at trial can also be very helpful to your attorney in many ways.

Be sure to check with the court for permission to use video equipment and computers, both for graphic demonstrations and for laptop use in the court-

Exhibit 12.6

Checklist for Determining the Status of a Case Before Trial

(   ) Suit Filed Date _____ Court _____

(   ) Defensive Pleadings—Suit Served on Defendant _____

    (   ) Should a Jury Trial Be Demanded? _____

    (   ) Answer & Pleadings Due_____ Filed _____

    Other Pleadings Filed   Hearing Date   Judge

    (   ) Demurrers _____

    (   ) _____

    (   ) _____

(   ) Stipulations

    (   ) Demurrers or Other Pleadings for Hearing—Date_____

    (   ) Case for Trial—Date_____ Is Special Order Needed? _____

    (   ) Reason _____

(   ) Discovery Procedures—Know Your Client Before Submitting

    (   ) Request for Admissions

    Served   Answers Due   Objection Hearing Date   Judge

    (   ) Interrogatories

    Served   Answers Due   Objection Hearing Date   Judge

    (   ) Depositions (Give Opposite Party Notice Required by Law. Check Law Regarding Time, Mileage & Attendance Fees in Subpoenaing Witnesses.)

    Name   Discovery or Other   Taken When & Where   Court Reporter

    (   ) Serve Above Witnesses With *Subpoena Duces Tecum* or Notice To Produce If Needed? (Check Statutory Notice as to Time & Service)

    (   ) Motions for Inspection & Copying Needed? _____

    (   ) Other Motions_____

(   ) Pretrial Procedures—Issued Resolved _____

(   ) Preparation for Trial

    (   ) Subpoena All Witnesses, Necessary Medical & Businesses Records

    (   ) Name   Address   Date   Mileage & Attendance Fee

    (   ) Prepare Exhibits & Enlarge Pictures for Use at Trial

    (   ) Prepare *Voir Dire* Questions

Source: Thomas W. Elliott and Agnes M. Elliott, *Tort Resume for Use in Prosecution and Defense of All Damage Claims* (Copyright 1965), pp. 24–25.

Exhibit 12.6

Continued

(   ) Obtain List of Prospective Jurors

(   ) Prepare Outline of Proof According to Witnesses

(   ) Prepare Trial Brief, Request to Charge & Tentative Argument to Jury

(   ) Jury Trial Before Judge_____ Date_____

      (   ) Verdict & Judgement _____ Date_____

(   ) Appellate Review

Motions, Preparation of Record & Briefs	Due	Filed	Service on Opposite Party	Hearing Result

      (   ) Final Appellate Court Decision & Direction—Date _____

(   ) Decision Made Judgment of Trial Court _____

room. Most federal and state judges have their own marshalling orders for exhibits, bench books, and trial books. Always check the local rules of the court in which the case is to be tried.

• For Trial: Case Status Checklist

Use the checklist in Exhibit 12.6 as a method to determine instantly the status of litigation after filing suit. Work closely with your attorney on items on which you need further direction. This checklist will give your attorney a quick overview of the case and should serve as a reminder of things that must be done prior to trial.

• Summary

Organizing your attorney's documents in preparation for trial not only saves him significant time, but knowing you are in control of all the papers involved will relieve him somewhat of the tremendous burden in preparing for trial. By being alert for new ways to help your attorney and by doing a good job, you will build the trust that is needed for him to delegate additional responsibility to you. Attention to detail will help you more than anything, and the forms in this chapter and those that you develop will help you in that aspect of your job.

13

How Computers Are Used in Litigation

• Introduction

In this chapter[1] you will learn how computer technology is used by law firms and the courts in the litigation process. You will be introduced to the different types of database software and the applications for which they are appropriate. Traditional applications such as docket control and conflict-of-interest checking are presented as elements of automated case management.

A litigation practice or department can benefit from automation as much, if not more, than any other legal specialty. The nature of litigation lends itself to an organized approach and demands a high degree of efficiency. There are several areas other than basic word processing where automation can provide benefits to litigation specialists, whether they are attorneys, paralegals, or secretaries. Indeed, automated litigation support is often one of the first systems a litigation firm implements. Litigation support as a system is discussed in detail in Chapter 14. (Of course, all systems that assist attorneys and paralegals in the litigation process could be considered litigation support.)

• Managing Information through Databases

Every law firm has information that can be better managed using a computer. Every attorney or department will have its own lists of information, which may include some of the following:

- Clients and matters, addresses and phone numbers.
- Mailing lists to be used for mass mailings.
- Expert witnesses and their areas of expertise.
- Wills kept in the firm's safe.
- Corporations and all related information necessary to file annual corporate returns.

---

[1]This chapter was co-authored by Paula F. Turner, CPA, MBA, partner in Holland Shipes Vann, P.C., Atlanta, Georgia, specializing in computer consulting to law firms. The chapter was edited by attorney Robert S. Hochdorf, Senior Litigation Specialist for the Atlanta office of The LITIDEX Company,™ a full-service automated litigation support company providing software and services to law firms and corporate legal departments. Contributions were also made by Joseph L. Hansen, Hansen Consulting, Atlanta, Georgia.

- Tax clients for whom the firm is responsible for filing returns.
- Employees and related data.
- Fixed assets such as furniture, computers and automobiles.
- Library books.

All of this information can be more easily managed by using a database management software program. A single program should be used throughout the firm to avoid duplication of effort and to allow sharing of information. For example, if the firm has a database of all clients and matters, the database can be expanded to identify those clients who have tax matters or which are corporations. The primary advantage of using a single database is that only one set of data must be maintained, and all systems thus become more efficient.

What Is a Database Software Program?

The concept of a database software program is easy to visualize. Imagine a file cabinet and the components of a filing system. Each cabinet contains a subset of information separated by file folders in some specific order. They may be in alphabetical, numerical, or chronological order. Inside each file folder are documents pertaining to a specific file. A database works like this filing system. Information is stored in electronic files, and all data is categorized by some meaningful system.

The primary difference between the electronic filing system and the manual system is the amount of space required for storage and the time required to locate and retrieve information. Millions of pieces of information can be stored inside your microcomputer, while physical copies of the same documents would require numerous file cabinets and significant wall space—plus probably some of the physical information would have to be stored on Rolodex® cards or on lists inside desk drawers. This decentralized method of storing information makes updating and locating it very time-consuming.

With a database program, you can do the following much more quickly than you could with a traditional filing system.

- Add new data.
- Change existing data.
- Locate specific data.
- Sort data in a specific order.
- Produce reports of desired data.

Some Basic Software Terms

All software programs contain an underlying database. If you understand the basic terminology of databases, you will understand the basic terminology of software in general. Here are some basic terms you should know:

1. *Field.* Each data item such as client name, matter number or attorney initials is a field.

2. *Record.* A collection of related fields, such as the client number, name, address and telephone number of a particular client.

3. *Files.* A collection of related records, such as all matters for the firm. Records may be kept in one *linear* file called a *flat file* or in several files arranged in either a *hierarchical* or *relational* structure.

Exhibit 13.1
•
Boolean Logic
(Logical Operators)

Operator	Description
AND	The AND operator narrows a search by producing a set whose components are common to both sets. For example, the expression APPLES AND ORANGES will operate on the set of records containing both the term APPLES and the term ORANGES. Both terms must be present.
OR	The OR operator expands a search by producing a set whose elements are found in either component set. For example, the expression APPLES OR ORANGES will produce a set of records where one or the other or both terms may be present.
NOT	The NOT operator produces a set whose elements are not identified by the specified term. In most systems NOT is equivalent to AND NOT. The expression APPLES NOT ORANGES will produce a set of records containing the term APPLES, but not also containing the term ORANGES.
XOR	Some software products include XOR (EXCLUSIVE OR) as an additional Boolean search operator. The search by the XOR operator produces a set whose elements include one of two terms, but not both terms in the same record. For example, the expression APPLES XOR ORANGES will produce a set of records containing either the word APPLES or the word ORANGES, but not both terms. XOR therefore initiates a search narrower than an OR search but perhaps broader than an AND search.

4. *Keys.* Database programs use keys (or *pointers*) to establish relationships between records. This is also referred to as *indexing* in some programs. A common key would be a client number. Each file containing data related to a specific client would contain a common data element, the client number. This helps the program search through all the records faster to locate data.

5. *Indexes.* To speed retrieval and allow greater search capabilities, nearly all database software programs create *inverted indexes,* which extract the searchable words or phrases from the linear, or flat, file and list them in a separate, alphabetically ordered files with pointers back to the appropriate record in the linear file. This index file provides rapid access to individual items.

6. *Tables.* These are words or shorthand codes of descriptive data, used frequently or repetitively, such as areas of law, personal or company names, departments, or attorneys.

7. *Validation.* Many programs also check the validity of data entered against tables of codes or actual data and notify the user if an error is found.

8. *Queries.* These are searches for specific data believed to be in the database file. Most database programs use *logical operators,* called *Boolean logic*[2] (see Exhibit 13.1) to define the conditions of a query. A second form of query is by way of *comparison* or *relational* operators (see Exhibit 13.2), or numeric search keys.

Specific Kinds of Database/Full-Text Software

The database/full-text product you choose will depend on your level of computer experience and what your firm's database needs are. Database software may be divided into categories of specialized use as follows:

1. Outliners/personal information managers.
2. Full text—deposition-specific.

---

[2]Logical operators are words that represent logical relationships between terms in a search statement. They are used in a system known as *Boolean logic,* named after the mathematician George Boole.

Exhibit 13.2
•
**Relational Comparison
Operators**

Relational Operators	Text Abbreviation	Description
=	EQ	Equal to
<> or #	NOT	Not equal to
>	GT	Greater than
<	LT	Less than
<=	LT EQ	Less than or equal to
>=	GT EQ	Greater than or equal to

3. Full text—generic.
4. Indexing/abstracting.
5. Integrated.

Outliners/Personal Information Managers

Personal information managers are best suited for simple lists of information. In addition to database management, personal information managers usually offer other capabilities like calendar control, outlining, to-do lists, telephone directory, and automatic dialing. They are also often referred to as *flat-file databases.*

If all the information you want to manage can be kept in a single file, then all you need is one of these simple products. Even though they can manipulate data in only one file at a time, they are entirely adequate for most purposes. They are designed for non-technical users and are easier to use than more complicated databases. Some of the more popular flat-file databases, or personal information managers, are as follows:

- DayFlo Tracker
- Professional File
- Q & A
- Act!
- Info-XL
- Lotus Agenda

A specific class of personal information manager software are referred to as *note takers.* These are *random access memory* (RAM) resident programs, meaning they operate in the background while you are working with a primary program. By pressing one key (also known as a *hot key*), you bring the note taker to the screen as a window. Note takers are used to document a phone call received while you are working on the computer. A word of caution: be careful to back up the note taker before turning off the computer or information will be lost. Three note-taker programs are Metro, Sidekick and InfoSelect.

Full-Text Deposition-Specific Software

Deposition-specific programs are designed specifically for use with the full text of depositions. All of the programs have unique approaches to functionality, but they all are designed to enhance searching the full text of depositions. It really depends on what your needs are and which program you feel the most comfortable with. The program's main advantage is that it handles line and page numbers, which means that what the attorney sees on the screen looks like a deposition. The programs can support as many depositions as your hard disk will hold. It is also possible to search multiple transcripts at one time.

CAT-Links and Discovery-ZX are two popular deposition-specific programs. Discovery lets you search up to 999 transcripts, with up to 500 pages in one search. The CAT-Links program has a menu-driven search program, while the Discovery program has a command line search system. Many lawyers find the CAT-Links menu easier to learn and use, but the tradeoff is that the Discovery search facility provides the user with more flexibility in doing searches. Basically, if you are familiar with software in general, you will probably find the Discovery program's command approach no more difficult to master than the CAT-Links menu approach.

Lawyers find that the use of these programs to manage depositions requires changing their methods for taking depositions. Remember, whatever you say in taking a deposition is exactly what will be indexed in the deposition when used with the full-text software. This means if your references throughout a deposition are not consistent and specific, it will be difficult to find all references in a deposition to a specific person, place, or event.

For example, if in asking a series of questions about John Smith, you gradually begin to refer to him as "he," your ability to search to all references to references to John Smith will be diminished. The computer cannot interpret "he" as meaning "John Smith."

The full-text software also makes traditional deposition digests unnecessary. The purpose of the digest is to present a summary of the deposition so that one need not read the entire deposition to find some desired information. The search capabilities of the software, however, serve the same purpose. If digests are used at all, they should be much more succinct—about one page of digest for every 75 pages of deposition transcript—and should stick to analysis of content rather than attempting to provide information that can be found through the software's searching capability. However, use of this software does not relieve the attorney of the obligation to read the depositions. Nothing replaces this requirement. The software is only a tool to use in light of one's overall knowledge of what is in the depositions based on having read them.

Generic Full-Text Software

An alternative to deposition-specific full-text software is generic full-text software. These programs do not specifically treat the full text of a deposition as a deposition. It is treated like any other text. Page and line numbers are not treated as functional parts of the deposition, and searching for information is not in direct reference to page and line numbers, although they will still be part of the information on the full-text page. Certainly, generic full-text programs show the line and page numbers if they exist in the original ASCII[3] file of the deposition.

The generic full-text programs do not contain the built-in features the deposition-specific programs have for creating notes or digests about depositions or for coding issues in depositions. But simply for searching for references in full text, these programs are entirely adequate. Indeed, they are preferred by many lawyers, who feel they are easier to use and provide less distraction with

---

[3]ASCII refers to the computer codes that define number and letter characters.

references to question-and-answer pairs. Some types of general full-text software follow:

- Folio Views
- Gofer
- Reference Set
- ZYIndex

Indexing and Abstracting Programs

Indexing and abstracting programs are used to create a synopsis or abstract about each document for the database, rather than using the full text in the database for each document. An abstract is used because it is a better tool for finding information in documents than the full-text approach. For example, if an attorney wants to find all documents authored by Smith, whose recipient is Jones, whose document date is in 1987, or 1988, and has a carbon-copy ("cc") list[4] containing the names Wilson or Murphy, a full-text search of documents, as opposed to document abstracts, cannot find the documents. The only way to search full text is for simple occurrences of information in text narrative. No particular "roles" or relationships of people in documents can be determined with a full-text search.

An abstract includes such information as:

- The date of the document.
- The author of the document.
- The recipient of the document.
- A letter reference or memo subject line.
- Names of persons mentioned in the document.
- cc/bc ("blind copy") names listed on the document.
- Who produced the document.
- An abstract of the document contents.

After all of the document records are loaded into the database, and provided to the attorney to load on the PC, the attorney will use the information contained in the database to prepare for trial. This preparation will initially focus on preparation for depositions. Attorneys can use the database to find all the documents that are in any way related to any witness to be deposed. Later, the focus will shift to preparation for trial and examination and cross-examination of witnesses during the trial. Some types of indexing/abstracting software follow:

- Ask Sam
- DataEase
- dBase IV
- INMAGIC
- LS/MC
- Nutshell Plus

---

[4]Carbon copies are rarely used in law firms today with the birth of photocopies, but the term "cc" is still used on correspondence to indicate who received copies.

- Paradox
- R:Base 5000
- Reflex
- Revelation
- Q & A

Integrated Programs

Integrated programs are integrated in the sense that they can handle both full-text and synopsis/abstract information. With an integrated program, all information, whether in abstract or full text, may be supported by one program. The prime advantage from the user's perspective is that since all information for each case is housed under one program, the user only has to learn one set of instructions for searching in both full-text and abstract data.

These programs are powerful and perform very well. However, you pay for this performance, as these programs running on minicomputers or mainframes can cost as much as $100,000. At the PC level several excellent integrated programs can be purchased for under $5,000. As you will see, some of these programs also integrate a third technology, document imaging, described in detail in Chapter 14. Some types of integrated software follow:

- BRS/Search-mini/mainframe/PC
- Basis-mini/mainframe
- Explorer-PC
- Interact-mini
- Inquire-mini/mainframe
- Litidex-PC
- MicroLS-PC
- MicroStairs/Concordance-PC
- Researcher-PC
- Summation-PC

Relational Databases

Relational databases can be used for more complicated sets of data where relationships between data need to be defined. However, you may need an experienced computer technician to help develop your application. Several "high-end" products offer the necessary programming power but are still relatively easy to use. They not only allow you to define the basic structure (field names, sorting rules, etc.) but also make it easy to design menus, data-entry screens, tables, and reports.

Many of the litigation support programs discussed in Chapter 14 are built using a relational structure for indices. The program allows users to define tables of key words and issues to use when coding documents gathered during the discovery process. Some types of relational database programs follow:

- R:Base for DOS
- DataEase
- Informix
- FoxPro
- Paradox

- dBase IV
- Summation
- Advanced Revelation
- Professional Oracle

Some programs for the Macintosh computer are:

- dBase Mac
- FoxPro + MAC
- File Maker

• Case Management Systems

Case management is a very broad category still being defined, but, in general, it refers to the use of hardware and software to streamline the litigation process. Attorneys are constantly under pressure from clients to keep fees and expenses low during the course of litigation. Case management software helps do this by facilitating communication among attorneys and paralegals. It also provides a means of maintaining case-related, non-accounting information, such as status of document production, opposing attorneys, court jurisdictions, the name of the person who referred a case, and the amount of the expected recovery or fee.

Some software companies have incorporated case management features into their time and billing systems. The typical case management product contains client information, a docket control system with court dates and scheduling information, and a system for checking for conflict-of-interest problems. These products are sometimes less accessible than those designed specifically for case management, because the information must often be requested from the accounting department.

Separate but integrated case management software puts the information directly at the attorneys' and paralegals' fingertips without assaulting them with unnecessary accounting information. Here is a step-by-step example of how a case management system might work in a litigation firm or department:

- **Step 1:** New case information would be entered as soon as a file or case is received.

- **Step 2:** The system would then perform a conflict-of-interest check and provide case information to the accounting department for the time and billing system.

- **Step 3:** The responsible attorney could review the level of associates' workloads and the status of their cases to determine which one has time to handle the new case.

- **Step 4:** Once assigned, the system could produce an initial set of documents, such as acknowledgement letters to the client, requests for medical information, standard interrogatories, and requests for production of documents, appearance notices to the court, and others.

- **Step 5:** The system would also generate docket notices for answer dates and other key events.

- **Step 6:** Over time, as events occurred, suitable entries to the system would, in turn, generate further documents, such as subpoenas and standard motions. Some systems would track time spent on a particular case while the system is being used to generate documents.

- **Step 7:** The time can then be electronically transferred to the billing system and the client charged with the cost.

Conflict-of-Interest Checking

Law firms must be careful to avoid situations that result in their representing two opposing parties, or persons or entities related to opposing parties, referred to as a *conflict of interest*. The opposing party and the related party may not be involved in the same case or matter. It can become more difficult to determine potential conflicts as a firm grows. If the firm establishes branch offices in other cities, it becomes even more difficult. Recently the courts have even ruled a paralegal who changes from one firm to another can create a conflict of interest if the two firms are involved in the same cases on opposing sides.[5]

Before computers were widely available to help review existing clients and opposing parties, word-of-mouth systems were used. Attorneys would ask each other if anyone was involved with litigation or other matters that might be a conflict of interest when a new client was accepted. In a small firm, an attorney might walk down the hall and ask each attorney, or bring it up in a firm business meeting. Many firms publish a listing of new clients and matters regularly so other attorneys can review them and spot possible conflicts. In larger firms, the review process includes writing a memo describing the new client, opposing and related parties, and the work to be done. You can see how this process can become unmanageable for a very large firm and for busy attorneys.

Computerization provides some assistance in conflict checking. Now when a new file is opened, all information about the new client and matter is entered into a conflict-of-interest program and checked against other names and entities in the system to see if there are any matches. If similar names are found, they are reviewed to make sure the firm is not representing both sides in some form. The new case may be a litigation matter, but the firm may represent a relative or employee of the opposing party in another matter such as a tax matter. If a conflict exists, the firm must decide which client it wants to keep, and the other client must be referred to another firm.

For a conflict-checking system to be effective, a law firm must develop a system for gathering the information and updating the database regularly. The new matter or new business form is the ideal tool to use. The form should be redesigned, if necessary, to ask for the following minimum information:

- Client name and number.
- Matter name and number.
- Nature of the matter.
- Names of opposing parties.

[5]Beatrice Motamedia, "In California, It's Better to Stay Put Than to Switch," *Legal Assistant Today* (May/June 1990), p. 37.

- Names of other related parties (shareholders, owners, etc.).
- Name(s) of opposing counsel.

The information can be added to the firm's time and billing database or a separate database set-up. Whichever method is used, it will be successful only if a single person is given the responsibility for keeping the data current. Whenever a new client or matter file is set up, the new business form should be forwarded to the person responsible for doing the conflict check. The date of the search and its results should be recorded on the form. The form should then be returned to the attorney responsible for the new matter. Only then can a decision be made about the advisability of accepting the new case.

Docket and Calendar Control

Attorneys have kept calendars as long as they have practiced law. Their calendar systems range from the manual desk and pocket calendar to the most sophisticated firm-wide system on a minicomputer or PC-based local area network. Regardless of the system used, responsibilities must be well defined, and data constantly updated to keep the information current.

Automated docket control or calendar software is designed to help attorneys and paralegals manage their time by tracking all appointments, meetings, court appearances, and other important dates individually and for the entire firm. Available software packages range in complexity. Some even allow users to check other person's schedules, broadcast information to pre-defined groups, and print out calendars with varying degrees of detail.

Departmental Versus Firm-Wide Calendar System

Each firm must decide whether to maintain a departmental or firm-wide calendar system. A litigation department may choose to keep its own centralized calendar, while the rest of the firm's attorneys may keep individual calendars. In many firm-wide systems, every document entering or leaving the firm is reviewed by a calendar clerk to capture information about scheduled events. There are, of course, pros and cons to this approach. The biggest complaint from attorneys is such review impedes the process of sending and receiving mail.

Computerized Record and File Management

Automation provides new approaches to managing client files and records. Current technology uses bar codes and scanning devices much like the ones used at the checkout counter in grocery stores. As a file is created, labels are printed with the information about the client and matter, file number, and other information in bar code form. The file room can then use this information to track the location of files. When files are removed from the file room, the label is scanned and the name of the person receiving the file is input, or a bar code with personal data is scanned. Later, if another person wants to locate the same file, the system can be queried and will show who has the file.

One of the greatest benefits of bar code technology is better management of file shelf space. If each shelf is identified with a bar code, then as files are placed on the shelves, the location can also be scanned. This eliminates alphabetical or numerical filing systems and the need to save enough space for replacing files. A file can be placed on any shelf with room for it, and the location bar code scanned.

Law firms also use imaging systems to convert paper files to electronic form. Microfilm has been used for years to store closed file information before closed records are sent to off-site storage or destroyed. Now even open, active client files' documents are scanned into electronic form. With the proper hardware and software combination, these images can be made available to many users in the firm simultaneously. This eliminates the need for movement of physical files from one location to another. There is still a lot of debate over the possibility of the "paperless office," but recent developments are certainly headed in that direction.

• Recent Developments in Computer-Assisted Legal Research

Years ago when attorneys and paralegals researched issues in a case, they would spend hours in the library searching for related cases, carrying heavy books, and making copies of pages with relevant information. While these methods continue in use, computer-assisted or on-line research has had a tremendous impact on the research process. The computer can search large databases of information very quickly and print out relevant information. By typing a word, name, or other search term into the computer and giving a command to search certain texts, a researcher can locate relevant information in seconds rather than hours. The search is also more thorough than a manual search and usually results in more pertinent information.

Care must be exercised to narrow the search to reduce the amount of data reviewed and to eliminate cases with no applicability to the issues. Once the relevant material is located, it can be printed or saved in an electronic file for later incorporation into a word-processing document. Because the research process is streamlined and the researcher's time significantly reduced, most law firms charge their clients for the use of the computer in addition to the hourly rate for the attorney or paralegal doing the research.

When the first databases were developed, most law firms did not have computers available for lawyers and paralegals to use. The owners of the databases developed and sold or leased dedicated terminals to law firms for use in their libraries. The terminals were equipped with the necessary modems and communication software. This allowed users to dial up the computers where the data was stored via regular telephone lines. Computer-aided research was done at these centrally located terminals or were in the library and required lawyers and paralegals to be away from their desks.

Things have changed. Today these dedicated terminals have been largely replaced with multi-purpose microcomputers. Law firms with *local area networks* (LANs), where lawyers and paralegals have their own computers often provide the necessary hardware and software to allow them to access research databases without leaving their desks. A centralized pool of modems connected to a communications server on the network provides this capability.

WESTLAW[6] and LEXIS[7] are the two major research services in use in law firms today, even though many other types of databases are being used. An-

---

[6]WESTLAW, West Publishing Company, 610 Opperman Drive, Eagan, MN 55123.
[7]LEXIS Document Services, Illinois Code Company, 2901 Normandy Road, Springfield, Illinois 62703.

Exhibit 13.3
•
Tips for Increasing Efficiency in Using WESTLAW and LEXIS

1. Check your search for typos before hitting the ENTER key.
2. Double check the information you are given to research. Make sure the attorney gives you clear directions. If specific information still isn't yielding the desired results, be prepared to admit that you may have been given wrong information and broaden your search accordingly.
3. Carefully think out your search before going on-line. Fill out a worksheet provided by *LEXIS*® and *WESTLAW*®, outlining your research goals and search strategies. Try to think through possible problem areas.
4. Start with a broad search and narrow down as you become confident you are proceeding in the right direction, particularly when using *LEXIS*. Remember, modifying a LEXIS search is free, creating a new one isn't.[a]
5. Use the toll-free reference attorney[b] numbers provided by the services. Explain your research problem and solicit advice.
6. If you hit a dead end in your research, exit the database and rethink your query off-line.
7. Do not sit and read while on-line. Print out cites and go to the books.
8. If the books are not available in your library, decide the most efficient way to proceed. Either make a printout of the full text or head to a full-service law library.
9. Exit the service before printing.
10. Attend training sessions on an on-going basis. Bring with you any current research problems you may be having, and ask the instructor to address those specific problems for you.
11. And don't forget the basics:
    a. Read the literature provided by *LEXIS* and *WESTLAW*. Stay up-to-date on the new databases, libraries and other services being offered by both companies.
    b. Take advantage of practice files and free time constantly provided by the services. Spend as much time as you can before you actually take on an assignment for a client.
    c. Learn the mechanics of traditional research. Familiarize yourself with the resources that are provided on-line. Know what they look like in book form.

[a]WESTLAW does not charge by the search.
[b]LEXIS has legally trained staff with some attorneys. WESTLAW has all attorneys.
Source: Lynx Braz, "Becoming More Efficient in Searching WESTLAW and LEXIS." Copyright 1992, James Publishing, Inc. Reprinted with permission from *Legal Assistant Todqy*. For subscription information, call (714) 755-5450.

other is Information America.[8] Each service has its strengths and weaknesses, and many firms choose to use both rather than choose one over another. Efficient searches require an understanding of the manual research method. It is very beneficial to paralegals and their firms to attend training classes provided by the vendors. Some ways to use the on-line services more efficiently and reduce charges to the firm are presented in Exhibit 13.3.

The next step in the evolutionary process of computer-assisted legal research will be the movement of these services into the law firm library itself. Instead of communicating over telephone lines with modems, you will have access to databases maintained in the firm's law library on CD-ROM disks. Depending on how the firm's computer systems are configured, researchers will be able to access the data without incurring on-line charges for the time spent querying the database. Currently West Publishing Company offers CD-ROM Libraries to law firms that include the material shown in Exhibit 13.4.

In addition to legal research databases, law firms need other general business information offered by other database services such as CompuServe, Dow Jones News/Retrieval Service and Dialog. (See Appendixes G through I for list-

[8]Information America® (IA®), One Georgia Center, 600 West Peachtree Street, N.W., Atlanta, Georgia 30308, (800) 235–4008 and (404) 892–1800.

Exhibit 13.4

West CD-ROM Libraries

FEDERAL TAX LIBRARY

Legislative Material
- IRS Code, Annotated
- IRS Regulations
- Tax Court and Claims
- Court Rules
- Legislative Acts
- Legislative History
- International Tax Agreements

Cases and Related Material
- Federal Court Cases on Tax
- Tax Court Cases
- Actions on Decisions

Administrative Material
- BNA Abstracts
- Revenue Rulings
- Revenue Procedures
- Private Letter Rulings
- Technical Advice Memoranda
- General Counsel Memoranda
- Administrative Orders

BNA TAX MANAGEMENT PORTFOLIOS LIBRARY

- Finding Tools
- U.S. Income Series
- Estate, Gifts and Trusts Series
- Foreign Income Series

GOVERNMENT CONTRACTS LIBRARY

- Federal Acquisition Regulation System (Title 48 C.F.R.)
- Supplemental Acquisition Regulations (including HRMR, Title 41 C.F.R.)
- U.S.C.A. Sections on Government Contracts
- Government Contract Cases (1945 to Date)
- Board to Contract Appeals Decisions (1953 to Date)
- Comptroller General Decisions (1921 to Date)
- Keyes: Government Contracts Under Federal Acquisitions Regulations
- Cibinic and Nash: Formation of Government Contracts, 2d Ed.
- Cibinic and Nash: Administration of Government Contracts, 2d Ed.

BANKRUPTCY LIBRARY

- Bankruptcy Cases
- Bankruptcy Code, Rules and Forms, Annotated
- Cowans: Bankruptcy and Law and Practice
- West's Bankruptcy Digest
- Bankruptcy Bibliography
- Bankruptcy Cases of Interest
- Bankruptcy Evidence Manual

FEDERAL CIVIL PRACTICE LIBRARY

- Wright & Miller: Federal Practice and Procedure
- Federal Rules Decisions
- Federal Practice Digest 2nd & 3rd
- (Topics of Federal Civil Procedure and Federal Courts)

Exhibit 13.4

Continued

MILITARY JUSTICE LIBRARY

Military Justice Reporter
Court-Martial Reporter, Vols. 1-50
West's Military Justice Digest
Manual for Courts-Martial 1984
Military Judge's Benchbook, Army Pamph. 27-9
Military Criminal Law Evidence, Army Pamph. 27-22
U.S.C.A.–Title 10 Armed Forces
C.F.R.–Title 32 National Defense

FEDERAL SECURITIES LIBRARY

Federal Securities Acts from U.S.C.A.
Federal Regulations on Federal Securities
S.E.C. Rules of Practice
S.E.C. No-Action Letters
S.E.C. Releases
Federal Securities Case
Commodity Futures Trading Com'n Decisions
Hazen: Securities Regulation, 2d Ed.

ings of some of the databases used by law firms.) WESTLAW can be used as a gateway to Dow Jones News/Retrieval Service. Approximately 400 of Dialog files are on the WESTLAW database.

• Special Software for Litigation

There are many special programs to assist lawyers and paralegals in litigation matters including:

- Bankruptcy.
- Debt collection.
- Expert-witness tracking.
- Spreadsheets.
- Graphic representations.
- Tax preparation.

There are several good sources for current information regarding these programs. One is the American Bar Association's *LOCATE*, "A Directory of Law Office Computer Software Vendors." This book is published annually by the ABA and provides product descriptions and vendor information on the most software developed for use in law firms. Another good source is *The Lawyer's PC*, "A Newsletter for Lawyers Using Personal Computers." This newsletter publishes an Annual Legal Software Directory and usually has many special programs not found in the ABA's *LOCATE*.

• Document Assembly

Document assembly is a new genre of software becoming popular in law firms with an existing sound technological base. Document-assembly systems allow law firms to delegate the production of legal work to less highly paid personnel in the firm once the attorney-expert has created a reusable document form or template. Attorney involvement in document production can be reduced by as much as two-thirds as segments of text are merged together to form new documents.

The successful implementation of a document-assembly system requires certain characteristics in the law firm. The most probable candidates are firms specializing in a few areas of law, producing many routine documents. Repetition seems to be the key. Here are some other characteristics indicating a firm may be suitable for document-assembly automation.

1. A solid technological base (state-of-the-art word processing, time and billing, use of databases, spreadsheets, etc.).
2. Attorneys with specialized knowledge, using PCs at their desks.
3. Willingness to make an initial investment of attorney time for document-assembly development.
4. Production of a lot of long, boilerplate documents.
5. Production of a large volume of documents.
6. Production of multiple documents for each transaction.

Document-assembly products can be categorized according to complexity, sophistication, and degree of flexibility. Although some of the really powerful systems are based on *artificial intelligence,* or *expert systems,* discussed later, others can be based on some of the advanced features in an existing word-processing program. In fact, most offices taking advantage of the power of today's word processors have already employed many document-assembly features.

Systems that work with word-processing software may use predefined forms and templates specific to that word-processing package. Custom forms designed for a specific area of law can be edited with the word-processing software, and the user can even create a standard library of form documents. Many of these systems make available multiple area-of-law or state modules.

Other document-assembly programs work directly with a word-processor's files. These systems link the files and produce documents fully formatted using various fonts, underlining, styles, and other features. They may use a decision-tree or menuing approach and distinguish decision input from data or variable entry. The user enters replacement information once, and all occurrences of the field are replaced throughout the document. The information can then be saved for use in other documents.

There are other programs with custom-designed forms for specific areas of law not directly integrated with word-processing software. Checklists or menu choices are used to determine the segments of text to be assembled. The document is then produced and printed in a format native to the document-assembly program. As an option, after the document is assembled, some of the packages allow it to be converted to the user's word-processing program for further editing and printing. Some of these products also include a correspondence system for automatic letter creation using the client-specific information entered in the assembly process.

The most sophisticated, and complicated to implement, document-assembly systems are known as *expert systems.* These systems provide a type of analysis or problem-solving model to handle problems the same way an expert would. The base of knowledge is provided by the attorney who is expert in a particular area of law. Once they are set up, the user has only to supply client data and answer questions relative to the client's circumstances. Using the knowledge previously supplied by the attorney-expert, the system then produces the required documents.

• Control through Document Management

Specialized document-management software was born out of the movement from minicomputers to PCs (microcomputers) and local area networks (LANs) to help manage word-processing documents. When word processing was done on minicomputers, legal secretaries were all using the same computer, and documents were stored in a central location. The software to name, describe, identify, and locate the documents was inherent in the minicomputer word-processing program. When law firms began to provide microcomputers to secretaries, however, connecting them together with networking hardware and software, the scenario was quite different. Now, every secretary had a computer, often with its own storage space on a local hard disk. Firms sometimes had multiple file servers and disks where the documents were stored. The PC-version of word-processing software did not provide the necessary features to allow secretaries to search across all the various disks to locate documents. When documents were named, the secretary was usually limited to the eight-character name allowed by the MS-DOS operating system. It was an administrative nightmare. Vendors who worked with law firms began to realize new software programs were necessary to help firms control their documents.

Today's document-management software provides control over the location, security, version, and status of word-processing documents created using PC-based word-processing systems. It is not unreasonable to assume that eventually document management will become an integral part of the word-processing programs themselves. Until then, separate programs will be necessary. Like most other software in use today, document-management software is a database of descriptive information about the documents, operators, attorneys, client, and matter numbers. All of these are available for queries to locate specific documents. Other features include automatic *archiving,* or deleting of old documents, tracking keystrokes or production time for charging word-processing time to clients, and automatic simultaneous backup to both local hard drives and central storage.

• Work-Product Retrieval System

Law firms that develop and use an internal *work-product retrieval system* are less likely to "reinvent the wheel" each time a case is researched or a document created. Attorneys have reused the products of their previous work for years but not always efficiently. Without automation if a law firm has previously handled a certain type of case, and a similar case is brought to the firm, one or more of the attorneys will have to remember the case in order for documents to be retrieved from storage for reuse. And it is always possible that the attorneys involved in the previous case are no longer with the firm. With automation, any attorney can query the firm's inventory of previous documents to see if similar situations were handled by the firm. An attorney may also check if there are any documents useful to expedite the current litigation and/or other matter. Because of automation, the firm does not have to rely on the memory or availability of any person, it develops its own corporate "memory."

To set up a work-product retrieval system, the firm must develop a database of documents similar to WESTLAW or LEXIS. This requires a full-text search and retrieval database program. It may be the same program used for document management. As documents are finalized, they can be added to the database for later use. Typically, only documents such as research memoranda, briefs, pleadings, contracts and similar documents are retained in the work-product retrieval system. Short memos and letters are archived, or deleted, after a case is closed. When an attorney or paralegal is researching an issue, the firm's internal work-product retrieval database can be searched along with other outside databases.

• Electronic Mail

One of the greatest time-savers in the law office is *electronic mail*, or *E-Mail*. This one automated application can greatly improve the efficiency of attorneys working on a single case. For example, it can be used to enhance a docket/calendar system by notifying attorneys of changes in scheduled appointments. As a paralegal you may be required to use services like the American Bar Association's ABA/Net, a special service for lawyers providing electronic mail and PC-to-fax transmission capability. It also allows multiple users to edit documents on-screen simultaneously.

• Computers in the Courts

Slowly, the courts are computerizing their records. Some major metropolitan areas have already converted much of their public record inventory to electronic forms. All 50 states and the U.S. Congress have begun automating their systems to allow researchers to track the status of a particular state bill. As electronic imaging systems and CD-ROM technology (Chapter 14) become more prevalent and affordable, the courts will be able to convert records from paper to electronic media. When this happens, the laborious task of searching titles, probate records, and other court records will become a thing of the past.

Soon attorneys and paralegals won't even have to enter the courthouse to search the records. They will access them the same way they do other databases such as WESTLAW and LEXIS—right from their own offices. The capability is already available in some metropolitan areas for title searches and name reservations with the secretary of state. Information America provides an on-line research capability as well as document delivery. Not all states provide the same level of access or information. Users can research the following types of data in California, Delaware, Georgia, Illinois, Nevada, Pennsylvania, and Texas:

- Uniform Commercial Code (UCC) and tax lien information.
- Basic corporate and limited partnership information from the secretary of state's office.
- Dun's Business Records for detailed company information.
- Bankruptcy court information.
- Courthouse records.

The document-delivery service uses electronic mail to place orders for documents such as a certificate of good standing for a particular company. This speeds the process considerably, and the documents are then delivered by local document delivery services in the participating cities.

ATTORNEY OR PARTY WITHOUT ATTORNEY (Name and Address):   TELEPHONE NO.:   COURT USE ONLY

ATTORNEY FOR (Name):

SUPERIOR COURT OF CALIFORNIA, COUNTY OF SAN DIEGO

☐ **CENTRAL COURT** S37000   ☐ **NORTH COUNTY** S37001   ☐ **EAST COUNTY** S37002   ☐ **SOUTH BAY** S37003

PLAINTIFF'S INITIAL FILING FORM–CIVIL PROCEEDINGS
(Civil Delay Reduction Program)

CASE NUMBER

DEFENDANT(S) NAMED IN COMPLAINT INCLUDING DBA AND/OR AKA, IF ANY:

1. _____
2. _____
3. _____
4. _____
5. _____
6. _____
7. _____
8. _____

☐ ADDITIONAL SHEET ATTACHED

NEW FILING

B51

CASE CATEGORY: [CHECK ONE BOX ONLY]   <u>CAUTION</u>: <u>MARKING AN INCORRECT BOX OR FILING AN INCORRECT FORM MAY RESULT IN A BREACH OF SAN DIEGO SUPERIOR COURT RULES.</u>

☐ PERSONAL INJURY, PROPERTY DAMAGE, WRONGFUL DEATH – MOTOR VEHICLE

A71

☐ PERSONAL INJURY PROPERTY DAMAGE WRONGFUL DEATH – OTHER

A72

☐ OTHER CIVIL COMPLAINTS

A60

☐ EMINENT DOMAIN* *TOTAL # OF PARCELS____

A73

☐ CIVIL PETITIONS WRITS, CIVIL HARRASSMENT CHG OF NAME, COMPEL ARB. GDN AD LITEM, ETC.

A61

E N D

ZA

<u>NOTICE TO ATTORNEYS:</u> PURSUANT TO DIVISION II, SECTION ONE, OF THE SAN DIEGO SUPERIOR COURT RULES, THIS CASE SHALL BE PROCESSED IN ACCORDANCE WITH THE TRIAL DELAY REDUCTION ACT OF 1986. THE RULES IN THIS SECTION APPLY, NOT WITHSTANDING ANY RULE IN THE CALIFORNIA RULES OF COURT THAT MAY CONFLICT (68612 G.C.)
WITHIN 60 CALENDAR DAYS OF THE DATE OF ITS FILING, THE COMPLAINT MUST BE SERVED ON ALL NAMED DEFENDANTS AND A CERTIFICATE OF SERVICE (SUPCT-345) FILED WITH THE COURT, UNLESS A CERTIFICATE OF PROGRESS (SUPCT-340) HAS BEEN FILED INDICATING WHY SERVICE HAS NOT BEEN EFFECTED ON ALL DEFENDANTS AND WHAT IS BEING DONE TO EFFECT SERVICE. (DIVISION II, RULE 1.4(a), SAN DIEGO SUPERIOR COURT RULES.)
NOTE: FILING OF AN AMENDED COMPLAINT AND/OR CROSS-COMPLAINT SHALL NOT EXTEND ANY DEADLINES IMPOSED BY SAN DIEGO SUPERIOR COURT RULES.

PLAINTIFF'S INITIAL FILING FORM–CIVIL PROCEEDINGS
(Civil Delay Reduction Program)

SUPCT-338 (REV. 10-90)

Exhibit 13.5

Plaintiff's Initial Filing Form—Civil Proceedings

Courtrooms are beginning to use automation to assist judges, lawyers, and court reporters in managing data. Computer terminals and printers are available to lawyers and paralegals in some courtrooms. Testimony is converted to electronic form as it is keyed by a court reporter and stored in a database. At the end of each day, during a trial in an automated courtroom, attorneys may leave with printed transcripts of the day's testimony. If an attorney wishes to review a witness's prior testimony, even if it occurred only minutes earlier, the testimony can be retrieved and displayed on the computer's screen. This changes the role of the court reporter dramatically and eliminates the need to read back a witness's testimony.

Previous testimony taken during depositions may be included in the database. Should a witness contradict previous testimony, the database can be queried, and the prior testimony located for use by the attorney. These tasks are often performed now by paralegals.

Computerized courtrooms also offer access to services such as WESTLAW and LEXIS, and the American Bar Association's ABA/Net to litigators and their paralegals. The computers may also be equipped with remote-access software to allow judges, lawyers, and paralegals to communicate with other computer systems in the courthouse or their offices. Remote access software is special communication software to allow a PC user to operate another PC-based local area network via telephone communications.

LEXIS now offers a similar service for document filing and searching. Searches for Uniform Commercial Code (UCC) filings, corporate records, tax lien information, and judgment searches can be done electronically using LEXIS Document Services.

Some courts are streamlining the handling of documents by using bar-code technology. When documents are filed, a form like the one in Exhibit 13.5 is required to be attached. Court personnel then enter descriptive information using the bar codes. For example, if a complaint is filed for personal injury, the attorney would check the block beside PERSONAL INJURY, PROPERTY DAMAGE, WRONGFUL DEATH, or OTHER, so court personnel would know to scan the lines underneath that description.

• Summary

If your firm's litigation department does not have any of the systems mentioned in this chapter, you should still become familiar with them for two reasons: (1) you will be able to spot the need for a particular system; and (2) should your firm purchase such a system, you will already be familiar with it.

Database software is quickly becoming a necessity in every law firm. Knowing the characteristics of relational databases and integrated programs will put you a step ahead even if your firm has not reached that point in its computerization. These types of software are where word-processing software was years ago, and they are quickly becoming familiar to attorneys.

Document retrieval has made many advances, as discussed in this chapter. Electronic mail is here to stay. Coming to work in the morning and checking your computer for mail will soon be an everyday occurrence. Computers are invading the court systems, and computer-assisted legal research is now individually accessible. To do your best as a paralegal and to advance in today's computerized world, you must overcome any reluctance you have toward using computers

Automated Litigation Support Systems

• Introduction

In this chapter[1] you will learn how computers are used in the litigation support process. The role of litigation support vendors will be explained and the basic hardware and software components of an automated litigation support system described. We will discuss how discovery documents are selected, screened, and coded for use during trial preparation; how computer searches are done to locate the desired information related to the issues of a case; and how security of case information is maintained both in the physical facilities and the computer system.

• Benefits of Automated Litigation Support

Litigation is a paper-intensive activity. The responsibility of managing the paper flow during a case usually falls on the paralegals. One helpful tool for handling massive amounts of paper is *automated litigation support (ALS),* which refers to the automated management and control of documents produced during the discovery process for later retrieval during trial preparation and trial. ALS systems allow attorneys and paralegals to spend less time searching for documents so that more time can be spent analyzing the information the documents contain. ALS systems are also designed to help manage oral testimony resulting from depositions and trials, written answers to interrogatories, and the firm's internal prior work product.

Several tests have been done to compare the efficiency of human management and control against computerized control. In one case, 20,000 documents were searched by paralegals for documents by a particular author, during a specific time frame on a specific topic. It took the paralegals 67 man-hours to locate 15 documents that qualified. The same documents were searched by the computer, and in milliseconds 20 documents were located.[2] The most striking

---

[1]This chapter was co-authored by Paula F. Turner, CPA, MBA, partner in Holland Shipes Vann, P.C., Atlanta, Georgia, specializing in computer consulting to law firms. The chapter was edited by Attorney Robert S. Hochdorf, Senior Litigation Specialist for the Atlanta office of The LITIDEX Company, a full-service automated litigation support company providing software and services to law firms and corporate legal departments.

[2]Deborah Shannon, "Law and Order." In *American Way,* American Airlines, Dallas/Fort Worth Airport, TX, 1989.

revelation of this experiment is not the speed of the computer's search but its accuracy. The paralegals were well trained, but they were also human, and human error accounted for their missing five of the documents.

Up until recently, cases with more than 10,000 documents to control were considered large enough to justify implementing a new ALS system. Also, when a firm had many cases that were similar (referred to as "cookie-cutter cases"), with the same or similar issues addressed in each case, they were considered ready for ALS. But today, with the prevalence of microcomputers throughout the law firm, the size of the case is no longer the primary factor in the decision to automate. There are other reasons to automate during litigation, including the following:

- A large number of documents are involved.
- There are complicated issues of fact.
- The client faces a high degree of exposure.
- There is a set schedule for discovery, deposition, and trial.
- The case involves several parties or multi-district litigation.
- It is too expensive or time-consuming to perform manual searches.
- The case may continue for several years.
- The firm already has ALS-system capabilities.

In summary, the more complex the litigation and the more the client has to lose, the more justification exists for implementing an ALS system.

Every ALS system has two basic purposes: (1) to manage and control documents and other information important to the case; and (2) to provide a mechanism for locating and retrieving the information when necessary. But an ALS system can go far beyond case-specific information management. Here is a list of functions you might expect from your litigation support system:

1. Searching of
   a. Documents produced by the opposition.
   b. Documents produced by adverse parties.
   c. Depositions and other oral testimony.
   d. Written answers to interrogatories.
2. Maintaining witness lists and linking them to relevant documents.
3. Helping to write and answer interrogatories.
4. Helping to prepare for taking depositions of others.
5. Organizing and indexing information according to a trial outline.
6. Allowing images to be scanned, managed, retrieved, and viewed by any user.
7. Providing inventory control of objects other than documents and images.
8. Providing a means of producing high-quality trial exhibits and charts.

Benefits include:

1. Conserving attorney time.
2. Providing a higher degree of security and confidentiality in long-term cases.

3. Providing continuity in long-term cases where personnel changes might otherwise cause discontinuity.
4. Providing a more cost-effective use of support personnel, facilities, and equipment.
5. Allowing attorneys to operate the system via telecommunications.

The sophistication of the ALS system needed will depend on the type of litigation in which your firm engages and its budget for hardware and software. Another consideration is the skill level of those who will operate it. If it is too complicated for the support staff to use, it will be ineffective. As a litigation paralegal, you can expect to be a decision maker and play a vital role in selecting, implementing, and operating the ALS system.

• Computer Resources for an Automated Litigation Support System

A law firm's decision to automate will be heavily influenced by the computer resources required to support the effort. There will naturally be a strong inclination to try to utilize existing computer hardware and software available in the firm. There are four possible approaches to setting up an ALS system:

1. Use existing hardware and software.
2. Upgrade current hardware and software.
3. Purchase new hardware and software.
4. Use an outside vendor to provide ALS services.

Remember, an ALS system that is unable to meet your information needs is much worse than a workable manual system.

Therefore, existing hardware and software should be used only if you are certain they will meet the needs of an adequate ALS system.

Litigation Support Vendors

Your law firm may consider using a consultant experienced in litigation support or bringing in an outside ALS system vendor to assist it. Many firms hire outside vendors to design or operate the system for them. Vendor support can take many different forms with varying degrees of responsibility and service.

Consultants
A *consultant* can help the firm define its requirements and locate the hardware and software to meet those requirements. Consultants can also help manage the implementation of the system and the training of the firm's staff in its use. Once the system is operating smoothly, the consultant may no longer be needed.

Specialty Services
In one form of vendor support, *specialty services*, a limited, distinct service such as document scanning or data entry is provided. A law firm may be able to handle its normal processing needs and may need only these types of specialty services when excessive demands are placed on its internal systems.

The advantage to using this type of vendor is that they are highly specialized and typically have the latest technology available. They have trained, experienced personnel in their specialty area. Disadvantages include difficulties in coordinating several different vendors, assigning responsibilities and assessing the effectiveness of the vendors' services. For very large cases, it may be wise to use a vendor capable of supervising the entire project, including other specialty vendors.

Full-Service Vendors

Full-service vendors provide all litigation support services, leaving the firm responsible only for management. The advantage of this arrangement is that the vendor, which offers a broad range of services, usually has measurement and control built into the internal structure of its organization, and at no additional cost. This "one-stop-shopping" concept saves time for the law firm. The full-service vendor typically has well-trained and experienced personnel, reducing or eliminating training and start-up time for the firm. The main disadvantage is the difficulty in defining the vendor's responsibility for performance while allowing enough flexibility to operate effectively.

Full-service vendors should be carefully evaluated to make sure their computer systems are adequate for the firm's needs. Some vendors use subcontractors to provide additional capacity during peak load times. This possibility should be discussed with the vendor in advance of entering into an agreement.

Program Management

Another type of vendor support is *program management* where a single vendor accepts complete responsibility for analyzing the data in the system and delivering the output of the system to the firm as requested. The vendor performs all of the technical support operations, coordination, and management required to control all information flow, including the searches and legal analysis of data. The computer systems, support personnel, and personnel trained in legal matters who can interpret results for the firm are supplied by the vendor. Consequently, this arrangement places the least burden on the firm's attorneys and support staff and provides the best expert witness trial during testimony. To best preserve the work-product protection privilege, a member of the litigation team should participate in the vendor's activities.

Selecting a Vendor

It is important to analyze a vendor's ability to deliver the services promised during litigation. The law firm should know who the vendor's personnel are, how they are trained, their experience levels, and exactly who will do the firm's work. Technical, data-processing, support, and management personnel must be evaluated. Focus the evaluation on determining the competence of the people assigned to do the firm's work. If some personnel, such as data-entry clerks, come out of a pool, find out what criteria are used for hiring such people.

Also, check whether the automation systems used by the vendor are state-of-the-art and whether they can handle the type of processing the firm requires. Ideally, the data provided by the vendor's system would be compatible with the firm's office automation systems, especially word processing. Software used by the vendor should include a full-featured and proven text-oriented *database management system* (DBMS). Find out what backup systems are available.

The vendor should sign a confidentiality agreement to ensure that all of the law firm's data are protected by the employees the vendor assigns to do the work. Inquiry should be made regarding the bonding of employees, the physical security arrangements at the vendor's offices, and the extent of the vendor's liability if a breach of confidentiality occurs.

Computer Hardware and Software Requirements

Every ALS system needs the same basic components consisting minimally of:

- Computer
- Disk storage
- Monitor (screen)
- Printer
- Operating system software
- Application software

A discussion of existing systems is not included here because systems change rapidly as technology advances. However, you should be aware of some hardware and software requirements. Hardware and software are configured in many ways, sometimes making it difficult to determine which components a firm should purchase. ALS systems will differ among firms depending on firm size, practice specialties, the size and number of cases to be automated, the ALS system budget, and what a firm expects to gain from the system. Unless a law firm has personnel experienced in technology issues, it will save significant time and money by consulting experts to set up a system. It can be as simple as a single personal computer, little different from the computer used by the secretaries for word processing. But more likely, the firm will be asking the system to do things other than word processing. The following discussion provides some general guidelines about the basic components of an ALS system.

Single-User versus Multi-User Systems

A single-user system can be used by only one person and usually consists of one microcomputer, or PC (personal computer). A multi-user system could be a group of PCs connected together on a network, or a larger, minicomputer. Up until recently, a multi-user system almost always involved a minicomputer, but now many law firms have installed *local area networks (LANs)*, a collection of PCs connected to a central file server and sharing data, documents, printers, and other computer resources.

The main attraction of PC-LANs is that each user's PC can operate as a stand-alone computer or as a workstation on the network and still share files. The result is better performance of the computer and more flexibility in utilizing the firm's computer resources.

When selecting ALS system hardware and software, the firm should consider whether the ALS system will be part of the firm's present or future PC-LAN. If so, then the hardware and software selected will need to be compatible with other network components. This is a time to rely heavily on the advice of outside consultants or in-house technical support personnel.

Usually, only very small firms or litigation departments can efficiently operate with a single-user system. It is a good idea for such a system to have a single operator who controls access and the processing schedule, since only one person at a time can sit at the computer. If there are more data to be entered than one person can handle, the firm should probably use a multi-user system. In other words, even if the firm has a computer with a large storage capacity, only one person at a time can enter that data, so the limiting factor is the keyboard input.

Speed or "Power" Issues

If your firm is considering the purchase of a PC-based ALS system, be sure to consider the speed of the processor and various other components of the PC. Because the computer will be storing and searching for a lot of data, the speed at which those searches occur will be of primary importance. Buy as much speed as your firm can afford.

RAM (random access memory) is another significant factor greatly affecting your computer's processing capability. Memory is often confused with storage size, both of which are expressed as kilobytes and megabytes. But RAM and disk storage capacity are very different. RAM provides only temporary storage of the computer's operating system, applications software, and data *while it is being used*. A good analogy is to think of storage capacity as a filing cabinet and RAM as the space on your desk. You take your papers out of the filing cabinet and work on your desk. RAM is the area that you temporarily use to work on your files. If there is not enough RAM, the computer slows down and may have to store part of what it needs on a disk. Extra time is therefore expended accessing and reading the disk when the information on it is required. Adequate RAM, properly managed, can greatly improve your computer's ability. Unless you are computer-literate, depend on your firm's computer vendor or its in-house technical staff to determine a configuration adequate to meet your needs.

Scanners

Law firms have used *scanners* for many years to input documents into word-processing systems and time-entry information into billing systems. Now scanners are playing new roles in law firms, especially in litigation support. Scanning is very similar to photocopying, but instead of the copied image being printed on paper, it is retained by the scanner in electronic form and transferred to the computer. Documents can be scanned into your ALS system as images or, using OCR (optical character recognition) (discussed next), as searchable text (also known as "full-text"). The OCR process is necessary, because even though an image is stored in the computer, you are not able to search the individual words contained in the document unless they are converted to characters.

The capabilities of scanners have increased, and the prices have decreased dramatically in recent times, making it possible for even the smallest firm to have good-quality scanning capabilities. Most scanners today have the higher-quality *grey-scale scanning* capabilities that allow even a photograph to be scanned and displayed in full detail on a high-quality video monitor.

Optical Character Recognition

If you want to convert the text on documents to searchable "full text" in your ALS system, *optical character recognition* (OCR) capabilities are required. OCR uses a combination of software and hardware to recognize characters. Words on paper exist as a combination of light and dark images. A scanner reads the differences in color intensity and converts them into digitized computer images. OCR software converts the text image into codes representing alpha characters, numbers, and other symbols.

Today's scanners and OCR software can recognize almost any style of type or font. If they cannot recognize the characters, they can be trained to read new fonts. Even with the excellent capabilities of scanners, however, the resulting text will need to be cleaned up after scanning. OCR may not detect all of the necessary codes in a document, such as tabs, indents, centers, boldface, underlining, and others.

Often there are errors, especially if the original document is not clear. The chance of error increases every time the document is copied. Even with a 98 percent accuracy rate, frequently cited by OCR software companies, extensive editing time will be required to produce a full-text file reliable enough for searching. Realistically, third-generation or worse copies are not OCR-scannable with existing technology—at least not for purposes of reliable full-text searching without extensive, time-consuming, and expensive editing.

Many experts believe it is more effective to analyze the documents and create abstracts or profiles because of the expense and time involved in the cleanup process. But if OCR capabilities improve, then, combined with the spell-checking abilities of most word processors, they may become more practical for firms to use.

Optical Disk Technology

Optical disk technology is changing the way law firms store and retrieve data. The optical disk employs the same technology as the music CD disk. It is called *optical* because instead of using a mechanical head to read information, like the heads in a tape player, the optical disk drive uses a laser light beam to read the information. This method of storing data and reading it optically allows the storage of more data than provided by a magnetic disk like those used in most computers.

The Imaging Revolution

Today's systems can store and retrieve not only document text, but document images and even voice recordings. Think of a document image as a digitized picture of each page of a document. Because the image is a picture, it is possible to examine handwritten marginalia or the signatures on letters or checks. Text, images, and voice can be stored together on a single optical disk. Descriptive summaries (also called *profiles, abstracts,* or *surrogates*) can be created for the images and voice recordings and searched the same way as text documents. When retrieved, the image can be displayed on the screen or printed, and the voice recording can be played audibly and analyzed. Many optical disk drives also have audio capability with jacks for earphones or external speaker connections.

The real impact of imaging is the ability of anyone with access to the system to be able to view a document in its original form immediately. It eliminates the need to have someone (usually the paralegal) locate the physical copy in the files for delivery to the researcher. Not only is the time to locate and look at a document reduced to seconds, but several people can review the same document simultaneously. Another benefit is the reduction in storage space required. Working copies are not required, as the image can be printed and used as the working copy, if needed. The originals (or original copies) can be protected and retrieved for use only during trial proceedings.

Printers

The printer you purchase for your ALS system should match the system's abilities. If your system stores images and you plan to print them, your printer needs may be different than if you want to print only straight text. Laser printers are commonly found in law firms and are preferable to dot matrix or impact printers because of their increased speed and quieter operation. Make sure the printer you purchase is supported by the application software you purchase.

In general, if you purchase name-brand computer components commonly in use in law firms (or those labeled "compatible with" a name brand), you will be safe. Do not be persuaded by a computer vendor to purchase an unknown printer even though it may have more capabilities than a well-known brand. If it is not supported by your ALS system software or other programs you will be using, you may waste a lot of time trying to make it work with your programs. This is one time to play it safe and stay with name brands.

Telecommunications

State-of-the-art telecommunications can be a substantial advantage to a practice with heavy emphasis in litigation. Generally speaking, there are two reasons for using telecommunications: (1) to enable persons outside to access your computer (with permission and with security precautions installed); and (2) to allow inside persons to access outside services such as databases like *WESTLAW*.

One specific reason that telecommunications are helpful to law firms is it allows litigators, who spend a lot of time out of the office during discovery, depositions, and trials, to communicate easily with the firm's office. Once you have set up your ALS system in the office, attorneys can use telephone lines to access it using a portable computer or another computer at home or from some other location. If they are traveling, they may access the firm's computer from their hotel room via the telephone lines.

To access the firm's ALS system, a *modem* and *communications software* are necessary on each computer. Special care should be taken to make sure the modems at both ends are *compatible*, meaning they are capable of operating at the same speed (measured in *baud*, as in 9600 baud) and using the same set of instructions. There are many more considerations, but if you purchase standard components, you will minimize your problems.

Communications software is relatively standardized but there are two basic kinds. With one you can call another computer and operate only one program. The Lexis and Westlaw programs are good examples of this type of access. Other communications programs allow a user at a remote site to control the host computer or network and run any program residing on the host (with proper security, of course). These are called *remote-access* communications programs. Two of the most popular are Procomm Plus and PCAnywhere IV.

Portable Computers

Portable computers can be taken to discovery sites for on-site data entry. In the future we may see portables used with bar-code printers and scanning wands and appropriate software to reduce the time required to log documents into the system and track them. Portables can also be taken into court, and images stored on disks can be projected onto large screens in court, if the judge allows it. Always ask in advance.

Software Required for ALS

The term *software* refers to the internal programs or routines that allow computers to provide functionality to their users. For most users, there are two types of software of importance—operating system software and application software. Every computer must have an *operating system*. Without it, the computer is nothing more than a collection of metal and plastic parts. The operating system supervises the operations of the computer and tells its components what to do. Examples of operating systems are MS-DOS (Microsoft Disk Operating System), OS/2 (IBM's multi-tasking operating system), and UNIX (AT&T's multi-user operating system).

Another level of operating system is necessary when a local area network (PC-LAN) is used. This is called the *network operating system*. A network operating system such as Novell Netware or Banyan VINES works in conjunction with MS-DOS or UNIX and cannot operate without these underlying operating systems. The operating system will be determined by the software you want to use for your ALS system.

Application software includes word processing, electronic spreadsheets, and accounting systems. Each application software program is developed to work with a specific operating system or systems. For litigation support, the application software required is called a *database manager*. Even the specialized litigation support programs you see advertised are developed using a database manager. Some firms purchase a database manager and design their own ALS system, while others purchase ALS system software already developed by a litigation-support software vendor.

Hypertext

Many of the available ALS systems and database managers have the ability to link data together for later retrieval. Suppose that you found a letter, memo, and photograph in your database were somehow related. If you link them together electronically, then when any one of them is retrieved as the result of a search, the user will be notified there are other related documents or objects available for review. This linking-and-retrieving process is commonly referred to as *hypertext*.

Work-Product Retrieval

Work-product retrieval refers to the reuse of a firm's prior work product. Just as information in databases such as Lexis and Westlaw can be searched, so can a search be made of the firm's database of documents prepared for prior cases. A search can be conducted for briefs, pleadings, research memos, expert-witness reports, arbitration evaluations, judges' profiles, or any other document in the system. This prevents the "reinvention of the wheel" and makes a firm operate more efficiently. The same software used for the ALS system is often used to store, search, and retrieve prior work product.

As documents are finalized, they are transferred to the database, indexed, and removed from the main disk storage area used for current documents. An electronic form of the document is retained off-line, but can be easily retrieved when needed. This is another area where optical disks are used because of their ability to store many thousands of pages of text on a single disk.

Selecting Litigation Support Software

Several good sources of information about litigation support software exist. Most of the products are advertised in magazines and other publications for lawyers and paralegals, such as *Legal Management*, a publication of the Association of Legal Administrators; *Legal Assistant Today*, a magazine for paralegals; and *Legal Economics*, a publication of the American Bar Association for attorneys involved in firm management. Another good source of information is a publication of the American Bar Association entitled *LOCATE* that describes many such software products and gives information about the companies selling them.

Once you have selected several products for review, you should compare the capabilities of each, and if possible, have someone who is knowledgeable about the programs demonstrate them. Refer to Appendix H for a list of features and functions you can look for when evaluating ALS system software. Depending on your firm's practice and budget, you may not require all of these capabilities, but you should know they are available. Look for the program with features most important to you.

Use of Client's Systems

Often a law firm's clients have sophisticated computer systems already equipped with database software necessary for ALS. In these situations agreements are often made to allow the law firm to use the client's computer for the client's litigation. The primary advantage to this arrangement is that the firm does not have to make a large investment in hardware and software. The firm may need to purchase the necessary computer terminal or PC and telecommunications components to access the client's computer, but this is usually a significantly smaller investment than purchasing a complete system.

Another advantage to using the client's computers is that the client will often have a technical staff to operate the system and train the law firm's staff in its use. This reduces the time required to get the system up and running efficiently. One disadvantage to using a client's computer is you will only be able to use it for that client's cases. If some of your other cases would benefit from ALS, you have to set them up on a different system and provide maintenance. You may also have to learn two software systems, if you are unable to use the same software as your client. Using two software systems can be confusing and is not an efficient way to operate.

• Implementing an Automated Litigation Support System

Planning is the key to a successful ALS system. Remember, computers can help you organize your work, but they cannot make you organized. Everyone involved in the project should be well trained before the ALS system is implemented. Quality-control procedures should be instituted. Proper attorney supervision is critical to the success of the project. The attorneys involved in the case must define the issues and then inform the paralegal staff about them. Although attorneys may be involved in document screening, they should not necessarily be involved in objective coding and input.

Integrated Software with Imaging

Some PC-based products now incorporate full-text, abstract, and image databases into one application designed for easy use by attorneys. Imaging is the newest technology lawyers are increasingly making use of. An image is a "digitized photograph" of the pages of an actual document. If a document contains handwritten notes, the attorney may "hot-key" to the image of the document to read the handwritten notes. In addition to litigation support, these programs may be used for other applications such as brief banks, library management, human resources, records management, and to track information on expert witnesses.

See Appendixes G, H, and I for list of image databases, personal information managers, relational database products, and database managers.

Document Production

Document production occurs during the discovery phase of a case. During field discovery, the discovery team, consisting of one or more attorneys, paralegals, and clerical staff, determines which of the opponent's documents will be copied for use in the litigation process. These documents constitute the predominant source of information for control and analysis. Our discussion of selection and screening of documents for an ALS system involves the same considerations as in cases supported by manual methods (see Chapter 8).

Documents produced during discovery may consist of correspondence, memorandums, client records, accounting records, or plat maps, blueprints, and drawings. Later, pleadings and briefs, and trial and deposition transcripts may be added to the database. Court reporting services today provide electronic versions of the transcripts of depositions or trial testimony. These can be imported into a litigation-support database as "full text" or can be summarized by a paralegal to create an abstract or profile.

As a member of the discovery team, the paralegal should pay close attention to quality-control procedures to reduce the need to return to the field discovery site and to ensure the document copies are of the highest quality. This is particularly important if document images or a full-text database will be created by scanning documents.

Document Selection

Document selection is the process of choosing which records will be pulled for screening and possible copying. Selection is not the process of choosing which records *will* be copied, but which records *may* be copied. At this stage it is useful to establish some objective criteria about the required documents, such as document type, author(s), recipient(s), or other characteristics that are easily recognizable.

Establishing these objective criteria often allows paralegals to administer the initial selection process rather than attorneys. Selection criteria are influenced by the relevance of an entire collection at a particular site, the size of the collection, the budget allocated for the collection, the index and organization of the records, and the skills of the key members of the field discovery team.

The type and volume of records will dictate the size of discovery operations and the methods employed to carry out the discovery functions. Large volumes of records produced will create demands for resources and time proportionate to the volume. For this reason, both the selection and screening of documents become more critical as document production increases.

Document Numbering

Every ALS system is based on a numbering system for the documents or other objects managed by the system. Every page of every document must be numbered. This can be done with a special numbering machine often referred to as a *Bates machine* or *Bates stamp*. These numbering machines produce sequential numbers automatically, or the computer may be used to print prenumbered labels. If the pages are not numbered, it will be difficult, if not impossible, to determine if a reviewed document is complete. Also, when a search produces a particular document with many pages, it will be difficult to locate the relevant search term contained without references to unique page numbers.

Document Screening

Document screening involves examination of the documents selected after the document production. Screening may take place either at the production site or back at the law firm's office. Likewise, the copying may occur at the discovery site or in the law firm if the originals can be removed from the discovery site. In either case, the screening of documents requires a decision on whether a particular document or class of documents is worth copying before it is returned to its source. Each document or class of documents should be analyzed individually. However, this does not mean each must be looked at individually. For example, if it is known that boxes 1 through 10 contain bank statements for the years 1990 and 1991, and these records are critical to proving part of the case, all of those records can be copied without individual examination.

When a decision is made to copy a particular document, it should be flagged. The most efficient method is to use a set of peel-off prenumbered labels with sequential numbers that correspond to the number on a *document logging form* like the one in Exhibit 14.1. These logging forms may also contain additional categories that form the basis for decisions about further processing of the documents once they are brought back to the office after copying. The document logging form can be as complex or as simple as needed. A "Remarks" section should be included so that special instructions or comments can be noted about particular documents that cannot be accommodated in the regular column headings. Here is a brief explanation of each column in the form:

- box = Insert the number of the box.
- item no. = Each document should be numbered. Insert the number of the first item.
- item thru = This is the number of the last page of the document. For example, if you have a three-page contract, insert the number 3 here.
- rec'd = Date received.
- b/c = Batch in control. Put a check here to indicate that you have made sure all the documents are labeled and/or date-stamped.
- prof = Profile. Put a check here to indicate that you have profiled the document.

Exhibit 14.1

Project Log Sheet

Box	Item No.	Item_thru	rec'd	b/c	prof	voc	itm	sub	sc	qc	#pgs	#profs	bckup	rtm'd	machine

- voc = Vocabulary check. Put a check here to indicate that the words have been checked.
- itm = Put a check here after you make sure that there is congruency and no overlaps in the database.
- sub = Subject. Use a code here, for example, "M" for memo.
- qc = Quality control. Put a check here if no problems exist.
- #pgs = Number of pages.
- #profs = Number of profiles.
- bckup = Backed up. Put a check here to indicate backup copy has been made.
- rtn'd = Put a check here to indicate documents have been returned to client.
- machine = The PC on which the database is located.

Consideration should be given to what copying will be needed and what are the available resources. Also, file boxes and supplies for packaging and shipping the copied documents will be necessary. Microfilm equipment may become necessary, because some documents cannot be easily copied. (*Microfilm* equipment stores the document images on a cartridge, as opposed to *microfiche*, which stores the documents on sheets. Microfilm is preferable to microfiche as the microfiche sheets are more easily damaged, misfiled, or lost.) *Imaging* of the documents may be even more useful, especially if you anticipate utilizing imaging as part of the litigation-support system. An additional possibility is imaging the documents in lieu of photocopying them. Using specially equipped photocopy machines, it is possible to print copies of document images at high speeds. Imaging documents in the field may also be faster than regular photocopying processes.

An even more difficult problem is the production of machine-readable data during discovery. Keep in mind that the value of most such data is not the actual computer tapes or software used to store the data, but rather the information in reports produced by the computer program. It is this information upon which a person acts, not the software used. The reports created are the real intelligence available, and they are what are used by an opposing party in its decision-making. In collecting such information, therefore, the focus should be on obtaining copies of all output reports, organizing, and labeling them clearly. Recent advances in imaging technology now allow such reports to be stored as images rather than in *hard copy* (paper) form. In this situation, either the firm or a specialty vendor will require the ability to view and print the images.

Document Marking

There are several methods of marking documents with pertinent information to assist in controlling them. After the documents have been copied, the copies can be written on using nonreproducible markers (the shade of pale blue that does not show on photocopies). This allows clean copies to be produced later without any markings showing. Another method is to use Post-It notes. A third method is to use labels with bar-coded information similar to those used on product packaging in the grocery store. This would require a small printer for printing labels, and an optical wand to scan labels for identifying documents. It is important that the bar-code labels print the document ID number and other iden-tifying information on the label itself, as well as the magnetic bar code. You will be seeing bar-code technology used more in law firms for file-tracking and document-tracking in the future.

Document Analysis and Coding

Selected documents are coded with objective and subjective information to de-scribe the contents of the document and also other identifying characteristics to provide location of documents during trial preparation. After the documents have been copied and numbered, the next step is to eliminate duplicate docu-ments and irrelevant material before coding begins. Special care should be taken to make certain apparent duplicate documents are actually exact duplicates. When several people have received the same document, for example, there may be personal markings or comments on them that differentiate them. These mark-ings are called *marginalia*. Documents that are without marginalia, and are, in fact, duplicates should be removed and stored elsewhere. Undue time and effort should not be devoted to eliminating duplicate documents, however. A small percentage of duplicate documents is not justification for a massive undertaking to weed them out. It frequently takes less time to code duplicates than to identify and remove them. Moreover, searches of the database will reveal duplication. Remember, though, no documents produced during the discovery process should be destroyed until the case is completed. Thus, duplicate documents do not have to be coded and entered into the ALS system database, but that does not mean they should be destroyed.

Coding Issues

Document production, numbering, screening, and logging is typically handled by the paralegal and clerical staff. The responsibility for objective coding may also fall to the paralegal staff, under the supervision of an attorney. However, experience has shown that data-entry personnel are best suited for actual data entry. They will achieve a much higher rate of productivity than paralegals and will generally do much higher-quality work. Also, data-entry clerks will cost the client much less than the hourly fees for paralegals. Paralegals are best used for supervising the work of data-entry clerks and providing subjective information for entry by the clerks.

While paralegals are more effective in supervising the work, the attorneys involved in the case are the only persons who can prevent wasted time working with irrelevant documents. Attorneys should provide advice in the setup of the objective coding system. They should also be responsible for identifying the issues in the case so that they may be used as a guideline for subjective coding. The issues should be reviewed by the attorney periodically throughout the life of the case, because they may change as the case progresses.

There is no right or wrong way to code documents as long as the coding meets the informational needs of a particular case. If the informational needs are met, then the coding was done correctly. If the coding done does not meet the information needs of the case, then the coding was done incorrectly. The only correct approach is to analyze the type of information a case requires and then develop a coding scheme to furnish the information. If the system is designed to handle many cases, it should provide the option of using as many of the coding approaches as the firm can afford. As discussed earlier, these coding schemes include abstracts, extracts, key words, images, and full-text storage.

Objective Coding

To decide on *objective coding*, that is, the bibliographic or objective information to be coded, it is important for attorneys, paralegals, and the ALS-system designer to discuss what is needed, its relative value, and a precise definition of what is meant by each term. For example, a decision must be made about whether all the recipients of a document, including those listed as receiving "cc" (carbon copies) and "bc" (blind copies), should be entered or just the primary recipient. To eliminate ambiguities, you must define each element of the database before coding begins. Exhibit 14.2 shows a representative list of objective elements and how they might be defined.

An excellent tool for precise documentation of coding procedures in a case is a *project* or *case manual*, which describes in writing all decisions made regarding coding conventions for that particular case. It is highly recommended that a case manual be developed for any case where the document population exceeds 10,000 documents. The case manual should contain a list of fields used to code documents such as DATE, DOCUMENT TYPE, AUTHOR, RECIPIENT, etc. It should also list all standardized lists of names, and/or abbreviations used for coding documents. Decisions regarding precisely where information will be placed in the fields should be documented. For example, if carbon-copy and blind-copy lists of names are coded separately from the main receiver of a document, the case manual should reflect this decision. Sample documents should be incorporated as exhibits to the case manual with notes for coding methods used with different classes of documents. The case manual serves as a blueprint for where and how information was entered into the database.

After defining the objective elements to be coded, you can create document coding forms like the one shown in Exhibit 14.3. These forms make it easier to enter the information into the computer. The most effective coding form will look similar to the screen used to enter the information, with each data element (field) in the same order on the form as it must be input. Likewise, it is also helpful to show the number of characters allowed for each field and include spaces for each person involved in the coding. In addition, the form should include a data-entry process for each person to sign off as his or her part is completed to eliminate duplication of effort and to allow determination of the status of any particular coding form.

However, coding forms are no longer the optimal method for data entry. Entering the data directly into the computer, while reviewing the document itself, is the fastest, most efficient method for building a database.

Coding forms add an extra, unnecessary step in the document-coding process. Usually, if a coding form is used, paralegals fill them out by hand. This process is extremely slow compared to heads-down data entry directly from a document. Data-entry clerks achieve document-coding rates two, three, and even four times greater than paralegals, given the appropriate environment.

The coding form also increases the possibility for human error. The person filling out the coding form may leave out information or record it wrongly or illegibly.

In addition, the case-specific knowledge paralegals possess may actually hinder the coding of *objective* (as opposed to *subjective*, discussed later) informa-

Exhibit 14.2
●
**Definitions—Objective
Coding Elements**

Item	Coding Term	Definition
1	Document ID	Unique control number assigned to the document during discovery and document production, often recorded on the logging form.
2	System index number	The number assigned by the computer system when the document coding information is input. May be the same as the Document ID.
3	Authors	The names of the persons who wrote the document. In some instances it is important to capture not only the name of the person who signed a document, but also other names of persons who did the actual writing.
4	Recipient	The names of persons who received the document. If those receiving copies are maintained separately, then this would include only those formally sent the document.
5	Type of document	Letter, memorandum, contract, accounting records, chart, bound documents, etc.
6	Document date	Date found on the document itself.
7	Subject line	In the case of a memo or report, the subject indicated on the document.
8	Source	From whom the document was obtained, or location of discovery.
9	Author's organization	Company or organization name.
10	Author's title	Usually found with signature.
11	Copyees	Persons receiving copies of the document.
12	Original or copy	Is the document in your possession the original or a copy of the original?
13	Number of pages	This is important for assuring the complete document is reviewed.
14	Attachments	Attachments may need to be entered as separate documents and cross-referenced, but should be identified here by type, number of attachments, and cross-index number.
15	Physical location	Where will the physical document be filed? Room, file cabinet, shelf, box, etc.
16	Marginalia	Does the document have handwritten notes added to it?

tion. A paralegal might neglect to record information that she views as unimportant based on her knowledge of the case. However, information that is unimportant today may suddenly become critical tomorrow. For example, the name of a minor player in the case might not be recorded—and three months later, it might be discovered that the person is actually a key player. A data-entry person would not make this mistake, since he or she will be making no subjective judgments about objective information. All names and other information will be captured precisely according to the instructions given.

Today most database software provides the user with an *audit trail* of data-entry activity, which can be used to identify errors in document coding in the

Exhibit 14.3

Document Coding Form

```
DOCUMENT_IDENTIFICATION:
CATEGORY:                      DATE:  /  /
ORIGINATOR:                         RECIPIENT:
COMPANY_REC:
AUTHOR'S ORGANIZATION:              AUTHOR'S TITLE:




EXH:
SUBJECT LINE:
SOURCE:
KEY_PEOPLE:                    TYPE OF DOC:
                               ORIG. OR COPY:
KEY_ENTITIES:                  NO. OF PAGES:
COPYEES:                       ATTACHMENTS:
MARGINALIA:                    PHYSICAL LOCATION:
ATTORNEY_COMMENTS:
```

same way completed coding forms have been used to compare with actual information in the database. The audit trail is much more useful, since it can be compared directly with the source document to check for accuracy of coding.

If your firm is large, it may hire data-entry personnel for objective coding from temporary employment services. The only qualifications are good use of the English language, the ability to print clearly if coding forms are used, and keyboard or typing skills if direct on-line data entry is used.

Subjective Coding

The other major type of coding is *subjective coding*. It may be entered as a second step, once an objective database is completed, or a short form may be attached to the document containing subjective information. The data-entry clerk may capture the subjective information from the form attached to the document at the same time objective information from the document is captured. This subjective information may take the form of abstracts, extracts, key-word coding, or document images. It requires subjective analysis of a document, taking that document out of the index class, which objective coding creates, and into a class known as a *document surrogate*.

In most cases, however, where documents provide key information to support or refute positions in a case, *objective* information may often lead the user to the relevant documents with little or no *subjective* coding. This is true because most actions taken by parties to litigation in the business setting are usually thoroughly documented, and the documentation creates startlingly vivid trails among the actors involved in a dispute. Accordingly, by searching an objective database for relatively simple author/recipient/bc/cc/date combinations, it is frequently possible to identify all essential documents. Participants in controversial circumstances interact with each other in a surprisingly consistent and detailed manner through business correspondence in the form of memoranda, letters, and reports of various kinds. No subjective coding is required to trace such distinct objective trails of interaction.

Of course, subjective coding does have its legitimate role to play. But since it is by its very nature expensive and time-consuming, and involves the value judgments of the individual performing it, it might be more valuable to initially consider using *quasi-subjective coding*. For example, in construction litigation, it might be useful to capture all change orders by their assigned numbers. While not standard objective information, change-order numbers are not exactly regular subjective information either. Yet in many construction cases a simple trail of documents referring to a major change order may hold the key to an important question of liability.

It is also advisable to do subjective coding as a second stage of document coding after building and using an objective database. Realistically, in most litigation matters many documents are coded containing little or no value to the case. Even with initial culling of documents produced by the other side prior to coding, relatively unimportant documents usually end up being included for coding. However, by initially using the objective database, it will be possible for the user to identify the more valuable documents that are worthy of the additional expense and effort involved in subjective coding.

Remember, objective coding is best accomplished by data-entry personnel, while subjective coding must be done by trained legal personnel, usually paralegals working on the case (unless a data-entry clerk is used to enter subjective data from a form prepared by the paralegal). This means subjective coding is an expensive process, since paralegal rates are much higher than those for data-entry clerks.

Another reason for waiting to do subjective coding as a second step after objective coding is that in almost all complex, lengthy cases, issues tend to change and come into focus more clearly after there has been time for discovery. This happens through interrogatories, requests for admissions, taking depositions, and narrowing issues for trial through the pleadings process in court. Therefore, subjective coding will be more effective if carried out in the latter stages of a case, when the more valuable documents can be identified by queries of the objective database.

As mentioned, subjective coding may take the form of abstracts, extracts, key-word coding, or document images. A short explanation follows.

Abstract.   An *abstract* is a short synopsis of a document of five to ten typed lines intended to take the place of the document itself by providing an informative condensed version of the document's contents. An *indicative* is a type of abstract that points to a document as containing or satisfying certain predefined subjective requirements. The indicative is not intended to take the place of the document as would a regular abstract, but rather to add bibliographic points that will direct the researcher to the document. The indicative abstract should be as short as possible, even though it may leave out some of the details and subject elements of the document.

Extracts.   Portions of the text, or *extracts*, may be reproduced verbatim and entered as the document surrogate instead of an abstract. The document coder looks for particular statements or discussions and enters them exactly as they appear in the document. The abstract and extract are created in different ways, but their uses in subjective coding are similar.

Key-Word Coding.   In *key-word coding*, various controlled vocabularies are used to code documents. A systematic classification scheme, or *taxonomy*, may be created so that you can use codes to indicate the presence of different subjective elements in the document. A set of such codes may be used to point to issues in the case. Another set may be used for the names of companies and people relevant to the case. A third set may be hierarchical to allow generalization of statements or contents without exact word matching. Alternatively, the hierarchy may use actual words and their hierarchical relationships. As a rule of thumb, taxonomies should not exceed 1,000 terms.

Thesaurus.   A more sophisticated form of key-word coding is the *thesaurus,* a collection of terms that allows additions both before and after the case begins, as necessary. A thesaurus does increase the preparation time needed to begin subjective coding, but it greatly increases the degree of precision attainable. The effort to create a thesaurus will only be justified for very large cases or in situations where the thesaurus can be used in support of several different cases that share the same or similar fact situations. If a firm specializes in patent-infringement suits, for example, a thesaurus geared to those types of cases might be a cost-effective undertaking.

Full-Text Storage and Retrieval

Full-text storage and retrieval involves the entry into the database of the entire document text verbatim and eliminates the need for key-word coding. This is becoming more common as the cost of electronic storage goes down and the time required for searches to locate documents decreases.

Building the ALS System Database

How the data is entered in the database will depend on many factors, especially who will be doing the data entry. If it will be a data-entry clerk, document-coding forms should be used for any subjective coding so the clerks won't be forced to make decisions for which they are untrained. Most objective information can easily be input directly into the computer. Avoid handling the documents or coding forms more than once. Accuracy is also critical, and all data input should be proofed after entry. Coding forms should be reviewed to make sure none were skipped or duplicated.

• Retrieving Information from an
Automated Litigation Support System

As the database develops, it can be searched for relevant information using several methods, depending on the type of system installed. This is the point at which the attorney responsible for the case must help develop the search criteria, since he or she is the one who knows best what information to look for.

The simplest searches are for single words, numbers, or dates. For example, a search may be conducted for all documents with a particular date or all documents authored by a particular individual. Every database manager has its own syntax for entering the search information, but many managers use simple English commands, and the request may resemble this: FIND DATE = 06/12/90 OR AUTHOR EQUAL "JERRY WHITMIRE."

This search request may result in numerous *hits* (findings of searched-for information) if there are any documents in the system dated June 12, 1990, or authored by Jerry Whitmire. Name searches may also be used to find related documents that should be linked together. For example, every time a new witness is designated to testify, a search can be done on the database for every document, deposition, or trial transcript containing the witness's name. This information can be examined and reviewed by the attorney to prepare for trial. These searches are examples of searches for objective information. Querying the database for subjective information (key words, abstracts, and extracts) requires more sophisticated techniques and the ability to compose a more complex search. The same taxonomy or thesaurus used to code the information can be used as a tool to prepare *search sets*, which are combinations of search requests used to locate a document or group of documents relating to a particular issue. The search set may contain a combination of both objective and subjective information.

Most systems have the ability to use Boolean connectors to formulate searches. As discussed earlier in this text, Boolean connectors include terms like AND, OR, and NOT. They help define logical relationships between different types of information. For example, a search might be composed to locate all documents NOT memos AND written by a particular author OR dated between a certain date range AND in which a certain issue is mentioned. If a search asks to see all documents that contain the words "dog" AND "cat," a system will interpret this to mean "find all the documents in the database that contain both the word 'dog' and the word 'cat.' " Both words must be present for the computer to retrieve the document as meeting the search criteria. On the other hand, if a search asks to see all documents containing the words "dog" OR "cat," the system will interpret this to mean "find all documents in the database containing either 'dog' or 'cat.' " Only one of the two words need be present for the computer to retrieve a document as meeting the search criteria. The difference between the two searches is that the AND search narrows the focus, while the OR search expands it.

The user language may also allow for searching of *adjacent terms* within a particular category of information. For example, a search to find the last names "adjacent to" the name TUCKER might produce the last names TINDAL, THOMPSON, THORNBERG, and TRAVIS, which occur alphabetically in front of TUCKER, and TURNER, TYLER, and TYSON, which occur alphabetically after TUCKER.

Another type of search is the *root search*, which involves searching for all words beginning with a particular set of characters. For example, a root search of "damag" might retrieve the words "damages, damaged, and damaging."

In full-text searching there is even more flexibility in locating information. You can search for words in the text by their proximity to other words and the order of occurrence to overcome ambiguities. An example of this *proximity searching* might be, FIND INJURY WITHIN 5 DEATH. This search would locate all occurrences of the word INJURY occurring within five words of the word DEATH. Another form of proximity searching is to locate words or phrases in the same sentence or same paragraph as other words or phrases.

However, in full-text searching, it is more difficult to refine the searches unless the documents have been profiled. The search for JERRY WHITMIRE in a full-text database would retrieve all documents with the name JERRY WHIT-MIRE instead of only those authored by him. Also, a search for a particular phrase, such as FIRE PROTECTION might miss relevant documents discussing FIRE SAFETY.

There are many other search techniques used with various systems. Most full-text search systems allow the user to use similar search criteria as found in Lexis, Westlaw, and other on-line databases. While it is important to know how to operate the computer, it is just as critical to know what is expected from the computer search. It is therefore necessary to have attorney supervision. If you aren't getting it, ask for it.

• Maintaining and Administering an Automated Litigation System

If the ALS system is maintained in-house, without vendor assistance or with limited vendor assistance, it will be essential for your firm to consider the support staff requirements of the system. If the firm is purchasing its own hardware and software, it will likewise have to train its existing staff or hire trained personnel to operate the system. Personnel constitute the most expensive and most important part of a successful ALS system. The number of support staff required will depend on the anticipated size and number of cases. You, the paralegal, for example, may be required to fill many roles.

In today's job marketplace, paralegals with experience in automation, especially automated litigation support, are in greater demand and can often command higher salaries. You should welcome the opportunity to become involved in your firm's litigation support system, even if it requires longer working hours and considerable frustration during the implementation. You will be rewarded in the long run by gaining additional marketable skills.

Maintaining System Security

Security is as important (or more so) as confidentiality during a client's litigation process. Not only is it important for a client's data to be kept confidential, the system must be secured so you can depend on it to operate properly when you need it. Computer disasters happen. The litigation process doesn't stop just because of a computer disaster. Consequently, it is vital you implement and follow security measures to ensure that important data will be available when required. Security involves physical security, access security, and data security.

Physical Security
Physical security involves controlling physical access to the computer and the facilities housing it. Access to the area containing the ALS system and the location of the documents themselves should be limited to only those persons who have a "need to know." Anyone not involved in the case should be prohibited from entering the filing area to avoid having documents inadvertently moved, lost, or destroyed. The simplest way to control physical access to the computer is with locks on the doors. Access to the documents shipped and received should also be carefully monitored and controlled.

Data Security
Once the information has been transferred to the ALS system and is stored electronically, different security issues emerge, those of *data security*. Now access to the electronic data must be limited. This is typically done by passwords and

the assignment of access rights in the software itself. Passwords should be carefully guarded and changed frequently. It is best to use nonsense words for passwords, since any computer hacker can use a dictionary of common English words to find a password. If your ALS system is operating on a local area network (LAN) and can be accessed from outside the office using modems and communications software, you are subject to greater security risks. Don't ignore this critical element of system administration.

Backup

If you are new to computers, you may have an important lesson to learn—frequent and proper backing up of data. Anyone who has ever lost important data or had to redo days' or even weeks' worth of computer work has already learned this lesson the hard way. You can avoid this disheartening experience by learning reliable backup techniques and using them every day. Never back up on top of yesterday's backup. Rotate your backup disks frequently—replacing the disks or tapes periodically (every few months). Your backups are critical to the success of the system. Make sure the media you are using is of the highest quality. And don't wait until you have a problem to test your "restore" function. Find out from your computer vendor or in-house technician how to restore data without writing over active data. Make sure the backup and restore functions work properly and that you know how to use them both.

Physical Facilities

The physical space required for an ALS system is not really any different from what is required for a manual system, except for the computer area. Indexers or coders need large surfaces for their work area. Large tables work best, but they should be the proper height for maximum comfort. The location of the computer will depend on who will be using it. If it is to be shared by several users, a central location is preferable. It should not be placed at anyone's permanent work-station, because that person will be continually displaced by other users. If your firm has a local area network (LAN) or other multi-user system, then it may reside on a central database server, and everyone who has a PC attached to the network may have access to it.

Physical Filing Systems

Once the data has been screened, coded, and input, the physical documents must be stored for later use. Because thousands of documents may need to be boxed and filed, open shelving is preferable to filing cabinets. The shelves should be arranged to eliminate the need to move some boxes to gain access to others. All boxes should be labeled on all sides so they can be read from any direction. Make it easy on yourself. Insist on proper physical filing facilities. If you need to locate a document on the bottom of a stack of heavy boxes, valuable time and effort will be wasted in retrieving it. Proper planning of physical filing facilities is the way to avoid this waste.

Using Off-Site Storage

Because of the rising cost of office space today, many law firms use off-site storage companies to store the hard copies of documents. These companies are themselves computerized to quickly locate and retrieve the boxes requested and will deliver them to your office. Someone should personally visit the off-site storage premises to make sure proper security measures are instituted and the storage areas are environmentally controlled. Often off-site storage is preferable to on-site simply because they do a better job of storing and retrieving boxes. Unless your firm has file room personnel to handle these tasks, it may be wise to use off-site storage.

• Summary

Because litigation is such a paper-intensive activity, computers are used to manage and control the numerous documents involved in a case. The paralegal is often responsible for the administration of the discovery process and the operation of the ALS system. Sometimes outside vendors are used to supplement a law firm's in-house ALS system or to provide all of the services necessary for ALS.

A law firm may be able to use existing hardware and software for its ALS system needs, but more likely it will need to purchase special components for ALS. The selection of new systems should involve the firm's technical support staff to ensure the ALS system fits well into the firm's overall automation strategy. Scanners and optical disk storage are becoming increasingly popular to implement document imaging systems. ALS systems require the use of database managers that allow not only the control of discovery documents, but also the firm's prior work product.

To implement an ALS system, it is important to plan each step to make sure information will be available to the attorneys during the trial proceedings. The discovery team selects the documents to be coded or scanned and works closely with the ALS system designer. If the documents are not stored in the ALS system as full text, they must be coded. Sometimes objective coding will suffice, but subjective coding may also be necessary. As the database grows, the attorneys or paralegals doing research can begin to search the database to locate information relevant to the case issues.

Learning how to implement and use ALS systems provides the paralegal with more marketable skills. Firm size and staffing resources determine the level of involvement a paralegal will have with ALS. Both physical security and data security are extremely important. Special facilities are usually not required unless there are numerous coders who need large work areas. Space for filing boxes of documents should have open shelving or may be at an off-site storage facility.

Automated litigation support systems are being used more and more in law offices. If your office doesn't currently use one, it most likely soon will, especially if the firm handles large cases. In the future, the systems will change and improve, and you should try to keep up with the advances of technology to do you job more effectively. The information in this chapter may be quickly outdated by technological advances. Do your own research to supplement what has been covered here.

Procedure and Practice After Judgment

• Introduction*

Once the judgment is obtained, the battle is not over. Now the judgment must be collected and enforced. After judgment, the plaintiff becomes the *judgment creditor* against the defendant. The defendant becomes the *judgment debtor*. Most judgment debtors will work out a plan to pay their debts if they don't have sufficient funds to pay the judgment in full. Some, however, try to have the judgment vacated or reversed at the trial level, or through appeal to higher courts. Others attempt to hide or transfer assets. The law provides various remedies for uncooperative judgment debtors. However, these post-judgment remedies vary considerably from state to state. Thus, in a creditor-oriented state, post-judgment remedies may be available in almost all actions. In a debtor-oriented jurisdiction, they will be restricted to particular actions and subjected to various procedural restrictions.

A federal court may use the post-judgment remedies available to the courts of the state in which it is sitting. However, the federal court may use them only to the extent the state remedies are not inconsistent with any other federal rule or statute.[1] This chapter will familiarize you with the various post-judgment remedies. In addition, you will learn effective methods of ascertaining the assets of a debtor and domesticating a foreign (from another state) judgment.

• Post-Trial Motions

Motions may be made in the trial court after the judgment has been entered by either party if the party is dissatisfied with or disagrees with the judgment. These motions may give either party an opportunity to request the court to set aside the judgment. If the judgment debtor seeks to appeal the judgment, he must obtain an order of *supersedeas* to stop the enforcement efforts while awaiting the outcome of his appeal—unless applicable law provides such a stay of judgment automatically.

Since post-trial motion practice varies from state to state, this chapter will be primarily based on the practice in the federal courts. Paralegals should always

---

*Contributions to this chapter were made by Francis M. Bird, Jr., attorney at law, Atlanta, Georgia.

[1] *Federal Rules of Civil Procedure*, Rule 64.

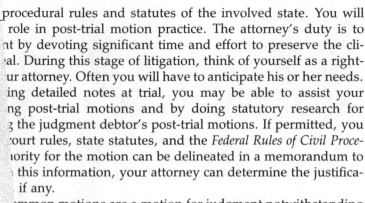

procedural rules and statutes of the involved state. You will
role in post-trial motion practice. The attorney's duty is to
nt by devoting significant time and effort to preserve the cli-
al. During this stage of litigation, think of yourself as a right-
ur attorney. Often you will have to anticipate his or her needs.
ing detailed notes at trial, you may be able to assist your
ng post-trial motions and by doing statutory research for
g the judgment debtor's post-trial motions. If permitted, you
ourt rules, state statutes, and the *Federal Rules of Civil Proce-*
iority for the motion can be delineated in a memorandum to
this information, your attorney can determine the justifica-
if any.

ommon motions are a motion for judgment notwithstanding
and a motion for a new trial. The primary purpose of these
e the judgment set aside by the party against whom the
entered. You might be asked to draft the initial motion and
obtain supporting affidavits. Be sure to enter the pertinent dates in the tickler,
docket control, or critical dates system. Your first draft can help your attorney
complete a final draft, at which time you can arrange for its service on the
opponent and its subsequent filing in court.

• Motion for Judgment Notwithstanding the Verdict (JNOV)

A *motion for judgment notwithstanding the verdict* (JNOV) (Exhibit 15.1) is made
after the jury has already rendered a verdict. Essentially, the judge is saying, by
accepting this motion, that no reasonable jury could have reached a verdict,
because there was not sufficient evidence on all the essential elements on which
to base a verdict. Before the verdict is rendered by the jury, a *motion for directed
verdict* may be made instead. By accepting this motion, the judge is saying that
the jury should not even get the case (or the particular issue), because there is
insufficient evidence on all elements.

Pursuant to Rule 50(b) of the *Federal Rules of Civil Procedure,* a party who has
moved for a directed verdict at the close of all evidence may file a motion for
JNOV. The motion must be filed within ten days after judgment has been entered.[2] The motion asks either that the judgment be set aside, combined with a
motion for a new trial (discussed next), or that judgment be entered in accordance with the previous motion for directed verdict. A motion for new trial may
also be filed separately.

A motion for JNOV is similar to a motion for a new trial (discussed next) in
that it challenges the legal sufficiency of the evidence, but it demands judgment
for the moving party rather than a new trial.

• Motion for New Trial

Under Rule 59 of the *Federal Rules of Civil Procedure,* a *motion for new trial* (Exhibits
15.2 and 15.3) must be filed within ten days of the entry of judgment. Typi-

---

[2]*Federal Rules of Civil Procedure,* Rule 50.

Exhibit 15.1

**Motion for Judgment
Notwithstanding
the Verdict (JNOV)**

IN THE UNITED STATES DISTRICT COURT FOR
THE ELEVENTH DISTRICT OF GEORGIA, NORTHERN DIVISION

SHARON RADEMAKER,	)	
	)	
Plaintiff,	)	
	)	Civil Action No. 578926
v.	)	
	)	
STEVEN N. REIFF,	)	
	)	
Defendant.	)	

MOTION FOR JUDGMENT NOTWITHSTANDING THE VERDICT

Plaintiff Sharon Rademaker moves the Court pursuant to Rule 50(b), *Federal Rules of Civil Procedure*, to set aside the verdict entered in the above-entitled action on October 30, 1992, (and the Judgment entered thereon on October 31, 1992) and to enter judgment in favor of Plaintiff Sharon Rademaker for the following reasons:

1. There was no substantial evidence offered by the Defendant Steven N. Reiff on the issue of breach of contract;
2. There was no substantial evidence offered by the Defendant Steven N. Reiff on the issue of fraud;
3. There was no substantial evidence offered by the Defendant Steven N. Reiff on the issue of damages; and
4. There was no substantial evidence offered by the Defendant Steven N. Reiff on the issue of intent.

Respectfully submitted,

John I. Bruno
Attorney for Plaintiff

[Certificate of Service]

cally, this motion alleges (1) procedural errors (improperly admitted or excluded evidence, improper argument by opposing counsel prejudicial jury instructions, etc.); and (2) a verdict contrary to law, excessive or inadequate damages, and other grounds.

As previously discussed, under the *Federal Rules of Civil Procedure* and most parallel state rules, a motion for JNOV may be joined with this motion. If a verdict was returned, the court may allow the judgment to stand. The court may also reopen the judgment and either order a new trial, or direct the entry of judgment as if the requested verdict had been directed. Making a motion for a new trial requires that the moving party have grounds. Some of these grounds may include:[3]

---

[3]William P. Statsky, *Torts: Personal Injury Litigation*, 2d ed. (St. Paul, MN: West Publishing Company, 1990), p. 221.

Exhibit 15.2

**Motion for New Trial
(Non-Jury Case)**

IN THE UNITED STATES DISTRICT COURT FOR
THE ELEVENTH DISTRICT OF GEORGIA, NORTHERN DIVISION

SHARON RADEMAKER,	)	
	)	
Plaintiff,	)	
	)	Civil Action No. 578926
v.	)	
	)	
STEVEN N. REIFF,	)	
	)	
Defendant.	)	

MOTION FOR NEW TRIAL IN NON-JURY CASE

Plaintiff Sharon Rademaker moves the Court to set aside the Findings of Fact, Conclusions of Law and Judgment pursuant to Rule 52(b), *Federal Rules of Civil Procedure,* and to grant Plaintiff a new trial pursuant to Rule 59(a), *Federal Rules of Civil Procedure* on the grounds that:

1. The court erred in ruling that. . . . . .
2. The Court erred in admitting the following evidence offered by the Defendant Steven N. Reiff over the objection of Plaintiff Sharon Rademaker. . . . . . .
3. The Court erred in excluding evidence of Plaintiff. . . . . .
4. The Court erred in admitting the following exhibits over objection for the following reasons. . . . . .
5. The Court erred in excluding the following exhibits. . . . . .
6. The Judgment is contrary to law in that. . . . . .

Respectfully submitted,

John I. Bruno
Attorney at Law

[Certificate of Service]

---

1. Prejudicial irregularities committed by the judge or by an attorney.
2. Excessive or inadequate damages.
3. Improper argument by opposing counsel.
4. Jury misconduct.
5. Surprise.
6. The verdict is manifestly against the weight of the evidence.
7. Fraud by a party.

Again, under Rule 59 of the *Federal Rules of Civil Procedure,* the motion must be supported by affidavit and filed within ten days of the entry of judgment. The opposing party is given ten days in which to file responsive affidavits. However, local court rules may vary.

Exhibit 15.3

Motion For New Trial (Jury Case)

IN THE UNITED STATES DISTRICT COURT FOR
THE ELEVENTH DISTRICT OF GEORGIA, NORTHERN DIVISION

SHARON RADEMAKER,	)	
	)	
Plaintiff,	)	
	)	Civil Action No. 578926
v.	)	
	)	
STEVEN N. REIFF,	)	
	)	
Defendant.	)	

MOTION FOR NEW TRIAL IN JURY CASE

Defendant Steven N. Reiff moves the Court pursuant to Rule 59(a) *Federal Rules of Civil Procedure,* to set aside the verdict of the Jury returned herein on October 30, 1992, and the Judgment entered on October 31, 1992, and to grant a new trial on the grounds that:

1. The verdict is contrary to law as follows. . . . .
2. The verdict is contrary to the evidence as follows. . . . . . .
3. The evidence in this case is totally insufficient to support a finding of breach of contract, fraud, damages and intent.
4. The verdict of the jury herein is excessive and appears to have been given under the influence of passion and prejudice as follows. . . . . . .
5. The Court erred in permitting the following testimony over objection of Defendant Steven N. Reiff. . . . . . .
6. The Court erred in refusing to allow witnesses to answer Defendant's questions as follows. . . . . . .
7. The Court erred in admitting the following exhibits for the following reasons. . . . . . .
8. The Court erred in excluding the following exhibits for the following reasons. . . . . . .

Respectfully submitted,

John I. Bruno
Attorney at Law

[Certificate of Service]

• Collecting and Enforcing the Judgment

The paralegal may play an active role in collecting and enforcing judgments. The process of finding and collecting the assets and liabilities of the judgment debtor can be systematized. The two most used remedies are *execution* through a *fi.fa.,* which is a record to constitute a lien on real estate and/or personal property, and *garnishment,* which is used to reach bank accounts and debts owed to the judgment debtor.

The necessity of acting quickly cannot be overemphasized to prevent the judgment debtor from hiding or dissolving her assets and thus becoming judgment-proof. For example, judgment debtors frequently transfer their assets into their spouse's name. If that spouse is not also a judgment debtor, this action makes it more difficult for the judgment creditor to collect. If there is any possibility that the judgment debtor will do this, the plaintiff may be able to institute *attachment* proceedings in some instances, wherein another's property can be seized to satisfy a judgment yet to be rendered. Check your local court rules, because the laws governing attachment are different in many states. Many states do not allow attachment under any circumstance.

Bill of Costs

The first step after the verdict or judgment is entered is to collect the receipts and prepare the bill of costs.[4] Costs are awarded to the predominant party unless the court directs otherwise. A litany of costs must be submitted to the clerk of the court. A copy is sent to the opposing attorney. Any objections to the bill or a motion for court review must be served within five days of the clerk's assessment of costs. Federal Form AO133 (Exhibit 15.4) is used in federal court, and similar forms are available in some state courts. Keep a running record of the costs to help you prepare the bill of costs when the judgment is rendered.[5]

Post-Judgment Interrogatories

Using the investigative techniques described in this chapter and Chapter 7, you can uncover many of the assets of the judgment debtor. The court can aid your investigation by means of *post-judgment interrogatories* (Exhibit 15.5) and post-trial *request for production of documents*. The request for production of documents may be submitted independently. You may request copies of all financial documents, including financial statements, tax returns, deeds, banking records, insurance policies, contracts, and most other financial information.

It is prudent to develop a flexible standard form of interrogatories that can be modified for use in various cases. You will want to make detailed inquiries into the following areas, keeping in mind any limits in your state as to the number of interrogatories:

1. Name, address, phone, social security number, and date of birth.
2. Present and previous employment or trade name and place of business during the past ten years (number of years).
3. Bank accounts, including savings and other accounts; safety deposit information; and trusts or potential inheritances.
4. Location and market value of personal and business assets, both tangible and intangible (royalties, stocks, patents, copyrights, life insurance); and information concerning the distribution or transfer of any assets.

---

[4]*Federal Rules of Civil Procedure,* Rule 54(d), and parallel state rules.
[5]McCord, *The Litigation Paralegal,* p. 444.

United States District Court

_____ DISTRICT OF _____

BILL OF COSTS

V.

Case Number: _____

_____

Judgment having been entered in the above entitled action on _____ against _____,
Date

the Clerk is requested to tax the following as costs:

Fees of the Clerk . . . . $ _____

Fees for service of summons and subpoena . . . .   _____

Fees of the court reporter for all or any part of the transcript necessarily obtained for use in the case   _____

Fees and disbursements for printing . . . .   _____

Fees for witnesses (itemize on reverse side) . . . .   _____

Fees for exemplification and copies of papers necessarily obtained for use in the case . . . .   _____

Docket fees under 28 U.S.C. 1923 . . . .   _____

Costs as shown on Mandate of Court of Appeals . . . .   _____

Compensation of court-appointed experts . . . .   _____

Compensation of interpreters and costs of special interpretation services under 28 U.S.C. 1828 . . .   _____

Other costs (please itemize) . . . .   _____

TOTAL $ _____

SPECIAL NOTE: Attach to your bill an itemization and documentation for requested costs in all categories.

DECLARATION

I declare under penalty of perjury that the foregoing costs are correct and were necessarily incurred in this action and that the services for which fees have been charged were actually and necessarily performed. A copy of this bill was mailed today with postage prepaid to:

_____.

Signature of Attorney: _____

Name of Attorney: _____

For: _____   Date: _____
Name of Claiming Party

Costs are taxed in the amount of _____ and included in the judgment.

_____   By: _____   _____
Clerk of Court   Deputy Clerk   Date

Form 15.4

Federal Form A0133—
Bill of Costs

NAME AND RESIDENCE	ATTENDANCE		SUBSISTENCE		MILEAGE		Total Cost Each Witness
	Days	Total Cost	Days	Total Cost	Miles	Total Cost	
					TOTAL		

WITNESS FEES (computation, cf. 28 U.S.C. 1821 for statutory fees)

NOTICE

Section 1924, Title 28, U.S. Code (effective September 1, 1948) provides:
"Sec. 1924. Verification of bill of costs."
"Before any bill of costs is taxed, the party claiming any item of cost or disbursement shall attach thereto an affidavit, made by himself or by his duly authorized attorney or agent having knowledge of the facts, that such item is correct and has been necessarily incurred in the case and that the services for which fees have been charged were actually and necessarily performed."

See also Section 1920 of Title 28, which reads in part as follows:
"A bill of costs shall be filed in the case and, upon allowance, included in the judgment or decree."

The Federal Rules of Civil Procedure contain the following provisions:
Rule 54 (d)
"Except when express provision therefor is made either in a statute of the United States or in these rules, costs shall be allowed as of course to the prevailing party unless the court otherwise directs, but costs against the United States, its officers, and agencies shall be imposed only to the extent permitted by law. Costs may be taxed by the clerk on one day's notice. On motion served within 5 days thereafter, the action of the clerk may be reviewed by the court."

Rule 6 (e)
"Whenever a party has the right or is required to do some act or take some proceedings within a prescribed period after the service of a notice or other paper upon him and the notice or paper is served upon him by mail, 3 days shall be added to the prescribed period."

Rule 58 (In Part)
"Entry of the judgment shall not be delayed for the taxing of costs."

Form 15.4

Continued

IN THE STATE COURT OF SHELBY COUNTY
STATE OF TENNESSEE

THE SONO GROUP, INC.,⁣   )
)
    Plaintiff,   )
)   CIVIL ACTION
)   FILE NO. 90–2118
AMELIA PRESS, INC.   )
)
    Defendant.   )
)

PLAINTIFF'S POST-JUDGMENT INTERROGATORIES
PROPOUNDED TO DEFENDANT AMELIA PRESS, INC.

TO: AMELIA PRESS, INC., and their attorney of record:

Joseph L. Hansen, Jr.
Hansen & Hansen
Attorneys at Law
1225 East Rock Springs Road, N.E.
Memphis, Tennessee 38102.

The following post-judgment interrogatories are submitted to you in accordance with the Tennessee Civil Practice § 69 and § 33 (*Tenn. Code Ann.* § 81A-169 and § 81A-133). You are required to answer same in accordance with said Civil Practice Act.

1. Please list and describe the real property presently owned by AMELIA PRESS, INC., whether partially, jointly, or entirely. Please include in said description the county where each piece of property is located and the total acreage thereof.

2. What liens are outstanding against real property presently owned by AMELIA PRESS, INC., either partially, jointly, or entirely, mentioned in your Answer to Interrogatory No. 1. Please state the name of lien holder, the date of the lien, the type of lien, and the amount of the lien.

    (a) Please designate each piece of property against which any of the liens are outstanding.

    (b) What are the amounts of each of the respective liens existing on any real property presently owned by AMELIA PRESS, INC., either partially, jointly, or entirely?

3. What real property has AMELIA PRESS, INC., transferred, conveyed, or had foreclosed at any time subsequent to April 4, 1989.

4. What is the present monthly income of AMELIA PRESS, INC.?

5. What income has AMELIA PRESS, INC., received subsequent to April 4, 1989?

    (a) From what source was such income received?

    (b) How much income was received from each source?

6. What automobiles, trucks, or other automotive equipment does AMELIA PRESS, INC., presently own?

    (a) What liens presently exist against any automobiles, trucks or other automotive equipment presently owned by AMELIA PRESS, INC.?

    (b) What is the tag number for each automobile, truck, or other automotive equipment presently owned by AMELIA PRESS, INC.?

7. At what bank(s) does AMELIA PRESS, INC., maintain an account(s)?

8. Does AMELIA PRESS, INC., have a safety deposit box?

9. What amount of money does AMELIA PRESS, INC., have on deposit in a savings account with a commercial bank(s)?

Form 15.5

Continued

10. What amount of money does AMELIA PRESS, INC. have on deposit in a savings account with a savings and loan association(s)?

11. What amount of money does AMELIA PRESS, INC. have on deposit in a regular checking account with any of the foregoing?

12. What amount of money does AMELIA PRESS, INC. have on deposit in any depository whatsoever?

13. Did AMELIA PRESS, INC. file federal income tax returns for the years 1988 and 1989?

14. If AMELIA PRESS, INC. filed federal income tax returns for the years 1988 and 1989, what amount of taxable income did it reflect as having been earned by AMELIA PRESS, INC. for each of said years?

15. Did AMELIA PRESS, INC. file a state or county *ad valorem* tax return for the years 1988 and 1989?

16. If AMELIA PRESS, INC. filed a state or county *ad valorem* return for the years 1988 and 1989, what property was scheduled thereon as being owned by AMELIA PRESS, INC.?

17. Who owns the furniture and equipment in AMELIA PRESS, INC.'s corporate offices, or any other offices or buildings presently owned or rented by AMELIA PRESS, INC.?

18. Please state the amount of AMELIA PRESS, INC.'s current assets and describe these assets in full detail.

19. Please state the amount of AMELIA PRESS, INC.'s current liabilities and describe these liabilities in full detail.

20. Please state the amount of AMELIA PRESS, INC.'s accounts receivable and describe these accounts receivable in detail.

21. Please state the amount of AMELIA PRESS, INC.'s accounts payable and describe these accounts payable in detail.

22. Were AMELIA PRESS, INC.'s financial records kept on a calendar or fiscal year prior to the change in tax laws?

23. If AMELIA PRESS, INC.'s financial records were kept on a fiscal year, on what date did the fiscal year of AMELIA PRESS, INC. end?

24. Please describe the personal property presently owned by AMELIA PRESS, INC. in detail.
   (a) What is the current market value of said personal property?
   (b) As to each piece of personal property, please describe all liens presently existing in detail. Include in the description the name of the lien holder, the date of the lien, the type of lien, and the amount of lien.

25. What negotiable instruments does AMELIA PRESS, INC., currently own?
   (a) What is the present value of said negotiable instruments?
   (b) Who are the makers of said negotiable instruments?

26. What stocks or bonds does AMELIA PRESS, INC., own?
   (a) What is the current market value of said stocks or bonds?

27. Has AMELIA PRESS, INC., transferred any personal, intangible or real property of any kind whatsoever to any person, corporation or any other entity, either by sale, trade, gift, foreclosure, or any other legal proceeding, subsequent to April 4, 1989?

28. If the answer to the foregoing Interrogatory is in the affirmative, please state:
   (a) Date of said transfer;
   (b) The name and address of the person or entity to which said property was transferred;
   (c) The description of said property;
   (d) The current market value of said property;
   (e) The terms of said transfer;

(f) The location of any documents pertaining to said transfer;

(g) The place of transfer; and

(h) The amount of money or value of property received by AMELIA PRESS, INC., as a result of said transfer.

Submitted this 26th day of November, 1992.

MILKEY, BROWN, SAMS & MILLER

By: _____

James A. Milkey
Attorney for Plaintiff
THE SONO GROUP, INC.

898 Miata Building
Memphis, Tennessee 38103
(901) 931–8277

CERTIFICATE OF SERVICE

This is to certify that I have served a copy of the foregoing PLAINTIFF'S POST-JUDGMENT INTERROGATORIES PROPOUNDED TO DEFENDANT AMELIA PRESS, INC., on its registered agent, John H. Jones, by depositing same in the United States Mail with adequate postage affixed thereto and addressed as follows:

John H. Jones, President
AMELIA PRESS, INC.
35 Briar Road, N.E.
Memphis, Tennessee 38103

This 26th day of November, 1992.

_____

James A. Milkey
Attorney for Plaintiff

5. Real estate (address, legal description, description, ownership, value of equity interest, and details of encumbrances).

6. Income tax returns and available financial statements (last two years).

7. Casualty losses.

8. Contracts.

9. General credit information.

10. Name of certified public accountant and firm.

11. Membership in pension, retirement fund, or profit-sharing plan.

12. Property exempt from forced sale.

13. Assignments.

Ascertaining Assets and Liabilities of Judgment Debtor

Locating the assets and determining the liabilities of the judgment debtor may be accomplished through post-judgment discovery and other informal investigative techniques. From the trial process and perhaps an appeal, much may be known about the judgment debtor already. A plaintiff who is seeking a money judgment should be on the alert from the commencement of the case to gather information about the defendant consistent with efforts toward trial—or settlement. These data not only contain some specific information on the assets and liabilities of the judgment debtor, but they also tell a lot about his or her life-style, and one's life-style is an excellent clue to possible assets and liabilities. Also, remember that the kind and extent of liability one assumes is often an indication of one's assets. That is, someone with a lot of liabilities probably has a lot of assets to cover those liabilities. Someone who rarely gets into debt probably has very little to risk. Of course, it is possible that the judgment debtor is overextended in liabilities and has little or nothing left for the judgment creditor to reach.

The judgment creditor or his successor in interest may obtain discovery from any person, including the judgment debtor. The *Federal Rules of Civil Procedure* or the practice of the state in which the district court is held governs this discovery (see also Chapter 8).

You need to find out about every asset the judgment debtor has, including the following:[6]

1. A description of each asset. Specify size, color, quantity, or any other identifying information.
2. The location of each asset. List the exact addresses and names of people who have possession of each asset, including the judgment debtor.
3. How the judgment debtor obtained an interest in the asset. Was it purchased, and if so, for how much? When was it purchased or acquired? Are there any supporting documents to the purchase?
4. The current, appraised, and/or fair market value of the asset. What would be its value if it were sold on the open market?

While frequently assets are thought of as either personal or real property, tangible or intangible, there are other types of assets, such as:

1. Property solely owned by the judgment debtor versus property in which others also have an interest.
2. Property in the possession of the judgment debtor versus Property in the possession of a third person.
3. Property in the state where the judgment was rendered (forum state) versus property in another state (foreign state).
4. Property the judgment debtor currently has versus property that will be received in the future.
5. Property the judgment debtor currently has versus property that the judgment creditor disposed of since the ligation began or just before it began.

---

[6]Statsky, *Torts: Personal Injury Litigation*, pp. 234–235.

6. Property that is exempt from creditor collection versus property not protected by exemption.

7. The debtor's interest in any estates, trusts, and other expectancies.

An asset may fall into more than one of these categories.

Execution

Execution is a process of executing on the assets of the judgment debtor for the payment of a certain amount of money. A writ of execution is commonly called a *fi. fa.* In some courts, it is automatically issued by the clerk after a mandatory brief period of time such as ten days.

When the *fi. fa.* is obtained from the court and recorded, the sheriff (or marshal in federal court) may take possession of or levy against the judgment debtor's assets, sell these assets, deduct the costs of execution, and return the balance of the proceeds to the judgment creditor. In the event the creditor receives the amount of the judgment plus interest, any balance is paid back to the judgment debtor.

Certain property of the judgment debtor will be exempt from collection. In some instances, the court acquires only limited jurisdiction over the case through the attachment of the judgment debtor's property in the state.

If a judgment is entered against certain public officers, such as a collector or other officer of revenue, or an officer of Congress,[7] the court may give a certificate of probable cause for his or her act as provided by statute. Execution shall not be issued against the officer or his or her property personally, but the final judgment shall be satisfied as provided in such statutes. Generally, public property is protected by governmental immunity, but some jurisdictions have provided special, though often limited, means to satisfy judgments.

Garnishment

In a *garnishment* proceeding, the assets of the judgment debtor that are in the possession of a third party are appropriated in order to satisfy the debt. These assets include only intangible property, such as wages, partnership interests, bank account proceeds, and/or claims against third parties, including any judgments. A writ of garnishment must be obtained so that the sheriff or other public official may inquire into the amount of money being held by the *garnishee* (the third person). The garnishee has a certain number of days to respond to the writ. When the amount is ascertained, an order for garnishment is requested, along with a writ for seizure of the property or a lien on the judgment debtor's property. This prevents the debtor from selling, transferring, or otherwise deposing of his property without satisfying the judgment held against him by the judgment creditor.

However, federal law prevents 75 percent of the employee's "disposable wages" (as defined by federal law) from being garnished. Disposable earnings include wages less withholding taxes, social security, and other regulated deductions. This protection is unavailable or restricted if the judgment is for sup-

---

[7]See Title 2, U.S.C.A., §118.

port or maintenance or "necessaries," as defined by law. Exhibit 15.6 shows a chart for keeping track of outstanding garnishments on one or more judgment debtors.

Supplementary Proceedings

Under the laws of most states, the judgment creditor will be allowed to conduct *supplementary proceedings* for the purpose of discovering the debtor's property and its application of the debt for which the execution is issued. Generally speaking, supplementary proceedings can be conducted (1) informally with the consent of the debtor, (2) by deposition, or (3) by other discovery methods.

Once the assets of the uncooperative judgment debtor are located, two primary processes are used for collection—execution and garnishment.

• Domesticating a Judgment in Another State

Domesticating a judgment is the legal process of bringing the judgment into another state and making it legally acceptable. In other words, it is the legal process of transferring a judgment of one court to a court in another jurisdiction for enforcement. If an action is removed from the state court, it will be prosecuted after removal pursuant to Rule 64 of the *Federal Rules of Civil Procedure*.

The paralegal's role in domesticating a judgment in another state may involve contacting the new state court clerk or correspondent firm for information on forms, filing fees, deadlines, the procedure for recording the judgment, and other processes. You also may inquire whether execution and garnishment is available, and what the exceptions are.

Although the particular procedure varies in each jurisdiction, it is relatively simple. An authenticated, or *exemplified*, copy of the original judgment, sometimes referred to as an *abstract of judgment*, must be filed with the court in the jurisdiction in which you wish to execute the judgment. Under the "full faith and credit" clause of the U.S. Constitution, Article IV, Section 1, states are required to give a foreign judgment such faith and credit as it had by law or usage of state of its origin.[8]

The judgment debtor has generally two defenses: (1) the original court lacked jurisdiction; or (2) the judgment has been paid in full. However, the judgment is presumed to be valid and, if the judgment debtor contests the judgment on either of these two defenses, she has the burden of proof to establish that the judgment was invalid. A state is not required by the Constitution to accept judgments patently in violation of the new state's public policy. For example, judgments on so-called *cognovit* notes may be refused on the grounds that public policy of the new state requires that a debtor may have a "day in court" and therefore may not validly "confess" judgment in advance, even though the old state may recognize such procedures as valid.

However, the judgment debtor cannot *collaterally* "attack," that is, attempt to retry any of the issues that were or should have been litigated in the initial action. She may not challenge the sufficiency of the evidence or attempt to show that errors were made in the initial action that caused her to lose.

---

[8]*First National Bank v. Terry*, 103 Cal. App. 501, 285 P. 336, 337.

Exhibit 15.6

Outstanding Garnishment Chart

Client Name & Matter: _____ File No.: _____ Responsible Attorney(s): _____ Date: _____

Name of Debtor/Defendant _____

Garnishment Served	Court of Garnishment	Garnishment No.	Creditor/Plaintiff	Garnishee	Amount Total Judgment*	Court of Judgment	Judgment No.	Answer Filed

Paralegal: _____

*Includes garnishment costs. With each succeeding garnishment by the same creditor, costs are added to total amount of judgment.

In establishing a defense of lack of jurisdiction in the initial action, the judgment debtor may attack the court's jurisdiction over either (1) the person of the defendant, (2) the subject matter of the litigation, (3) the remedy afforded, or (4) geographical limitations. Again, the judgment debtor has the burden to show lack of jurisdiction in the initial action.

Because the court is reluctant to allow the prevailing party to enforce the judgment before the defendant exhausts or waives his post-trial remedies, the judgment will usually grant a 30-day stay against entry of judgment or a 10-day stay of execution on the judgment. Of course, if an appeal is filed and the appellant posts a sufficient bond or undertaking, the court will grant a stay of execution on the judgment.

• Appointment of Receivers

The *appointment of a receiver* provides for a custodian or manager of disputed property *pendente lite*, or while the suit is pending. A primary reason for this remedy is defendant's actual or potential insolvency. Another appropriate use of the remedy is to preserve property pending litigation when there is the threat of fraud, or a substantial danger that the property will be removed from the state, lost, materially injured, or destroyed.[9]

An action wherein a receiver has been appointed will not be dismissed except by order of the court. Under Federal Rule 66, the practice in the administration of estates by receivers or by other similar officers appointed by the court must be in accordance with the practice followed in the U.S. courts as provided in the rules of the district courts. In all other respects the action in which the appointment of a receiver is sought or which is brought by or against a receiver is governed by Federal Rule 66. The rights, duties, and liabilities of a receiver are discussed in Section 959(b) of Title 28 of the *United States Code*.

• Summary

To be helpful to your attorney in motion practice, you will have to be assertive in asking for certain responsibilities. Attorneys are used to handling this phase of litigation all by themselves. You therefore need to educate your attorney on what you can do and then do it right to build her confidence in you. Working with post-trial motions and post-judgment discovery is much like the work you are probably already doing in discovery. Motions must be researched, and they must be accurate. Be sure to clarify any confusion you have with your attorney. You will probably work more closely with your attorney in this important phase of litigation than in many others.

---

[9]John J. Cound, Jack H. Friedenthal, and Arthur R. Miller, *Civil Procedure*, 2d ed. (St. Paul, MN: West Publishing Co., 1974), p. 977.

How to Provide Support in Appellate Practice

• Introduction

Because of the cost involved, few cases are appealed. If you are called upon to assist with an appeal, you will find the procedures in filing an appeal, governed by the *Federal Rules of Appellate Procedure*, to be very definitive. One of your primary values in assisting in this area is your organizational abilities. This chapter will help you become familiar with some basic principles and terminology and give you a step-by-step procedure for perfecting an appeal in federal court.[1]

• Appellate Procedure

A person who feels that he has been wronged by the decisions of the trial judge may appeal the judgment. Even the prevailing party may file an appeal if he is unhappy with the damages he was awarded. Also, if a cause of action was stricken by the trial judge or dismissed before the case was tried, a party may decide to appeal.

The appellate court will review only legal questions, not questions of fact decided by the trial court judge or jury. In some issues, such as whether the verdict goes against the weight of the evidence, the appellate judgment must review the evidence, but the question remains a question of law—was the verdict so erroneous that, as a matter of law, it must be reversed.[2]

The person initiating the appeal, that is, the aggrieved party is called the *appellant*. The person defending against the appeal is the *appellee* or *respondent*. The procedure for appeal is similar to motion procedures but far more complicated. After giving notice of his intention to appeal, the appellant files an opening brief, the respondent files a brief opposing the appeal, and the appellant closes with a reply brief. The appellant presents argument that the trial court either erred in applying the law or engaged in some misconduct.[3]

---

[1]Contributions to this chapter were made by Francis M. Bird, Jr., attorney at law, Atlanta, Georgia.

[2]James W. H. McCord, *The Litigation Paralegal* (St. Paul, MN: West Publishing Company, 1988), pp. 470–471.

[3]Susan Burnett Luten, *California Civil Litigation* (St. Paul, MN: West Publishing Company, 1989), p. 350.

• Findings of Facts and Conclusions of Law

In some states, judges must make detailed *findings of fact* and *conclusions of law* in non-jury cases. In other states, exceptions require that findings of facts and conclusions of law also be filed in non-jury cases as a prerequisite to the appellate procedure. The exceptions are then argued to the trial judge, and two other judges, who will decide the issues raised for appeal after briefing by the counsel for the parties.

However, the federal courts do not require the filing of exceptions to findings of fact and conclusions of law. For this, the party in a non-jury case in the federal courts would appeal directly to the appropriate federal court of appeals.

• Perfecting the Appeal

There are seven steps to "perfect" or take an appeal in a civil case within the period of time specified by the *Federal Rules of Appellate Procedure* (FRAP). According to Rule 31(c), if the appellant fails to follow these procedures in a timely manner, the appellee may file a motion in the court of appeals to dismiss the appeal.

• Step 1:   File notice of appeal.

The *notice of appeal* must be filed in the district court that heard the case within 30 days from the date of the entry of the judgment or the order being appealed. If the United States, or an officer of an agency of the United States is a party, the notice of appeal may be filed by any party within 60 days of such entry.[4]

Appellee has seven days after service of petition to file opposition for leave to appeal. (In the event the appeal is taken from an administrative agency, a *petition for review* is filed instead of a notice of appeal.)

• Step 2:   File appeal bond for costs.

In order to stay a judgment or order, the moving party must file a *supersedeas* bond or other appropriate security in the district court.

A *supersedeas* bond is an undertaking or promise, with a surety, made in a court proceeding for the purpose of obtaining a suspension of the judgment of a court and a delay in its execution, pending the outcome of an appeal. The bond provides that the appellant and surety, usually an insurance company or other person, agree to pay to the appellee any damages sustained by reason of the delay if the appellant is not successful. The court sets the amount of the bond based on the monetary value of the risk to the appellee should the appellant be unsuccessful in his appeal.[5]

If no *supersedeas* bond is filed, unless the appellant is exempted by law, he is required to file a bond for costs or equivalent security in the district court with the notice of appeal. However, security is not required of an appellant who is not

---

[4]*Federal Rules of Appellate Procedure*, Rules 3 and 4.
[5]Ibid., Rule 8(b).

subject to costs. The bond or equivalent security must be in the sum of $250 unless the district court fixes a different amount.[6]

Both parties may enter into a stipulation waiving the appeal bonds. A *waiver* is beneficial to the respondent because if he loses the appeal, usually the cost of the bond is borne by him.

• Step 3:   Order the transcript.

Within 10 days after the filing of the notice of appeal, the appellant must order the transcript of those parts of the proceedings in the district court not already on file with the appellate court that the appellant wants to include in the record. The appellant must pay the costs of the transcript.

The appellant must file and serve on the appellee a description of the parts of the transcript that she intends to include in the record and a statement of the issues she intends to present in the appeal within 10 days after filing the notice of appeal.[7]

• Step 4:   Transmit the record.

The record on appeal consists of all original papers. These may include pleadings, exhibits filed in the district court, the transcript or partial transcript of the proceedings, if any, and a certified copy of the docket entries prepared by the clerk of the district court in which the case was heard.

Within 40 days after the filing of the notice of appeal, the record on appeal must be transmitted by the clerk of the district court to the court of appeals. It is the duty of the appellant to make sure that all relevant papers have actually been included in the court's record prior to its transmission by the clerk of the applicable district court.[8]

• Step 5:   Docket the appeal.

Within 40 days after the filing of the notice of appeal, the appellant must pay the docket fee to the clerk of the court of appeals, and the clerk will enter the appeal on the docket of the court.[9]

After the appeal has been docketed, the clerk will file the record. Notice will be given to all parties by the clerk of the date of the filing of the record on appeal.

• Step 6:   Prepare briefs and oral argument.

The appellant's brief must be filed and served within 40 days after the date on which the record is filed. If the brief is not filed on time, the appellee may move for dismissal of the appeal. File 25 copies of all briefs.[10] The appellee's brief must be filed and served within 30 days.[11] An extension of 40 days may be filed in

---

[6]Ibid., Rule 7.

[7]Ibid., Rule 10(b).

[8]Ibid., Rule 11(a)(b).

[9]Ibid., Rule 12(a).

[10]Ibid., Rule 31.

[11]Ibid., Rule 31(a).

Exhibit 16.1

Checklist for Filing Appeals in Federal Court

○ File notice of appeal within 30 days of judgment or order, or within 60 days if the United States or an officer or agency thereof is a party.[a]

○ File bond with notice of appeal.

○ Transmit record within 40 days after filing notice of appeal.

○ Docket the appeal within 40 days after filing notice of appeal.

○ Pay docket fee at the time of docketing the appeal.

○ All papers except briefs and appendices may be filed by mail but they must be *received* by the clerk within the time fixed for filing.

○ Briefs and appendixes are deemed filed on the day of mailing by the most expeditious form of delivery by mail, excluding special delivery.

○ In motions requesting relief that may be granted by a single judge, the judge may allow the motion to be filed with him or her, dated the same day, and transmitted to the clerk.

[a]*Federal Rules of Appellate Procedure*, Rule 41 (a) (1).

district court. File and serve the appellant's reply brief within 14 days after service of the appellee's brief.[12]

The merits of the case will be argued orally, but the brief will be the permanent record of each party's position on appeal. After the oral argument, the court will decide the case, either in a written opinion, or merely *per curiam* (a decision without an opinion).

• Step 7:   Initiate post-appellate decision procedures if necessary.

After the appellate court has made its decision, the losing party may petition for a rehearing. It is unusual for an appellate court to grant such a rehearing, however. Where the decision has been made by an intermediate appellate court, there may be a right of appeal to the highest court, or the highest court may have discretion as to whether or not it will permit the appeal.[13]

When you are assisting your attorney in filing civil appeals, it is imperative that you follow the procedural rules meticulously. Whether the appeal is filed in the state court or the federal court, make certain that you clearly understand the procedural rules. Since they vary in the state appellate courts, it is difficult to discuss them here in general, but many are patterned after the *Federal Rules of Civil Procedure*. Therefore, understanding the federal procedures will enable you to understand and apply the procedural rules of the applicable state court. The discussion in this section is based upon the *Federal Rules of Appellate Procedure* as well as the *Federal Rules of Civil Procedure*. Use the checklist in Exhibit 16–1 as a guide to avoid errors in filing an appeal in the federal court of appeals.

[12]Ibid., Rule 31(a).

[13]Mark I. Weinstein, *Introduction to Civil Litigation*, 2d ed. (St. Paul, MN: West Publishing Company, 1986), p. 271.

Service of Required Papers

All papers filed by a party, except for those required to be filed by the clerk, must be served by that party upon all parties to the appeal or their respective counsel. This service may be personal or by mail. *Personal service* may be accomplished by serving a copy to a clerk or other responsible person at the office of the counsel. *Service by mail* is complete on the date of mailing, excluding special delivery. Proof of service or an acknowledgment of service by the person served must accompany all papers presented for filing (see Chapter 2).

Computation of Time

Time is computed as follows:[14] Do not include the day of the act, event, or default from which the designated period of time begins to run, but do include the last day of the period unless it is a Saturday, Sunday, or legal holiday. If the last day is a Saturday, Sunday, or legal holiday, extend the period of time until the end of the next day that is not a Saturday, Sunday, or legal holiday. If the period of time is less than seven days, exclude intermediate Saturdays, Sundays, and legal holidays.

Extension of Time

Unless it is specifically authorized by law, an extension of time must be requested by a motion for extension of time, except for the filing of:[15]

- Notice of appeal.
- Petition for allowance.
- Petition for permission to appeal.
- Petition to enjoin.
- Petition to set aside.
- Petition to modify or otherwise review.
- Notice of appeal from an order of an administrative agency, board, commission, or officer of the United States.

Additional Time After Service by Mail

An additional three days are added to the prescribed period of time after service of a paper by mail upon a party when the party is required or permitted to do a particular act within a prescribed period.[16]

Procedure of Motions

An application for an order or other relief must be made by filing a motion with proof of service on all other parties, unless otherwise stated in the rules. All required papers, briefs, and/or affidavits must be served and filed with the

---

[14]*Federal Rules of Civil Procedure,* Rule 26(a). See also Chapter 2.

[15]Ibid., Rule 26(b).

[16]Ibid., Rule 26(c).

Exhibit 16.2

●

**Summary of Contents of
Appellate Briefs**

Description	Appellant	Appellee

1. Table of contents
  a. Table of cases (in alphabetical order)
  b. Table of statutes and authorities
	Yes	Yes

2. Statement of the issues	Yes	If appellee disagrees with appellant's statement

3. Statement of the case
  a. Nature of the case
  b. Course of proceedings
  c. Disposition in the court below
  d. Statement of the relevant facts
	Yes	If appellee disagrees with appellant's statement

4. Argument
  a. May be preceded by a summary
  b. Must contain the contents of appellant or appellee with respect to the issues
  c. Must contain the reasons for such contentions
  d. Must contain citations to the authorities, statutes, and parts of the record relied on
	Yes	Yes

5. Conclusion a. Stating precise relief sought	Yes	No

ᵃPage references to record in appendix must be indicated (Rule 30(a))

motion. Response in opposition to a civil motion other than one for a procedural order must be filed within seven days after service of the motion.

A summary of the contents of Appellate Briefs is shown in Exhibit 16.2. The sample appellate excerpt in Exhibit 16–3 illustrates the format for an appellate brief in the U.S. Court of Appeals.

• Appendix to the Brief and Other Papers

Specific rules in the *Federal Rules of Appellate Procedure* govern the preparation of the appendix to the briefs and other papers. It is the appellant's duty to prepare and file the appendix, which must contain the following:

1. The relevant docket entries in the proceedings.
2. Any relevant portions of the pleadings, charge, findings, or opinion.
3. The judgment, order, or decision in question.
4. Any other parts of the record to which the parties wish to direct the particular attention of the court.

Ten copies of the appendix must be filed with the clerk, and one copy must be served on counsel for each party separately represented, unless the court rules otherwise.

The parties are encouraged to agree as to the contents of the appendix. If the parties do not reach an agreement within ten days after the date of the filing of the record, the appellant must serve on the appellee a notice designating the part of the record that he intends to include in the appendix and a statement of the issues that he intends to present for review.

The appellee may, within ten days after receipt of the designation by the appellant, serve upon the appellant a designation of those parts to which he wished to direct the particular attention of the court not designated by the appellant.

In absence of an agreement to the contrary, the cost of producing the appendix must be initially paid by the appellant. If the appellant considers the parts of the record designated by the appellee for inclusion as unnecessary for the determination of the issues presented, the appellee must pay the cost of including those parts.

The court may by rule dispense with the requirement of an appendix and permit the appeals to be heard on the original record; however, the court may require that copies of the record, or relevant parts, be submitted.

Arrangement of Appendix

The appendix should be organized as follows:

1. List the parts of the record in the order in which the parts are set out, with references to the appropriate pages of the appendix.
2. Set out docket entries in the order of the list of contents.
3. Set out other parts in chronological order following the docket entries.
4. Indicate in brackets the page number of the reporter's transcript of the proceedings immediately before the particular item set out.
5. Indicate omissions in the text of papers or of the transcript by asterisks.
6. Omit immaterial matters such as captions, subscriptions, acknowledgments, etc.
7. Put the question and its answer in a single paragraph.

Exhibits in Appendix

Exhibits may be contained in a separate volume, or volumes, but they must be indexed. Four copies must be filed with the appendix, and one copy must be served on counsel for each party. The transcript of an administrative proceeding may be used as an exhibit.

Front Cover of Brief and Appendix

The front cover of the briefs and of appendixes, if separately printed, shall contain:

1. The name of the court and the number of the case.
2. The title of the case.
3. The nature of the proceeding in the court, for example, appeal, petition for review.
4. The title of the document, for example, brief for appellant, appendix.
5. The names and addresses of counsel representing the party on whose behalf the document is filed.

Petitions for Rehearing, Motions, and Other Papers

Petitions for rehearing must be produced in the same manner as briefs and appendixes. Motions and other papers may be produced in the same manner, or

Exhibit 16.3

**Sample Appellate
Brief Format**

(Cover Sheet)

IN THE UNITED STATES COURT OF APPEALS
FOR THE ELEVENTH CIRCUIT

CASE NO. 90-8625

MARY ANN NEUMANN,
Plaintiff-Appellee,

v.

UNITED STATES OF AMERICA,
Defendant-Appellant.

ON APPEAL FROM THE UNITED STATES DISTRICT COURT
FOR THE SOUTHERN DISTRICT OF GEORGIA

BRIEF OF PLAINTIFF-APPELLEE

CHARLES R. ASHMAN	DON C. KEENAN
JEFFREY W. LASKY	DAVID S. BILLS
THE KEENAN ASHMAN FIRM	THE KEENAN ASHMAN FIRM
120 W. Liberty Street	148 Nassau Street, N.W.
Savannah, Georgia 31412	Atlanta, Georgia 30303
(912) 232-6423	(404) 523-2200

ATTORNEYS FOR PLAINTIFF-APPELLEE

NO PREFERENCE

(Certificate Page)

CERTIFICATE OF INTERESTED PERSONS

The undersigned hereby certifies that, to the best of his information and belief, the following is a complete list of interested persons, pursuant to 11th Cir. R. 28-2(b):

The Honorable Anthony A. Alaimo
United States District Judge
Southern District of Georgia
Brunswick, Georgia

Defendant-Appellant

United States of America
United States Department of Army
Major Joseph K. Lawrence, M.D.
United States Attorney's Office,
    Southern District of Georgia, Savannah, Georgia
United States Department of Justice, Washington, D.C.
Hinton R. Pierce, Esq.
Lawrence B. Lee, Esq.
Melissa S. Mundell, Esq.

Plaintiff-Appellee

Mary Ann Neumann
Captain James A. Neumann, M.V.D.
The Keenan Ashman Firm, P.C., Atlanta and Savannah, Georgia
Don C. Keenan, Esq.
Charles R. Ashman, Esq.
Jeffrey W. Lasky, Esq.
David S. Bills, Esq.

Respectfully submitted,

THE KEENAN ASHMAN FIRM

_____

DON C. KEENAN
Attorney for Plaintiff-Appellee

Exhibit 16.3

Continued

148 Nassau Street, N.W.
Atlanta, Georgia 30303
(404) 523-2200

STATEMENT REGARDING ORAL ARGUMENT

Plaintiff-Appellee submits that oral argument would be of material benefit to the Court in understanding the issues presented on this appeal.
(End of Page)

(Table of Contents Page)
TABLE OF CONTENTS

I. The Trial Court correctly applied Georgia law in concluding that genuine issues of fact existed as to the alleged medical negligence of Defendant's agents and employees; and the Court's findings of negligence were fully supported by substantial evidence.

II. The Trial Court correctly applied Georgia law in concluding that a genuine issue of fact existed as to the foreseeability of Plaintiff's vestibular injury; and the Court's finding that Plaintiff's injury was foreseeable was fully supported by substantial evidence.

III. The Trial Court's findings with regard to Plaintiff's economic and non-economic damages were fully supported by substantial evidence.

(Authorities Page)
TABLE OF AUTHORITIES

Exhibit 16.3

Continued

STATEMENT OF JURISDICTION

The jurisdiction of this Court is provided at 28 U.S.C. § 1291.

STATEMENT OF ISSUES PRESENTED FOR REVIEW

I. Whether or not the Trial Court correctly applied Georgia law in concluding that genuine issues of fact existed as to the alleged medical negligence of Defendant's agents and employees; and whether or not the Court's findings of negligence were clearly erroneous based upon the evidence.

II. Whether or not the Trial Court correctly applied Georgia law in concluding that a genuine issue of fact existed as to the foreseeability of Plaintiff's vestibular injury; and whether or not the Court's finding that Plaintiff's injury was foreseeable was clearly erroneous based upon the evidence.

III. Whether or not the Trial Court's findings with regard to Plaintiff's economic and non-economic damages were clearly erroneous based upon the evidence.

STATEMENT OF THE CASE[8]
A. COURSE OF PROCEEDING AND DISPOSITION BELOW:

Plaintiff Mary Ann Neumann, the wife of James A. Neumann, D.V.M., a Captain in the United States Army, brought this action for medical malpractice in the United States District Court for the Southern District of Georgia, pursuant to the Federal Tort Claims Act, 28 U.S.C. §§ 1346(b), 2671, *et seq.* The Complaint, filed on 10 May 1989, alleged that Plaintiff sustained injury in October 1987 due to the negligent administration of the antibiotic Gentamicin, while hospitalized for treatment for a post partum (i.e., after child birth) pelvic infection at Winn Army Community Hospital, Fort Stewart, Georgia. Plaintiff alleged that due to the negligent administration of Gentamicin, she sustained an ototoxic vestibular injury, being permanent disabling damage to her equilibrium and balance. (R1–1).

On 7 July 1989, Defendant United States of America filed its Answer, denying liability and asserting various defenses. (R1–9).

---

[8]According to the Federal Rules of Civil Procedure 28 (g) - In the statement of the case, as in all other sections of the brief, every assertion regarding matter in the record shall be supported by a reference to the volume document number and page number of the original record where the matter relied upon is to be found.

Exhibit 16.3

Continued

The trial was presented to the District Court on Thursday, 1 February 1990 through Saturday, 3 February 1990. An advisory jury, empaneled by the Court pursuant to Fed. R. Civ. P. 39(c), returned a verdict in favor of Defendant. (R1–47; R6–149–150).[9] Thereafter, the parties each submitted Proposed Findings of Fact and Conclusions of Law. (R1–49, 51). On 3 May 1990, the Court entered its Findings of Fact and Conclusions of Law. (R1–52).

On 4 May 1990, Judgment was entered in favor of Plaintiff, awarding compensatory damages in the total amount of $1,674,495.00. (R1–53).

Defendant filed its Notice of Appeal on 29 June 1990. (R1–58).

B. *STATEMENT OF FACTS:*[10] (Not all facts are included in this example.)

Facts stipulated by the parties included the following:

1) Plaintiff Mary Ann Neumann was thirty-two (32) years of age at the time of her injury and had a life expectancy of 47.77 years;

2) At all relevant times, Ms. Neumann was the wife of James A. Neumann, M.V.D., a Captain in the United States Army;

3) At all relevant times, Joseph K. Lawrence, M.D., was a licensed physician and a Major in the United States Army;

4) At all relevant times, Dr. Lawrence was a staff physician in the Obstetrics-Gynecology Department of Winn Army Community Hospital, which is operated by Defendant United States of America, by and through the Department of the Army, at Fort Stewart, Georgia.

5) At all relevant times, Dr. Lawrence was the primary treating physician of Ms. Neumann.

6) At all relevant times, all nurses participating in the care and treatment of Ms. Neumann at Winn Army Community Hospital were employees of the United States of America.

7) On 6 October 1987, Ms. Neumann presented at the emergency room at Winn Army Community Hospital with complaints of a sudden onset of chills, fevers, and lower abdominal pain;

8) At the time of her presentation at the emergency room, being approximately 5:00 p.m., Ms. Neumann's temperature was measured and found to be 103.4 degrees fahrenheit; and prior to being transferred out of the emergency room, her temperature was again measured and was found to be 101.7 degrees fahrenheit;

9) At the time of her admission to the hospital, Dr. Lawrence reached a tentative diagnosis of Ms. Neumann's condition as post partum endometritis;

C. *STATEMENT OF STANDARD OF REVIEW*[11]

The standard of review applicable to this action is set forth at Fed. R. Civ. P. 52(a), which provides in relevant part as follows: "Findings of fact whether based on oral or documentary evidence shall not be set aside unless clearly erroneous, and due regard shall be given to the opportunity of the Trial Court to judge the credibility of witnesses."

The law of the State of Georgia governs as to questions of substantive law, if any, raised in this appeal.

SUMMARY OF THE ARGUMENT[12]

Under the well-established standard of review, this Court must properly decline to engage in a *de novo* assessment of the evidence. Further, under the well-established

---

[9]Although not reflected in the record on appeal, counsel for Plaintiff-Appellee hereby certify that Defendant-Appellant twice declined the Trial Court's invitation to consent to be bound by the verdict of the advisory jury.

[10]A proper statement of facts reflects a high standard of professionalism. It must state the facts accurately, those favorable and those unfavorable to the party. Inferences drawn from the facts must be identified as such.

[11]A statement of the standard or core of review for each contention. For example, where the appeal is from an exercise of district court discretion, there shall be a statement that standard of review is whether the district court abused its discretion.

[12]The opening briefs of the parties shall also contain a summary of argument, suitably paragraphed, which should be clear, accurate and succinct.

Exhibit 16.3

Continued

standard of review, this Court must properly review all of the evidence and give due regard to the opportunity of the Trial Court to judge the credibility of witnesses, in determining whether the Trial Court's findings of fact were clearly erroneous. Fed. R. Civ. P. 52(a).

The various legal and factual issues presented on this appeal by Defendant-Appellee are each without merit and provide no proper ground for reversing the Judgment entered in favor of Plaintiff-Appellee.

ARGUMENT AND CITATIONS OF AUTHORITY[13]

Fed. R. Civ. P. 52(a) provides in relevant part as follows: "Findings of fact, whether based on oral or documentary evidence, shall not be set aside unless clearly erroneous, and due regard shall be given to the opportunity of the trial court to judge the credibility of the witnesses."

It is well-established that the Trial Court's findings of fact may not properly be set aside as clearly erroneous except when, after reviewing all of the evidence, this Court is "left with the definite and firm conviction that a mistake has been committed." *United States v. Gypsum Co.*, 333 U.S. 364, 395, 68 S.Ct. 525, 542, 92 L.Ed. 746 (1948); *Anderson v. City of Bessemer City, N.C.*, 470 U.S. 564, 573, 105 S.Ct. 1504, 84 L.Ed 2d 518 (1985). This Court may not properly substitute its interpretation of the evidence for that of the Trial Court.

Notwithstanding these well-established principles of review, Defendant has taken this appeal for the evident purpose of attempting to relitigate the trial of this action, urging this Court to engage in a *de novo* assessment of the evidence, reweighing and reinterpreting the evidence, reassessing the credibility of the witnesses, and substituting its judgment for that of the Trial Court.

As is shown by the extensive Statement of Facts set forth in this Brief, *supra*, Plaintiff presented a substantial amount of evidence as to each and every issue in this action. The Trial Court, as the trier of fact, had the opportunity to fully assess the credibility of all the witnesses, to determine which witnesses' testimony should be given credit, and to resolve where the preponderance of the evidence may lie. As such determinations are inherently within the province of the finder of fact, it is submitted that this Court must properly decline to substitute its judgment for that of the Trial Court.

I. THE TRIAL COURT CORRECTLY APPLIED GEORGIA LAW IN CONCLUDING THAT GENUINE ISSUES OF FACT EXISTED AS TO THE ALLEGED MEDICAL NEGLIGENCE OF DEFENDANT'S AGENTS AND EMPLOYEES; AND THE COURT'S FINDINGS OF NEGLIGENCE WERE FULLY SUPPORTED BY SUBSTANTIAL EVIDENCE.

As to the standard of care issues, Defendant first argues that where there is evidence that a physician's care is in accord with one accepted school of medical thought, then, as a matter of law, any contrary evidence may constitute only a mere difference in view between physicians; and that such a mere difference of view regarding the standard of care is insufficient, as a matter of law, to raise genuine issues of fact. Thus, Defendant asserts that the Trial Court erred in construing and applying Georgia law as to the standard of care.

Defendant's said argument is wholly without merit. Under well-established Georgia law, where a plaintiff in an action for medical malpractice presents expert opinion testimony that the defendant physician has breached the standard of care, then the issues are to be determined by the finder of fact. As has been shown, Defendant's denials of liability were directly and repeatedly controverted by the competent testimony of Plaintiff's expert witnesses. Therefore, the Trial Court correctly recognized the standard of care issues to constitute factual issues. *Shea v. Phillips*, 213 Ga. 269, 271, 98 S. E.2d 552 (1957); *Killingsworth v. Poon*, 167 Ga. App. 653, 307 S.E.2d 123 (1983); *Crumbley v. Wyant*, 188 Ga. App. 227, 372 S.E.2d 497 (1988).

---

[13]Citations of authority in the brief shall comply with the rules of citation in the latest edition of the *Maroon Book* or *A Uniform System of Citation*. State case references should also cite national reporter cross references. (*Maroon Book* is published by the Lawyers Co-operative Publishing Co. and Mead Data Central, Inc. *A Uniform System of Citation*, published since 1926 by a consortium of law reviews led by Harvard and Columbia law schools.)

Exhibit 16.3

Continued

Defendant next engages in transparent efforts, grossly distorting and mischaracterizing the record, to establish that the Trial Court's findings of medical negligence were not supported by substantial evidence. In essence, Defendant's arguments are merely that Plaintiff's expert witnesses were not credible, but that Defendant's expert witnesses were credible and absolutely established all matters to which they testified.

In this regard, Defendant repeatedly suggests that the Trial Court was required to fully accept all testimony offered by its expert witnesses, since specific findings discrediting those witnesses were not entered. Not surprisingly, Defendant cites no authority for this proposition.

II. THE TRIAL COURT CORRECTLY APPLIED GEORGIA LAW IN CONCLUDING THAT A GENUINE ISSUE OF FACT EXISTED AS TO THE FORESEEABILITY OF PLAINTIFF'S VESTIBULAR INJURY; AND THE COURT'S FINDING THAT PLAINTIFF'S INJURY WAS FORESEEABLE WAS FULLY SUPPORTED BY SUBSTANTIAL EVIDENCE.

Under Georgia law, foreseeability is virtually without exception held to constitute a factual issue. The Courts have repeatedly noted:

> [I]n Order for a party to be held liable for negligence, it is not necessary that he should have been able to anticipate the particular consequences which ensued. It is sufficient if, in ordinary prudence, he might have foreseen that some injury would result from his act or omission, and that consequences of a generally injurious nature might result.

Swofford v. Cooper, 184 Ga. App. 50, 54, 360 S.E.2d 624 (1987). *See also Williams v. United States*, 352 F.2d 477, 481 (5th Cir. 1965); *Harden v. United States*, 485 F.Supp. 380 (S.D. Ga. 1980) (under Georgia law, foreseeability is talismanic for purposes of determining whether there has been a breach of duty of care). Foreseeability is held to constitute an issue of law only where the evidence is plain, palpable and indisputable. *Levangie v. Dunn*, 182 Ga. App. 439, 656 S.E.2d 88 (1987).

The Trial Court's finding that Plaintiff's vestibular injury was foreseeable is not clearly erroneous and must, therefore, be properly affirmed by this Court.

III. THE TRIAL COURT'S FINDINGS WITH REGARD TO PLAINTIFF'S' ECONOMIC AND NON-ECONOMIC DAMAGES WERE FULLY SUPPORTED BY SUBSTANTIAL EVIDENCE.

As with all questions of fact, the amount of damages found by the Trial Court as having been sustained by Plaintiff is not to be set aside unless clearly erroneous. Fed. R. Civ. P. 52(a); *Neal v. United States*, 562 F.2d 338 (5th Cir. 1977); *Ferrero v. United States*, 603 F.2d 510, 512 (5th Cir. 1979); *Davis v. Marsh*, 807 F.2d 908, 913 (11th Cir. 1987); *Cole v. United States*, 681 F.2d 1261, 1263 (11th Cir. 1988).

As to the award of economic damages, Defendant asserts that the annual income figure of $42,000, utilized by the Trial Court for computation of future lost earnings, was unsupported; and that the Trial Court erred in reducing Plaintiff's work life expectancy by only fifty percent. These assertions are, however, clearly without merit.

Plaintiff submits that the Court's findings with regard to damages, when properly viewed in light of all of the evidence presented at trial, are supported by substantial evidence, are in no way "exorbitant and flagrantly outrageous", are indeed exceptionally conservative, and must, therefore, be properly affirmed by this Court.

CONCLUSION

Based upon the foregoing, Plaintiff-Appellee respectfully submits that the Judgment of the District Court must properly be affirmed in all respects.

This _____day of October 1990.

Exhibit 16.3

Continued

Respectfully submitted,
THE KEENAN ASHMAN FIRM

_____

DON C. KEENAN

_____

DAVID S. BILLS

THE KEENAN BUILDING
148 Nassau Street, N.W.
Atlanta, Georgia 30303
(404) 523–2200

_____

CHARLES R. ASHMAN

_____

JEFFREY W. LASKY
Attorneys for Plaintiff-Appellee

THE ASHMAN BUILDING
120 W. Liberty Street
Savannah, Georgia 31412
(912) 232–6423

CERTIFICATE OF SERVICE

This is to certify that I have this day served the following individuals with a copy of the foregoing Brief of Plaintiff-Appellee, by mailing a copy through the United States Mail with adequate postage attached thereto:

Lawrence B. Lee, Esq.
United States Attorney's Office
P.O. Box 8999
Savannah, Georgia 31412

This _____ day of October 1990.

THE KEENAN ASHMAN FIRM

_____

DAVID S. BILLS
Attorney for Plaintiff-Appellee

THE KEENAN BUILDING
148 Nassau Street, N.W.
Atlanta, Georgia 30303
(404) 523-2200

Exhibit 16.3

Continued

APPENDIX
TABLE OF CONTENTS

Transcript Page No.		Page No.
T-1	Complaint	1
T-5	Answer	6
T-8	Plaintiff's First Continuing First Interrogatories to Defendant	8
T-12	Defendant's Answers to Plaintiff's First Continuing Interrogatories	18
T-18	Defendant's First Continuing Interrogatories to Plaintiff	22
T-22	Plaintiff's Answers to Defendant's First Continuing Interrogatories	31
T-28	Plaintiff's Motion for Summary Judgment	42
T-30	Judgment	44

they may be typewritten upon opaque, unglazed paper 8½ × 11 inches, with double spacing. Consecutive sheets must be attached at the left margin. Legible copies may be used for filing and service. Motions or other papers must use a caption that sets forth (1) the name of the court; (2) the title of the case; (3) the file number; and (4) a brief descriptive title indicating the purpose of the paper.

• Summary

Since most of the drafting done during the appeal stage is done solely by the attorney, she will need you primarily to double-check the accuracy of her citations and the organization of her brief. You may be asked to do some limited research. Another area in which you can be of tremendous assistance will be in helping your attorney follow the finite procedures of the appellate court, including ensuring that the proper format is followed in the brief and that the proper number of copies are made. You may be asked to research certain procedures and make inquiries for information. You also may assist by gathering and organizing the exhibits to the brief.

List of Appendixes

A. Paralegal Skills Inventory Test
B. Sample Paralegal Evaluation
C. Affirmation of Responsibility of the National Federation of Paralegal Associations, Inc. (NFPA)
D. Member Associations of the National Federation of Paralegal Associations, Inc. (NFPA)
E. Code of Ethics and Professional Responsibility of the National Association of Legal Assistants, Inc. (NALA)
F. National Association of Legal Assistants, Inc. Affiliated Associations
G. Databases Used by Law Firms
H. Litigation Support Software Evaluation Form
I. Relational Databases
J. Federal Agencies
K. State Agencies
L. Local Agencies
M. Useful Abbreviations of Legal Terms and Law Office Terminology
N. Trite Words and Phrases to Avoid

Note: The directory of paralegal schools contains more than 700 schools and is too voluminous to include as an appendix. For a complete up-to-date list of paralegal schools, please contact the National Federation of Paralegal Associations, Inc., 5700 Old Orchard Road, First Floor, Skokie, Illinois 60077-1057 (816) 941-4000.

Paralegal Skills Inventory Test

DATE: _____

NAME: _____ EDUCATION: _____

FIRM: _____ LOCATION: _____

DEPT: _____ YEARS EXP: _____

PHONE: (Office) _____ (Home) _____

INSTRUCTIONS:

Please complete the following questionnaire relating to your current specific tasks and duties. If you have experience in more than one practice area, please complete the portion of the questionnaire relating to that area also.

If you have not had experience in a particular area but have had enough exposure to the specific task through your educational training, please check "O"

KEY

F = Frequently   O = Occasionally   N = Never

I. GENERAL or special skills used in your present or prior jobs (Please check):

☐ Client contact (telephone, correspondence, personal)
☐ Draft documents
☐ Computer/word processing
☐ Spreadsheet (Lotus/Multiplan, etc.)
☐ Financial computations
☐ Research: Statutory
☐ Foreign language translation
☐ Supervise nonattorney staff
☐ Train nonattorney staff
☐ Maintain library
☐ Handle billing for attorneys/firm
☐ Notarizing
☐ Tickler control

☐ Bookkeeping
☐ Filing
☐ Office administration
☐ Personnel hiring
☐ Attorney recruitment
☐ Other (Please specify:) _____

II. LITIGATION

On which specific types of litigation matters have you worked?

☐ General Civil
☐ Criminal
☐ Antitrust
☐ Breach of Contract
☐ Fraud

□ Personal Injury/Wrongful Death
□ Product Liability
□ Medical/Legal Malpractice
□ Employment Discrimination
□ Bankruptcy/Creditors' Rights

□ Environmental/Asbestos
□ Trademark/Patent Disputes
□ Securities

Please check each task as it relates to the performance of your present and previous job experience:

F = Frequently   O = Occasionally   N = Never

□ F □ O □ N Interview clients
□ F □ O □ N Organize and index files
□ F □ O □ N Work with litigation support
□ F □ O □ N Organize and index documents
□ F □ O □ N Digest/summarize depositions
□ F □ O □ N Analyze/summarize factual information (e.g., wages)
□ F □ O □ N Review files to suggest documents to be produced and witnesses to interview
□ F □ O □ N Obtain documents through subpoena or request to produce
□ F □ O □ N Calendar due dates and maintain "tickler" calendar
□ F □ O □ N Maintain and update form files
□ F □ O □ N Locate witnesses
□ F □ O □ N Interview witnesses
□ F □ O □ N Arrange for expert witnesses
□ F □ O □ N Prepare drafts of expert witness' testimony or charts/graphs
□ F □ O □ N Arrange for attorney or investigator to interview witnesses
□ F □ O □ N Trace documents and other physical evidence
□ F □ O □ N Examine public records
□ F □ O □ N Perform statistical research
□ F □ O □ N Perform factual research
□ F □ O □ N Perform statutory research
□ F □ O □ N Perform case research
□ F □ O □ N Perform *LEXIS* research
□ F □ O □ N Draft complaints/answers
□ F □ O □ N Draft interrogatories/answers to interrogatories
□ F □ O □ N Draft requests for admission and/or responses to requests
□ F □ O □ N Draft notices to produce
□ F □ O □ N Gather and prepare documents in response to notices/motions to produce
□ F □ O □ N Attend document productions
□ F □ O □ N Prepare *subpoenas duces tecum*
□ F □ O □ N Draft, file, serve and prepare return of service

□ F □ O □ N Arrange witness' depositions and subpoenas
□ F □ O □ N Prepare preliminary drafts of depositions questions for attorney
□ F □ O □ N Attend depositions with attorney
□ F □ O □ N Attend production of documents in lieu of attorney
□ F □ O □ N Draft motions to compel discovery
□ F □ O □ N Draft pretrial statements and/or settlement conference memoranda
□ F □ O □ N Assist in the preparation of *voir dire*
□ F □ O □ N Review attorney briefs to check accuracy of factual information from file
□ F □ O □ N Draft legal memoranda and briefs
□ F □ O □ N Cite check and/or shepardize
□ F □ O □ N Assist attorney in preparing trial book
□ F □ O □ N Organize trial exhibits
□ F □ O □ N Arrange witness' attendance at trial
□ F □ O □ N Prepare charts/graphs for trial exhibits
□ F □ O □ N Attend trial to take notes, etc.
□ F □ O □ N Represent clients at administrative hearings

OTHER: Please list task and frequency of performance:

□ F □ O □ N _____
□ F □ O □ N _____
□ F □ O □ N _____
□ F □ O □ N _____

III. CORPORATE

Please check each task as it relates to the performance of your job:

□ F □ O □ N Check availability of proposed corporate name and prepare letter to reserve name
□ F □ O □ N Draft articles of incorporation
□ F □ O □ N Draft minutes of initial meetings
□ F □ O □ N Draft corporate by-laws
□ F □ O □ N Obtain corporate seal, minute book, and stock certificates
□ F □ O □ N Prepare documents to open corporate bank account

☐ F ☐ O ☐ N   Draft minutes of directors' meetings

☐ F ☐ O ☐ N   Draft corporate resolutions

☐ F ☐ O ☐ N   Draft notice of shareholders meetings, proxy statements, ballots, agenda, etc.

☐ F ☐ O ☐ N   Draft shareholder agreements

☐ F ☐ O ☐ N   Draft stock option plans

☐ F ☐ O ☐ N   Draft pension and profit sharing plans

☐ F ☐ O ☐ N   Draft trust agreements

☐ F ☐ O ☐ N   Draft tax returns

☐ F ☐ O ☐ N   Draft closing papers on corporate acquisitions

☐ F ☐ O ☐ N   Draft employment agreements

☐ F ☐ O ☐ N   Prepare documents for qualification to do business in foreign jurisdictions

☐ F ☐ O ☐ N   Prepare documents to amend articles of incorporation or by-laws

☐ F ☐ O ☐ N   Draft documents for corporate divestitures and dissolutions

☐ F ☐ O ☐ N   Draft sections of annual report

☐ F ☐ O ☐ N   Assist in research of Blue Sky requirements

☐ F ☐ O ☐ N   Assist in obtaining tax exempt status

☐ F ☐ O ☐ N   Draft general and limited partnership agreements

☐ F ☐ O ☐ N   Draft and file statements and certificates of partnership

☐ F ☐ O ☐ N   Prepare, file and have published fictitious business name statements

☐ F ☐ O ☐ N   Prepare minutes of partnership meetings

☐ F ☐ O ☐ N   Draft amendments to agreements and agreements for dissolution

☐ F ☐ O ☐ N   Draft termination of fictitious business name

☐ F ☐ O ☐ N   Draft notice of termination of partnership

☐ F ☐ O ☐ N   Keep track of legislation

☐ F ☐ O ☐ N   Summarize/digest files

☐ F ☐ O ☐ N   Extract designated information from corporate records and documents

☐ F ☐ O ☐ N   Assemble financial data from records on file at SEC and state agencies

☐ F ☐ O ☐ N   Calendar due dates and maintain "tickler" calendar of important dates

☐ F ☐ O ☐ N   Maintain and update form files

☐ F ☐ O ☐ N   Act as liaison with Secretary of State

IV. REAL ESTATE

Please check each task as it relates to the performance of your previous job experience:

A. CLOSING WORK:

1. *General Information Gathering*

☐ F ☐ O ☐ N   Directly for client

☐ F ☐ O ☐ N   From supervising attorney

☐ F ☐ O ☐ N   From courthouse

☐ F ☐ O ☐ N   From lenders

☐ F ☐ O ☐ N   From adverse party

2. *Title Work*

☐ F ☐ O ☐ N   Public records search

☐ F ☐ O ☐ N   Prepare title certificate

☐ F ☐ O ☐ N   Review title reports and commitments

☐ F ☐ O ☐ N   Ascertain necessary corrective title work

☐ F ☐ O ☐ N   Prepare title clearance documents

☐ F ☐ O ☐ N   Order title policies and endorsements

3. *Survey Work*

☐ F ☐ O ☐ N   Order surveys

☐ F ☐ O ☐ N   Draft legal descriptions

☐ F ☐ O ☐ N   Review surveys against legal descriptions

4. *Appraisals*

☐ F ☐ O ☐ N   Order appraisals

☐ F ☐ O ☐ N   Follow-up on completion of appraisal

☐ F ☐ O ☐ N   Existing files

☐ F ☐ O ☐ N   Existing loan documentation

☐ F ☐ O ☐ N   Existing leases

☐ F ☐ O ☐ N   Analyze the above items and determine necessary action(s)

5. *Document preparation and drafting*

a. *Acquisition transactions (raw land and improved property)*

☐ F ☐ O ☐ N   Sales contracts

☐ F ☐ O ☐ N   Option agreements

☐ F ☐ O ☐ N   Exchange agreements

☐ F ☐ O ☐ N   Deeds

☐ F ☐ O ☐ N   Affidavits

☐ F ☐ O ☐ N   Corporate resolutions

☐ F ☐ O ☐ N   Easement agreements

☐ F ☐ O ☐ N   Purchase money notes

☐ F ☐ O ☐ N   Purchase money deeds to secure debt

☐ F ☐ O ☐ N   Bills of sale

□ F   □ O   □ N   Transfer & assignment instrument

□ F   □ O   □ N   Restrictive covenants

□ F   □ O   □ N   Management agreement

□ F   □ O   □ N   Commission agreements

□ F   □ O   □ N   Escrow agreements

□ F   □ O   □ N   Powers of attorney

b. *Loan transactions (acquisition and development, construction, preclosed, gap, and permanent)*

□ F   □ O   □ N   Loan commitments

□ F   □ O   □ N   Loan agreements

□ F   □ O   □ N   Tri-party & buy-sell agreement

□ F   □ O   □ N   Promissory notes

□ F   □ O   □ N   Security deeds

□ F   □ O   □ N   Security agreements

□ F   □ O   □ N   Financing statements

□ F   □ O   □ N   Pledge agreements

□ F   □ O   □ N   Collateral assignments

□ F   □ O   □ N   Modification agreements

□ F   □ O   □ N   Participation agreements

□ F   □ O   □ N   Indemnification agreements

□ F   □ O   □ N   Affidavits

□ F   □ O   □ N   Lien waivers

□ F   □ O   □ N   Loan transfer documents

□ F   □ O   □ N   Subordination agreements

□ F   □ O   □ N   Estoppel certificates

□ F   □ O   □ N   Opinions of counsel

6. *Coordination of closings and follow-up work*

□ F   □ O   □ N   Draft closing statements (obtain loan payoffs and assumptions; calculate prorations)

□ F   □ O   □ N   Closing memoranda

□ F   □ O   □ N   Schedule closings and notify involved parties

□ F   □ O   □ N   Prepare closing checklist and coordinate requirements

□ F   □ O   □ N   Organize documents for closing

□ F   □ O   □ N   Copy documents

□ F   □ O   □ N   Assist attorney at closings

□ F   □ O   □ N   Notarize documents at closings

□ F   □ O   □ N   Attend closings

□ F   □ O   □ N   Disburse funds

□ F   □ O   □ N   Send documents to record

□ F   □ O   □ N   Monitor post-closing title work

B. LEASE DRAFTING (RESIDENTIAL AND COMMERCIAL)

□ F   □ O   □ N   Leases and subleases

□ F   □ O   □ N   Subordination agreements

□ F   □ O   □ N   Attornment and nondisturbance agreements

□ F   □ O   □ N   Tenant estoppel certificates

□ F   □ O   □ N   Lease assignments

□ F   □ O   □ N   Surety and guaranty agreements

C. FORECLOSURES AND DEEDS IN LIEU OF FORECLOSURE

□ F   □ O   □ N   Draft notice letters

□ F   □ O   □ N   Draft demand letters

□ F   □ O   □ N   Draft notices of sales under power

□ F   □ O   □ N   Proofread newspaper ads

□ F   □ O   □ N   Attend foreclosure sales

□ F   □ O   □ N   Draft deeds under power

□ F   □ O   □ N   Draft foreclosure affidavits

□ F   □ O   □ N   Draft deeds in lieu of foreclosure

D. LEGAL ANALYSIS

Review and Summarize the following:

□ F   □ O   □ N   Loan commitments

□ F   □ O   □ N   Contracts

□ F   □ O   □ N   Submitted closing documents

□ F   □ O   □ N   Leases

E. ADMINISTRATIVE

□ F   □ O   □ N   Revise and prepare real estate forms

□ F   □ O   □ N   Maintain form files

□ F   □ O   □ N   Open files

□ F   □ O   □ N   Prepare departmental procedural memoranda

□ F   □ O   □ N   Monitor developments in specific areas of real estate law

□ F   □ O   □ N   Interview paralegal applicants

□ F   □ O   □ N   Train new paralegals

□ F   □ O   □ N   Draft index

□ F   □ O   □ N   Copy documents

□ F   □ O   □ N   Put tabs on divider sheets

□ F   □ O   □ N   Assemble binders

□ F   □ O   □ N   Forward original documents closing binders to appropriate parties

□ F   □ O   □ N   Prepare final bill

□ F   □ O   □ N   Close file

_____ % of my real estate workload involves residential transactions

_____ % of my real estate workload involves commercial transactions

OTHER: Please list each task and frequency of performance:

☐ F   ☐ O   ☐ N   _____

☐ F   ☐ O   ☐ N   _____

☐ F   ☐ O   ☐ N   _____

☐ F   ☐ O   ☐ N   _____

F. Do your answers to the above questions reflect all of your present and past work responsibilities? _____ Yes _____ No

If not, please describe what other areas you have worked in, the type of work which these areas require, and how much of your time is spent in these other areas:

_____

_____

_____

G. My involvement in the preparation of documents referred to above has been:

☐ F   ☐ O   ☐ N   Drafting

☐ F   ☐ O   ☐ N   Typing

☐ F   ☐ O   ☐ N   Proofing

H. To what extent have you been involved in negotiations and meetings with clients and/or the adverse parties?

☐ F   ☐ O   ☐ N   Attend meetings with attorney

☐ F   ☐ O   ☐ N   Attend meeting and take notes

☐ F   ☐ O   ☐ N   Prepare memoranda summarizing the agreements reached

☐ F   ☐ O   ☐ N   Rely on own notes to draft and/or change documents

☐ F   ☐ O   ☐ N   Participate in negotiations

☐ F   ☐ O   ☐ N   Attend meetings with the attorneys

☐ F   ☐ O   ☐ N   Handle negotiations

If you have been asked to handle negotiations or attend meetings without an attorney, please describe briefly the type of transactions involved:

_____

_____

_____

_____

V. TRUSTS AND ESTATES

Please check each task as it relates to the performance of your previous job experience:

☐ F   ☐ O   ☐ N   Assist in audits of estate tax returns

☐ F   ☐ O   ☐ N   Prepare accountings

☐ F   ☐ O   ☐ N   Maintain financial records of estate

☐ F   ☐ O   ☐ N   Obtain Certificate of Release from State Controller

☐ F   ☐ O   ☐ N   Calculate distributive shares of heirs

☐ F   ☐ O   ☐ N   Assist in closing documents

☐ F   ☐ O   ☐ N   Prepare documents for Petition for Letters of Conservatorship

☐ F   ☐ O   ☐ N   Prepare inventory and appraisement for conservatorship

☐ F   ☐ O   ☐ N   Arrange for transition from conservatorship to estate proceedings

☐ F   ☐ O   ☐ N   Assist in preparation of accountings for conservatorships

☐ F   ☐ O   ☐ N   Calendar due dates and maintain "tickler" calendar

☐ F   ☐ O   ☐ N   Maintain and update form files

☐ F   ☐ O   ☐ N   Act as liaison with tax referees and Probate Court

☐ F   ☐ O   ☐ N   Keep track of legislation involving and estates

☐ F   ☐ O   ☐ N   Collection of data for estate planning

☐ F   ☐ O   ☐ N   Draft wills and/or trusts

☐ F   ☐ O   ☐ N   Investment analysis for estate planning

☐ F   ☐ O   ☐ N   Supervise preparation of documents to be filed with probate court

☐ F   ☐ O   ☐ N   Obtain certified copies of death certificate, will, marriage certificate

☐ F   ☐ O   ☐ N   Notify beneficiaries

☐ F   ☐ O   ☐ N   Notify creditors

☐ F   ☐ O   ☐ N   Arrange for payment of funeral expenses

☐ F   ☐ O   ☐ N   Arrange for opening and inventorying of decedent's safe deposit box

☐ F   ☐ O   ☐ N   Check insurance coverage

☐ F   ☐ O   ☐ N   Trace financial history of decedent

☐ F   ☐ O   ☐ N   Collect and enumerate assets

☐ F   ☐ O   ☐ N   Obtain date of death valuations of assets

☐ F   ☐ O   ☐ N   Compare date of death valuations with alternative valuations

☐ F   ☐ O   ☐ N   Analyze and summarize provisions of will

☐ F   ☐ O   ☐ N   Arrange for appraisals and bond

☐ F   ☐ O   ☐ N   Make preliminary tax estimate

☐ F   ☐ O   ☐ N   Prepare State Inheritance Tax forms

☐ F   ☐ O   ☐ N   Prepare Federal Estate Tax Return

☐ F   ☐ O   ☐ N   Prepare Federal and State Fiduciary Returns

☐ F   ☐ O   ☐ N   Prepare decedent's last personal income tax returns

OTHER: Please list each task and frequency of performance:

☐ F   ☐ O   ☐ N   _____

☐ F   ☐ O   ☐ N   _____

☐ F   ☐ O   ☐ N   _____

☐ F   ☐ O   ☐ N   _____

Sample Paralegal Evaluation

Paralegal _____

Attorney _____

Evaluation Period _____

GENERAL INSTRUCTIONS:

In order to obtain a full evaluation of this paralegal, you are urged to observe the following principles: Each item should be answered by selecting the appropriate objective answer with some brief comment, or "N.O." (Not Observed). "N.O." should be reserved only for those cases where not even a slight observation has been made, as there may be small observations by more than one lawyer which will cumulatively indicate a subtle talent, potential or problem, that should be brought out to help the paralegal in his/her development.

	Excellent	Good	Acceptable	Unacceptable
1. Quality of Performance:				
a. (1) Legal and Factual Analysis	☐	☐	☐	☐
(2) Ability to apply legal reasoning to problems	☐	☐	☐	☐
Comments:				
b. Preparation of Pleadings and Discovery:				
(1) Understanding of State Statutes and *Federal Rules of Civil Procedure* regarding pleadings and discovery	☐	☐	☐	☐
(2) Use of legal style and approach	☐	☐	☐	☐
(3) Conciseness and clarity	☐	☐	☐	☐
(4) Follows instructions	☐	☐	☐	☐
Comments:				
c. Other Written Materials: (Letters, Digests, etc.)				
(1) Absence of typos, grammatical errors, sentence structure problems, etc.	☐	☐	☐	☐
(2) Follows instructions	☐	☐	☐	☐
(3) Conciseness and clarity	☐	☐	☐	☐
Comments:				
d. Files:				
(1) Ability to functionally organize a file	☐	☐	☐	☐
(2) Use of personal diary system	☐	☐	☐	☐
(3) Ability to follow-up on unconcluded matters without having to be reminded	☐	☐	☐	☐
Comments:				
e. Professional Demeanor:				
(1) Initiative	☐	☐	☐	☐
(2) Motivation	☐	☐	☐	☐

(3) Professionalism	☐	☐	☐	☐
(4) Career attitude and orientation	☐	☐	☐	☐

Comments:

f. Rapport with Clients and Others:

(1) Dealing with clients	☐	☐	☐	☐
(2) Dealing with witnesses	☐	☐	☐	☐
(3) Effectiveness as an investigator	☐	☐	☐	☐

Comments:

2. Attitude and Identity with Firm: ☐ ☐ ☐ ☐

a. Hours—Attendance

—Availability	☐	☐	☐	☐
—General willingness to work overtime	☐	☐	☐	☐
—Willingness to assist in legal emergency requiring nights, weekends, etc.	☐	☐	☐	☐

Comments:

b. Quantitative—Workload	☐	☐	☐	☐
—Output	☐	☐	☐	☐

Comments:

c. Timeliness—Completion of Assignments ☐ ☐ ☐ ☐

Comments:

d. Cooperation and Assistance to Other Lawyers and Paralegals ☐ ☐ ☐ ☐

Comments:

e. Relations With Nonlegal Personnel ☐ ☐ ☐ ☐

Comments:

3. Personal: ☐ ☐ ☐ ☐

a. Responsibility, judgment and initiative

Comments:

b. Speech and expression ☐ ☐ ☐ ☐

Comments:

4. Development:

a. Does this paralegal generally take less, more or as much time to do a task as you would expect a paralegal to spend, or instruct him or her to spend?

_____

_____

b. Does this paralegal generally follow your instructions as to what you want done on a specific file, or do you have to repeat instructions or have work done over later?

_____

_____

c. Does this paralegal understand the legal process and procedures in his or her area of specialization? _____

_____

_____

d. What are this paralegal's strongest areas? _____

_____

_____

e. What are this paralegal's weakest areas? _____

_____

_____

_____

_____

f. General evaluation _____

_____

g. Special commendation _____

_____

h. Other comments _____

_____

_____

_____

Attorney

_____ Date

C

Affirmation of Professional Responsibility of the National Federation of Paralegal Associations, Inc. (NFPA)

• Preamble

The National Federation of Paralegal Associations, Inc. (NFPA) recognizes and accepts its commitment to the realization of the most basic right of a free society, equal justice under the law.

In examining contemporary legal institutions and systems, the members of the paralegal profession recognize that a redefinition of the traditional delivery of legal services is essential in order to meet the needs of the general public. The paralegal profession is committed to increasing the availability and quality of legal services.

NFPA has adopted this Affirmation of Professional Responsibility to delineate the principles of purpose and conduct toward which paralegals should aspire. Through this Affirmation, NFPA places upon each paralegal the responsibility to adhere to these standards and encourages dedication to the development of the profession.

• I. Professional Responsibility

A paralegal shall demonstrate initiative in performing and expanding the paralegal role in the delivery of legal services within the parameters of the unauthorized practice of law statutes.

Discussion: Recognizing the professional and legal responsibility to abide by the unauthorized practice of law statutes, NFPA supports and encourages new interpretations as to what constitutes the practice of law.

• II. Professional Conduct

A paralegal shall maintain the highest standards of ethical conduct.

Discussion: It is the responsibility of a paralegal to avoid conduct which is unethical or appears to be unethical. Eth-

ical principles are aspirational in character and embody the fundamental rules of conduct by which every paralegal should abide. Observance of these standards is essential to uphold respect for the legal system.

• III. Competence and Integrity

A paralegal shall maintain a high level of competence and shall contribute to the integrity of the paralegal profession.

Discussion: The integrity of the paralegal profession is predicated upon individual competence. Professional competence is each paralegal's responsibility and is achieved through continuing education, awareness of developments in the field of law, and aspiring to the highest standards of personal performance.

• IV. Client Confidences

A paralegal shall preserve client confidences and privileged communications.

Discussion: Confidential information and privileged communications are a vital part of the attorney, paralegal and client relationship. The importance of preserving confidential and privileged information is understood to be an uncompromising obligation of every paralegal.

• V. Support of Public Interests

A paralegal shall serve the public interests by contributing to the availability and delivery of quality legal services.

Discussion: It is the responsibility of each paralegal to promote the development and implementation of programs that address the legal needs of the public. A paralegal shall strive to maintain a sensitivity to public needs and educate the public as to the services that paralegals may render.

• VI. Professional Development

A paralegal shall promote the development of the paralegal profession.

Discussion: This Affirmation of Professional Responsibility promulgates a positive attitude through which a paralegal may recognize the importance, responsibility, and potential of the paralegal contribution to the delivery of legal services. Participation in professional associations enhances the ability of the individual paralegal to contribute to the quality and growth of the paralegal profession.

———

D. Member Associations of the National Federation of Paralegal Associations, Inc. (NFPA)

• Region I

Alaska Association of Legal Assistants
P.O. Box 101956
Anchorage, AK 99510-1956

Arizona Association of Professional Paralegals, Inc.
P.O. Box 25111
Phoenix, AZ 85002

Central Coast Legal Assistant Association
P.O. Box 93
San Luis Obispo, CA 93406

Hawaii Association of Legal Assistants
P.O. BOX 674
Honolulu, HI 96809

Juneau Legal Assistants Association
P.O. Box 22336
Juneau, AK 99802

Los Angeles Paralegal Association
P.O. Box 241928
Los Angeles, CA 90024

Oregon Legal Assistants Association
P.O. Box 8523
Portland, OR 97207

Sacramento Association of Legal Assistants
P.O. Box 453
Sacramento, CA 95812-0453

San Diego Association of Legal Assistants
P.O. Box 87449
San Diego, CA 92138-7449

San Francisco Association of Legal Assistants
P.O. Box 26668
San Francisco, CA 94126-6668

Washington Legal Assistants Association
2033 6th Avenue, Ste. 804
Seattle, WA 98121

• Region II

Dallas Association of Legal Assistants
P.O. Box 117885
Carrollton, TX 75011-7885

Greater Denton Legal Assistants Association
101 S. Locust, Ste. 601
Denton, TX 76201

Illinois Paralegal Association
P.O. Box 857
Chicago, IL 60690

Kansas City Association of Legal Assistants
P.O. Box 13223
Kansas City, MO 64199

Kansas Legal Assistants Society
P.O. Box 1675
Topeka, KS 66601

Legal Assistants of New Mexico
P.O. Box 1113
Albuquerque, NM 87103-1113

Minnesota Association of Legal Assistants
2626 E. 82nd Street, Suite 201
Minneapolis, MN 55425

New Orleans Paralegal Association
P.O. Box 30604
New Orleans, LA 70190

Paralegal Association of Wisconsin, Inc.
P.O. Box 92882
Milwaukee, WI 53202

Rocky Mountain Legal Assistants Association
P.O. Box 304
Denver, CO 80201

• Region III

Baltimore Association of Legal Assistants
P.O. Box 13244
Baltimore, MD 21200

Cincinnati Paralegal Association
P.O. Box 1515
Cincinnati, OH 45201

Cleveland Association of Paralegals
P.O. Box 14247
Cleveland, OH 44114

Columbia Legal Assistants Association
P.O. Box 11634
Columbia, SC 29211-1634

Georgia Association of Legal Assistants
P.O. Box 1802
Atlanta, GA 30301
Greater Dayton Paralegal Association
P.O. Box 515, Mid-City Station
Dayton, OH 45402
Indiana Paralegal Association
Federal Station, P.O. Box 44518
Indianapolis, IN 46204
Legal Assistants of Central Ohio
P.O. Box 15182
Columbus, OH 43215-0182
Lexington Paralegal Association, Inc.
P.O. Box 574
Lexington, KY 40586
Louisville Association of Paralegals
P.O. Box 962
Louisville, KY 40201
Memphis Paralegal Association
P.O. Box 3646
Memphis, TN 38173-0646
Michigan Paralegal Association
P.O. Box 11458
South Bend, IN 46634
Middle Tennessee Paralegal Association
P.O. Box 198006
Nashville, TN 37219
National Capital Area Paralegal Association
1155 Connecticut Ave. N. W., Ste. 300
Washington, DC 20036
Roanoke Valley Paralegal Association
P.O. Box 1505
Roanoke, VA 24001

• Region IV

Central Connecticut Association of Legal Assistants
P.O. Box 230594
Hartford, CT 06123-0594
Central Massachusetts Paralegal Association
P.O. Box 444
Worcester, MA 01614
Central Pennsylvania Paralegal Association
P.O. Box 11814
Harrisburg, PA 17108

Connecticut Association of Paralegals, Fairfield County
P.O. Box 134
Bridgeport, CT 06601
Connecticut Association of Paralegals, New Haven
P.O. Box 862
New Haven, CT 06304-0862
Delaware Paralegal Association
P.O. Box 1362
Wilmington, DE 19899
Legal Assistants of Southeastern Connecticut
P.O. Box 409
New London, CT 06320
Long Island Paralegal Association
P.O. Box 80
Kings Park, NY 11754
Massachusetts Paralegal Association
P.O. Box 423
Boston, MA 02102
Paralegal Association of Northwestern Pennsylvania
P.O. Box 1504
Erie, PA 16507
Paralegal Association of Rochester
P.O. Box 40567
Rochester, NY 14604
Philadelphia Association of Paralegals
1411 Walnut Street, Suite 200
Philadelphia, PA 19102
Pittsburgh Paralegal Association
P.O. Box 2845
Pittsburgh, PA 15230
Rhode Island Paralegal Association
P.O. Box 1003
Providence, RI 02901
South Jersey Paralegal Association
P.O. Box 355
Haddonfield, NJ 08033
Southern Tier Association of Paralegals
P.O. Box 2555
Binghamton, NY 13901
Western Massachusetts Paralegal Association
P.O. Box 30005
Springfield, MA 01102
Western New York Paralegal Association
P.O. Box 207, Niagara Square Station
Buffalo, NY 14202
West/Rock Paralegal Association
P.O. Box 101 - 95 Mamaroneck Ave.
White Plains, NY 10601

Code Of Ethics and Professional Responsibility of National Association of Legal Assistants, Inc.

Preamble

It is the responsibility of every legal assistant to adhere strictly to the accepted standards of legal ethics and to live by general principles of proper conduct. The performance of the duties of the legal assistant shall be governed by specific canons as defined herein in order that justice will be served and the goals of the profession attained.

The canons of ethics set forth hereafter are adopted by the National Association of Legal Assistants, Inc., as a general guide, and the enumeration of these rules does not mean there are not others of equal importance although not specifically mentioned.

Canon 1 — A legal assistant shall not perform any of the duties that lawyers only may perform nor do things that lawyers themselves may not do.

Canon 2 — A legal assistant may perform any task delegated and supervised by a lawyer so long as the lawyer is responsible to the client, maintains a direct relationship with the client, and assumes full professional responsibility for the work product.

Canon 3 — A legal assistant shall not engage in the practice of law by accepting cases, setting fees, giving legal advice or appearing in court (unless otherwise authorized by court or agency rules).

Canon 4 — A legal assistant shall not act in matters involving professional legal judgment as the services of a lawyer are essential in the public interest whenever the exercise of such judgment is required.

Canon 5 — A legal assistant must act prudently in determining the extent to which a client may be assisted without the presence of a lawyer.

Canon 6 — A legal assistant shall not engage in the unauthorized practice of law and shall assist in preventing the unauthorized practice of law.

Canon 7 — A legal assistant must protect the confidences of a client, and it shall be unethical for a legal assistant to violate any statute now in effect or hereafter to be enacted controlling privileged communications.

Canon 8 — It is the obligation of the legal assistant to avoid conduct which would cause the lawyer to be unethical or even appear to be unethical, and loyalty to the employer is incumbent upon the legal assistant.

Canon 9 — A legal assistant shall work continually to maintain integrity and a high degree of competency throughout the legal profession.

Canon 10 — A legal assistant shall strive for perfection through education in order to better assist the legal profession in fulfilling its duty of making legal services available to clients and the public.

Canon 11 — A legal assistant shall do all other things incidental, necessary, or expedient for the attainment of the ethics and responsibilities imposed by statute or rule of court.

Canon 12 — A legal assistant is governed by the American Bar Association Model Code of Professional Responsibility and the American Bar Association Model Rules of Professional Conduct.

NALA Affiliated Associations*

• Alabama

Legal Assistant Society of Southern Institute
Chris Christ
Southern Institute
115 Office Park Drive
Birmingham, AL 35223-2401

Alabama Association of Legal Assistants
Lynn Reynolds, CLA, President
Sirote & Permutt, PC
PO Box 55727
Birmingham, AL 35255

Phyllis Coggin, NALA Liaison
Sirote & Permutt, PC
PO Box 55727
Birmingham, AL 35255-5727

• Alaska

Fairbanks Associations of Legal Assistants
Sally Lowery, CLA, President
FALA
PO Box 70810
Fairbanks, AK 99707

Barbara A. Johnson, NALA Liaison
101 Oak Drive
Fairbanks, AK 99709-3161

• Arizona

Arizona Paralegal Association
John Steiner, President
Law Offices of William Mark Jacobs
111 W Monroe,
Suite 1220
Phoenix, AZ 85003

Marian Johnson, CLA, NALA Liaison
1425 East Libra
Tempe, AZ 85283

Legal Assistants of Metropolitan Phoenix
Terri L. Mortensen, President
2407 E Cinnabar
Phoenix, AZ 85028

Beverly Kane, NALA Liaison
6821 N. 24th Drive
Phoenix, AZ 85015

Southeast Valley Association of Legal Assistants
Sandra Gail Slater, CLA, President
1707 N. Temple
Mesa, AZ 85203

Tucson Association of Legal Assistants
Linda S. Patrou, CLA, President
Patrou Professional Services
4301 East 5th Street
Tucson, AZ 85711

Mary Butera, CLA, NALA Liaison
3011 E Helen Street
Tucson, AZ 85716

• Arkansas

Arkansas Association of Legal Assistants
Alice C. Cook, CLA, President
Mitchell Law Firm
1000 Savers Federal Bldg.
320 W Capital Ave.
Little Rock, AR 72201

Katibel C. Perdue, NALA Liaison
Eilbott Law Firm
PO Box 8948
Pine Bluff, AR 71611-8948

*As of June 11, 1992

• California

Legal Assistants Association of Santa Barbara
Lynn M. Mollie CLA, President
519 1/2 W. Valerio St.
Santa Barbara, CA 93101

JoEllen Alderson, NALA Liaison
Robert Sanger, Law Office
233 E. Carrillo St., Ste. C
Santa Barbara, CA 93101-2187

Paralegal Association of Santa Clara County
Tita Brewster, President
PO Box 26736
San Jose, CA 95159

Jo Ellen Floch, NALA Liaison
129 Parkwell Court
San Jose, CA 95138-1633

Ventura County Association of Legal Assistants
Leslie McGuire, CLA, President
1000 Towne Ctr. Drive, 6th Floor
Oxnard, CA 93030

Cynthia J. Adams, NALA Liaison
Edward J. Lacey, Attorney at Law
56 E. Main St. #200
Ventura, CA 93001

• Colorado

Association of Legal Assistants of Colorado
Donna Coble, CLAS, President
910 41 Avenue
Greeley, CO 80634

• Florida

Florida Legal Assistants, Inc.
Catherine J. Scott, CLAS, President
William T. Kirtley, P.A.
702 Sarasota Quay
Sarasota, FL 34236

Kathleen J. Foos, CLAS, NALA Liaison
L.A.S., Inc.
1201 U.S. Hwy. 1, Ste. 430
West Palm Beach, FL 33408

Bay Area Legal Academy Student Association
Ned Schroeder
Bay Area Legal Academy
Sabal Business Center
3924 Coconut Palm Drive
Tampa, Fl 33619-9925

Darline R. Root, NALA Liaison
Bay Area Legal Academy
Sabal Business Center
3924 Coconut Palm Drive
Tampa, FL 33619-9925

Dade Association of Legal Assistants
Marie Wilson, CLA, President
9301 SW 92 Avenue #C-209
Miami, FL 33176

Lori Allen, CLA, NALA Liaison
9720 W. Bay Harbor Drive
Bay Harbor Islands, FL 33154

Jacksonville Legal Assistants
Gina M. Wynn, President
Taylor, Day & Rio
10 S. Newnan Street
Jacksonville, FL 32202

Donna A. Hoffman, CLA, NALA Liaison
The Charter Company
PO Box 17707
Jacksonville, FL 32245-7707

Orlando Legal Assistants
Cindy L. Taylor, President
Orlando Legal Assistants
PO Box 1107
Orlando, FL 32802

Catherine A. Perry, CLAS, NALA Liaison
4627 Darwood Drive
Orlando, FL 32812

Pensacola Legal Assistants
Rhonda Barkley, President
David Sapp, Attorney
5043 Bayou Blvd., Suite B
Pensacola, FL 32503

Donna Johnson, CLA, NALA Liaison
Levin, Middlebrooks, Marbie, et al
PO Box 12308
Pensacola, FL 32581

Volusia Association of Legal Assistants
Rosemary E. Hallman, CLA, President
1950 Red Cedar Circle
S. Daytona, FL 32119

Mary J. Harrington, NALA Liaison
98 Fairway Drive
Ormond Beach, FL 32176

• Georgia

Professional Paralegals of Georgia
Donita C. Berckemeyer, CLA, President
King & Spalding
191 Peachtree Street
Atlanta, GA 30303-1763

Deborah L. Thompson, NALA Liaison
King & Spalding
191 Peachtree Street
Atlanta, GA 30303-1763

Southeastern Association of Legal Assistants of Georgia
Debra R. Sutlive, CLA, President
2215 Bacon Park Drive
Savannah, GA 31406

Diann Beasley, NALA Liaison
Route 2, Box 181
Guyton, GA 31312

South Georgia Association of Legal Assistants
Martha H. Tanner, President
L. Andrew Smith, P.C.
PO Box 1026
Valdosta, GA 31603-1026

• Idaho

Idaho Association of Legal Assistants
Nancy L. Schwend, CLA, President
5076 Tinker
Boise, ID 83709

Virginia B. Rayne, CLA, NALA Liaison
11224 Valley Heights Circle
Boise, ID 83709

• Illinois

Central Illinois Paralegal Assocation
Carolyn S. Pitts, CLA, President
Ostling, Ensign, Barry & Glenn
102 S East St. #200
Bloomington, IL 61701-5247

Rose M. Lanter, CLA, NALA Liaison
Reno, O'Byrne & Kepley, PC
501 W Church Street
PO Box 693
Champaign, IL 61824

• Indiana

Indiana Legal Assistants
Dorothy M. French, CLA, President
14669 Old State Road
Evansville, IN 47711

Randall Forsythe, NALA Liaison
Komyatte & Freeland
9650 Gordon Drive
Highland, IN 46322

• Kansas

Kansas Association of Legal Assistants
Jimmie Sue Marsh, CLA, President
Foulston & Siefkin
700 Fourth Financial Center
Wichita, KS 67202

Stephanie G. Rahm, CLA, NALA Liaison
Foulston & Siefkin
700 Fourth Financial Center
Wichita, KS 67202

• Louisiana

Northwest Louisiana Paralegal Association
Cindy Vucinovich, President
Cook, Yancey, King & Galloway
PO Box 22260
Shreveport, LA 71120-2260

Katherine J. Griffis, CLA, NALA Liaison
Sockrider, Bolin, Anglin
327 Crockett Street
Shreveport, LA 71037

• Maine

Maine Association of Paralegals
Julie Sawtelle, CLA, President
65 Vesper Street
Portland, ME 04101

Michele A. Fossett, NALA Liaison
81 Beech Street
Augusta, ME 04330

• Michigan

Legal Assistants Association of Michigan
Cora S. Webb, President
Woll, Crowley, Berman, et al
315 S Woodward, Ste. 200
Royal Oak, MI 48067

Vicki V. Voisin, CLA, NALA Liason
Simpson & Moran, P.C.
202 Clinton
Charlevoix, MI 49720

• Minnesota

Minnesota Paralegal Association
Maria C. Adamson, President
505 Marquette Bank Bldg.
PO Box 549
Rochester, MN 55903-0549

Muriel L. Hinrichs, NALA Liaison
611 Marquette Bank Bldg.
PO Box 968
Rochester, MN 55903-0968

• Mississippi

Mississippi Association of Legal Assistants
Connie M. Cavanaugh, President
PO Box 651
600 Heritage Bldg.
Jackson, MS 39205

Sharon Gowan, NALA Liaison
Brunini, Grantham, Grower & Hewes
PO Box 119
Jackson, MS 39205

Society for Paralegal Studies
Laura Lilly, President
USM Paralegal Society
S S Box 5108
Hattiesburg, MS 39406-5108

Ronald G. Marquardt, NALA Liaison
USM Paralegal Society
S S Box 5108
Hattiesburg, MS 39406-5108

• Missouri

St. Louis Association of Legal Assistants
Carol Young, President
527 Willoughby Lane
St. Louis, MO 63119

Lucy E. Ebersohl, CLA, NALA Liaison
The Stolar Partnership
911 Washington Ave.
St. Louis, MO 63101

• Nebraska

Nebraska Association of Legal Assistants
Carol E. Nielsen, President
1853 S 50th St.
Lincoln, NE 68506

Linda A. Walker, CLA, NALA Liaison
McGill, Gotsdiner, Workman, et al
10010 Regency Circle, Suite 300
Omaha, NE 68114

• Nevada

Clark County Organization of Legal Assistants, Inc.
Sue E. Fogleboch, CLA, President
Nevada Power Company
Legal Department
6226 West Sahara Avenue
Las Vegas, NV 89102

Janet L. Sanford Baker, NALA Liaison
Vargas & Bartlett
3800 Howard Hughes Pkwy., 7th Fl.
Las Vegas, NV 89109

Sierra Nevada Association of Paralegals
Candace R. Jones, CLA, President
Phyllis Halsey Atkins
300 Booth Street #5011
Reno, NV 89509

Merrilyn Marsh, CLA, NALA Liaison
69 Skyline Circle
Reno, NV 89509-3901

• New Hampshire

Paralegal Association of New Hampshire
David Tucker, President
Wiggin & Nourie
PO Box 808
Manchester, NH 03105

Frances Dupre, NALA Liaison
Wiggin & Nourie
PO Box 808
Manchester, NH 03105

• New Jersey

The Legal Assistants Association of New Jersey, Inc.
John Shufro, CLA, President
11 Welshman Court
Caldwell, NJ 07006

Diane B. Mitchell, CLA, NALA Liaison
38 Cottage Lane
Clifton, NJ 07012

• North Carolina

Coastal Carolina Paralegal Club
Rose Egan, President
506 Sarah Court
Jacksonville, NC 28540

Col. Robert E. Switzer, NALA Liaison
Coastal Carolina Comm. College
Paralegal Technology Dept.
444 Western Blvd.
Jacksonville, NC 28546

North Carolina Paralegal Association, Inc.
T. William Tewes, Jr., President
Fuller & Corbett, PA
PO Box 1121
Goldsboro, NC 27533-1121

Linda L. Waldrop, CLA, NALA Liaison
403 Magnolia Lane
Hudson, NC 28134

• North Dakota

Red River Valley Legal Assistants
Jeanine L. Rodvold, CLA, President
Conmy, Feste, Bossart, et al
400 Norwest Center, Fourth & Main
Fargo, ND 58126

Susan McKigney, NALA Liaison
Conmy, Feste, Bossart, et al
400 Norwest Center
Fargo, ND 58126

Western Dakota Association of Legal Assistants
Vicki J. Kunz, CLAS, President
Wheeler Wolf Law Firm
116 North 4th Street
P. O. Box 2056
Bismarck, ND 58502

Jane K. Rieger, CLA, NALA Liaison
605 19 Ave. Ste. #A
Minot, ND 58701

• Ohio

Toledo Association of Legal Assistants
Denise Conrad, President
Jones & Bahret
First Federal Plaza
701 Adams Street, Ste. 709
Toledo, OH 43624

Constance M. Gensbechler, CLAS, NALA Liaison
Connelly, Soutar & Jackson
1600 Ohio Citizens Bank Bldg.
Toledo, OH 43604

• Oklahoma

Oklahoma Paralegal Association
Stephanie Mark, CLAS, President
Hall Estill
4100 BOK Tower
Tulsa, OK 74172

Denise L. Newsom, CLA, NALA Liaison
McKnight & Gasaway
201 N Grand Street, 4th Floor
PO Box 1108
Enid, OK 73702

Rose State Paralegal Association
Judy Shaw
6420 SE 15th Street
Midwest City, OK 73110

Student Association of Legal Assistants
Roger State College
Lenneice Marshall, President
Rogers State College
Will Rogers & College Hill
Claremore, OK 74017-2099

Pamela Pavatt, Faculty Advisor
Rogers State College
Will Rogers & College Hill
Claremore, OK 74017-2099

TJC Student Association of Legal Assistants
Judy Tucker
TJC—Legal Assistant Program
909 S Boston, Rm. #429
Tulsa, OK 74119

Tulsa Association of Legal Assistants
Toni G. Hammerton, CLAS, President
605 South Indianwood Avenue
Broken Arrow, OK 74012

Sue R. McInnis, CLAS, NALA Liaison
2645 Raintree Circle
Sapulpa, OK 74066-9312

• Oregon

Pacific Northwest Legal Assistants
Tracy Drullinger, CLA, President
Bruce C. Moore
96 E Broadway
Eugene, OR 96401

Linda J. Triden, CLA, NALA Liaison
Ackerman, DeWinter & Huntsberger
870 West Centennial
Springfield, OR 97477

• Pennsylvania

Keystone Legal Assistant Association
Catrine Nuss, President
3021 Guineveer Drive, Apt. B4
Harrisburg, PA 17110

Peggy S. Clements CLA, NALA Liaison
1114 Garden Avenue
Lebanon, PA 17042

• South Carolina

Greenville Association of Legal Assistants
Debbie S. Massingil, President
Fluor Daniel, Inc.
100 Fluor Daniel Dr.- C303F
Greenville, SC 29607-2762

Amanda A. Folk, CLA, NALA Liaison
Bozeman, Grayson, Smith & Price
301 College St., Ste. 400
Greenville, SC 29601

• South Dakota

South Dakota Legal Assistants Association, Inc.
Louise A. Peterson, CLA, President
May, Johnson, Doyle & Becker, PC
PO Box 1443
Sioux Falls, SD 57101-1443

Leann M. Niebuhr, CLA, NALA Liaison
6601 N. Cliff Avenue
Sioux Falls, SD 57104

• Tennessee

Tennessee Paralegal Association
Janet Davey, President
Miller & Martin
Volunteer State Life Building
Suite 1000
Chattanooga, TN 37402

Martha S. Wedgeworth, CLA, NALA Liaison
Neely, Green, et al
65 Union Avenue, Suite 900
Memphis, TN 38103

• Texas

Capital Area Paralegal Association
Maria Hernandez, President
Salmanson, Smith, Travis & Schrager, P.C.
101 E 9th Street #900
Austin, TX 78701-2435

Sara Richardson, NALA Liaison
UT Legal Assistant Certificate Program
PO Box 7870
Austin, TX 78713-7879

El Paso Association of Legal Assistants
Martha G. Parton, CLA, President
Mounce & Galatzan
Texas Commerce Building
El Paso, TX 79950-1977

Randi Brewer, NALA Liaison
Mayfield & Perrenot
First City Bank Bldg.
300 E Main, 5th Floor
El Paso, TX 79901

Legal Assistant Assocation/Permian Basin
Darla J. Fisher, President
P.O. Box 10506
Midland, TX 79702

Jana G. Clift, CLA, NALA Liaison
Steven L. Clack, Attorney At Law
300 N Main
PO Box 1179
Andrews, TX 79714

Northeast Texas Association of Legal Assistants
Javan Johnson, CLA, President
PO Box 2284
Longview, TX 75606

Genevieve McFadden, CLA, NALA Liaison
PO Box 2284
Longview, TX 75606

Nueces County Association of Legal Assistants
Alice Simons, CLA, President
U.S. Courthouse, 2nd Floor
521 Starr Street
Corpus Christi, TX 78401

Elaine Edwards, NALA Liaison
McMains & Constant
PO Box 2846
Corpus Christi, TX 78403

Wichita County Student Association
Kathy M. (Parker) Adams, CLA, President
4717 Cypress Avenue
Wichita Falls, TX 76310

Billie Ruth Goss, NALA Liaison
Midwestern State University
Continued Education
3400 Taft Blvd.
Wichita Falls, TX 76308

Southeast Texas Association of Legal Assistants
Martha Maze, CLA, President
470 Orleans Street
Beaumont, TX 77701

Grace M. Guillot, CLA, NALA Liaison
Mehaffy & Weber
PO Box 16
Beaumont, TX 77704

Texarkana Association of Legal Assistants
Diane Plunkett, CLA, President
1012 Olive
Texarkana, TX 75501

Myra J. Conaway, CLA, NALA Liaison
Smith, Stroud, McClerkin, et al
6 State Line Plaza, Suite 6
Texarkana, AR 75502

Texas Panhandle Association of Legal Assistants
Lisa Clemens, President
Culton, Morgan, Britain & White
Box 189
Amarillo, TX 79105

Marilyn A. Commons, CLA, NALA Liaison
6019 Elmhurst
Amarillo, TX 79106

West Texas Association of Legal Assistants
Marilyn Dean, CLA, President
Crenshaw, Dupree & Milam
PO Box 1499
Lubbock, TX 79408

Eyvonne Crenshaw Palmer, CLAS, NALA Liaison
P. O. Box 352
Brownfield, TX 79316

• Utah

Legal Assistants Association of Utah
Kay D. Bateman, President
Suitter, Axland, et al
175 South West Temple #700
Salt Lake City, UT 84101

Suzanne J. Addison, CLA, NALA Liaison
Woodbury & Kesler, PC
265 East 100 South #300
Salt Lake City, UT 84111

• Virginia

Peninsula Legal Assistants, Inc.
Phyllis T. Anderson, CLAS, President
Jones, Blechman, Woltz & Kelly, P.C.
Habour Centre
2 Eaton Street, Suite 700
Hampton, VA 23669

Diane Morrison, CLA, NALA Liaison
Jones, Blechman, Woltz & Kelly, P.C.
PO Box 12888
600 Thimble Shoals, Suite 200
Newport News, VA 23612-2888

Richmond Association of Legal Assistants
Patricia S. Stout, CLA, President
Signet Bank Corporation
PO Box 25970
Richmond, VA 23260

Nellie J. Foley, CLA, NALA Liaison
Stuart A. Simon & Associates
4900 Cutshaw Avenue
Richmond, VA 23230

Tidewater Association of Legal Assistants
Claire S. Isley, CLA, President
Willcox & Savage, P.C.
1800 Sovran Center
Norfolk, VA 23510

Carol S. Pakradooni, NALA Liaison
4501 Sir John's Lane
Virginia Beach, VA 23455

• Virgin Islands

Virgin Islands Paralegals
Eula Castleberry-Hymes, President
PO Box 990
St. Thomas, VI 00804-0990

Betty L. King, NALA Liaison
PO Box 9121
St. Thomas, VI 00801

• Washington

Association of Paralegal of Washington State-Spokane
Sheila M. White, CLAS, President
2622 E 61 Avenue
Spokane, WA 99223-6912

Columbia Basin College Paralegal Association
Janet E. Taylor, CLA, President
1206 Cottonwood Drive
Richland, WA 99352

Kerri Wheeler Feeney, CLAS, NALA Liaison
7720 W. River Blvd.
Pasco, WA 99301-1739

• West Virgina

Legal Assistants of West Virgina, Inc
Elizabeth B. Gorrell, President
Bowles, Rice, McDavid, et al
PO Box 1386
Charleston, WV 25325

Joanna W. Olds, CLA, NALA Liaison
#6 Warren Place
Charleston, WV 25302

• Wyoming

Legal Assistants of Wyoming
Michele D. Doyle, President
PO Box 548
Jackson, WY 83001

Nancy R. Hole, CLAS, NALA Liaison
Brown & Drew
123 W First, Suite 800
Casper, WY 82601

Databases Used by Law Firms

Following are descriptions of databases used by many law firms:

BRS Information Technologies
1200 Route 7
Latham, NY 12110
(800) 345-4277 (toll-free in continental U.S.)
(518) 783-7251 (collect calls accepted from outside continental U.S.)

This service makes information services available through a wide range of terminals and microcomputers. Telecommunication services are available through TELENET, TYMNET, and UNINET. BRS offers many different private database services, covering a wide variety of disciplines and subjects, through private suppliers. Contact BRS for a list of offerings.

Business Dateline
UMI/Data Courier
620 S. Third Street
Louisville, KY 40202-2475
(800) 626-2823
(502) 589-5575

This service offers a compilation of the full text of articles from more than 180 U.S. and Canadian business publications. It is available on CD-ROM and on-line through DIALOG, Dow Jones News/Retrieval, OCLC Epic, Human Resource Information Network, Nexis and Vu/Text.

BusinessWire
44 Montgomery Street #2185
San Francisco, CA 94104
(800) 227-0845
(415) 986-4422

This service offers the full text of press releases issued by companies, research institutions, and universities announcing information such as new products, research findings, and financial results. It is updated daily and is available on-line from CompuServe, Delphi, DialCom, DIALOG, Dow Jones News/Retrieval, FYI News, NewsNet, Nexis and Vu/Text.

Chemical Abstracts Service (CAS)
2540 Olentangy River Road
P.O. Box 3012
Columbus, OH 43210
(614) 421-3600

Search Assistance Desk:
(800) 848-6533 (toll-free continental U.S. outside OH)
(800) 848-6538 (toll-free in OH)
(614) 421-3698

This service offers bibliographic and chemical structure searching on a wide range of terminals and microcomputers. Optional graphics input and display require Tektronix Plot 10 vector graphics compatibility. Telecommunications services are available through TELENET, TYMNET, and Datex-P (Germany).
On-line databases include *CA File,* which offers journal articles; patents; proceedings from meetings, symposia and edited collections; technical reports; deposited documents; dissertations; and books, and *Registry File,* which offers registry of substances, including unique CAS registry number, molecular structure diagram, molecular formula, structurally descriptive CA index name and synonyms.

CompuServe Information Services
5000 Arlington Centre Blvd.
P.O. Box 20212
Columbus, OH 43220
(800) 848-8199

This service is an on-line information service with over 1,500 databases, including news, weather, electronic mailbox, encyclopedias, shareware, and public domain software.

DIALOG® Information Services, Inc.
3460 Hillview Avenue
Palo Alto, CA 94304
(415) 858-3785
(800) 334-2564

This service provides over 370 databases for access to current and historical information on companies, products, industries, medicine, patents, trademarks, expert witnesses, chemicals, and more. It also provides the complete text of over 800 publications.

Disclosure, Inc.
5161 River Road
Bethesda, MD 20816
(212) 581-1414

This service provides approximately 230 financial-data items on more than 12,000 publicly owned U.S. companies whose securities are traded on the New York Stock Exchange, the American Stock Exchange, NASDAQ, and the OTC National Market System. It is updated monthly and is available on CD-ROM or on-line from BRS Information Technologies, CompuServe, CDC Business Information Services, DataStar, Dow Jones News/Retrieval, Lexis, Quotron Systems, Reuters Historical Information Division and Warner Computer Systems.

Dow Jones News/Retrieval Services
Dow Jones & Co., Inc.
P.O. Box 300
Princeton, NJ 08543-0300
(609)520-4000

This service provides access to 63 different databases covering stock quotes, business related stories and general information. Information can be retrieved concerning a historical text of past filings, past estate values, and past quotes in order to assess the value of a client's estate on a given date.

Dow Jones Business and Finance Report
Dow Jones & Co., Inc.
P.O. Box 300
Princeton, NJ 08543-0300
(609) 520-4000

This service offers the full text of published articles from the *National Business and Employment Weekly* and is updated weekly. It is available on-line from DIALOG and Dow Jones News/Retrieval services.

Information America
600 West Peachtree Street, NW
12th Floor
Atlanta, GA 30308
(404) 892-1800
(800) 235-4008

This service provides on-line access to information used to complete commercial transactions. The information includes secretary of state corporate records, UCC filings, Dun's Business Records Plus, national documents ordering (DOX), People Finder, bankruptcy records, and local courthouse records in some communities.

Legislative Retrieval System
308, The Capitol
Albany, NY 12224
(518) 455-7672
(800) 356-6566

This is the official electronic source of the New York State Legislature. The on-line service offers complete text to NYS consolidated Laws, Bill Text and Bill Status, NYS Chapters, the New York City Code and Charter, and Code of Rules and Regulations of New York State.

Martindale-Hubbell
121 Chanlon Road
New Providence, NJ 07974
(908) 665-6717

Martindale-Hubbell Law Directory provides personal and firm information on over 800,000 lawyers in the United States and is available in book form (16 volumes) or on CD-ROM.

Mead Data Central, Inc.
P.O. Box 933
Dayton, OH 45401
(800) 227-4908

LEXIS is one of the leading computer-assisted legal research services and has extensive files of state and federal case law, codes and regulations. *NEXIS* has the full text of more than 750 publications.

National Library of Medicine
MEDLARS Management Section
8600 Rockville Pike
Bethesda, MD 20894
(800) 638-8480 (toll-free in U.S. and outside MD)
(301) 496-6193

Information services are available through a wide variety of terminals and microcomputers. Telecommunication services are available through TELENET, TYMNET, and UNINET.

The National Library of Medicine, through its *MEDLARS* service, offers a wide variety of medical-related databases. Call the MEDLARS Management Section for further information on available databases.

NewsNet®
Independent Publications
945 Haverford Road
Bryn Mawr, PA 19010
(800) 345-1301 (toll-free in continental U.S. outside PA)
(215) 527-8030

Information services available through a wide range of terminals and microcomputers. Telecommunications services are available through TELENET, TYMNET, and UNINET.

NewsNet oers full-text newsletters, PR (Press Release) Newswire, and UPI (United Press International) Newswire, although UPI is not available for interactive searching. *News-Flash,* an electronic clipping service, allows the user to specify up to ten words or phrases for constant monitoring of all incoming information, including from UPI. Successful matches result in storage and display of headlines for the user at the next time of sign-on, at which point the user may read, delete, or save them.

NewsNet also oers a private database service known as Closed User Group (CUG) with many dierent databases services, covering various disciplines and subjects. Contact NewsNet® for a list of oerings.

Newsearch
Information Access
362 Lakeside Drive
Foster City, CA 94404
(800) 227-8431
(415) 378-5329

This service is an index of 4,000 current news stories, articles, and book reviews on companies, industries, products, economies, and finance. It is updated daily and is available on-line from DIALOG and BRS Information Technologies.

Prentice-Hall Online
1900 East Fourth Street
Suite 130
Santa Ana, CA 92705
(800) 333-8356

This service is an on-line public-record database of corporate, limited partnership, UCC filings, bankruptcy, and other local public-record information such as tax liens, judgments, notice of default and foreclosure. Data are compiled from major state and county jurisdictions nationwide.

Standard & Poor's News
25 Broadway
New York, NY 10004
(212) 208-8622

This service supplies financial and operational information such as interim earnings, management changes, new issues of securities, acquisitions, and buyouts for more than 12,000 companies. It is updated daily and is available on-line from DIALOG, Knowledge Index, Lexis and Nexis.

Thomson & Thomson
500 Victory Road
North Quincy, MA 02171
(617) 479-1600
(800) 692-8833

Two on-line trademark searching services are available: *Compu-Mark Online* provides a fully automatic, menu-driven search of a proposed mark, including the retrieval of phonetically identical marks and other marks with similar prefixes and suffixes, substituted vowels, and anagrams. *Trademarkscan* federal and state databases are available through DIALOG Information Services, both on-line and on CD-ROM, providing searches for trademark names, designs/logos, owner names, goods and services, including those in the United Kingdom.

Trademark Research Corporation
300 Park Avenue South
New York, NY 10010
(212) 228-4084
(800) TRC-MARK

This service provides personalized trademark research services and is affiliated with CCH-Legal Information Services.

West Publishing Company
610 Opperman Drive
Eagan, MN 55123
(800)937-8529 (WESTLAW)

WESTLAW is one of the leading computer-assisted legal research services and provides access to current files of state and federal case law, codes and regulations, including full-text opinions. In addition, WESTLAW allows the user to search by key number and to perform certain kinds of digest searches more easily. You can shepardize on WESTLAW and find the most current case history in West's *Insta-Cite.* Over 200 DIALOG databases are available on WESTLAW. This is helpful for obtaining general legal background information for a case.

WILSONLINE
The H. W. Wilson Company
950 University Avenue
Bronx, NY 10452
(800) 622-4002 (toll-free in U.S. outside NY)
(800) 538-3888 (toll-free in NY)
(212) 588-8998 (collect calls accepted from Canada)

Information services are available through a wide range of terminals and microcomputers. Telecommunication services are available from TELENET and TYMNET.

WILSONLINE databases include: applied science and technology; art index; bibliographic index; biography index; biological and agricultural index; business periodicals index; book review digest; cumulative book index; education index; general science index; humanities index; index to legal periodicals; library literature; social sciences index; subject file associated with each of the preceding databases; journal directory; publishers' directory and name authority file.

H
Litigation Support Software Evaluation Form

Feature/Function	Comments
System Specifications	
Operating system required	You will want to make sure the operating system is compatible with current hardware and software.
Operating system version required	Operating systems are continuously improved and upgraded, and all software has a minimum version requirement. If you are considering putting the software on present equipment, you should check your present operating system to make sure it meets these requirements.
Minimum RAM required	The minimum RAM is not necessarily all the RAM you will need. Most programs today benefit from additional RAM.
Can the system use expanded or extended memory? How?	The use of expanded and extended memory (RAM) usually improves performance.
Minimum hard disk capacity recommended	The programs may reside on your computer's hard disk while the data may be stored on optical disks. You should check the amount of disk space on your hard disk necessary for the programs. If you plan to keep the database on your hard disk as well, you will have to calculate the amount of required disk space. The software vendor can help you with this.
Diskette drive required	Make sure the diskette drive you have is compatible with the media you will receive from the vendor with the programs, updates, and fixes.
Color monitor/card required or supported (VGA high resolution)	Most systems require VGA or better resolution, especially if imaging is used.
Printers required and/or supported?	The software vendor will have a list of printers supported. Make sure the printer you will be using is supported by the software before you buy. Otherwise you may have to buy new printers.
Is the system multi-user?	Multi-user systems can be used by more than one person at a time. You need to know if the software will operate on a PC-LAN, under UNIX, or other multi-user operating system on a minicomputer.
Network operating systems are supported	Make sure the network operating systems that your firm uses, or plans to use, are supported by the software.
Can more than one user work on the same case/database at one time?	Even if a system is multi-user, that doesn't always mean you can use the same database at the same time. Some systems restrict access. Check it out.
Are there limitations on the size of the database/number of abstracts/number of full-text pages?	All litigation support systems are limited by the user's disk storage space. A program cannot handle more files than there is room to store and manipulate. Extremely large databases require the use of external storage media such as CD-ROM disks and/or optical jukebox systems. Image files can require extremely large amounts of permanent storage files; it is not usual for a single image file to be as large as 1 megabyte.

Feature/Function	Comments
Does the system support removable/optical/laser disks?	Full-text documents and images are stored on removable/optical drives with the index stored on the system's hard drive. After a hit,[1] the full-text document or image must be accessed through a hardware interface from the storage device and, in the case of images, displayed on a system specifically designed for the purpose.
Does the system use inverted file software architecture?	Inverted file software architecture refers to a database structure to speed sorting of large and complex databases. It requires less disk space for temporary sort files.
Is file security built into the system by the use of passwords and/or user codes?	Some programs have their own built-in security, others use the security features of the network operating system, and some use both.

User Interface and Help Features

Feature/Function	Comments
Does the system support a mouse?	The mouse interface is becoming more popular for use with graphical user interfaces (GUI).
Is the user interface designed specifically for the legal industry and for litigation support?	Not all products used for litigation support were designed for the legal industry. Those designed for use by lawyers and paralegals with familiar terminology may be easier to learn and use.
Does the user interface use menus?	Menus allow users to select the function they wish to perform rather than having to know special and often cryptic commands.
Do menus support different levels of users?	Not everyone will use all the functions of the system. Lawyers will not input data and data-entry clerks may not search for data. Some systems allow only certain functions to be displayed, depending on the user.
Is the system licensed to use *LEXIS* or other well-known menu clones?	Some systems use well-known menu clones to reduce user learning time and because familiar menus are "friendlier."
Can the user modify existing menus?	Sometimes it is desirable to change the menus to eliminate some of the functions, say, for data-entry clerks. It is desirable for them to have only the functions on their menus they should have access to.
Can the user create menus?	You may want to create special menus for a particular group of users to make it easier for them to use the system.
Is there a command-line interface for experienced users?	After a user has become experienced with a system, menus can slow down the search process. A command-line interface allows the user to turn off or bypass menus and type in standard search or reporting commands.
Is there an on-line help function?	On-line help means the help information displays on the screen when a particular key or combination of keys is pressed.
Is the help function context-sensitive?	Context-sensitive help functions contribute to the overall efficiency of a well-designed program because help is available about the particular feature in use at the time the help key is pressed without the user having to choose from a menu of help subjects.

Profiles and Abstracts

Feature/Function	Comments
Can profiles or abstracts be completed for each document/image in the system?	The terms *profiles, abstracts, surrogates* and *headers* all refer to the summary of information the user enters about each document entered. The profiles can be used alone if the system is used primarily for file management or in conjunction with full-text indexing in more sophisticated litigation support systems.
Are sequential numbers automatically assigned to every profile?	If the system assigns the numbers automatically, it eliminates the necessity for you to keep track of the next available number manually.
Are defined fields used in the profiles?	Without defined fields such as "author" or "recipient," searches cannot be refined; the searcher will have to look at every occurrence of the term, whether or not the occurrence falls within a prescribed definition (a letter written by X rather than a letter mentioning X in the text, for example).
Is the profile screen a fixed, predefined field system?	Fixed field systems contain a certain number of predefined fields in the profile. The labels can be changed by the user, but the number of fields cannot be changed without special customized programming ($). Fixed field programs are limiting in certain respects but eliminate the need for profile design.
Are data fields user-definable?	When creating a profile, you may want to define the fields as used for text, numbers, dates, currency, etc.

[1]A "hit" is the term used for each time a document or other object in the database meets the search criteria and is retrieved for review by the researcher.

Feature/Function	Comments
Can automatic profiles be generated by the system when the file is indexed?	Sometimes it is quicker to let the system create a profile as documents are added to the system. The profile may consist only of the file name, date, and the first lines of the text. These profiles can be edited and finalized later. Automatic profiles are used in full-text systems.
Can different profiles be used for each different type of document on the system?	Sometimes it is preferable to have different profiles for memos, letters, briefs, depositions, transcripts, etc.
Can printouts be created that list information contained in profile "hits"?	Once the system has located profiles meeting the search criteria, it is desirable to print out the profile information.
Can the information to be printed out be defined by the user?	The system should have a report writer or other facility to allow the user to create reports of any information in the system, at any time.
Are the information choices presented in menu form, or must the user have knowledge/training in report-writing techniques?	You should review how easy it is to design your own reports.
Can the profile field labels be altered by the user?	If the system has fixed profiles, can the user change the name of any of the fields?
Can the field type be controlled by the user?	Field type refers to whether or not the field can be designated *alpha, numeric, date,* or *dollar amount.* Only alpha characters are allowed in an alpha field; only validated data information is allowed in a field designated as a date field.
Can the profile fields be validated by the use of a validation table?	A validation table can be a list of possible choices for a field that the user chooses from when completing the profile, or it can be a table to which the program refers to verify whether information has been entered correctly. Validation tables help eliminate erroneous entries due to misspelling and typographical error, etc.
Does the system have a speed-entry feature?	Speed-entry tables allow the user to choose from a menu of possible choices and enter the information by typing a corresponding number or highlighting the information and pressing the ENTER key.
Does the system include a concordance?	A concordance is nothing more than a listing of all indexed words.
Does the concordance listing display the number of times each word appears in the database?	It is often helpful to know how many times a word occurs in all the documents and profiles in the database.
Is the concordance listing alphabetized?	The concordance should be alphabetized.
Can speed entries be made from the concordance listing for searches?	It is useful for the user to be able to review the concordance to see what words are in the database and select one or more of the words to be included in the search request without having to type in the word. This is usually accomplished by placing the cursor on the word and pressing the ENTER key.
Does the system have a thesaurus to display synonyms for copying to the search line for use during word searches?	A thesaurus can make your searches more effective by including words with the same or similar meaning as the search term you are using.
Can the user add words and synonyms to the thesaurus?	A thesaurus is more effective if the user can add words to it as it becomes necessary.
Does the system provide space for attorney comments in each profile?	If the user designs the profiles, then a comments section can be included. The thing to consider here is that comment sections require a lot of disk space.
Can words in the attorney comments be searched and retrieved?	Just because the attorney adds comments doesn't mean they become searchable. Make sure they become a part of the searchable database.

Indexing

Is the system capable of full-text indexing?	Full-text indexing is not necessarily a substitute for well-planned document profiles. More words can be searched with full-text indexing, but it is more difficult to carefully define a search to eliminate unwanted material, because words are used in so many different ways within documents. Since full-text indexing eliminates dependency on coding and keywords, however, the system may be searchable sooner than a system requiring coding.
Can fully indexed documents be profiled?	It may be preferable to create a profile, or summary, of a document so the researcher can review it instead of having to read the entire document to know what the subject matter is.
Can material be keyed directly into the system and then be indexed and searched?	Some systems allow the user to key data directly into comment fields, and index the data for later searches.
Can the system handle both paper documents and electronic transcript files?	If the system you are reviewing can't handle electronic transcripts, it is obsolete and you should not consider purchasing it.

Feature/Function	Comments
Does the system require proprietary data files for indexing?	ASCII files must be in a specific format for most programs if they are to be handled properly. Some programs require a proprietary format—a format only the program or service produces or uses. This requirement can severely limit the use of court transcript files prepared in ASCII and increase the cost of including such documents in the system.
Does the system require special page-break codes in ASCII files before the document is indexed?	Some programs require a document to be specially page-marked by a separate software product after it has been converted to ASCII format and before it is indexed. Some programs have the capability of handling embedded page numbers or can generate page numbers whenever a form feed is detected in the file or when any user-defined number of lines are read.
How are paper documents transferred to the system for indexing?	Scanning is not built into basic litigation support systems. A scanner must be bought as a separate piece of equipment, and the cost depends on scanning speed and the quality of output desired. In addition to the scanner itself, special optical character recognition (OCR) software must be purchased to convert the printed page to electronic files for use in indexing. Additional computer hardware (a board or card) is sometimes required as well.
Is editing required before the scanned document can be indexed?	Documents can be indexed before editing but the integrity of the database is compromised unless each indexed document is first carefully checked for accuracy and edited where necessary. The spell-checking feature of word processing software facilitates this. Also, some OCR software has a built-in spell-check feature.
Can the system convert word-processing files to ASCII files automatically for indexing?	Some systems require a word-processing document to be converted to ASCII by the word-processing software before transfer to the litigation-support system for indexing. Others have the ability to do the conversion within the litigation support program with the user specifying the word-processing software and version used to create the document.
Can multi-document files be indexed and stored without having to split the file into separate files?	Although multi-document files can be indexed and stored without having to split the documents into multiple files, some programs will retrieve the entire file if it matches the search criteria instead of only the sub-document matching the search.
Can new files be indexed automatically without having to specify individual files to be indexed?	Is it possible to tell the system to index all files in a certain subdirectory, or other group without having to type in the names of the files one at a time?
Is automatic indexing optional?	You may want to select specific files to be indexed.
Can adding new documents to the system be delayed for batch input?	The indexing process is sometimes lengthy and requires the database not be accessed by other users. It is preferable in these situations to do the indexing at night or at other times when there is not heavy use of the database for research.

Hypertext and Notes

Can word-processing files be retrieved from within the system?	This feature allows a word-processing document to be viewed and edited within the word-processing software, "launched" from within the litigation-support software.
Can the litigation support system be accessed from within word-processing software?	This feature allows a search to be made on word-processing documents and then the word-processing file to be retrieved from within the word-processing program with all formatting intact.
Can documents and images be linked through a hypertext feature?	This feature allows multiple related documents or images to be retrieved at one time with one set of search criteria; notes can be created, attached, and retrieved with documents stored on the system.
Can notes be created and linked to stored files and then searched?	Sometimes documents can be linked, but the attorneys' notes cannot be linked to any document other than the one in which they were created.
Can "cut and paste" operations be performed on notes and word processing files?	"Cut and paste" is simply a way of moving or copying text from one part of a document to another, or from a document to a note or different document.

Witness Lists

Does the system provide witness and/or potential witness information?	Some systems allow names to be input and categorized as "witnesses" through the use of codes in the profile or header information. Reports can then be produced on witnesses and the documents pertaining to them.
Is witness information automatically created from document entry?	Can codes be used to develop witness lists as documents are added to the system?

Feature/Function	Comments
Can subjective information be included about witnesses?	This would fall into the area of *hypertext*, or the ability to add notes about the documents or text retrieved during a search. The notes would then be linked to the witness's name and would appear when the hypertext key is pressed to reveal any attachments.
Can the results of witness information searches be printed?	If a separate function is used to review witness information, make sure the information can be printed just like other "hits."

Searches	
Can individual words be searched?	Obviously, this is a very basic function.
Can partial words be searched?	A partial word might be a "root" search or any other part of a word.
Does the system automatically search for all variants of the word (rooting) including plural, past, and future tense, etc.?	"Root" searches are a form of partial word searches.
Are common words such as THE, etc. excluded from indexing?	Common words used in almost every document are sometimes referred to as *stopwords* and are not indexed in some programs. The user should be able to edit the stopword list to prevent elimination of common words when desired in a particular case.
Can numbers in the text of a document be indexed and searched?	Again, this is a basic function, but don't assume the system can do it. Check it out.
Can phrases be searched?	A phrase might be referred to as a *string*.
Is a distinction always made between profiles and full text in searches?	Is the program separated into two distinct parts, with no overlap between operations performed on profiles and operations performed on full text?
Can a distinction be made between information in a profile and full text for searches?	If the program doesn't distinguish between them, is it possible for the user to specify a search on profiles only or full-text only.
Can Boolean operators be used in searches?	Boolean operators allow searches to be refined using search terms such as AND, OR, NOT, and SAME SENTENCE or SAME PARAGRAPH.
Is proximity searching available?	Proximity searching refers to searching for a word within a certain number of words, lines, sentences of another word or phrase.
Can date ranges be searched?	Many systems allow searches for specific dates, but not for a range of dates.
Can ITEM ranges be searched?	ITEM refers to the document ID assigned by the system to each document indexed. It is sometimes helpful to search for a group of documents within a certain range of ITEM numbers.
Are question-and-answer pairs kept together in searches?	The system should keep question-and-answer pairs of written or oral testimony together to facilitate a better understanding of the text. An answer may be meaningless without reference to the question answered. Some systems allow the user to code the data to keep question-and-answer pairs together.
Can wild-card searches be made?	A wild-card search is specified by putting an asterisk "*" after the character(s) keyed. Example: RE* returns RENT, REVENUE, REAL, etc.
Can the user zoom to finer and finer levels of detail of the document or file?	Zooming refers to moving to different levels of a document. The first level may be the profile, the second may be specific paragraphs containing the term searched for, and another level may be the sentence level.
Can words of interest be returned ranked in presumed order of relevance?	Some systems allow the user to specify which terms are more important and the results of the search to be ranked in a similar order.
Can a search be made for similar documents ranked according to similarity?	A similar document would be a duplicate, or near duplicate, or a document following the same format with many of the same words or terms.
Are programs used to display document or images launched from within the litigation support system?	In some programs, it is possible to move out of the litigation support program and to "view" the document as an image, word-processing document, spreadsheet, or desktop publishing document in the program used to create the document. This is called *launching*.
Can the user scroll through the directory listing of documents found in a search?	If the system locates many "hits," it may be preferable to review the names of the documents to select the ones for further analysis.
Can the results of searches be printed?	Review the format of reports to make sure the information is clearly presented in an easy-to-understand format. Reports should be uncluttered.
Can the user choose which portion of the search results are to be printed?	You may want to print only the first 50 documents or block a group of "hits" and print only those.
Can searches be restricted to recently added documents only?	In some programs, searches can be confined to recently input documents more easily than others. You should ask how easy this is to do.

Feature/Function	Comments
Can document hits be sorted into user-specified order according to profile information?	Once the search has retrieved relevant material, it is useful to sort the documents in various ways based on the fields in the profile. You may want them sorted by date, author, document type, etc.
Can ASCII text of document or image files be printed after a search?	It is not always easy (or quick) to print an image file, and considerable attention should be given to the hardware configuration necessary to permit this.
Can partial text of documents be printed after a search?	Some programs allow the user to block certain sections of text to be saved, moved, and printed.
Can search sets be saved for use at a later time.	Defining the terms of a search is time-consuming, so the product you select should allow you to save the search set you have defined for later use.

Imaging

Does the system handling imaging?	A litigation-support system capable of "handling" images does not necessarily store and display images within the main software framework. Some create descriptive profiles about the image and related relevant information. Others handle text files and images within the same database.
Are profiles used to keep track of and search for images?	Most likely profiles will be used to describe the images and also to facilitate searching.
Are image files stored within the same case database?	Some systems store images separately from the main database, with the profiles stored in the main database. This is done to improve performance, because the image files are so large.
Can images be viewed without leaving the main litigation support system where profile searches are performed?	Some systems require the user to exit the system to use a different program to view the images. Newer programs don't require this extra step (and extra time).
Are images compressed to reduce the amount of storage space required?	If images aren't compressed, don't buy the system.
Can the system decompress image files on demand?	When an image is selected for viewing, the software should automatically decompress it without the user having to go through a separate step.
Can images be displayed with pan and scroll?	Pan and scroll are ways for the user to control the screen and move about the image more easily than the single-space cursor movement for text.
Can the system print raster images?	Images are stored in different formats, sometimes referred to as raster images or tiff header files. Make sure your printer and software can print these if you plan to print images.
Can the system handle "voice" recordings?	Combinations of voice recordings, images, and text are the wave of the future and can all be stored on the same optical disk.
Can images be input via a "paint" program?	A "paint" program refers to one of the many graphics programs available for PCs.

System Utilities

Does the system provide maintenance utilities?	Maintenance utilities consist of file utilities, database reorganization, etc.
Does the system provide a backup and restore facility?	If you aren't putting the software on a centralized system such as a PC-LAN, you will be responsible for backing up the system periodically. In this event, it is good to have the backup functions as an integral part of the program.
Does the system provide for data transfer from active to inactive storage?	This is commonly known as archiving. Once documents or other data are no longer needed in the database, there should be a means of removing them and saving them elsewhere. If this is not done periodically, the database will grow and grow until performance of the system degrades.
Does the system create and manage computer directories and subdirectories for cases automatically?	The program should create the necessary subdirectories without the user having to go to the operating system level to do so.
Can the system generate document number labels?	These are the labels used in the document logging process. Labels are to be placed on the documents as they are entered into the system and a document ID is assigned.
Can the database be reorganized by the user to speed up retrieval or reduce time needed to add documents to the system?	Most systems have a database reorganization feature. The question here is really how easy it is to utilize the reorganization function.

Feature/Function	Comments
Services	
Does product support include litigation support services *per se?*	Some vendors selling database products also are in the business of helping law firms develop their litigation support system, while others simply sell the software.
Will the vendor create the database for you?	The level of vendor support and service should be balanced against your firm's needs.
Does the vendor offer product training?	Some of the database products don't really require formal training, depending on the user's level of computer expertise.
Does product training include training in database development as well, and in how to use the program once the database has been constructed?	Database construction is probably the area where most users need training. A properly constructed database is the key to a good litigation support system.
Are training manuals provided?	A good tutorial is helpful if you are not going to have training by the vendor.
Are training videos provided?	Training videos are nice because you can be "trained" at a time convenient to you. They can also be used for all staff who will use the system and as new staff are hired.
Is there an 800 number for product support?	Most vendors offer an 800 number for toll-free support. But the support itself is usually not free.
Are there annual or monthly maintenance fees?	Annual support agreements are common and will entitle you to a certain level of support from the vendor. Also, as the product is improved and corrected, the upgrades may be made available to you at no additional charge.
Are there other costs involved in ongoing support?	Hourly fees and out-of-pocket expenses are often in addition to support/maintenance agreements.

Relational Databases

• Image Databases

Justlaw, Inc. (Annotate)
950 Third Avenue
28th Floor
New York, NY 10022
(212) 888-1160

The LITIDEX Company (LITIDEX)
The LITIDEX Building
Suite 200, One Park Ten Place
Houston, Texas 77084
(800) 548-4339
(713) 578-8800

• Personal Information Managers[1]

Act!
Conductor Software, Inc.
9208 West Royal Lane
Irving, TX 75063
(800) 627-3958
(214) 929-4749
Price: $395

DayFlo Tracker
DayFlo Software Corporation
17701 Mitchell Avenue
North Irvine, CA 92714
(800) 367-5369
Price: $249

Info-XL
Valor Software Corporation
2005 Hamilton Avenue
San Jose, CA 95125
(408) 559-1100
Price: $295

Lotus Agenda
Lotus Development Corporation
55 Cambridge Parkway
Cambridge, MA 02142
(617) 572-8500
Price: $395

Professional File
Software Publishing Corporation
1901 Landings Drive
P.O. Box 7210
Mountain View, CA 94039
Price: $299

Q&A
Symantec Corporation
10201 Torre Avenue
Cupertino, CA 95014
(408) 253-9600
Price: $349

• Relational Database Products

Advanced Revelation
Revelation Technologies
3633 136th Place, SE
Bellevue, WA 98006
(206) 643-9898
Price: $950

---

[1]Prices are approximate and as of the date of publication.

DataEase
DataEase International, Inc.
7 Cambridge Drive
Trumbull, CT 06611
(203) 374-8000
(800) 243-5123
Price $600; LAN version $700

DBASE IV 1.0
Ashton-Tate Corporation
20101 Hamilton Ave
Torrance, CA 90502
(210) 329-8000
Price: $795

Justlaw, Inc.
950 Third Avenue
28th Floor
New York, NY 10022
(212) 888-1160
Price: $1,000; LAN version $1,000-$1,750

Paradox
Ansa—A Borland Company, Inc.
4585 Scotts Valley Dr.
Scotts Valley, CA 95066
(408) 438-8400
Price: $725; LAN version $995

R:Base for DOS
Microrim, Inc.
3925 159th Avenue, NE
P.O. Box 97022
Redmond, WA 98052-9722
(206) 885-2000
Price: $725; LAN version up to $2,695

Professional Oracle
Oracle Corporation
20 Davis Drive
Belmont, CA 94002
(415) 598-8000
Price: $1,295

Summation
Summation Legal Technologies
Suite 2050
595 Market Street
San Francisco, CA 94105
(800) 735-7866
Price: $1195; LAN version $3495

• Field Oriented Database Products

Inmagic
Inmagic Inc.
2067 Massachusetts Avenue
Cambridge, MA 02140
(617) 661-8124
Price: $1400

• Database Managers for Apple Macintosh

DBASE MAC
Ashton-Tate Corporation
20101 Hamilton Ave
Torrance, CA 90502
(210) 329-8000
Price: $795

File Maker
Claris
440 Clyde Avenue
Mountain View, CA 94043
(415) 960-1500
Price: $295

FoxBASE Plus-MAC
Fox Software
118 W. South Boundary
Perrysburg, OH 43551
(419) 874-0162
Price: $395

Federal Agencies

The following federal agencies may be helpful in obtaining information regarding the investigation of a lawsuit.

Federal Aviation Administration (FAA), Department of Transportation, Washington, D.C. Provides national guidance and policy on accident prevention in general aviation. Provides reports and information regarding airplane accidents, airplane safety standards, airplane schedules and routes. For information on all accidents and incidents involving aircraft, contact the Accident/Incident Analysis Branch, Air Traffic Service, Federal Aviation Administration, Department of Transportation, Washington, D.C.

National Highway Traffic Safety Administration, Department of Transportation, Washington, D.C. This department carries out programs relating to the safety performance of motor vehicles and related equipment, motor vehicle drivers, and pedestrians. Administers programs and studies aimed at reducing economic losses in motor vehicle crashes and repairs, through general motor vehicle programs. Also administers the federal odometer law, and a uniform national maximum speed limit, and promulgates average fuel economy standards for passenger and nonpassenger motor vehicles.

Federal Highway Administration, Washington, D.C. This department maintains information regarding automobile safety and highways, including safety standards of trucking companies, such as driver practices (e.g., necessity for regular rest periods), and other safety regulations.

National Weather Service, The National Oceanic and Atmospheric Administration (NOAA), Department of Commerce, Washington, D.C. You can obtain certified copies of the weather reports for any given date.

Branch of Distribution, Geological Survey, Federal Center, Denver, Colorado. You can obtain topographical maps for each state and territory.

Internal Revenue Service. You can locate tax rates and schedules from prior years.

Department of Agriculture, Washington, D.C. You can obtain literature regarding poisonous plants, animals, insects, or other species. (For example, one paralegal was requested to research information on blackbirds in a nuisance action where the birds were disturbing the peace and quiet).

Census Bureau, Department of Commerce, Washington, D.C. You can acquire statistics and other information regarding the population of cities, states, and towns in the United States. The Census Bureau has numerous other miscellaneous statistics regarding ages, employment, number of persons in household, and other standard information listed on the census questionnaire for the requested year. You can also get some of this information from your state archives, local chamber of commerce, or from the historian for the local chapter of the Daughters of the American Revolution.

Occupational Safety and Health Administration (OSHA), Department of Labor, Washington, D.C. You can obtain information regarding safety standards of particular products.

Employment Standards Administration, Department of Labor, Washington, D.C. You can request information regarding wages and working conditions, including workers' compensation, child labor standards, and equal employment opportunity requirements.

Department of Justice, Antitrust Division, Washington, D.C. This department can assist you in inquiries regarding antitrust practices.

Federal Trade Commission, Washington, D.C. This agency offers assistance regarding credit discrimination practices, and matters involving fraud, monopoly or restraints on trade, or unfair or deceptive trade practices.

Patent and Trademark Office, Department of Commerce, Washington, D.C. Information and communications involving patent and trademark infringements can be coordinated through this office. The Office of Enrollment and Discipline, Patent and Trademark Office, Washington, D.C., will provide a list of patent attorneys.

State Agencies

The following state agencies may be able to provide you useful information when conducting an investigation of a lawsuit:

Department of Streets and Highways. You can request blueprints of state highways, tunnels, and bridges. You also may be able to secure information regarding speed limits and traffic signs and lights in a particular area.

Department of Motor Vehicles. In some states, this department will provide driver's license information and individual driving records to attorneys at a nominal cost.

Department of Labor and Industry. You can obtain copies of pamphlets with rules and regulations concerning industrial accidents and safety standards in various industries. (For example, in an action involving persons injured from a falling scaffold, this information would be helpful.)

Geology Department. You can obtain geological surveys upon request for a nominal charge.

Department of Corporations, Secretary of State. You can request general information regarding domestic and foreign corporations that are qualified to do business in that particular state, such as the registered agent and address for service of process, principal place of business, officers, the county and date of incorporation, and information regarding annual reports.

Department of Vocational Rehabilitation. You can request information such as the potential ability for a disabled person to become rehabilitated. For example, if your client is being sued by a person who was injured and consequently disabled, this information would be useful in determining the potential for that person to become fully or partially rehabilitated and able to work. You could estimate the value of the future earning potential of the injured person based on this information.

Department of Employment. You can obtain information from this department regarding possible employment opportunities for a particular skill or trade based on an individual's qualifications. This information is useful for estimating future earning potential.

Department of Insurance. You can request information regarding the state's requirements for individual personal automobile liability insurance coverage, or general information regarding requirements of insurance companies doing business in the state.

Department of Business and Professions. You can request general information regarding licensing requirements of particular trades and businesses.

Bureau of Vital Statistics. You may obtain certified copies of birth and death records for a fee.

Department of the State Revenue Commissioner. This department maintains records of state taxes paid by individuals on personal property. In some states, for a nominal fee this department will provide you with the following information regarding an individual's ownership of personal property, such as automobiles, boats, trailers, campers, and mobile homes:

1. Identification number.
2. Current title number.
3. Year, make, and model.
4. Number of cylinders of automobile and engine number.
5. Legal owner.
6. Registered owner.
7. Information regarding any liens on the property, such as name of lien holder, amount of lien, date of lien, and type of lien.
8. The last date any action was taken on the property, e.g., if it was sold or the title was transferred.

Copies of any documents filed relating to this information are available by request in some states. Requests for an information search may be made by either supplying a name or an automobile license tag number.

L | County and Local Agencies

The following county and local agencies can be found in most states, and typically, will provide the information indicated.

County Tax Assessor's Office. This department has public records on property ownership that includes the title in which the property is held, lot and block number, street address, tax assessment number, and the rate at which the property is assessed. If you know either the location of the property or the name of the owner, you can find this information easily.

Voter Registrar. Voter registration records are available to the public by request and usually include the following information: name and address of the individual, date or year of birth, sex, race, and voting precinct.

District Attorney's Office. This office retains information regarding individual criminal records. You may need your attorney to make the initial contact with this office, because it might be reluctant to release information to a non-lawyer that is not a matter of public record.

Bureau of Missing Persons. This agency is often a part of the local police department. You must file an official report of a missing person before it can assist you.

City Attorney's Office. The city attorney has information only on misdemeanors and violations of city ordinances. However, often the city attorney has personal knowledge of certain persons in the community, especially if the plaintiff, defendant, potential witness, or missing person whom you are investigating is of ill repute. In addition, this office can frequently refer you to additional sources of information in the community or to those persons or agencies who can do so.

County Coroner's Office. This office retains extensive records on circumstances surrounding deaths. If an open inquest was held on the particular death you are investigating, you may obtain copies of the transcript of the testimony. You may ob-

tain copies of the affidavits involved for a closed inquest. If you can arrange for an interview, you might be able to obtain information regarding the coroner's office personnel's personal observations on the circumstances of the death.

In any death case, find out if an inquest will be held by contacting the coroner's office immediately, and find out if it will be open to the public so that you may attend. Also, check to see whether there will be an autopsy, and ask whether you can obtain copies of the autopsy report.

City Chamber of Commerce. This office retains a storehouse of information regarding local businesses and their products and services. It often provides various free maps, charts, and brochures.

Better Business Bureau. This is a reliable source for inquiring into the business reputation of local businesses, because this office regularly receives complaints from previous customers and consumers of local businesses. Most reputable local businesses are members of this organization. It may be able to provide you with information regarding previous criminal schemes conducted in the area and name those persons involved in such criminal schemes. You might inquire whether there are any other consumer groups in the area that can also assist you.

City Department of Public Works (Transportation). You can usually obtain blueprints or diagrams (to scale) of streets, roads, and highways located in the city to help you locate and thus obtain a description of the scene of an accident. Also, local public transportation routes are available.

City Traffic Department. This department is an invaluable source of information regarding the sequence and timing of traffic lights at any location in the city. Often computers control traffic lights. This department conducts regular checks and maintains reports on these signals, reflecting, for example, how many seconds each light or turn signal is on. Such information might be used to impeach the testimony of a plaintiff, defendant, or witness who testifies to a particular sequence of the light.

In some cities traffic department personnel will accompany you to the scene of the accident to explain the sequence and time-cycle of the traffic signals. They often will appear in court to testify as expert witnesses. In some cities you may obtain copies of the traffic count (density of traffic) at a particular accident scene.

Credit Bureaus. More credit bureaus are making information available to consumers and creditors. Dun and Bradstreet, for example, provides credit reports to companies for a fee.

M

Useful Abbreviations of Legal Terms and Law Office Terminology*

Affidavit	afdt	Estate	est
Agency hearing	ct	Examine	rev
Agent	ag	Executive Committee	E.C.
Agreement	K		
Assignment	asmt	Federal	fed
Attorney	atty	Foreclosure	forc
Bank	bk	General Counsel	G.C.
Bankrupt	br		
Because	b/c	Hearing Preparation	tpr
Beneficiary	benef		
Between	b/t	Investigation	res
Bill of Sale	b/s		
Board of Directors	B of D	Judgment	judg
Bona fide purchaser	bfp		
Building	bldg	Landlord	LL
		Letter from	lf
Chairman of Board	C of B	Letter to	lt
Client	cl	Liable	l
Community Property	com prop or cp	Lien Holders	lienhs
Concerning, with respect to	re:		
Conference with	cw	Mechanics' lien (materialman's lien)	m/m
Consideration	con	Memorandum from	mf
Contract	K	Memorandum to	mt
Copy of letter from	clf	Miscellaneous	misc
Corporation	corp	Mortgage	mtg
Correspondence from	lf	Motion for Summary Judgment	msj
Correspondence to	lt	Motion to Dismiss	m(d)
Court	ct		
Court Appearance	cta	Necessary (necessaries)	neces
Creditor	cr	Negligence (negligent)	neg
		Not	nt
Damages	dams		
Debtor	dr	Opinion	ops
Defendant	D or △	Opposing Attorney	tratty
Deposition	dpn		
Director	dtr	Plaintiff	P or π
District	dist	Preparation for	prep
Draft, drafting	dft	Preparation of	dft

---

*Many of these abbreviations can be used on time slips and records.

Presumption . . . . .pr
Principle; principal . . . . .prin
Purchaser. . . . . .pur

Receiver . . . . .rcr
Regarding, regards . . . . .re
Research . . . . .res
Reviewing, review of . . . . .rev

Security deed. . . . . .s.d.
Shareholder/stockholder .sh
State. . . . . .st
Study . . . . .rev

Telephone call from. . . . . .tf
Telephone call to. . . . . .tt

Telephone conference with . . . . .tcw
Tenant. . . . . .t
Travel. . . . . .tvl
Trial preparation . . . . .trp
Trustee . . . . .tee

Warranty . . . . .wy
Warranty deed. . . . . .w.d.
With . . . . .w/
Withdrawn . . . . .w/d
Without . . . . .w/o

Year. . . . . .yr

N

Trite Words and Phrases to Avoid

Instead of	Use
a majority of	most
a number of	numerous or many
along the lines of	like
are of the same opinion	agree
as is the case	as
as of this date	today
as to	about
at an earlier date	previously or before
at the present time	now or currently
at this point in time	now or today
based on the fact that	because
by means of	by
completely full	full
definitely proved	proved
despite the fact that	although
due to the fact that	because or since
during the course of	during
fewer in number	fewer
finalize	end
first of all	first
for the purpose of	for
for the reason that	because, since
from the point of view of	for
give rise to	cause
has the capability of	can, may
in a satisfactory manner	satisfactorily
in a very real sense	(leave out)
in case	if
in close proximity	close, near

Glossary

Abstract A short synopsis of a document used in litigation support to take the place of the document itself.

Abstract of Judgment An authenticated or *exemplified* copy of the original judgment.

Acknowledgment of Service (Proof of Service) A statement acknowledging that the particular pleading or other paper was received by a party or his/her attorneys.

Admission A statement made in a pleading or in discovery admitting the truth of the allegations made by the opponent.

Affidavit A sworn statement in writing that is sometimes attached to and supports a pleading or motion.

Affirm An act by the appellate court declaring a judgment, decree, or order is valid and right and must stand as rendered.

Affirmative Defense A response to the plaintiff's claim that attacks the plaintiff's legal right to bring an action while not attacking the truth of the claim.

Allegation A statement made by a party who claims it can be proved as a fact.

Amend To change or improve. An amended pleading may set forth new facts, omit facts, or change the facts as previously presented.

Annotated Describes a document or book that lists cases that interpret the statutes.

Answer A pleading in response to a complaint that may admit or deny allegations made.

Appeal The procedure for seeking review in a superior (i.e., appellate) court of an inferior (i.e., trial) court's decision.

Appearance The coming into court as the party of a suit, either in person or represented by an attorney, whether as plaintiff or defendant.

Appellant The person initiating an appeal.

Appellate Court A court having jurisdiction over the appeal and review of decisions of lower courts.

Appellate Jurisdiction The authority to hear an appeal from the lower courts.

Appellee The person defending against an appeal.

Arbitration The process used to resolve disputes in which a neutral third party (arbitrator) renders a decision after both parties have had an opportunity to be heard.

ASCII Computer codes that define number and letter characters.

Assumption of the Risk A doctrine meaning that a plaintiff cannot recover for an injury to which he or she assents.

Attachment The legal process of seizing another's property for the purpose of securing satisfaction of a judgment yet to be rendered.

Automated Litigation Support A system referring to the management and control of documents produced during the discovery process for later retrieval during the trial preparation and trial phase.

Averments Allegations in a pleading.

Bankruptcy The procedure under federal law in which a debtor's remaining assets are distributed among the creditors, thereby discharging the debtor from any further obligation, or a procedure in which the debtor's debt structure is reorganized.

Bates Machine Numbering machines that produce sequential numbers automatically.

Blueback Heavy paper used to cover complaints. Some bluebacks have return-of-service forms printed on one side. Many states no longer use bluebacks.

Bond A written agreement to pay a certain amount of money on or before a certain future date. In an appeal, a bond insures the appellee that he or she will be paid if any damages are incurred because of the delay caused by the appellant's appeal, assuming it is not successful in overturning the decision of the trial court.

Boolean Logic A system of logic that establishes rules for relationships between computer search terms.

Brief   A written document that states the facts and points of law that are an attorney's basis for argument before a court.

Burden of Proof   The duty of affirmatively proving a fact or facts in dispute on an issue raised between the parties in a cause. If the burden is not met, the party with the burden will lose the issue or the case.

Causes of Action   The claim upon which relief may be granted in an action. In other words, a "right to sue."

CD-ROM   A compact disc on which a large amount of digitized read-only data can be stored.

Certiorari **(Writ of Petition for)**   Commonly used to refer to the Supreme Court of the United States, which uses the writ of certiorari as a discretionary device to choose the cases it wishes to hear.

Challenge   There are two types of challenges: A juror may be *challenged for cause* when it can be shown that he or she probably cannot render an impartial judgment. A *peremptory challenge* may be executed against a juror without any reason given. Challenges for cause are unlimited in number; peremptory challenges are usually limited in number.

Charge (Jury Instruction, Jury Charge, or Point for Charge)   An instruction to the jury given by the judge after the closing argument that instructs the jury on the law. Usually these are prepared by counsel for both parties and selected by the court.

Circumstantial Evidence   Circumstantial evidence allows the inference that a certain thing has occurred.

Class Action   A lawsuit brought in the name of one party on behalf of a large group of plaintiffs or against a large group of defendants brought together because of common characteristics.

Code Pleading   If code pleading governs in the applicable jurisdiction, the answer must contain more detail than in a notice-pleading jurisdiction.

Comparative Negligence   This doctrine permits a plaintiff who is contributorily negligent to recover based upon the percentage of the plaintiff's negligence.

Complaint   A written pleading that commences the lawsuit and sets the cause of action.

Concurrent Jurisdiction   When two courts have jurisdiction over the same case, they have concurrent jurisdiction.

Conflict of Interest   Situations whereby the representation by counsel of two opposing parties, or persons or entities related to opposing parties, would be unethical.

Conform   To conform a signature in a complaint is to indicate that it was signed by inserting "/s/" together with the person's name, either typed or printed.

Contract   An agreement between two or more parties for the doing or not doing of something specified.

Contributory Negligence   A defense to negligence based on the claim that the act or omission of the plaintiff was a contributing factor to the injury caused by the defendant's negligence.

Counterclaim   A claim presented by the defendant in opposition to or as a deduction from the claim of the plaintiff.

Counts   In a complaint, each separate claim or cause of action is set forth as a separate count. A complaint may contain several counts.

Crossclaims   A claim made by co-defendants or co-plaintiffs against each other, and not against an opposing party in the litigation.

Database   A collection of organized data in electronic form that can be accessed and manipulated by specialized computer software.

Default Judgment   Judgment entered by the clerk or the court against a party who has failed to defend against a claim that has been brought by another party.

Defendant   The party against whom a lawsuit has been instituted.

Demand   (1) The portion of the pleading that requests relief, usually occurring at the end of the pleading. (2) The assertion of a legal right; a legal obligation asserted in the courts.

Demurrer   An allegation by the defendant that even if the facts stated in the complaint were true, there is no legal basis for the action.

Denial   A response by the defendant to material alleged by plaintiff in the complaint.

Deponent   Testifying party.

Deposition   A formal procedure whereby a party or witness answers questions under oath prior to trial.

Digest   A summary of testimony obtained during a deposition.

Directed Verdict   A request by counsel upon motion that a decision be rendered by the court because there is insufficient evidence on all elements for the case to go to the jury for consideration.

Discovery   A formal procedure governed by court rules and sanctions in which opposing counsel exchange information in the lawsuit.

Diversity of Citizenship   Exists when parties of a lawsuit are citizens of different states and the matter in controversy exceeds $50,000.

Docket   (1) The record in the clerk's office kept to record the pleadings and activities of a case. (2) In the law office, the system for controlling the documents and activities of a case.

Document Surrogate   A class of coding using abstracts, extracts, key-word coding, or document images.

Domesticating a Judgment The legal process of bringing the judgment into another state and making it legally acceptable.

Domicile The place that is the fixed and permanent home and principal establishment of an individual.

Duty The obligation of due care owed by one person to another.

E-Mail (Electronic mail) Messages between individuals on a computer network.

Equity Based on English law, equity is justice administered according to fairness as opposed to the strict rules of common law.

Estoppel A principle that bars an individual from alleging or denying a fact because of that individual's previous conduct.

Evidence The means by which an act is established; testimony.

Ex Parte A statement prepared for, on behalf of, or on the application of one party only.

Exclusive Jurisdiction The right of one court to hear specific types of cases to the exclusion of other courts.

Execution The process of obtaining the assets of the judgment debtor for the payment of a certain amount of money. A writ of execution, commonly called a *fi. fa.* is obtained.

Exhibit A document or object used as evidence at trial, such as letters or objects.

Expert A witness with established credentials who gives an opinion based on his or her expertise.

Extracts Portions of the text taken verbatim and entered as the document surrogate instead of an abstract.

Federal-Question Jurisdiction The basis for federal-question jurisdiction is the U.S. Constitution, a federal law, or a treaty of the United States.

Fi. Fa. (Fieri Facias) Writ of execution directing the sheriff to satisfy a judgment from the debtor's property.

Field Designates a certain type of information such as client name, matter number, or attorney initials.

File A collection of related information stored on a computer disk.

Foreign Corporation A corporation incorporated in a state other than the one in which it is doing business.

Forum A court of justice; a place of jurisdiction.

Forum Shopping The process whereby attorneys pick the forum they believe would best suit their client's interests.

Full-Text Storage The entry into the database of the entire document text verbatim; this eliminates key-word coding.

Garnishee A person who has money or property of the judgment debtor in his or her possession, or who owes the judgment debtor a debt to which money or property is attached.

Garnishment A proceeding to recover money or property belonging to or being held by a third person, which property is owed to the defendant debtor in a lawsuit.

General Denial A blanket denial of all the allegations in the entire complaint. It may be used to respond to an unverified complaint.

General Jurisdiction The power of a court to hear all controversies brought before it within the legal bounds of rights and remedies.

Guardian *ad litem* A person appointed by a court to have the control or management of the person or property, or both, of an infant or a person deemed incompetent.

Habeas Corpus A writ requiring a person to appear before the court. Used more frequently in criminal law to seek protection against illegal custody or imprisonment. (Latin for "you have the body.")

Headnotes The header at the beginning of the case in the law book that delineates the issues relevant in the case.

Hearsay A repetition of a statement made by another and offered in evidence by the witness while testifying at a trial or hearing to prove a matter. Hearsay is generally inadmissible.

Hit A term used to refer to each time a search request is found in an automated litigation support system.

Imaging Input storage transmission and output of graphic images with a computer.

Index A collection of searchable words or phrases from linear or flat files, listed in a separate, alphabetically ordered file to speed retrieval.

Indicative Bibliographic pointers to a file that contain certain predefined requirements that will direct the researcher to the document.

Injunction A writ issued by a court or a judge that restrains an individual or other entity from a certain act.

Interrogatories Written questions to an opponent during the discovery phase of the lawsuit that must be answered in writing and under oath.

Joinder (1) The addition of a party to a lawsuit. (2) The uniting of parties making claims or defending against an action as co-plaintiffs or co-defendants.

Joint Tort-Feasor Two or more persons jointly or severally liable in tort for the same injury to person or property.

Judgment Creditor After judgment in his or her favor, the plaintiff becomes the judgment creditor against the defendant.

Judgment Debtor After judgment against the defendant, the plaintiff becomes the judgment debtor.

Judgment Notwithstanding the Verdict (JNOV) A judgment rendered by the judge after the jury has already rendered a verdict. Essentially, the judge is saying that no reasonable jury could have reached a verdict, because there was not sufficient evidence of all the essential elements upon which to base a verdict.

Jurisdiction   The authority or power of a court to hear a particular cause of action and to render a lawful and binding judgment against one or more defendants.

Jury Instruction   An instruction to the jury on the applicable law of a case that it must use in rendering a decision. Also known as a *jury charge* or a *point for charge*.

Key-Word Coding   The use of various controlled vocabularies to code documents in automated litigation support.

Key-Number System   West Publishing Company's key-number system provides designated numbers to quickly locate cases when performing legal research.

Keys   Items of data used to specify search criteria, for example, birthdate or client number and birthdate.

Laches   Negligence, or unreasonable delay, in pursuing a legal remedy, concurrent with a resultant prejudice to the opposing party, whereby a person forfeits his or her right.

LANs (Local Area Networks)   A computer network confined to a limited area, linking computers so that programs, data, peripheral devices, and processing tasks can be shared.

Last Clear Chance   The doctrine that applies when the plaintiff is in a position of danger, and the defendant knows that the plaintiff cannot save himself. If the defendant has such knowledge in sufficient time to enable him to prevent the injury by the exercise of reasonable care, but thereafter fails to exercise due care, the plaintiff may recover.

Levy   The act of a sheriff in subjecting property to the satisfaction of a court judgment or to the lien of a court attachment.

Lien   A claim against the real or personal property of a judgment debtor.

Logical Operators   Words that represent logical relationships between terms in a computer search statement, such "AND" or "OR".

Long-Arm Statutes   Laws that give a court personal jurisdiction over nonresident defendants who commit civil wrongs in a state other than the state in which they reside.

Marginalia   Personal markings or comments written on documents.

Mediation   A procedure for resolving disputes out of court by an outside party or parties.

Memorandum of Law (Memorandum of Points and Authorities)   *Points* are the argument, and *authorities* are the citations to the law. There are three parts to a memorandum: statements of law, fact, and argument.

Microfiche   Documents stored on small plastic sheets that can be viewed with a viewer.

Microfilm   Documents stored on a cartridge as opposed to microfiche.

Motion   A request made by an attorney, either orally or in writing, for the court take a particular action in a case.

Negative Pregnant   A common error in pleading in which an allegation is denied in such a manner as to imply an admission of part of the allegation. It is an express denial "pregnant" with an implied admission.

Negligence   The failure to use ordinary care, under the particular factual circumstances revealed by the evidence in a lawsuit.

Neonate   A newborn infant up to one month of age.

Notice Pleading   Abbreviated form of pleading authorized by the *Federal Rules of Civil Procedure* and parallel state rules.

Objective Coding   Bibliographic or objective information used to code documents in automated litigation support.

Official Cite   The first citation to appear in an authority as recognized by the courts.

On Point   A term used to identify a precedent that supports the case being researched. (Translates as "on all fours.")

Original Jurisdiction   Possessed by the court that has the authority to hear a case originally, that is, the court where the suit is commenced.

Peremptory Challenge   Eliminates a prospective juror without a reason given. Peremptory challenges are usually limited in number.

Perfect   To file an appeal in a civil case within the period of time specified by the *Federal Rules of Appellate Procedure*.

Personal Jurisdiction   The jurisdiction of the court over the individual parties, corporations, fiduciaries, or other litigants.

Plaintiff   The person who initiates a lawsuit against another.

Pleading   Formal papers filed with the courts that state the facts each party will try to prove as to the other party's claim or defense.

Post-Judgment Remedies   Means of collecting the judgment from the judgment debtor through executions, garnishments, injunctions, etc.

Post-Trial   That period of time after trial of a case but prior to a final decision being entered by the court.

Precedent   A former case that may serve as an example or reason for another case.

Pretrial Order   An order resulting from action taken at a pretrial conference, governing the conduct of the trial and binding the parties unless the judgment modifies it.

Prima Facie   The plaintiff must present sufficient evidence that he or she is entitled to require defendant to proceed with the case. (Latin for "at first sight.")

Probable Cause   Reasonable cause; required for a valid search and/or seizure or arrest. That is, a good reason is required for a search and/or seizure or arrest.

Procedural Law   Defines the steps that must be followed in a lawsuit.

Prohibition (Writ of)   That process by which a superior court prevents an inferior court possessing judicial or quasi-judicial powers from exceeding its jurisdiction in matters not within its jurisdiction to hear or determine.

Proof of Service   Evidence submitted by a process server that he or she has made service on a defendant in an action.

Proximate Cause   In tort law, that which caused the injury. In other words, the injury was the result of a natural and continuous sequence of this cause, and without it, would not have occurred.

Proximity Searching   The search for words in the text according to their proximity to other words.

Queries   Searches for specific data believed to be in the database file.

RAM (Random Access Memory)   Computer memory used for running programs and temporarily storing data.

Receiver   A person who is appointed to act as a custodian or manager of disputed property *pendente lite,* i.e., while the suit is pending, of defendant's actual or potential insolvency.

Record   In automated litigation support, a collection of related fields, such as the client number, name, address, and telephone number of a particular client.

Relational Databases   An electronic database organized according to relational principles that allow relationships between items of information to be easily created and later used for queries.

Release   A formal document by which one or more executing parties relinquishes all or certain claims against one or more specified parties.

Remand   An action by a higher court sending back a case to a lower court for further proceedings.

Removal   The process of removing a case from the state court and sending it to the federal court that had jurisdiction in the first place.

Request for Admission   Written statements of facts concerning a case submitted to the opposing party during discovery to admit or deny.

Request for Production   Written requests submitted by one party in a lawsuit requesting the opposing party during discovery to produce certain written documents and things for inspection.

Res Judicata   Literally, a thing judicially acted upon or decided. After judgment has been entered and all appeals have been exhausted or expired, any subsequent lawsuit is barred on the same subject matter.

Respondent (Appellee)   The person defending against the appeal.

Root Search   The search for all words beginning with a particular set of characters.

Rule *Nisi*   Similar to the standard form of a notice of motion.

Sanctions   A penalty or punishment imposed by law for failure to comply with the law or with rules or regulations.

Search Set   A combination of search requests used to locate a document or group of documents relating to a particular issue.

Service of Process   The physical delivery of writs, summonses, and subpoenas to a party or witness involved in a lawsuit. Can also be done by publication or mailing.

Settlement Brochure   A written compilation of factual information and materials used as a tool to encourage settlement.

Settlement Distribution Statement   A written statement substantiating the financial disbursements of the settlement proceeds.

Settlement Precis   A written summary or abstract used as a tool in settlement proceedings.

Sheparizing   The act of checking a set of books titled *Shepard's Citations* to determine the history and subsequent treatment of a published opinion.

Situs   Literally, the location.

Slip Laws   New laws still in bill forms.

Special Damages   The actual "out-of-pocket" expenses incurred by the damaged party in a lawsuit.

Specific Denial   In an answer, a specific admission or denial of each allegation.

Statutes   Laws enacted by the legislature.

Statutes of Limitations   Laws setting forth certain periods of time within which one must file a lawsuit to prevent "stale" claims that make it more difficult to locate evidence and available witnesses.

Stay   (1) To stop an enforcement of an order. (2) To prevent a case from proceeding.

Stipulation   An agreement between opposing litigants that certain facts are true or that certain acts may take place.

Subject-Matter Jurisdiction   The court's power to hear and determine cases on the general subject involved in the action.

Subjective Coding   This step analyzes the entire document using subjective criteria.

Subpoena   A command to appear at a certain time and place to give testimony upon a certain matter.

Substantive Law   Defines the duties owed by one person to another and concerns the rights of the parties as opposed to the procedure for enforcing that law.

Summary Judgment   Procedural device that allows a judgment or a voluntary dismissal before the trial goes any further if the discovery process reveals no basis for the lawsuit.

Summons   The written instrument served upon a party to acquire jurisdiction in order to commence a civil action.

Supersedeas Bond   A means of security to stay a judgment or order filed by the moving party.

Taxonomy   Created to allow codes to indicate the presence of different subjective elements in the document.

Thesaurus   A collection of similar terms to which additional terms can be added both before and after the case begins.

Third-Party Defendant   When a defendant in a lawsuit wants to add another party to the lawsuit, the original defendant may file a *third-party complaint* bringing the *third-party defendant* into the lawsuit.

Tickler System   A manual or computerized reminder system for important dates, activities, and events.

Tort   A civil wrong for which the court provides a remedy through action for damages.

Unofficial Citation   The second citation to appear in an authority as recognized by the courts.

Validation   Program for checking the validity of data entered against tables of codes or actual data and notifying the user if an error is found.

Venue   Place or location, i.e., city, county, district, or other geographical division, in which an action is to be heard and tried.

Verdict   The decision reached by a jury or judge at the conclusion of a legal proceeding.

Verification   A short oath concluding a pleading that affirms the pleader is ready to prove his or her allegations.

Voir Dire   A preliminary oral examination of a prospective juror conducted by the attorneys to all parties prior to trial.

Waiver   The surrender, either expressed or implied, of a right to which one is entitled by law.

With Prejudice   The dismissal of a case whereby the party may *not* file any further action based on the issue or issues in the former action.

Without Prejudice   This dismissal of a case whereby the party may file a subsequent action on the same issue or issues in the former action.

Writ of *Certiorari*   *See* Certiorari.

Writ of Execution   A written instrument used to enforce a judgment for money.

Writ of *Mandamus*   A writ issued by a superior court commanding an inferior court to perform a duty imposed by law.

Index of Exhibits, Checklists, and Forms

———— • ————

Index

• D

• E